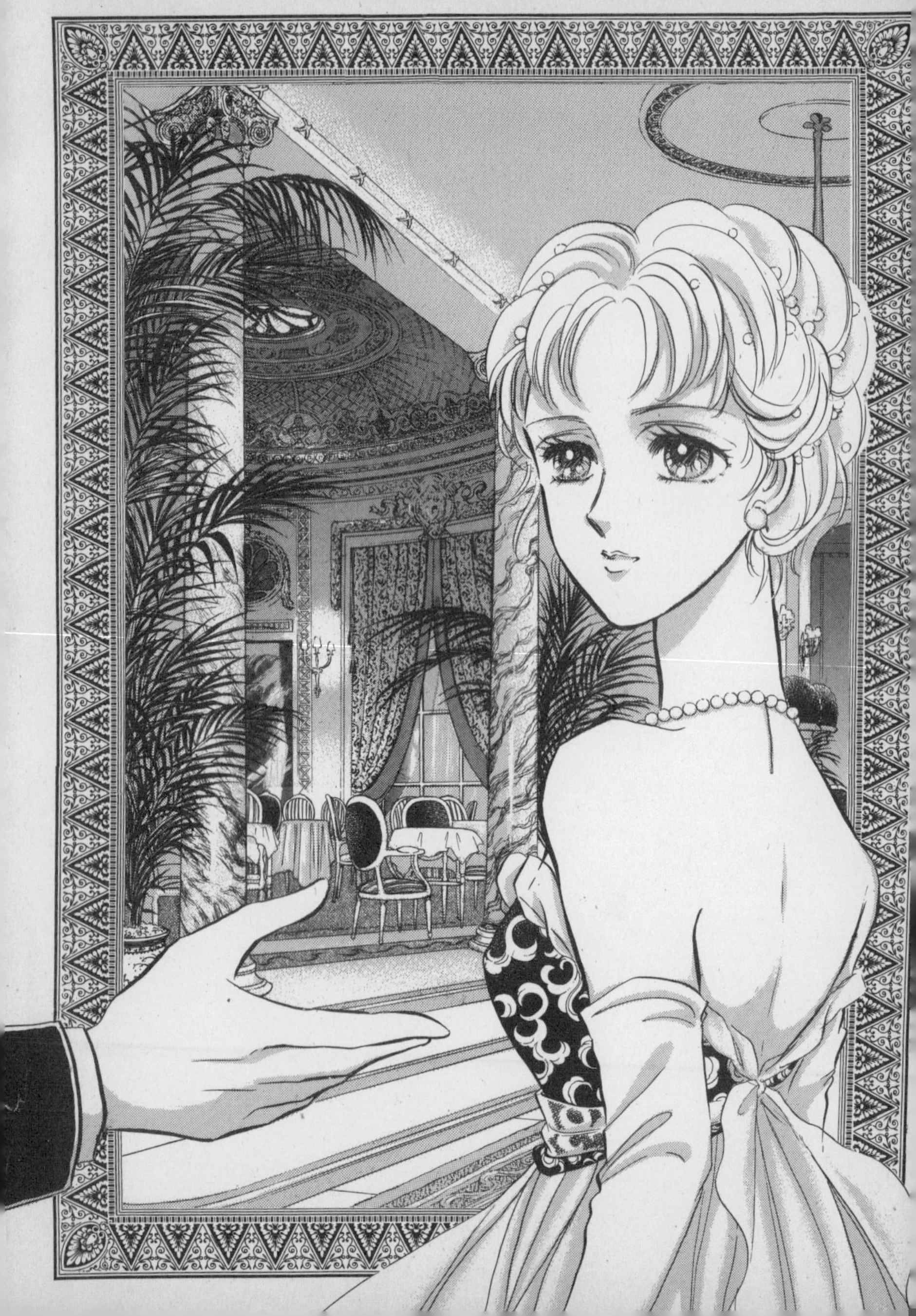

# Idol Dreams

Based on an original novel by
**Charlotte Lamb**

Art by
**Yoko Hanabusa**

HARLEQUIN PINK:

# IDOL DREAMS

HARLEQUIN®
Ginger Blossom

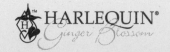

# IDOL DREAMS
*based on an original novel
by Charlotte Lamb*

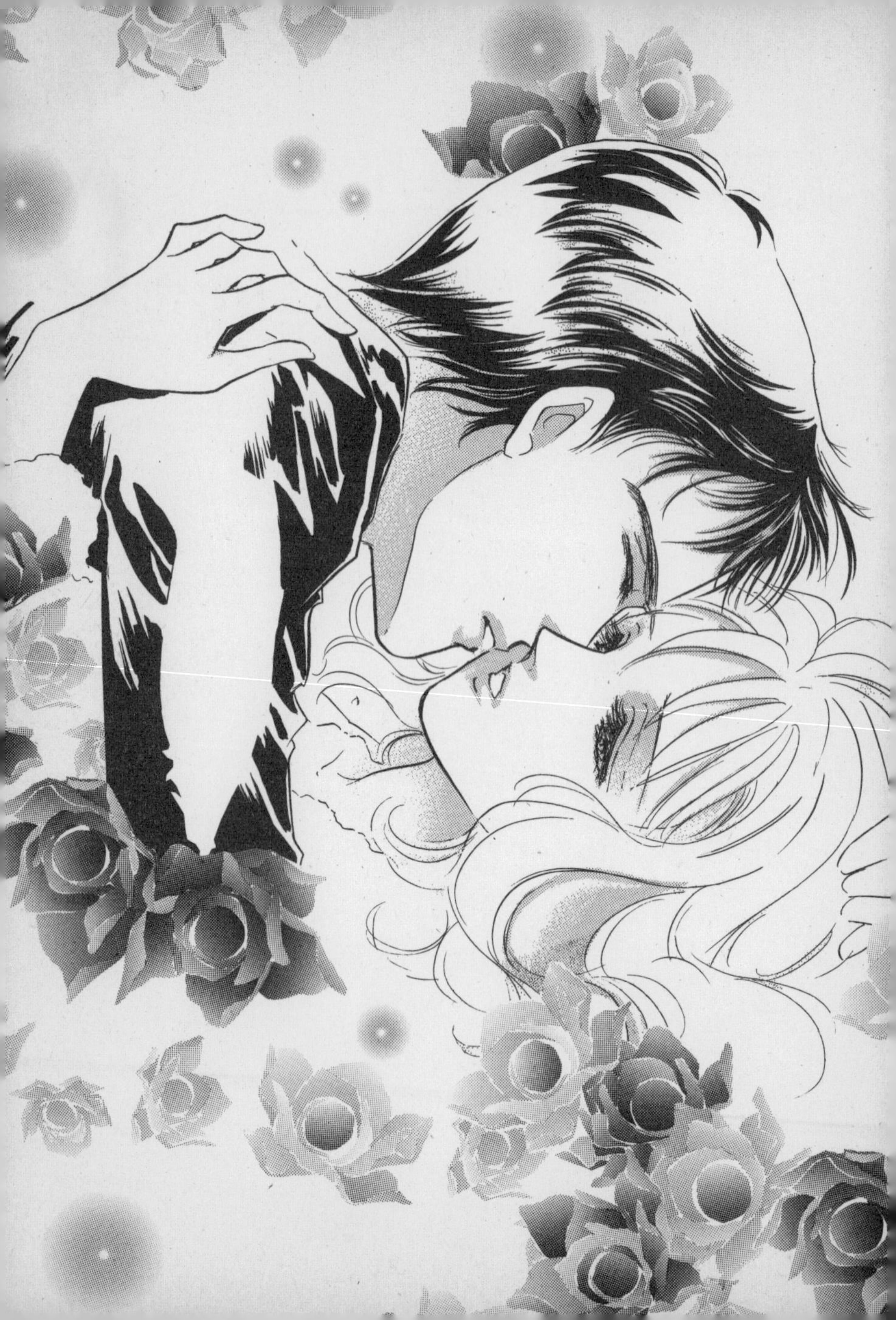

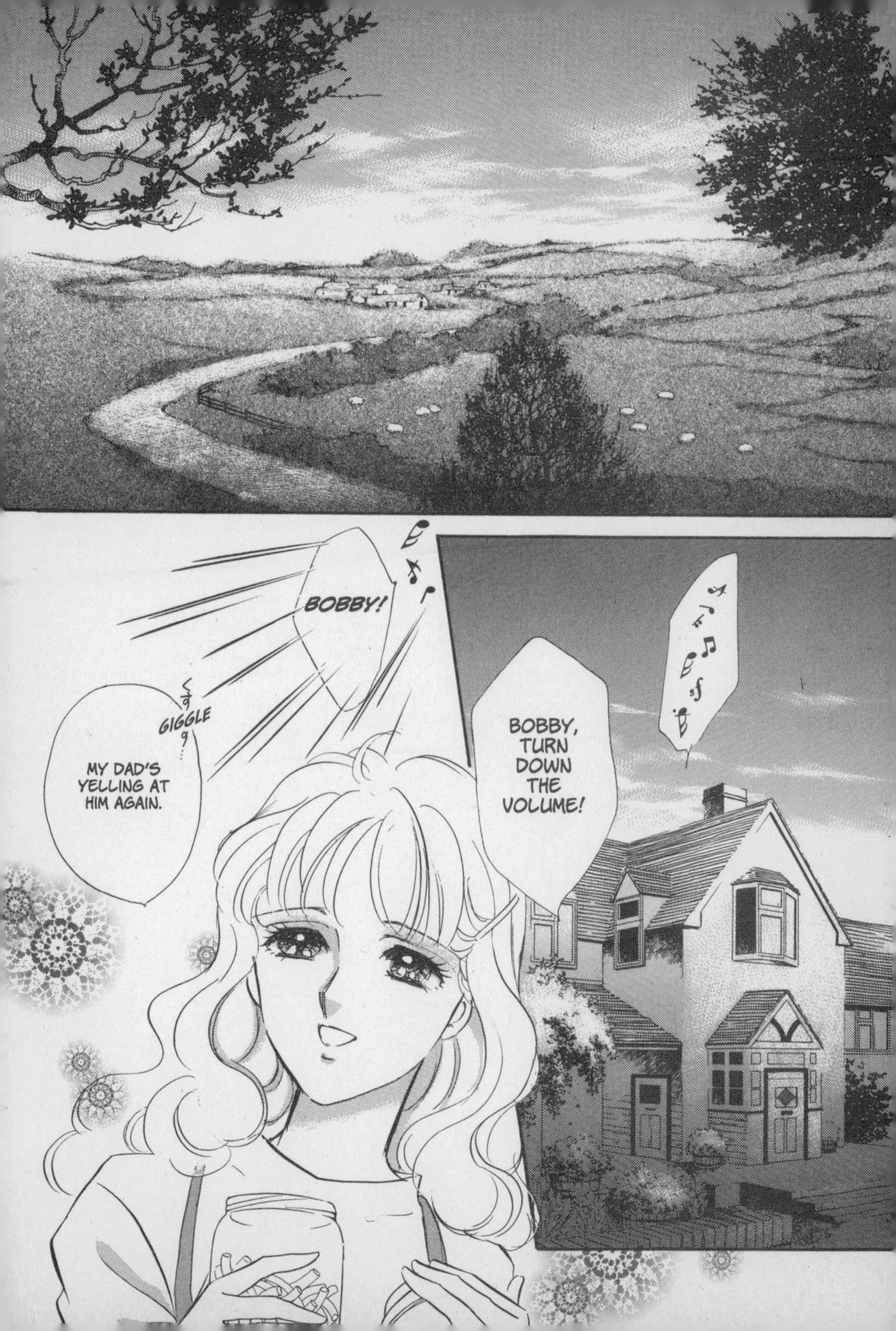
BOBBY, TURN DOWN THE VOLUME!
BOBBY!
くす
GIGGLE
MY DAD'S YELLING AT HIM AGAIN.

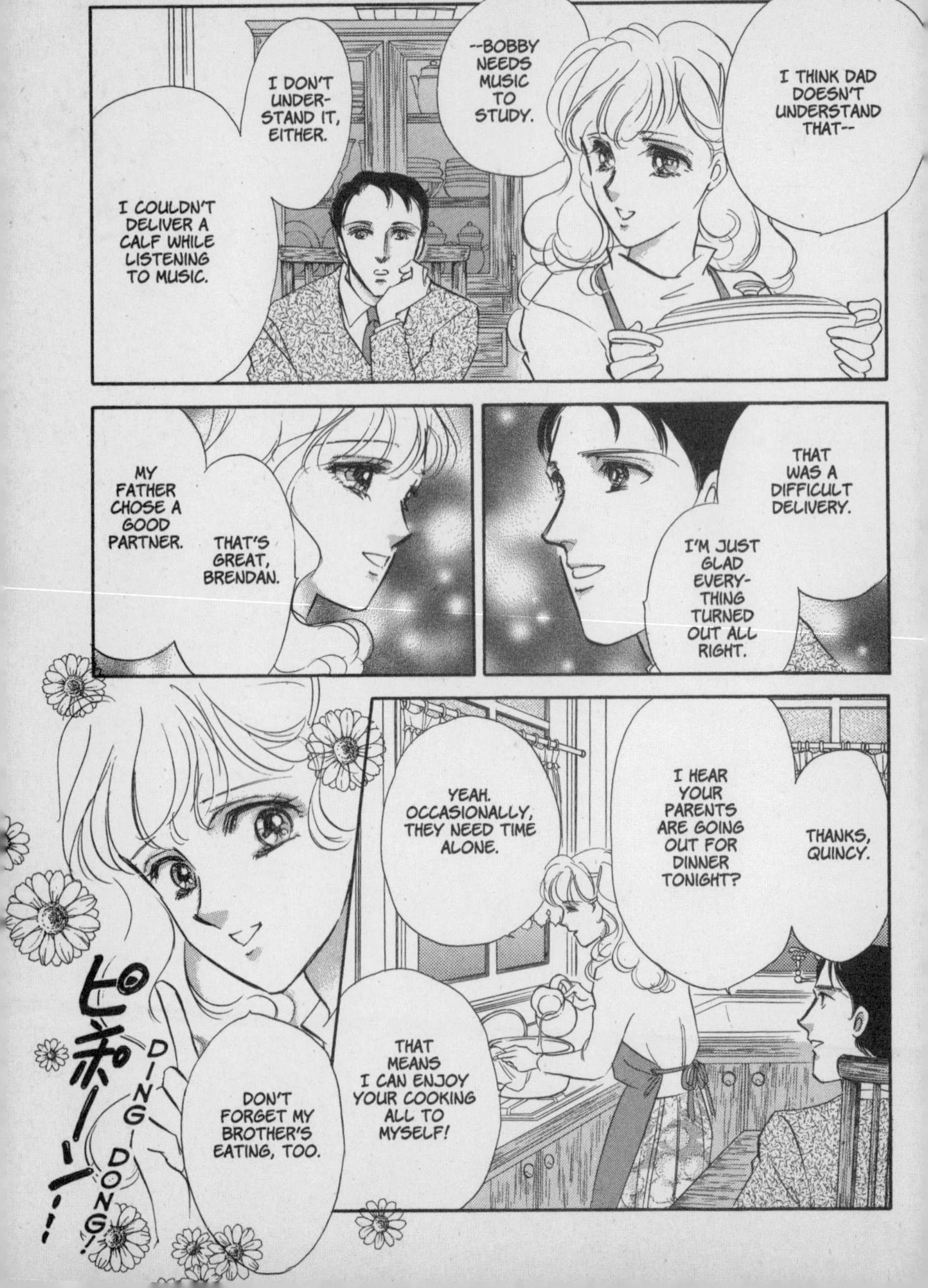
I THINK DAD DOESN'T UNDERSTAND THAT--
--BOBBY NEEDS MUSIC TO STUDY.
I DON'T UNDERSTAND IT, EITHER.
I COULDN'T DELIVER A CALF WHILE LISTENING TO MUSIC.
THAT WAS A DIFFICULT DELIVERY.
I'M JUST GLAD EVERYTHING TURNED OUT ALL RIGHT.
THAT'S GREAT, BRENDAN.
MY FATHER CHOSE A GOOD PARTNER.
THANKS, QUINCY.
I HEAR YOUR PARENTS ARE GOING OUT FOR DINNER TONIGHT?
YEAH. OCCASIONALLY, THEY NEED TIME ALONE.
THAT MEANS I CAN ENJOY YOUR COOKING ALL TO MYSELF!
DON'T FORGET MY BROTHER'S EATING, TOO.
ピンポーン!!
DING-DONG!

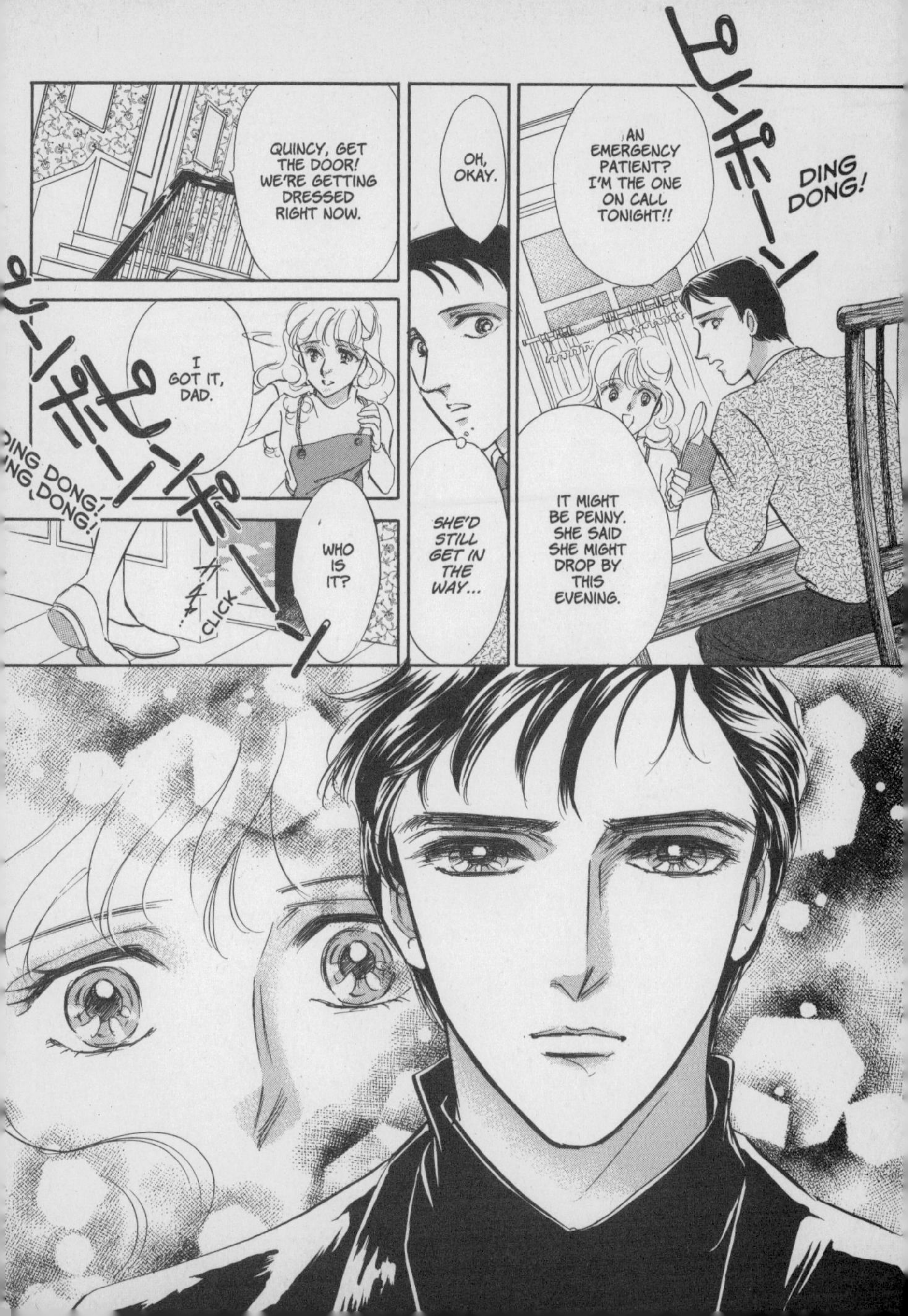
ピンポーン
DING DONG!
AN EMERGENCY PATIENT? I'M THE ONE ON CALL TONIGHT!!
IT MIGHT BE PENNY. SHE SAID SHE MIGHT DROP BY THIS EVENING.
OH, OKAY.
SHE'D STILL GET IN THE WAY...
QUINCY, GET THE DOOR! WE'RE GETTING DRESSED RIGHT NOW.
I GOT IT, DAD.
ピンポーンピンポーン
DING DONG! DING DONG!
WHO IS IT?
CLICK

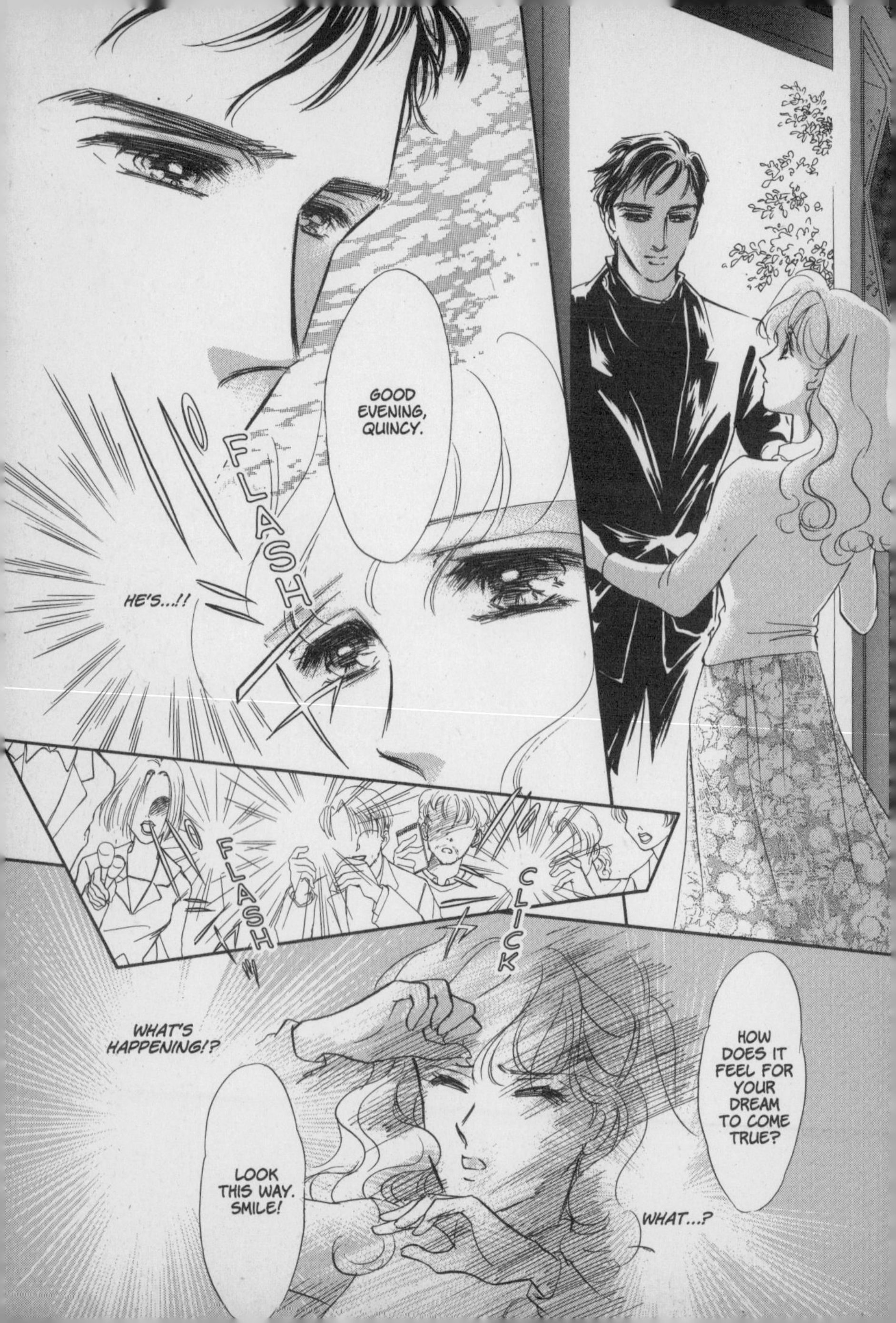
GOOD EVENING, QUINCY.
FLASH
HE'S...!!
CLICK
FLASH
HOW DOES IT FEEL FOR YOUR DREAM TO COME TRUE?
WHAT'S HAPPENING!?
LOOK THIS WAY. SMILE!
WHAT...?

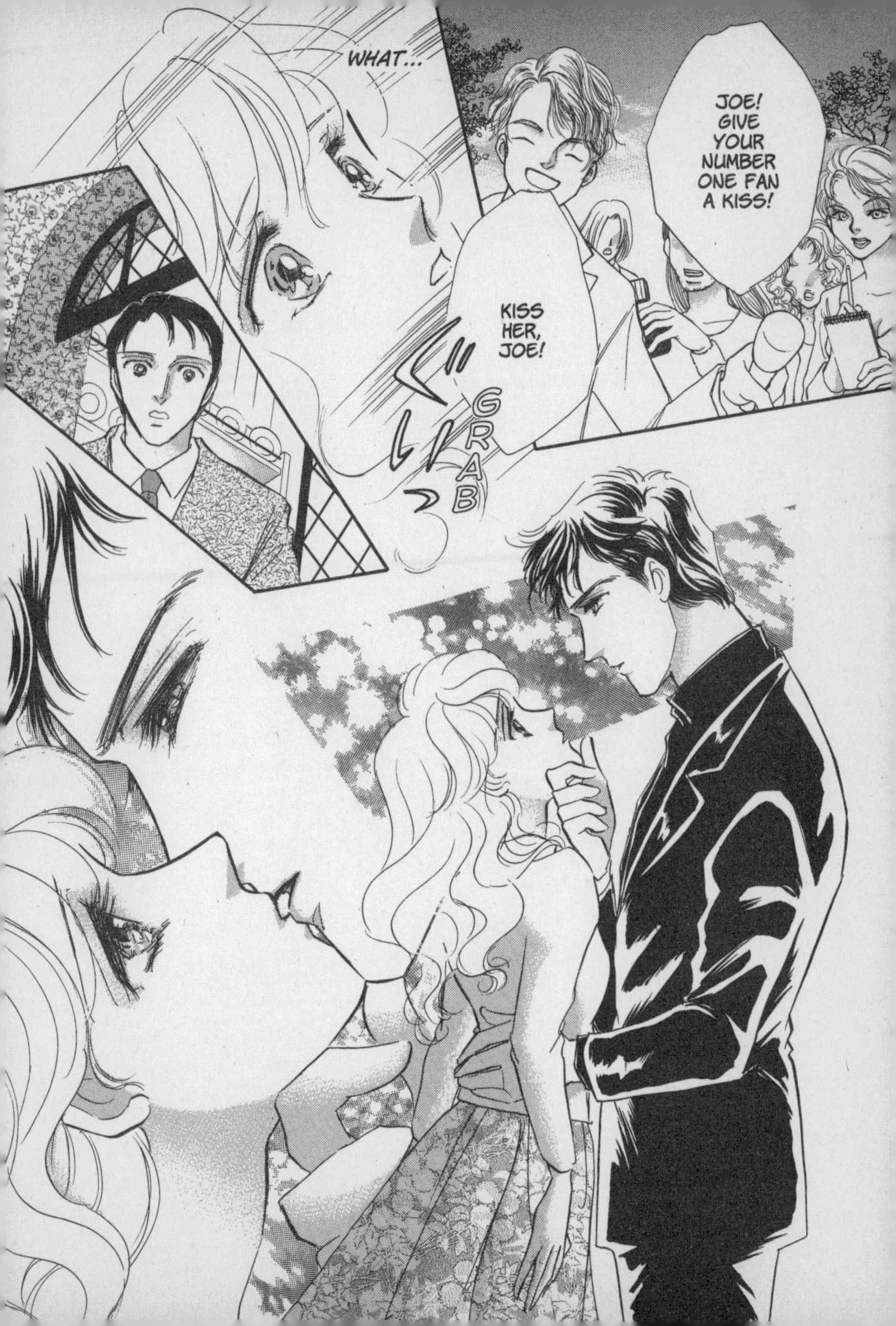
JOE! GIVE YOUR NUMBER ONE FAN A KISS!
KISS HER, JOE!
WHAT...
GRAB

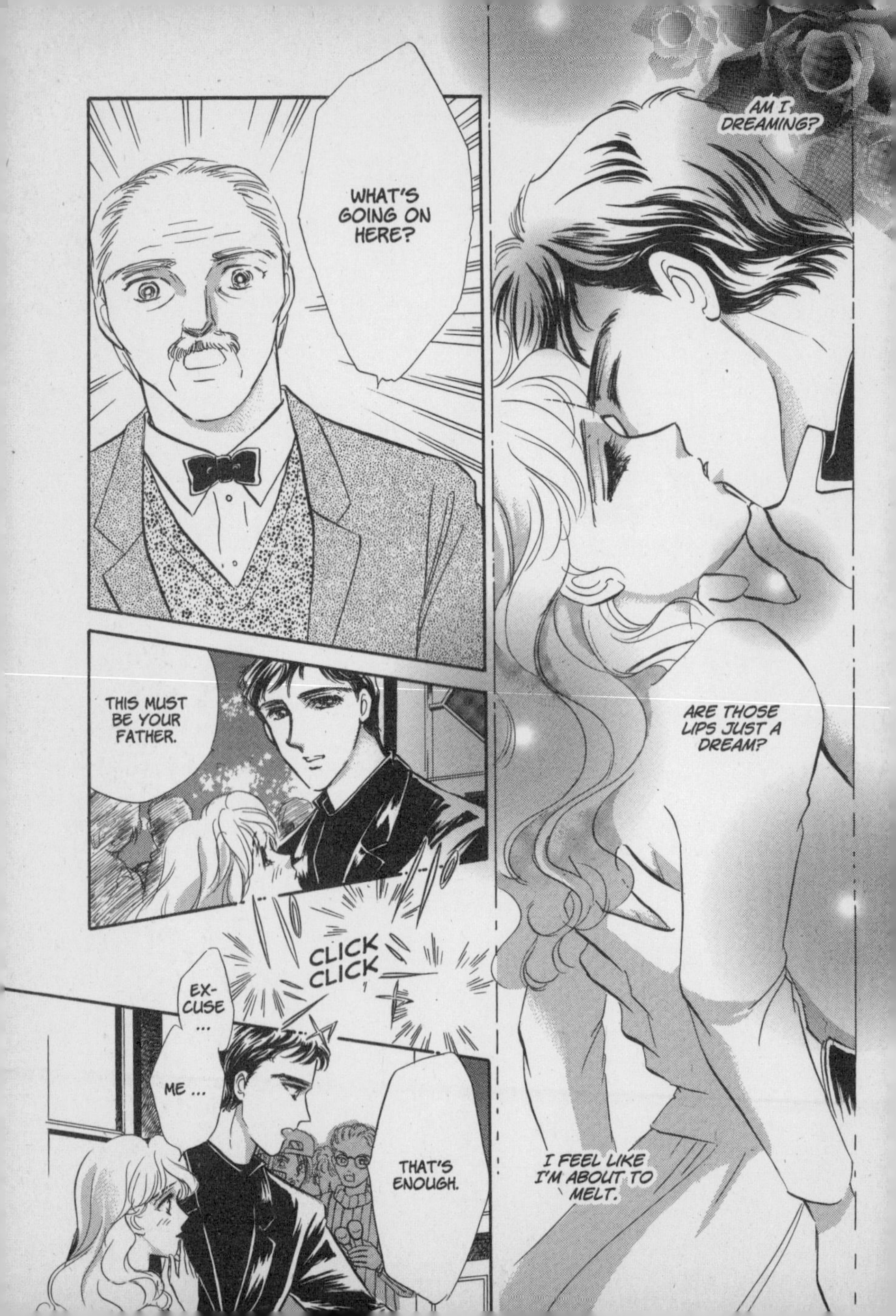
AM I DREAMING?
ARE THOSE LIPS JUST A DREAM?
I FEEL LIKE I'M ABOUT TO MELT.
WHAT'S GOING ON HERE?
THIS MUST BE YOUR FATHER.
CLICK CLICK
EX-CUSE ...
ME ...
THAT'S ENOUGH.

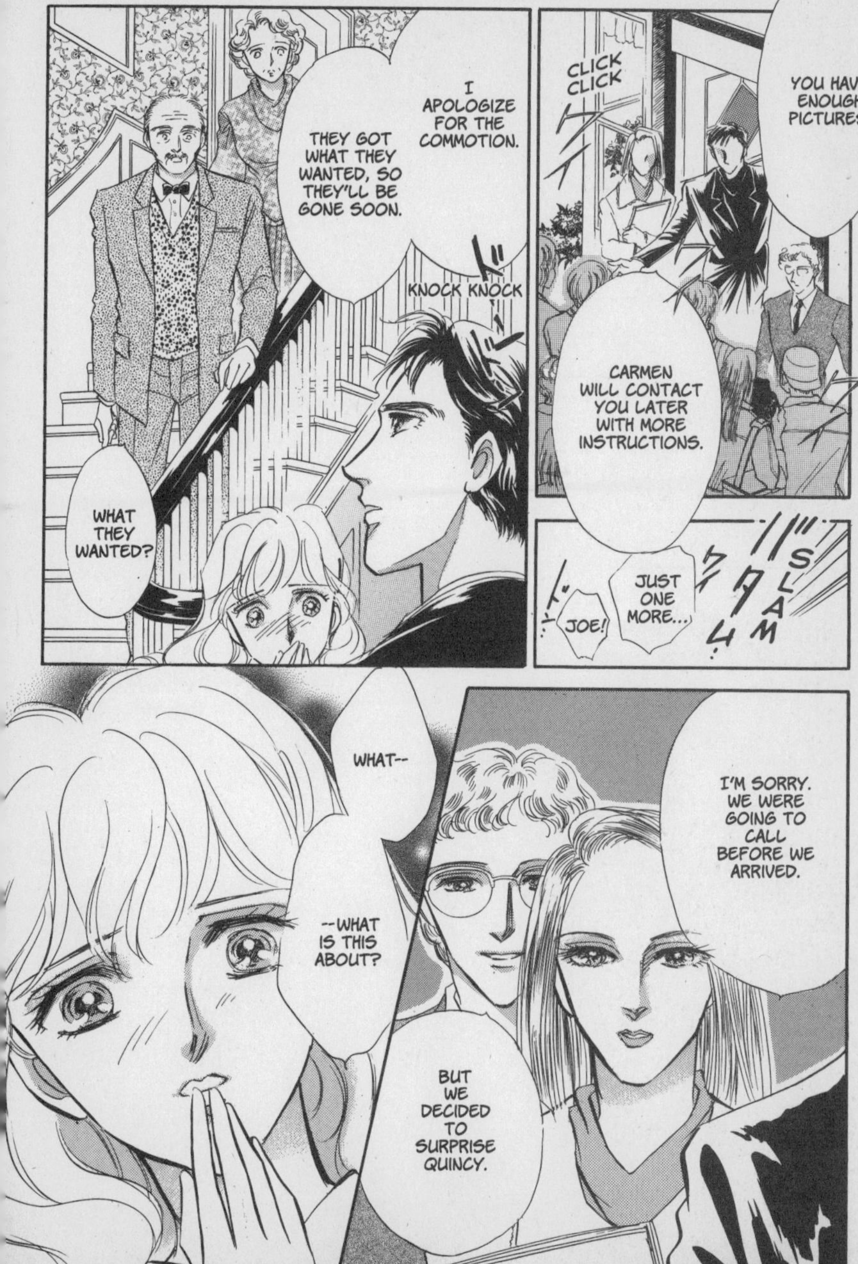
YOU HAVE ENOUGH PICTURES.
CLICK CLICK
CARMEN WILL CONTACT YOU LATER WITH MORE INSTRUCTIONS.
JUST ONE MORE...
JOE!
SLAM
I APOLOGIZE FOR THE COMMOTION.
THEY GOT WHAT THEY WANTED, SO THEY'LL BE GONE SOON.
KNOCK KNOCK
WHAT THEY WANTED?
I'M SORRY. WE WERE GOING TO CALL BEFORE WE ARRIVED.
BUT WE DECIDED TO SURPRISE QUINCY.
WHAT--
--WHAT IS THIS ABOUT?

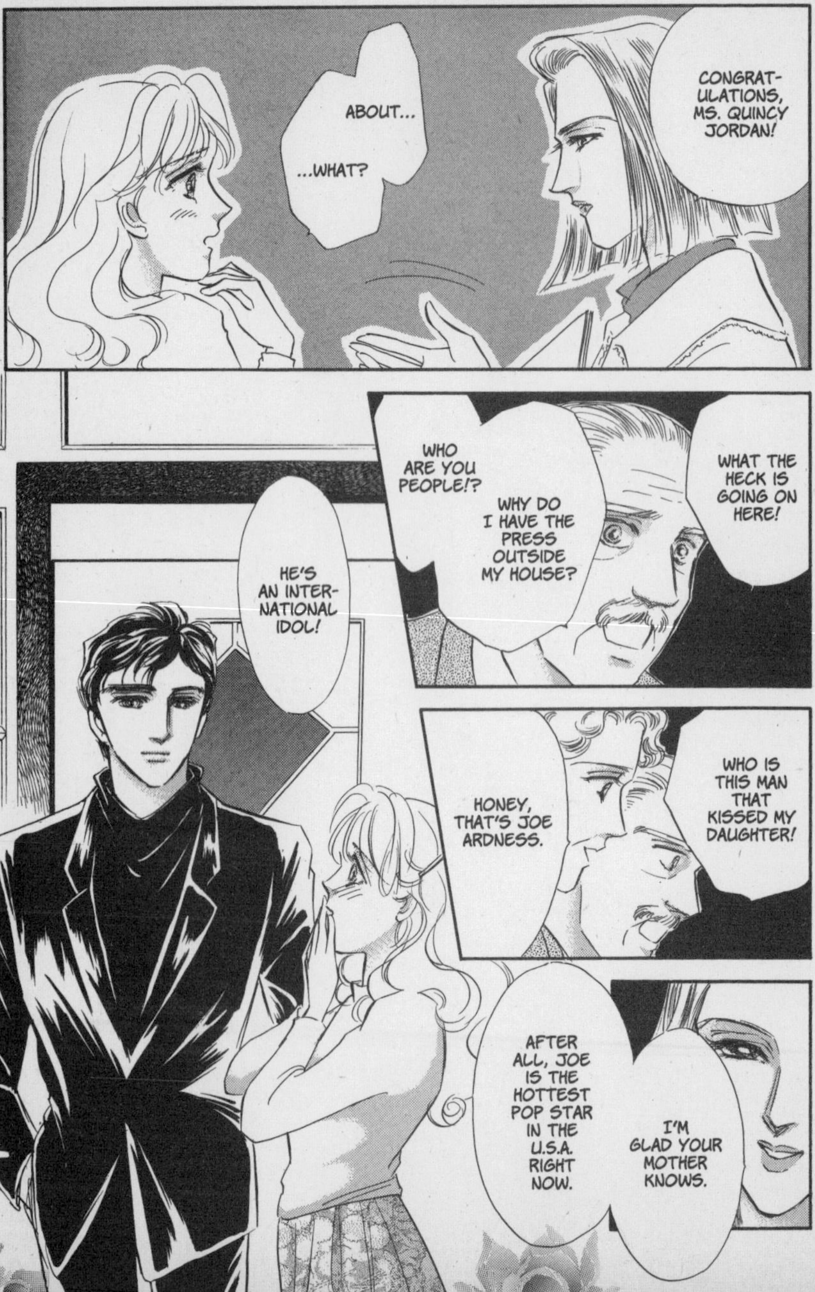
CONGRATULATIONS, MS. QUINCY JORDAN!
ABOUT...
...WHAT?
WHAT THE HECK IS GOING ON HERE!
WHO ARE YOU PEOPLE!?
WHY DO I HAVE THE PRESS OUTSIDE MY HOUSE?
WHO IS THIS MAN THAT KISSED MY DAUGHTER!
HONEY, THAT'S JOE ARDNESS.
I'M GLAD YOUR MOTHER KNOWS.
AFTER ALL, JOE IS THE HOTTEST POP STAR IN THE U.S.A. RIGHT NOW.
HE'S AN INTERNATIONAL IDOL!

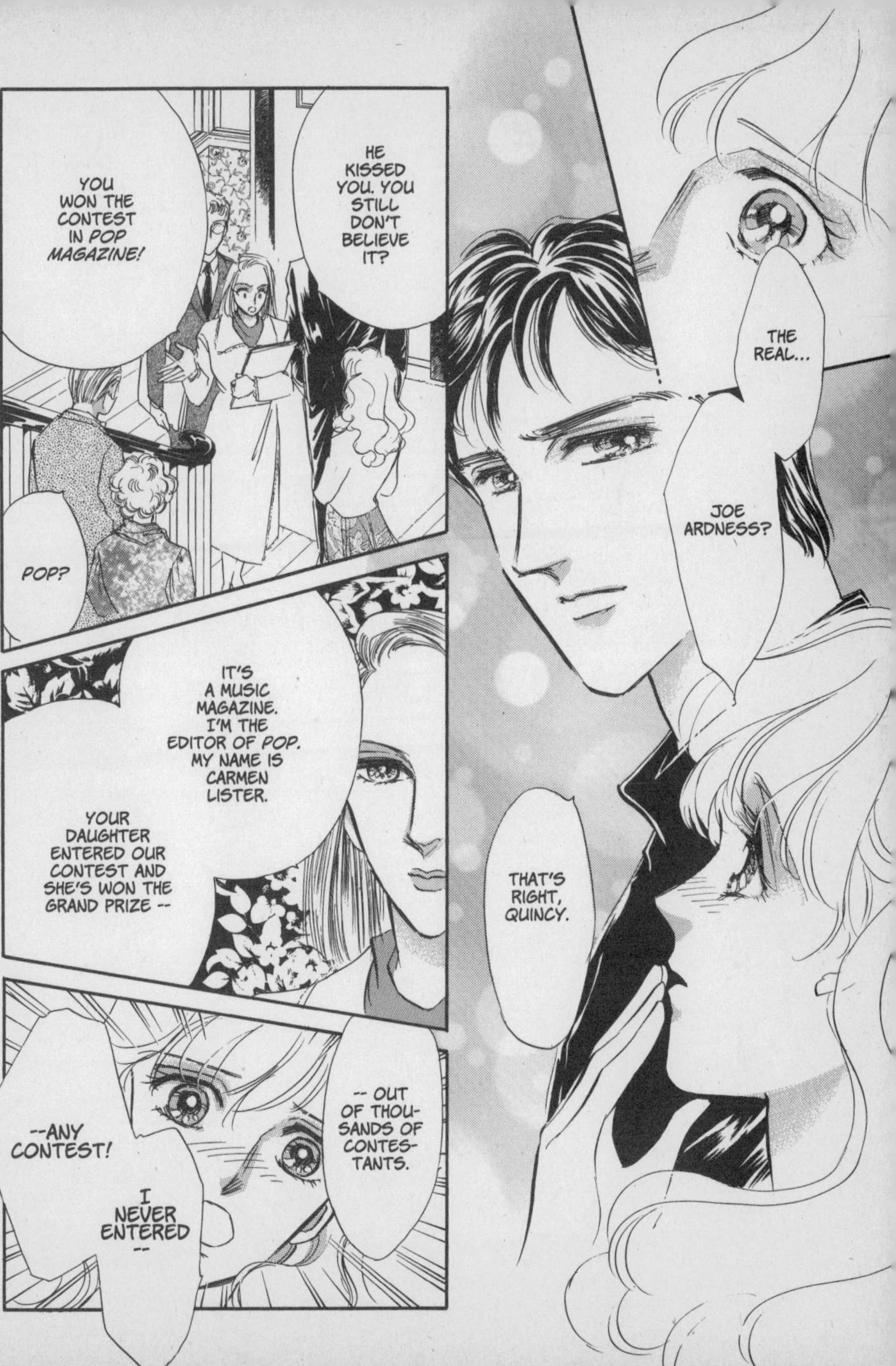
THE REAL...
JOE ARDNESS?
THAT'S RIGHT, QUINCY.
HE KISSED YOU. YOU STILL DON'T BELIEVE IT?
YOU WON THE CONTEST IN *POP MAGAZINE!*
*POP?*
IT'S A MUSIC MAGAZINE. I'M THE EDITOR OF *POP*. MY NAME IS CARMEN LISTER.
YOUR DAUGHTER ENTERED OUR CONTEST AND SHE'S WON THE GRAND PRIZE --
-- OUT OF THOUSANDS OF CONTESTANTS.
I NEVER ENTERED --
--ANY CONTEST!

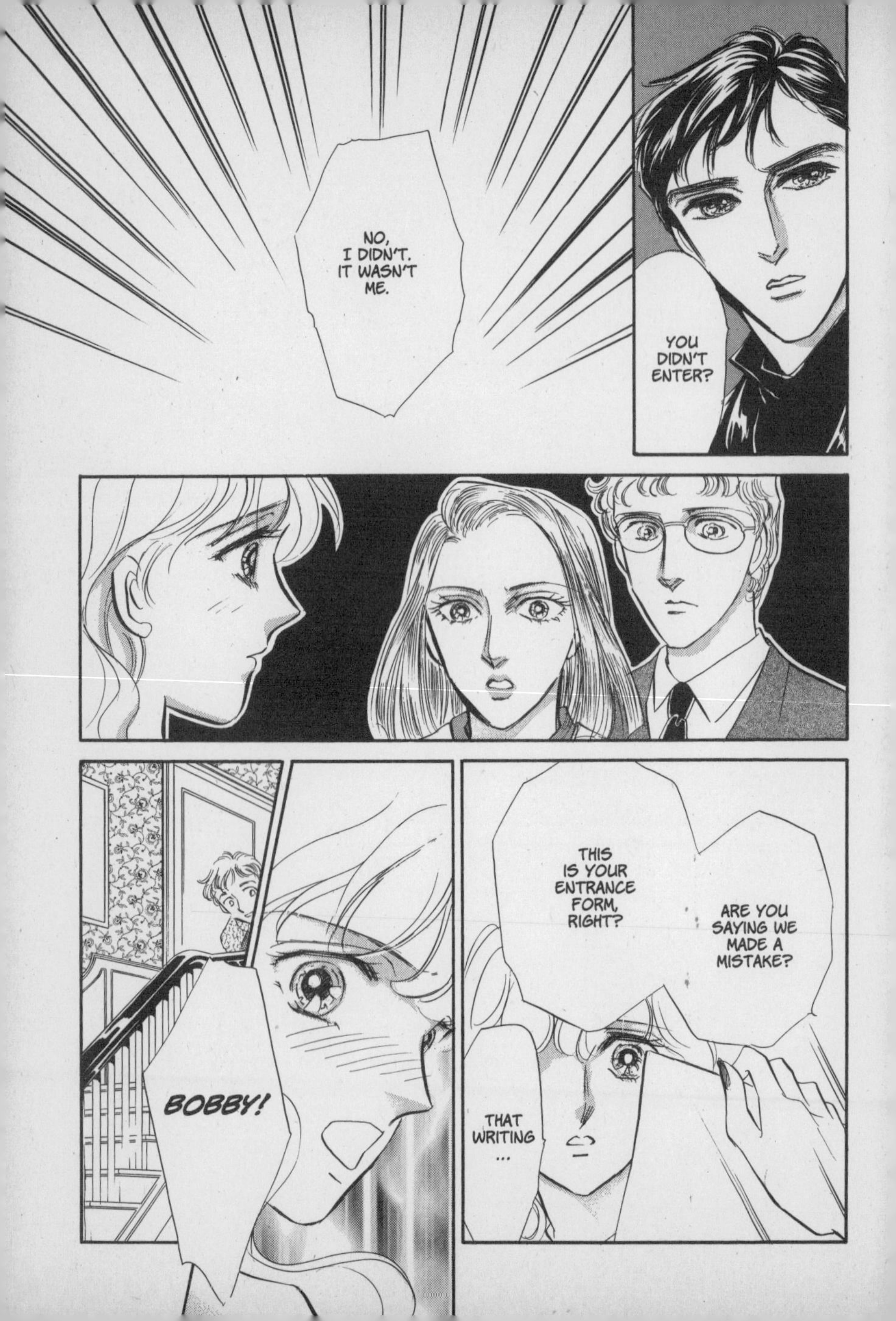
YOU DIDN'T ENTER?
NO, I DIDN'T. IT WASN'T ME.
THIS IS YOUR ENTRANCE FORM, RIGHT?
ARE YOU SAYING WE MADE A MISTAKE?
THAT WRITING ...
BOBBY!

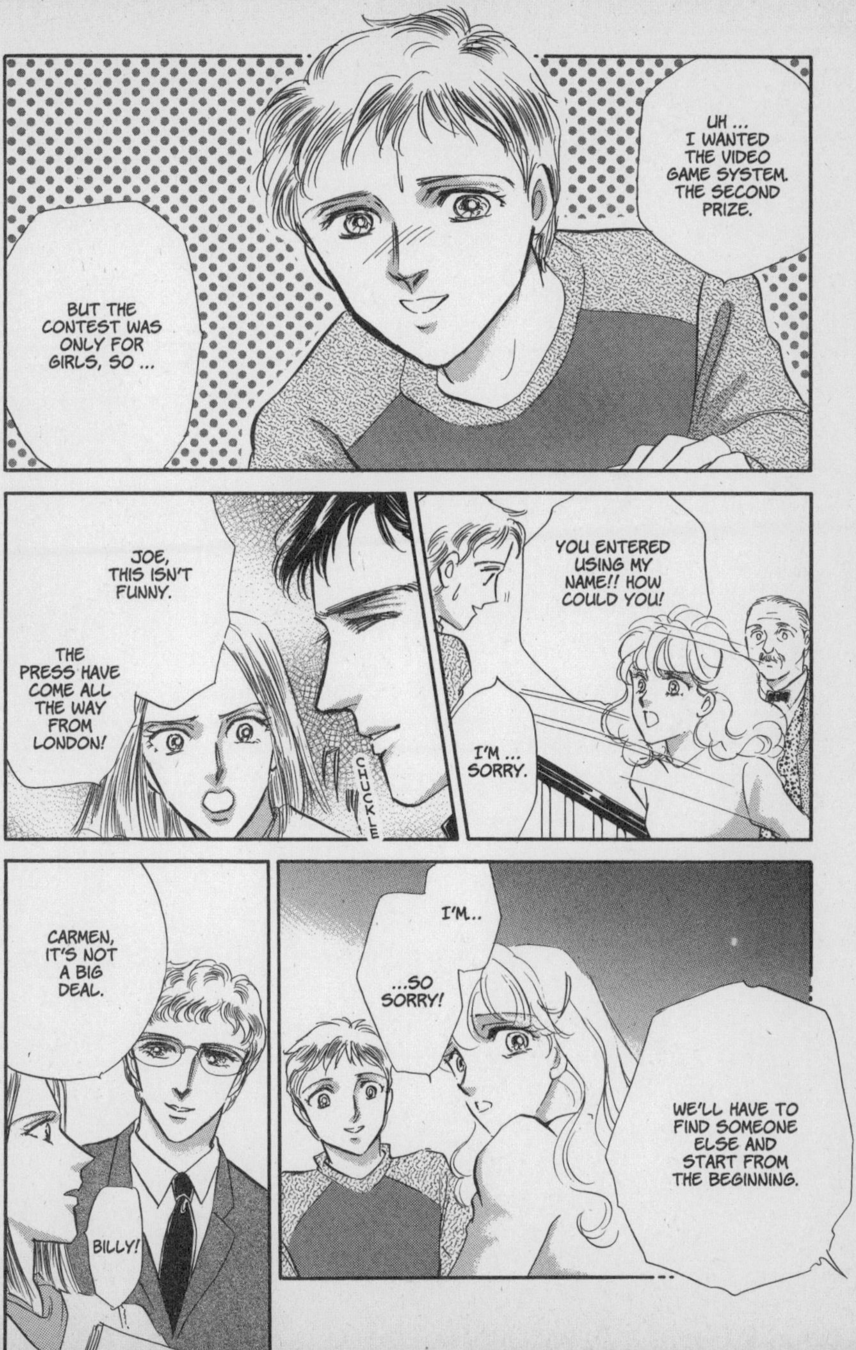
UH ... I WANTED THE VIDEO GAME SYSTEM. THE SECOND PRIZE.
BUT THE CONTEST WAS ONLY FOR GIRLS, SO ...
YOU ENTERED USING MY NAME!! HOW COULD YOU!
I'M ... SORRY.
JOE, THIS ISN'T FUNNY.
THE PRESS HAVE COME ALL THE WAY FROM LONDON!
CHUCKLE
I'M..
...SO SORRY!
WE'LL HAVE TO FIND SOMEONE ELSE AND START FROM THE BEGINNING.
CARMEN, IT'S NOT A BIG DEAL.
BILLY!

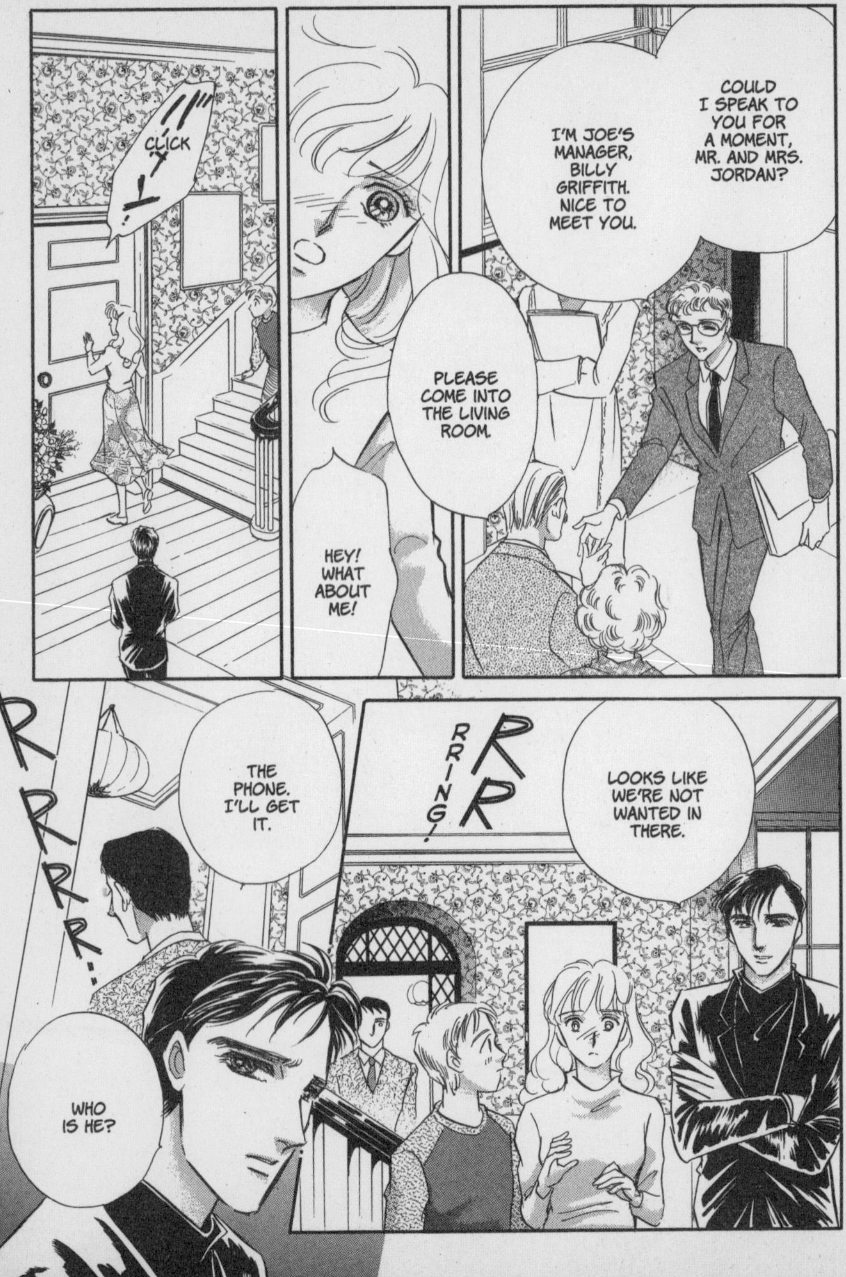
COULD I SPEAK TO YOU FOR A MOMENT, MR. AND MRS. JORDAN?
I'M JOE'S MANAGER, BILLY GRIFFITH. NICE TO MEET YOU.
PLEASE COME INTO THE LIVING ROOM.
HEY! WHAT ABOUT ME!
CLICK
RRING! RR
LOOKS LIKE WE'RE NOT WANTED IN THERE.
RRRRR...
THE PHONE. I'LL GET IT.
WHO IS HE?

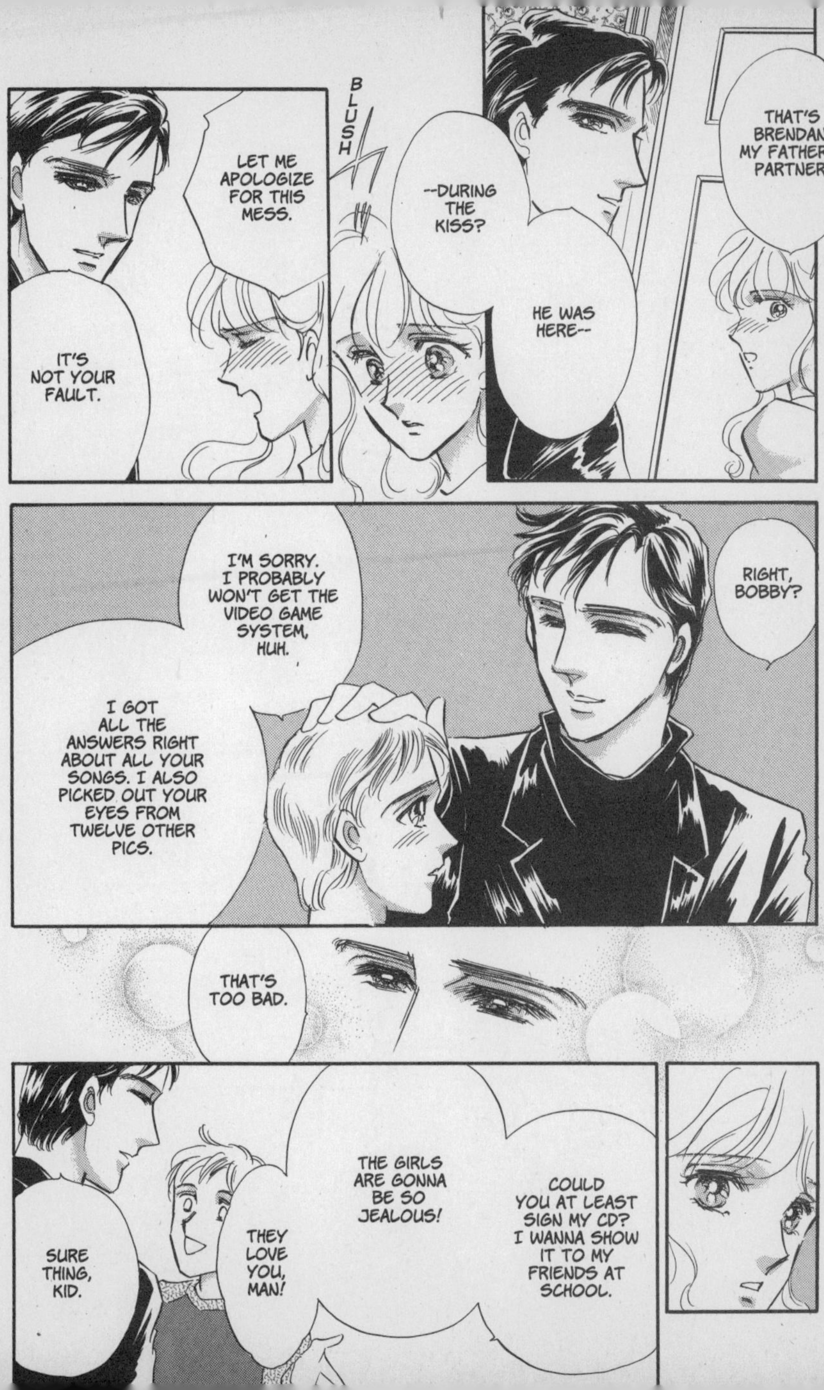
THAT'S BRENDAN. MY FATHER'S PARTNER.
HE WAS HERE--
--DURING THE KISS?
BLUSH
LET ME APOLOGIZE FOR THIS MESS.
IT'S NOT YOUR FAULT.
RIGHT, BOBBY?
I'M SORRY. I PROBABLY WON'T GET THE VIDEO GAME SYSTEM, HUH.
I GOT ALL THE ANSWERS RIGHT ABOUT ALL YOUR SONGS. I ALSO PICKED OUT YOUR EYES FROM TWELVE OTHER PICS.
THAT'S TOO BAD.
COULD YOU AT LEAST SIGN MY CD? I WANNA SHOW IT TO MY FRIENDS AT SCHOOL.
THE GIRLS ARE GONNA BE SO JEALOUS!
THEY LOVE YOU, MAN!
SURE THING, KID.

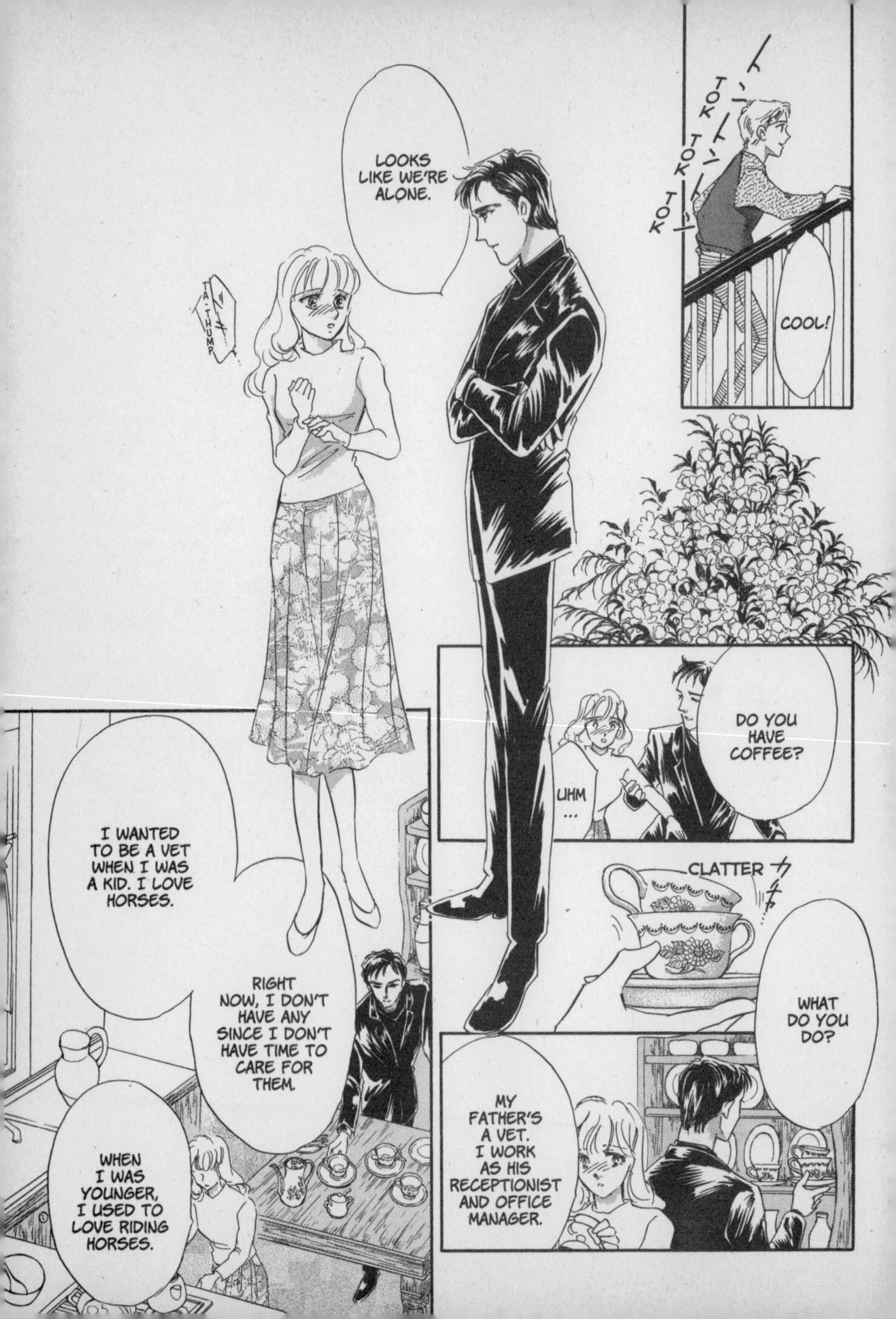
TOK TOK TOK
COOL!
LOOKS LIKE WE'RE ALONE.
TA-THUMP
DO YOU HAVE COFFEE?
UHM ...
CLATTER
WHAT DO YOU DO?
MY FATHER'S A VET. I WORK AS HIS RECEPTIONIST AND OFFICE MANAGER.
I WANTED TO BE A VET WHEN I WAS A KID. I LOVE HORSES.
WHEN I WAS YOUNGER, I USED TO LOVE RIDING HORSES.
RIGHT NOW, I DON'T HAVE ANY SINCE I DON'T HAVE TIME TO CARE FOR THEM.

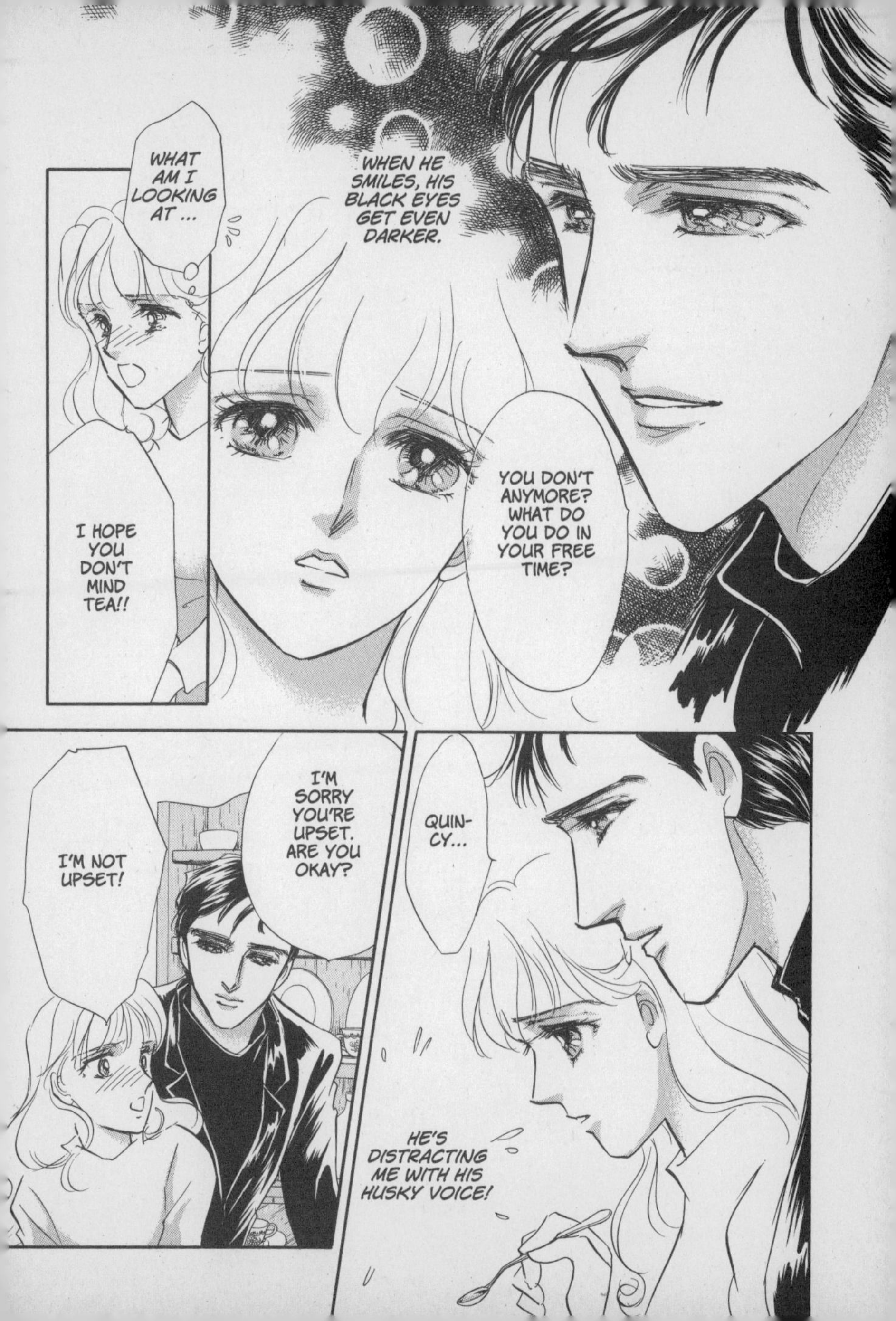
YOU DON'T ANYMORE? WHAT DO YOU DO IN YOUR FREE TIME?
WHEN HE SMILES, HIS BLACK EYES GET EVEN DARKER.
WHAT AM I LOOKING AT ...
I HOPE YOU DON'T MIND TEA!!
QUIN-CY...
HE'S DISTRACTING ME WITH HIS HUSKY VOICE!
I'M SORRY YOU'RE UPSET. ARE YOU OKAY?
I'M NOT UPSET!

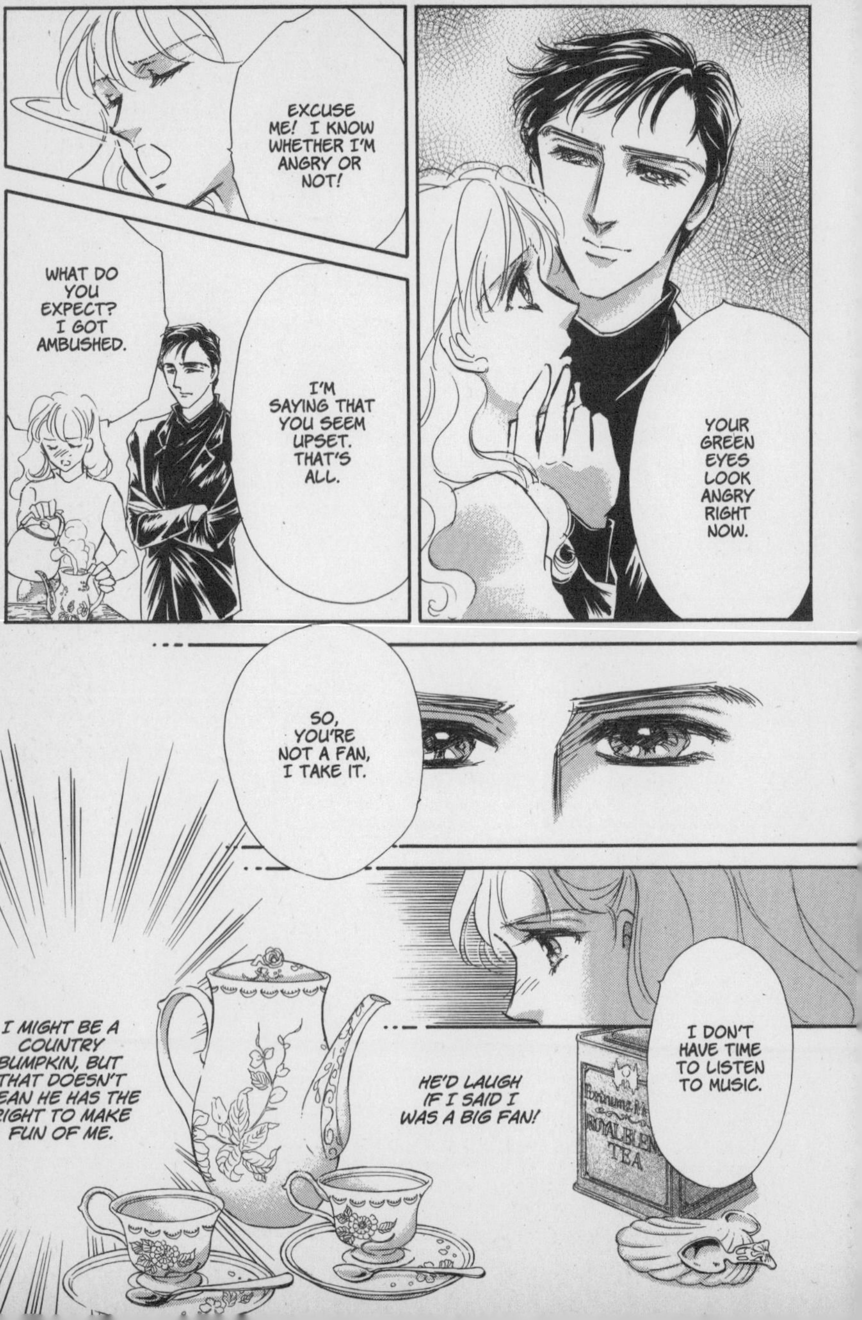
YOUR GREEN EYES LOOK ANGRY RIGHT NOW.
EXCUSE ME! I KNOW WHETHER I'M ANGRY OR NOT!
I'M SAYING THAT YOU SEEM UPSET. THAT'S ALL.
WHAT DO YOU EXPECT? I GOT AMBUSHED.
SO, YOU'RE NOT A FAN, I TAKE IT.
I DON'T HAVE TIME TO LISTEN TO MUSIC.
HE'D LAUGH IF I SAID I WAS A BIG FAN!
I MIGHT BE A COUNTRY BUMPKIN, BUT THAT DOESN'T MEAN HE HAS THE RIGHT TO MAKE FUN OF ME.

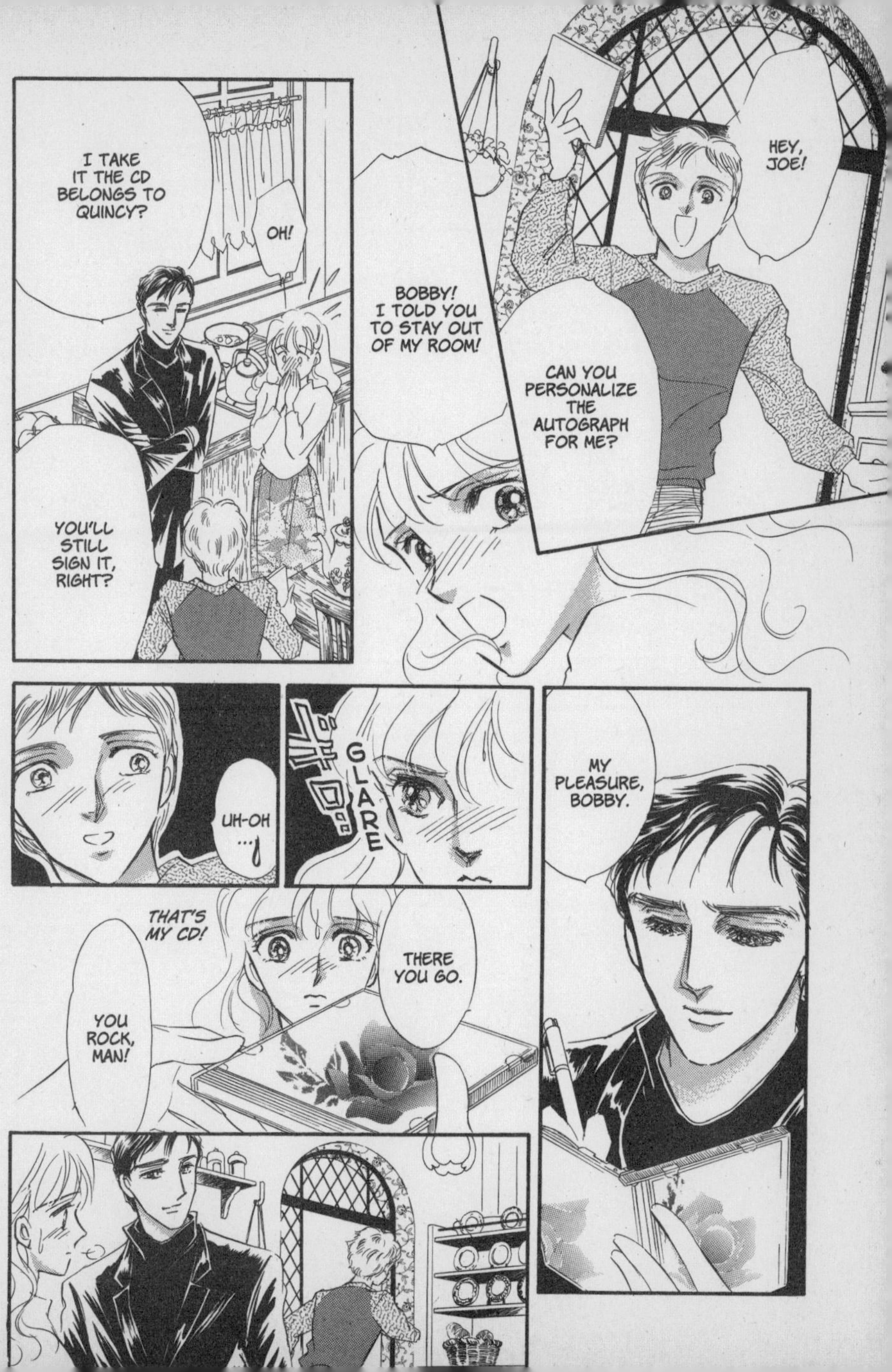
HEY, JOE!
CAN YOU PERSONALIZE THE AUTOGRAPH FOR ME?
BOBBY! I TOLD YOU TO STAY OUT OF MY ROOM!
I TAKE IT THE CD BELONGS TO QUINCY?
OH!
YOU'LL STILL SIGN IT, RIGHT?
MY PLEASURE, BOBBY.
GLARE
UH-OH ...
THERE YOU GO.
THAT'S MY CD!
YOU ROCK, MAN!

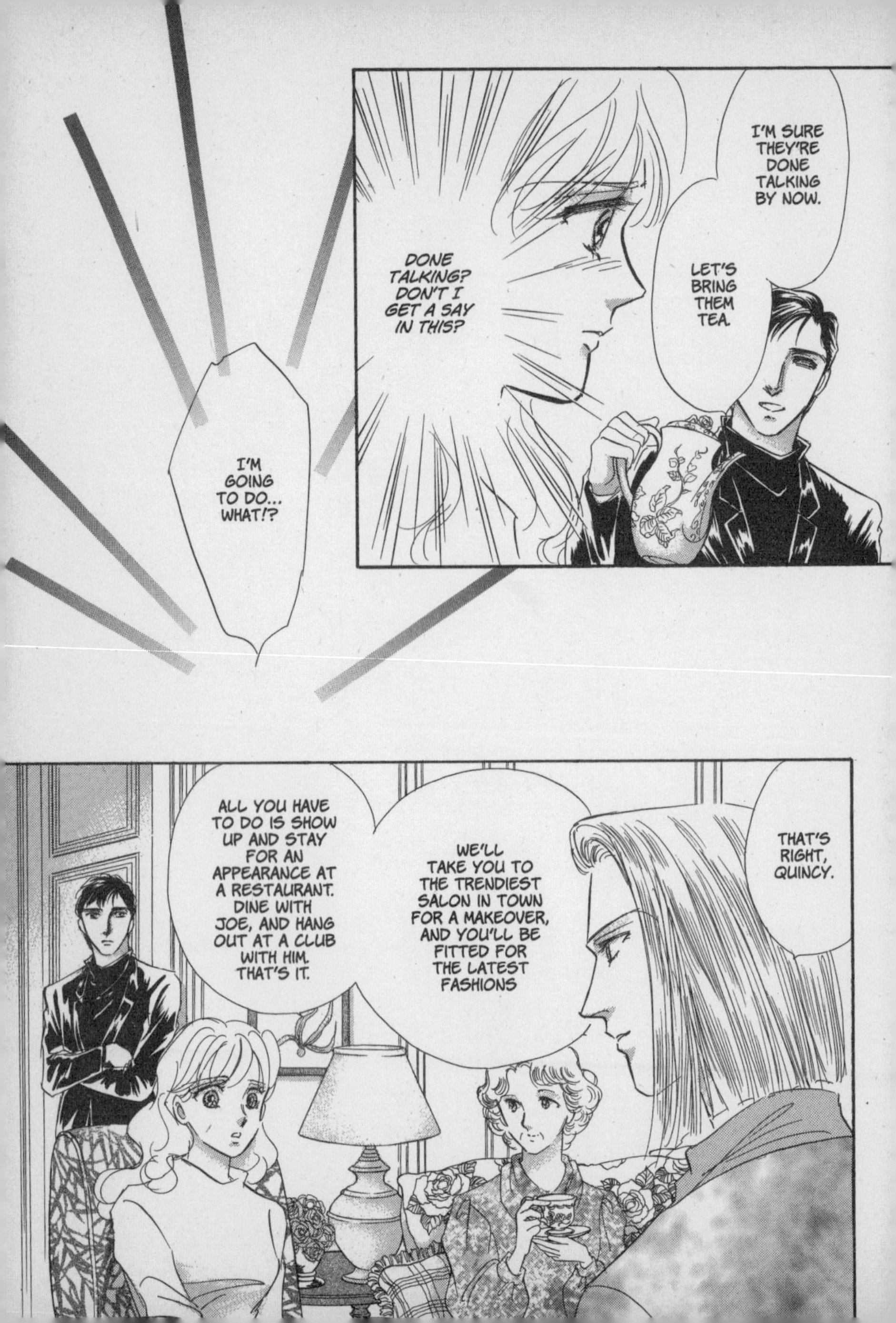
I'M SURE THEY'RE DONE TALKING BY NOW.
LET'S BRING THEM TEA.
DONE TALKING? DON'T I GET A SAY IN THIS?
I'M GOING TO DO... WHAT!?
THAT'S RIGHT, QUINCY.
WE'LL TAKE YOU TO THE TRENDIEST SALON IN TOWN FOR A MAKEOVER, AND YOU'LL BE FITTED FOR THE LATEST FASHIONS
ALL YOU HAVE TO DO IS SHOW UP AND STAY FOR AN APPEARANCE AT A RESTAURANT. DINE WITH JOE, AND HANG OUT AT A CLUB WITH HIM. THAT'S IT.

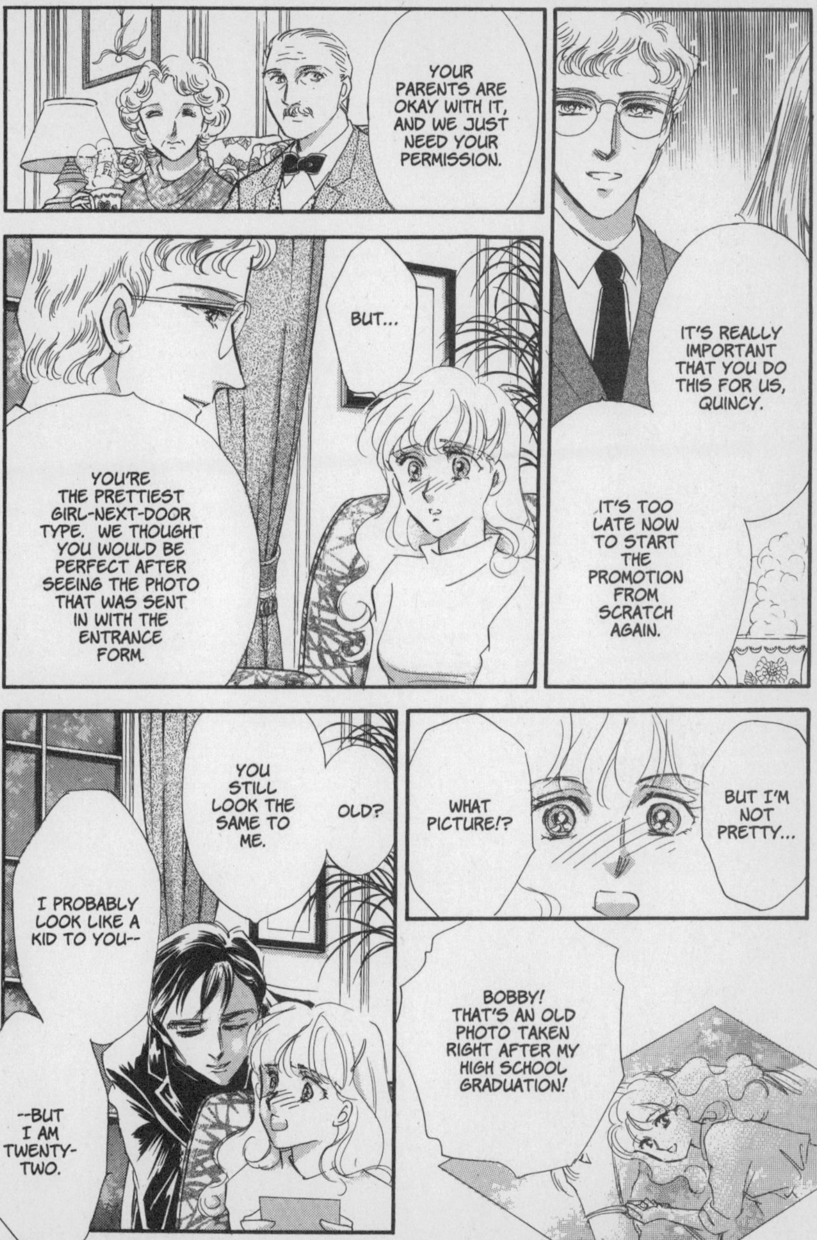
IT'S REALLY IMPORTANT THAT YOU DO THIS FOR US, QUINCY.
IT'S TOO LATE NOW TO START THE PROMOTION FROM SCRATCH AGAIN.
YOUR PARENTS ARE OKAY WITH IT, AND WE JUST NEED YOUR PERMISSION.
BUT...
YOU'RE THE PRETTIEST GIRL-NEXT-DOOR TYPE. WE THOUGHT YOU WOULD BE PERFECT AFTER SEEING THE PHOTO THAT WAS SENT IN WITH THE ENTRANCE FORM.
BUT I'M NOT PRETTY...
WHAT PICTURE!?
BOBBY! THAT'S AN OLD PHOTO TAKEN RIGHT AFTER MY HIGH SCHOOL GRADUATION!
OLD?
YOU STILL LOOK THE SAME TO ME.
I PROBABLY LOOK LIKE A KID TO YOU--
--BUT I AM TWENTY-TWO.

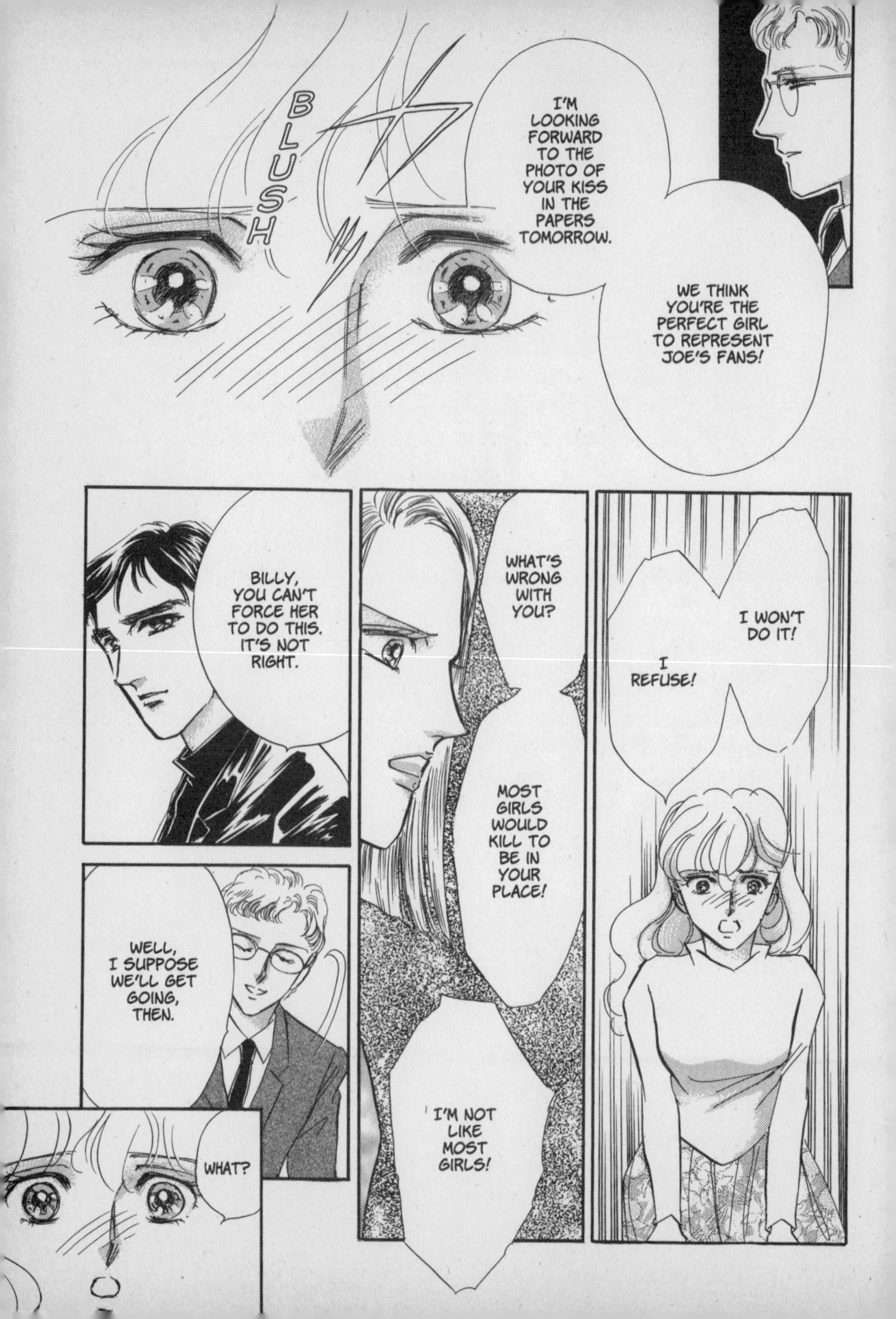
I'M LOOKING FORWARD TO THE PHOTO OF YOUR KISS IN THE PAPERS TOMORROW.
WE THINK YOU'RE THE PERFECT GIRL TO REPRESENT JOE'S FANS!
BLUSH
I WON'T DO IT!
I REFUSE!
WHAT'S WRONG WITH YOU?
MOST GIRLS WOULD KILL TO BE IN YOUR PLACE!
I'M NOT LIKE MOST GIRLS!
BILLY, YOU CAN'T FORCE HER TO DO THIS. IT'S NOT RIGHT.
WELL, I SUPPOSE WE'LL GET GOING, THEN.
WHAT?

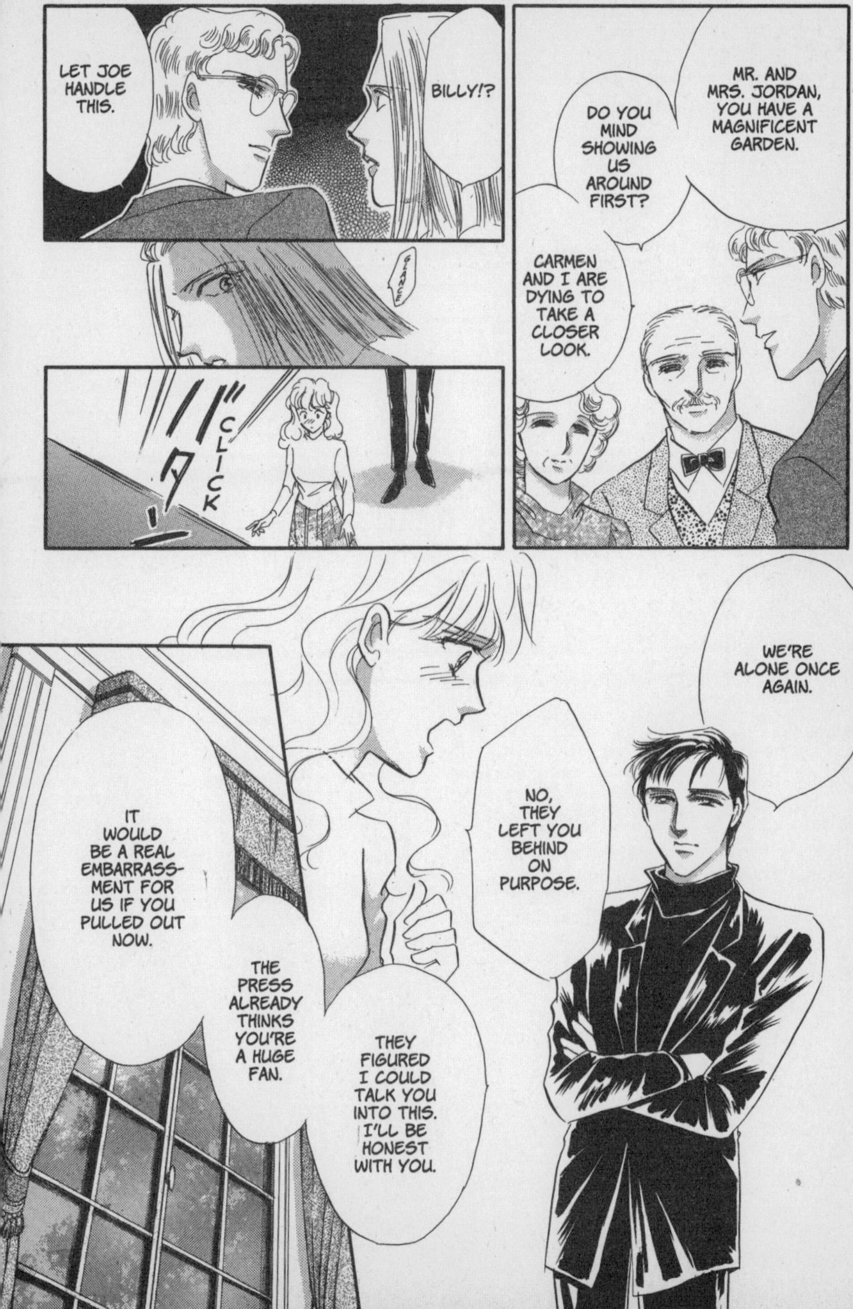
MR. AND MRS. JORDAN, YOU HAVE A MAGNIFICENT GARDEN.
DO YOU MIND SHOWING US AROUND FIRST?
CARMEN AND I ARE DYING TO TAKE A CLOSER LOOK.
BILLY!?
LET JOE HANDLE THIS.
GLANCE
CLICK
WE'RE ALONE ONCE AGAIN.
NO, THEY LEFT YOU BEHIND ON PURPOSE.
THEY FIGURED I COULD TALK YOU INTO THIS. I'LL BE HONEST WITH YOU.
IT WOULD BE A REAL EMBARRASS-MENT FOR US IF YOU PULLED OUT NOW.
THE PRESS ALREADY THINKS YOU'RE A HUGE FAN.

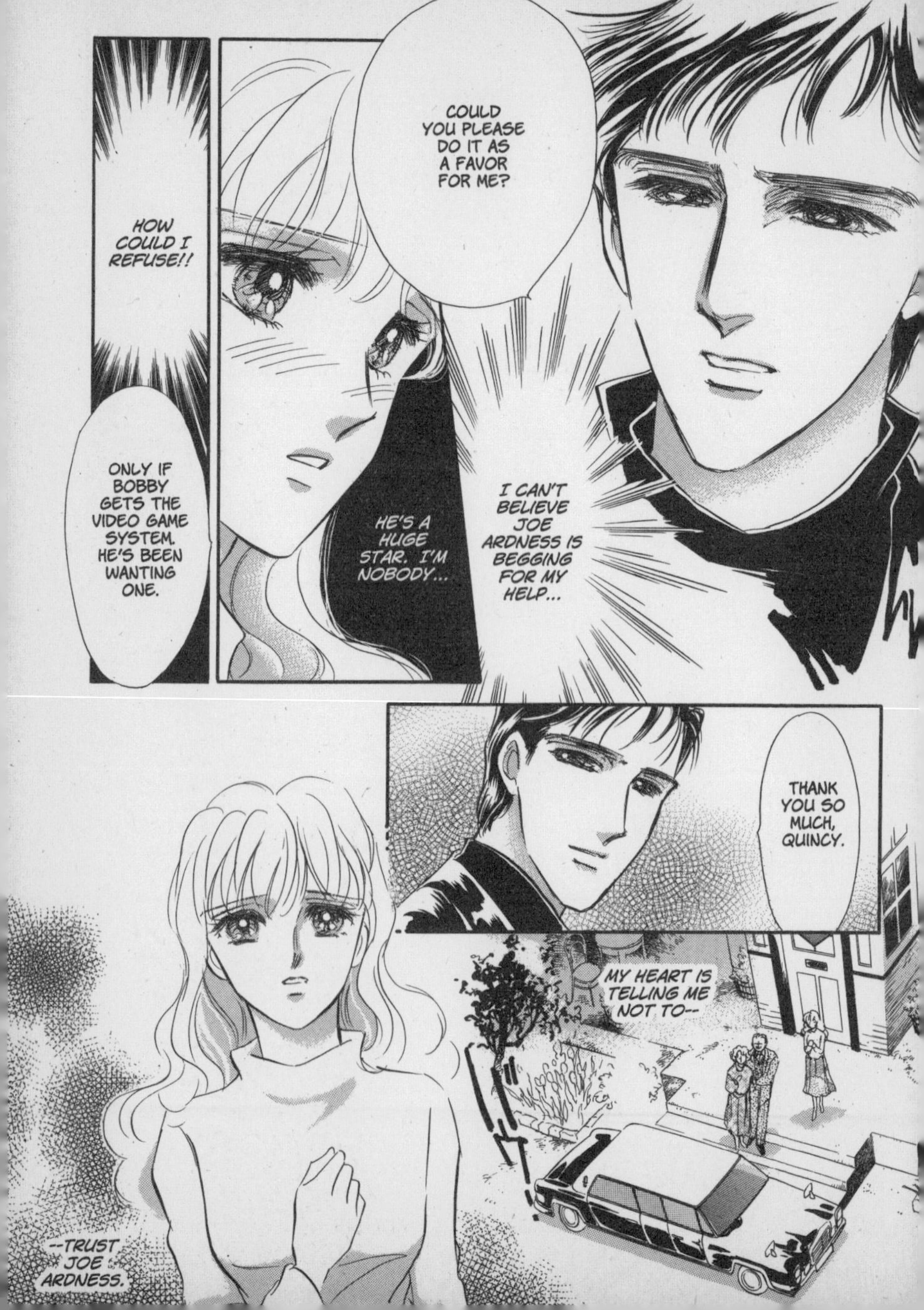
COULD YOU PLEASE DO IT AS A FAVOR FOR ME?
I CAN'T BELIEVE JOE ARDNESS IS BEGGING FOR MY HELP...
HE'S A HUGE STAR. I'M NOBODY...
HOW COULD I REFUSE!!
ONLY IF BOBBY GETS THE VIDEO GAME SYSTEM. HE'S BEEN WANTING ONE.
THANK YOU SO MUCH, QUINCY.
MY HEART IS TELLING ME NOT TO--
--TRUST JOE ARDNESS.

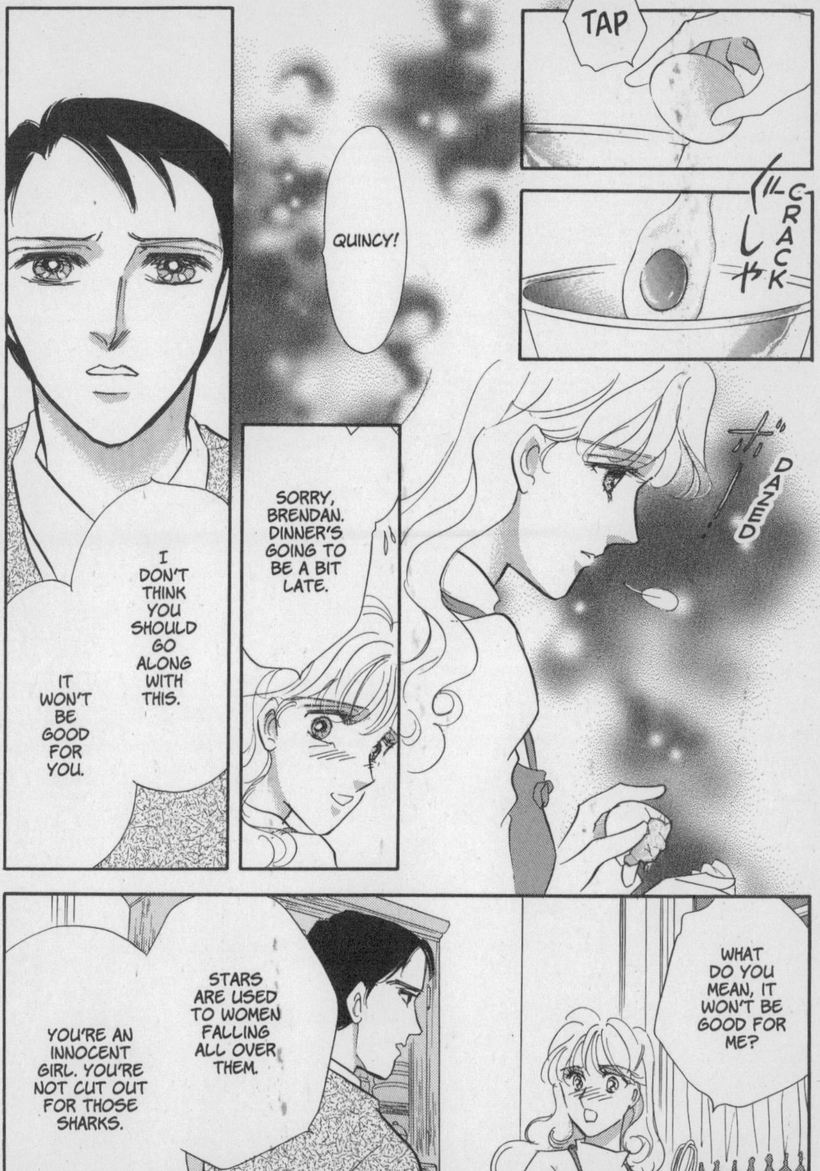
TAP
CRACK
DAZED
QUINCY!
SORRY, BRENDAN. DINNER'S GOING TO BE A BIT LATE.
I DON'T THINK YOU SHOULD GO ALONG WITH THIS.
IT WON'T BE GOOD FOR YOU.
WHAT DO YOU MEAN, IT WON'T BE GOOD FOR ME?
STARS ARE USED TO WOMEN FALLING ALL OVER THEM.
YOU'RE AN INNOCENT GIRL. YOU'RE NOT CUT OUT FOR THOSE SHARKS.

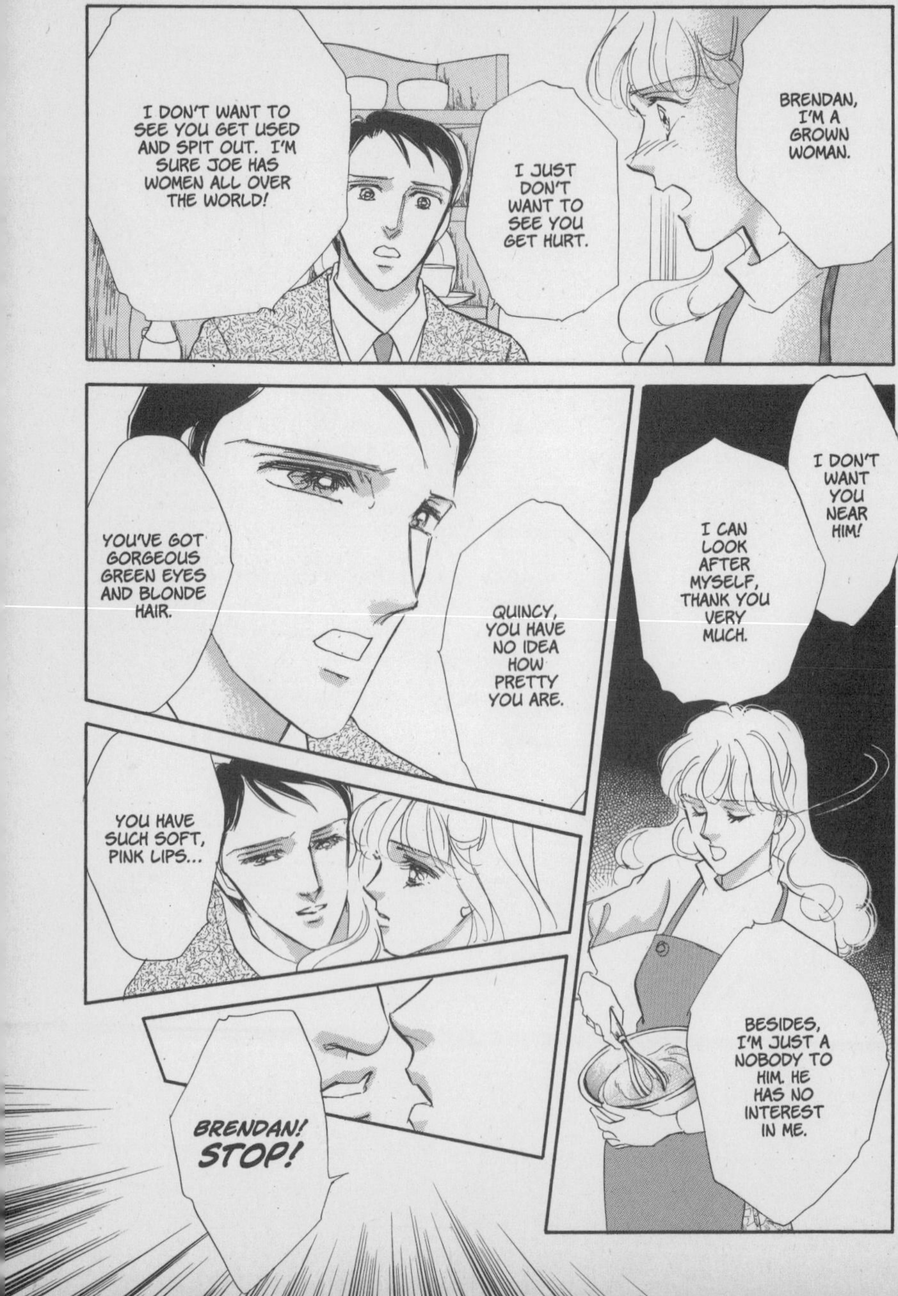
BRENDAN, I'M A GROWN WOMAN.
I JUST DON'T WANT TO SEE YOU GET HURT.
I DON'T WANT TO SEE YOU GET USED AND SPIT OUT. I'M SURE JOE HAS WOMEN ALL OVER THE WORLD!
I DON'T WANT YOU NEAR HIM!
I CAN LOOK AFTER MYSELF, THANK YOU VERY MUCH.
BESIDES, I'M JUST A NOBODY TO HIM. HE HAS NO INTEREST IN ME.
QUINCY, YOU HAVE NO IDEA HOW PRETTY YOU ARE.
YOU'VE GOT GORGEOUS GREEN EYES AND BLONDE HAIR.
YOU HAVE SUCH SOFT, PINK LIPS...
BRENDAN! STOP!

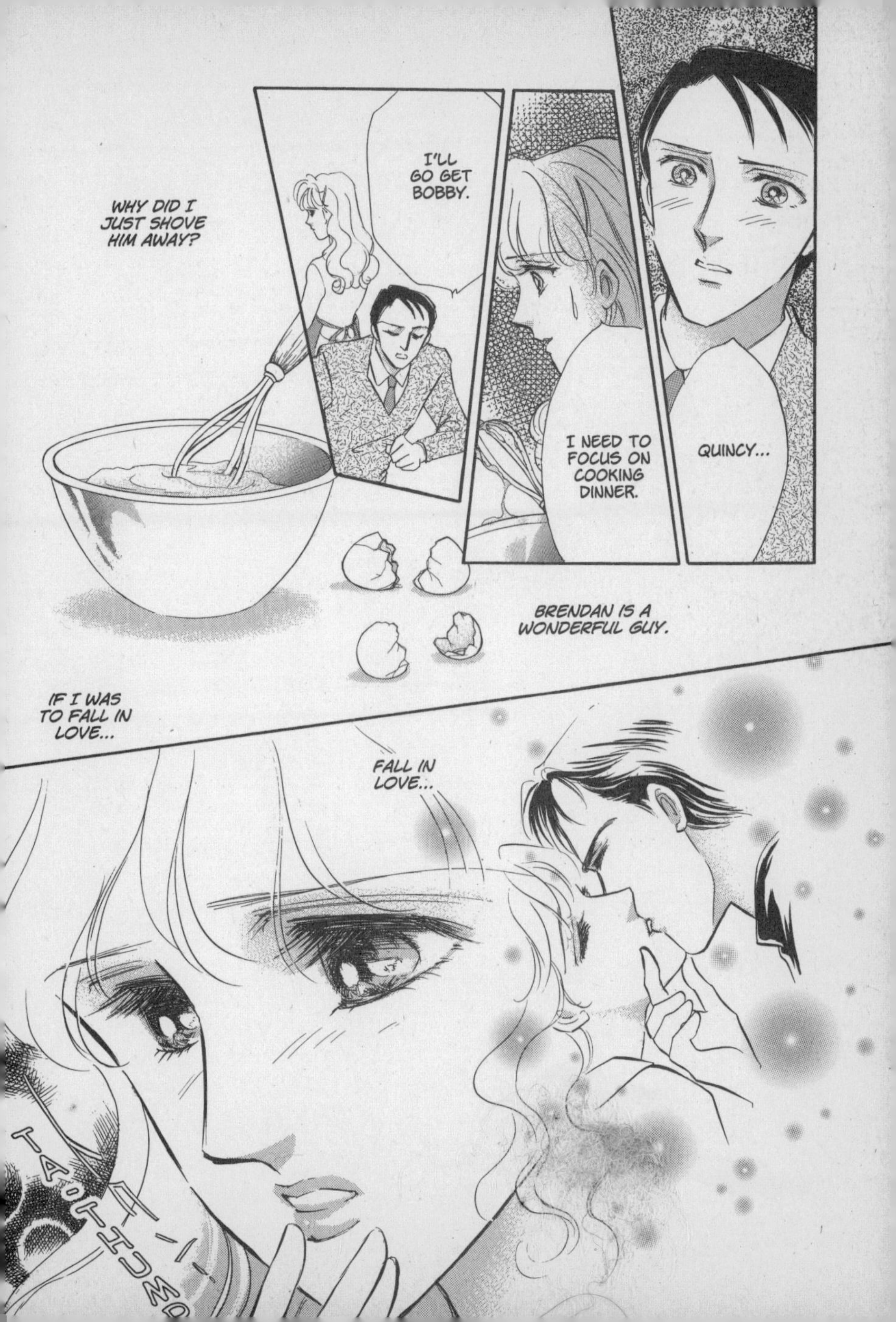
QUINCY...
I NEED TO FOCUS ON COOKING DINNER.
I'LL GO GET BOBBY.
WHY DID I JUST SHOVE HIM AWAY?
BRENDAN IS A WONDERFUL GUY.
IF I WAS TO FALL IN LOVE...
FALL IN LOVE...

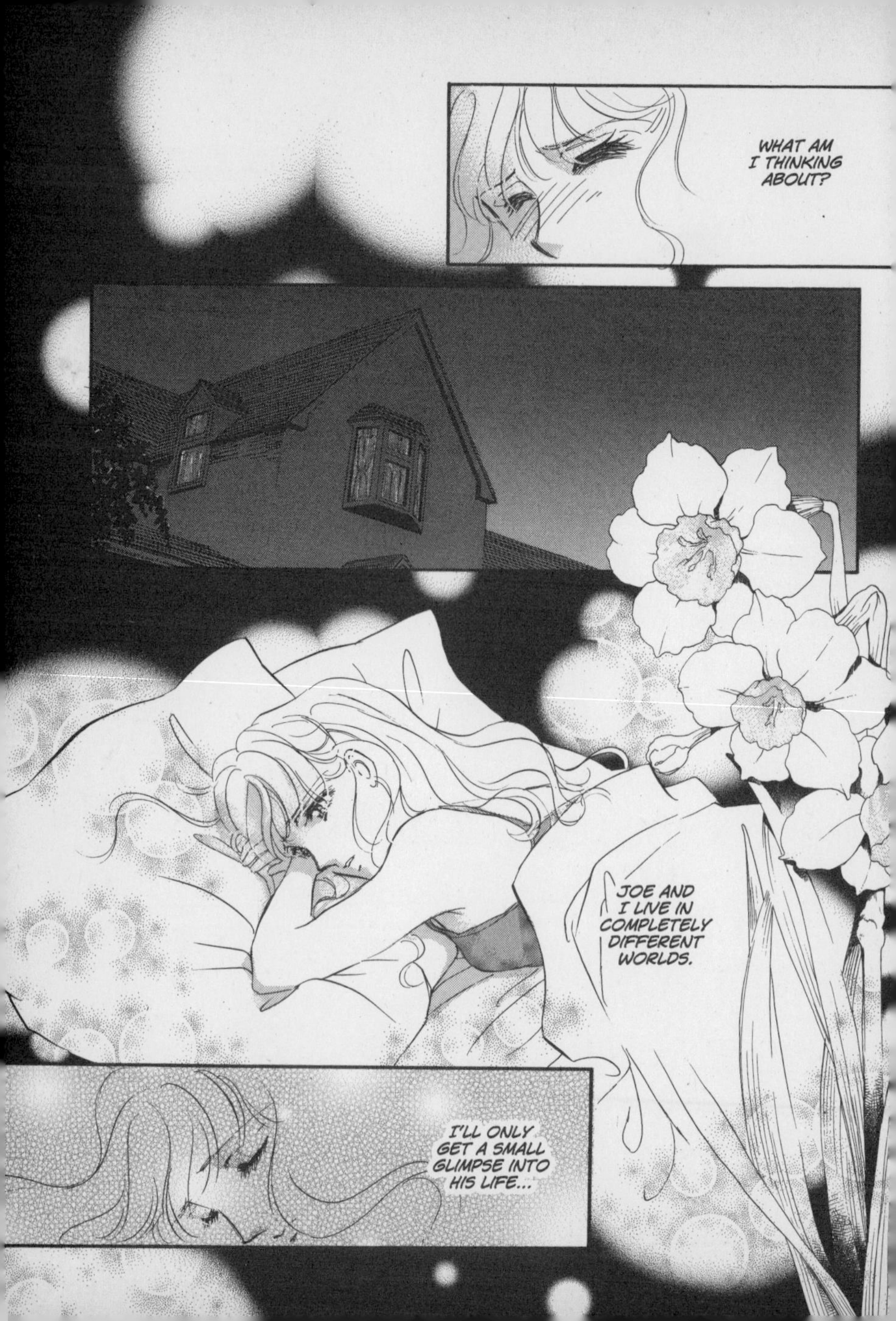
WHAT AM I THINKING ABOUT?
JOE AND I LIVE IN COMPLETELY DIFFERENT WORLDS.
I'LL ONLY GET A SMALL GLIMPSE INTO HIS LIFE...

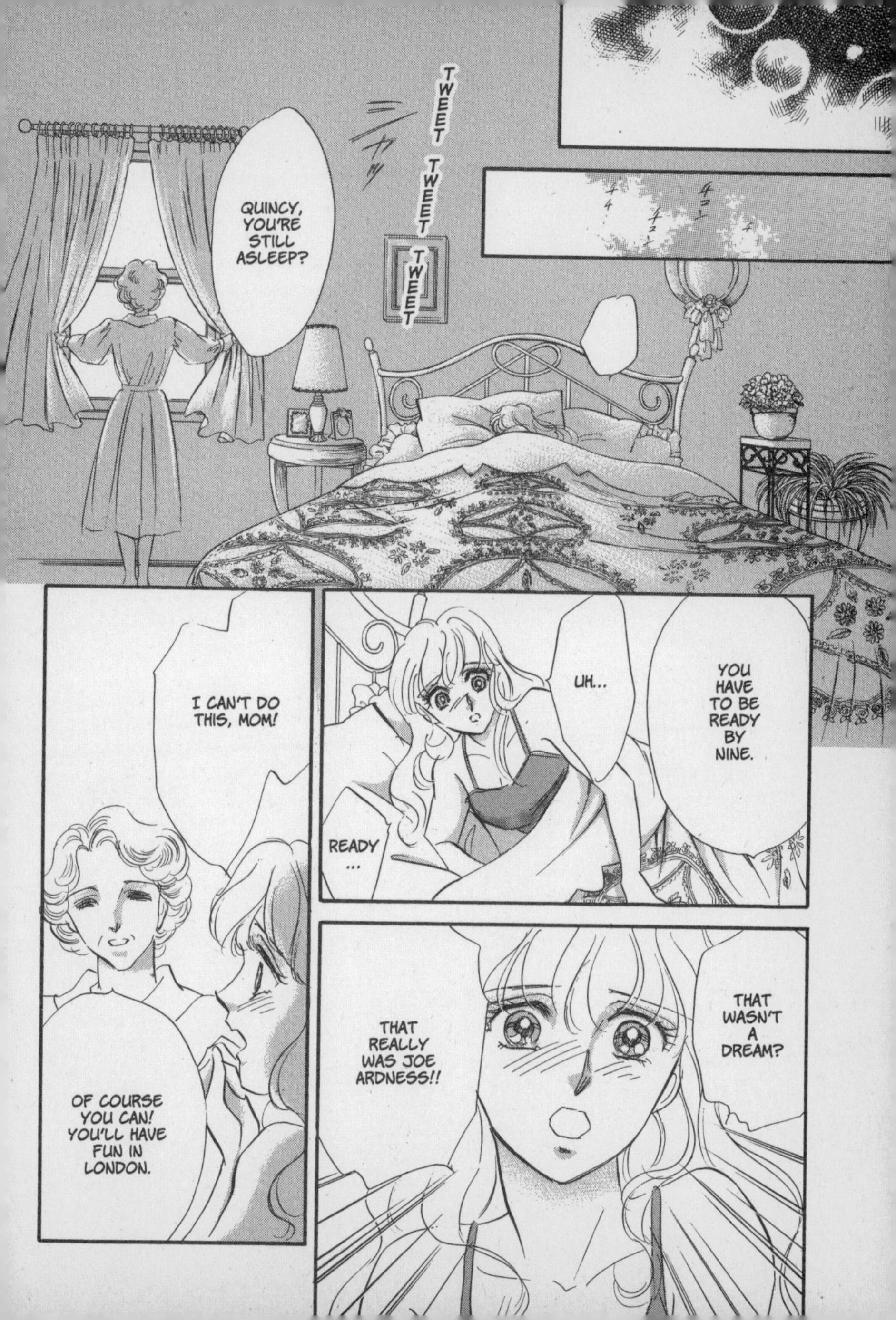
TWEET TWEET TWEET
QUINCY, YOU'RE STILL ASLEEP?
YOU HAVE TO BE READY BY NINE.
UH...
READY ...
THAT WASN'T A DREAM?
THAT REALLY WAS JOE ARDNESS!!
I CAN'T DO THIS, MOM!
OF COURSE YOU CAN! YOU'LL HAVE FUN IN LONDON.

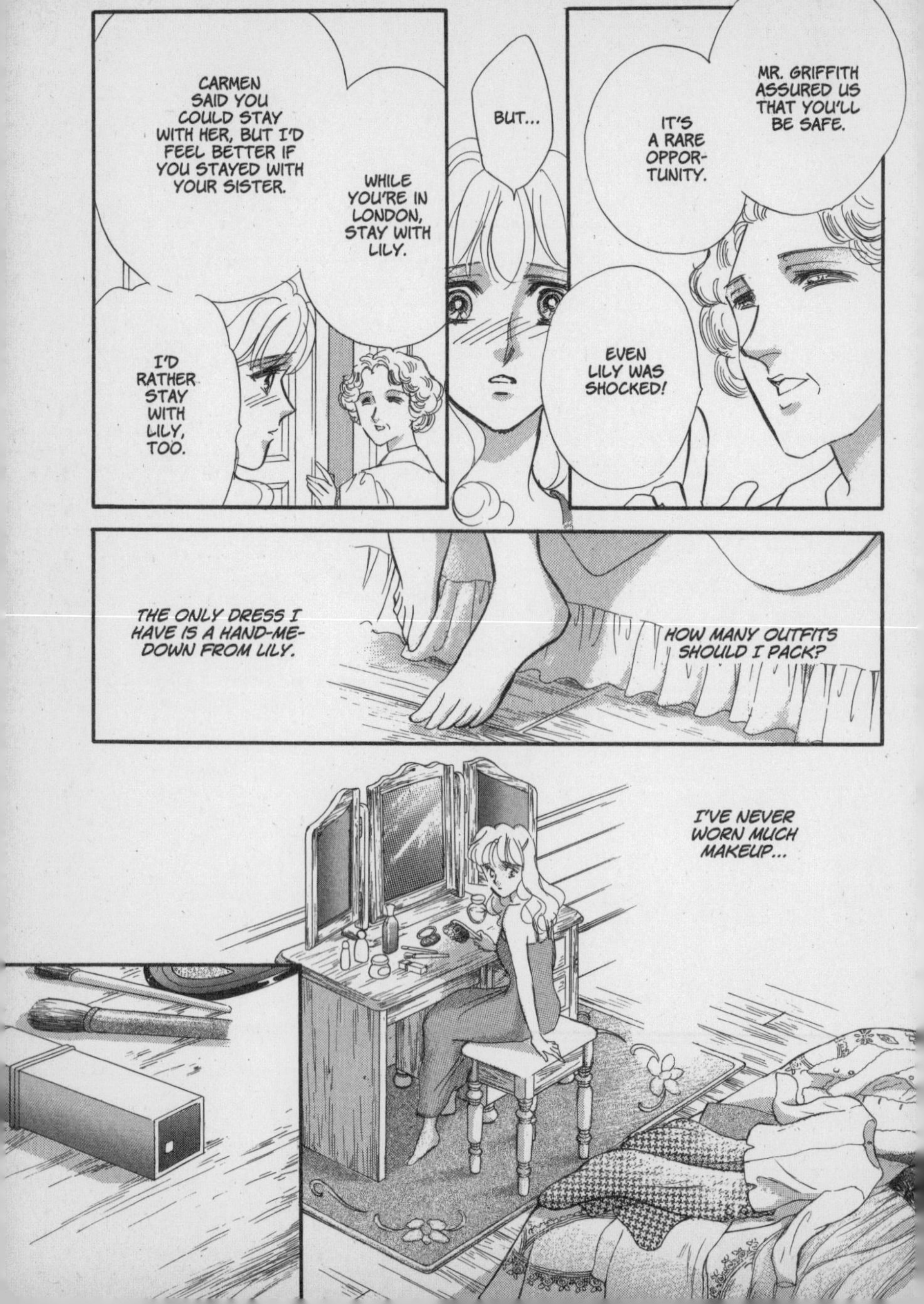
MR. GRIFFITH ASSURED US THAT YOU'LL BE SAFE.
IT'S A RARE OPPOR-TUNITY.
EVEN LILY WAS SHOCKED!
BUT...
WHILE YOU'RE IN LONDON, STAY WITH LILY.
CARMEN SAID YOU COULD STAY WITH HER, BUT I'D FEEL BETTER IF YOU STAYED WITH YOUR SISTER.
I'D RATHER STAY WITH LILY, TOO.
HOW MANY OUTFITS SHOULD I PACK?
THE ONLY DRESS I HAVE IS A HAND-ME-DOWN FROM LILY.
I'VE NEVER WORN MUCH MAKEUP...

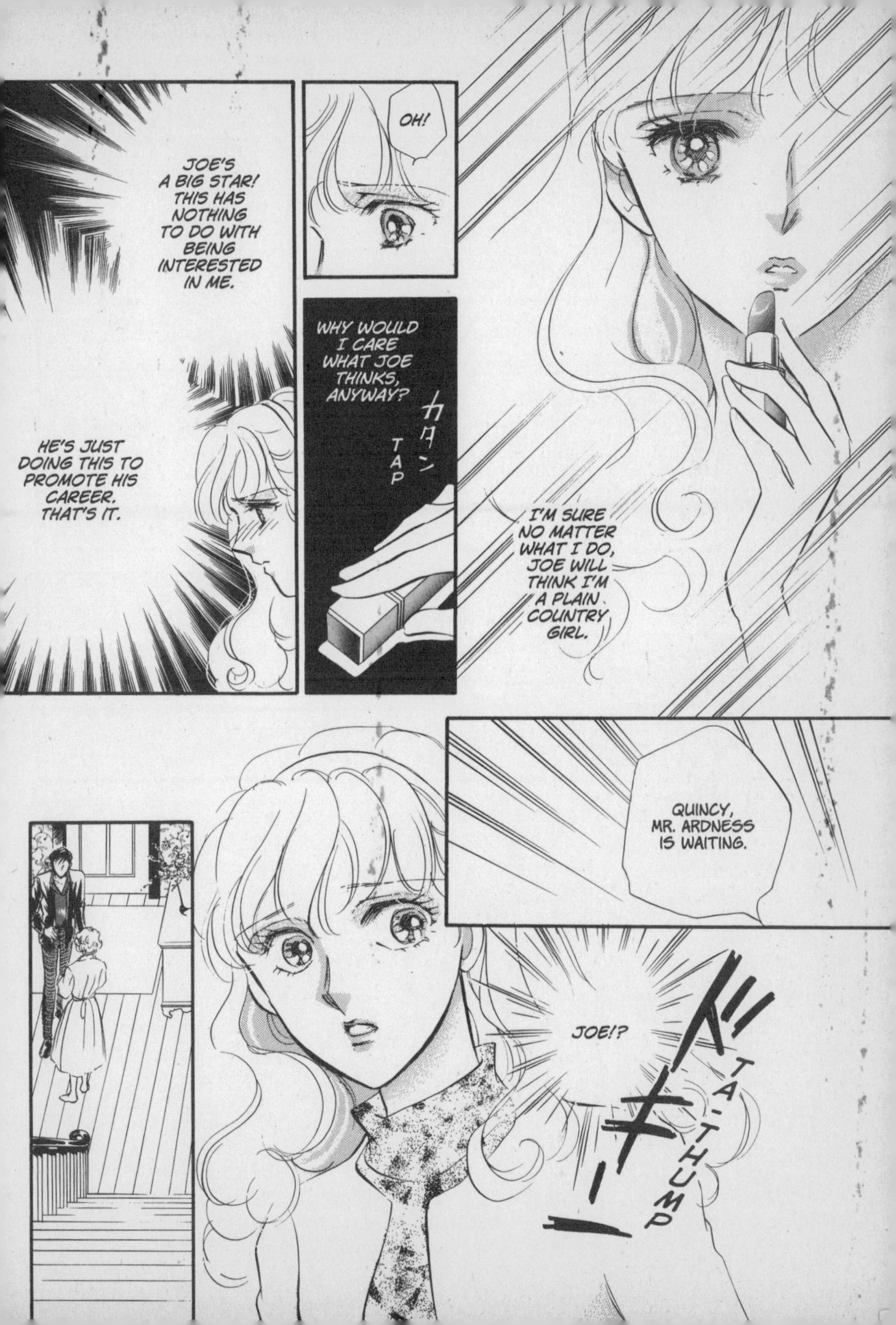
I'M SURE NO MATTER WHAT I DO, JOE WILL THINK I'M A PLAIN COUNTRY GIRL.
OH!
WHY WOULD I CARE WHAT JOE THINKS, ANYWAY?
カタン
TAP
JOE'S A BIG STAR! THIS HAS NOTHING TO DO WITH BEING INTERESTED IN ME.
HE'S JUST DOING THIS TO PROMOTE HIS CAREER. THAT'S IT.
QUINCY, MR. ARDNESS IS WAITING.
JOE!?
TA-THUMP

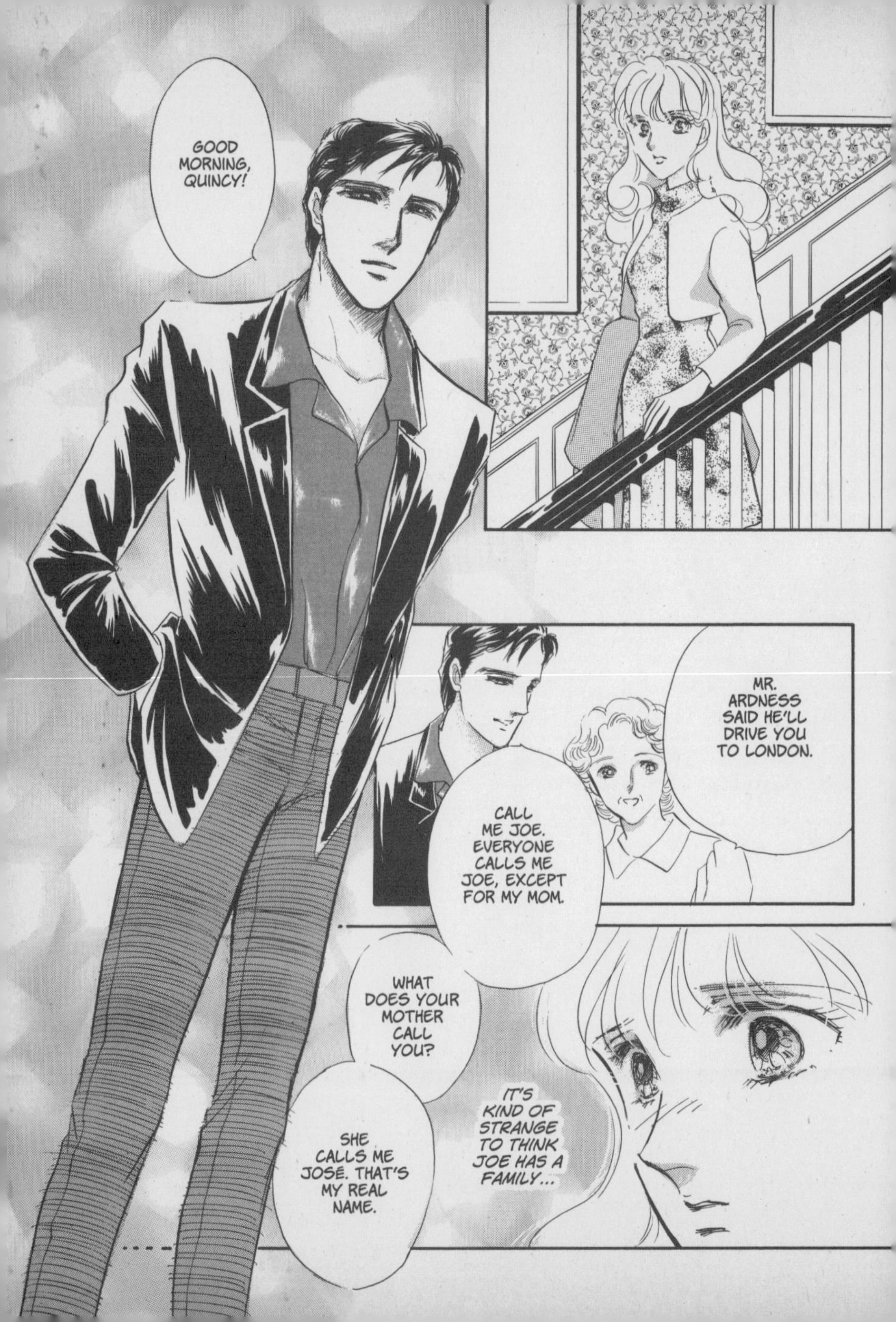
GOOD MORNING, QUINCY!
MR. ARDNESS SAID HE'LL DRIVE YOU TO LONDON.
CALL ME JOE. EVERYONE CALLS ME JOE, EXCEPT FOR MY MOM.
WHAT DOES YOUR MOTHER CALL YOU?
SHE CALLS ME JOSÉ. THAT'S MY REAL NAME.
IT'S KIND OF STRANGE TO THINK JOE HAS A FAMILY...

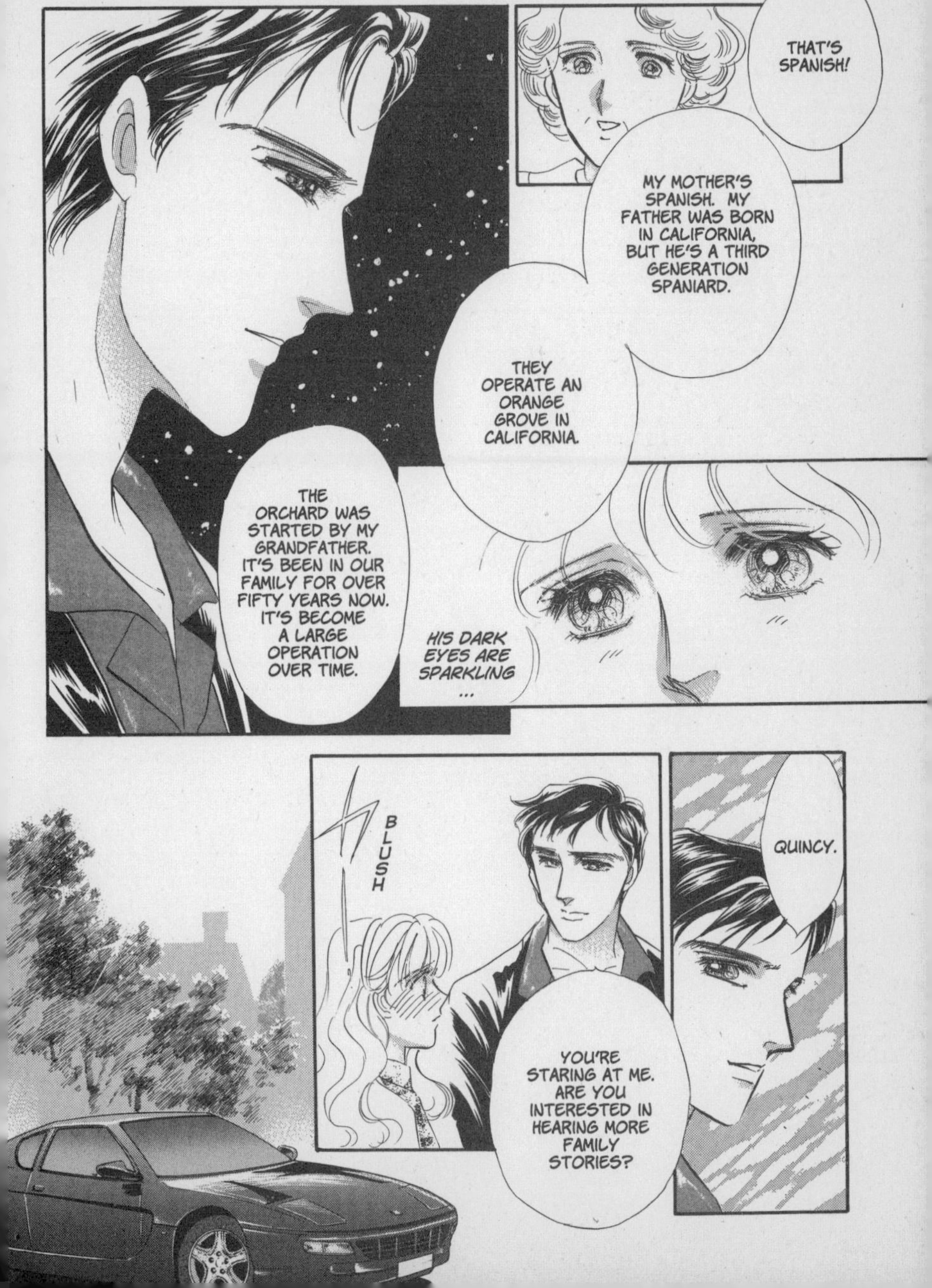
THAT'S SPANISH!
MY MOTHER'S SPANISH. MY FATHER WAS BORN IN CALIFORNIA, BUT HE'S A THIRD GENERATION SPANIARD.
THEY OPERATE AN ORANGE GROVE IN CALIFORNIA.
HIS DARK EYES ARE SPARKLING ...
THE ORCHARD WAS STARTED BY MY GRANDFATHER. IT'S BEEN IN OUR FAMILY FOR OVER FIFTY YEARS NOW. IT'S BECOME A LARGE OPERATION OVER TIME.
QUINCY.
YOU'RE STARING AT ME. ARE YOU INTERESTED IN HEARING MORE FAMILY STORIES?
BLUSH

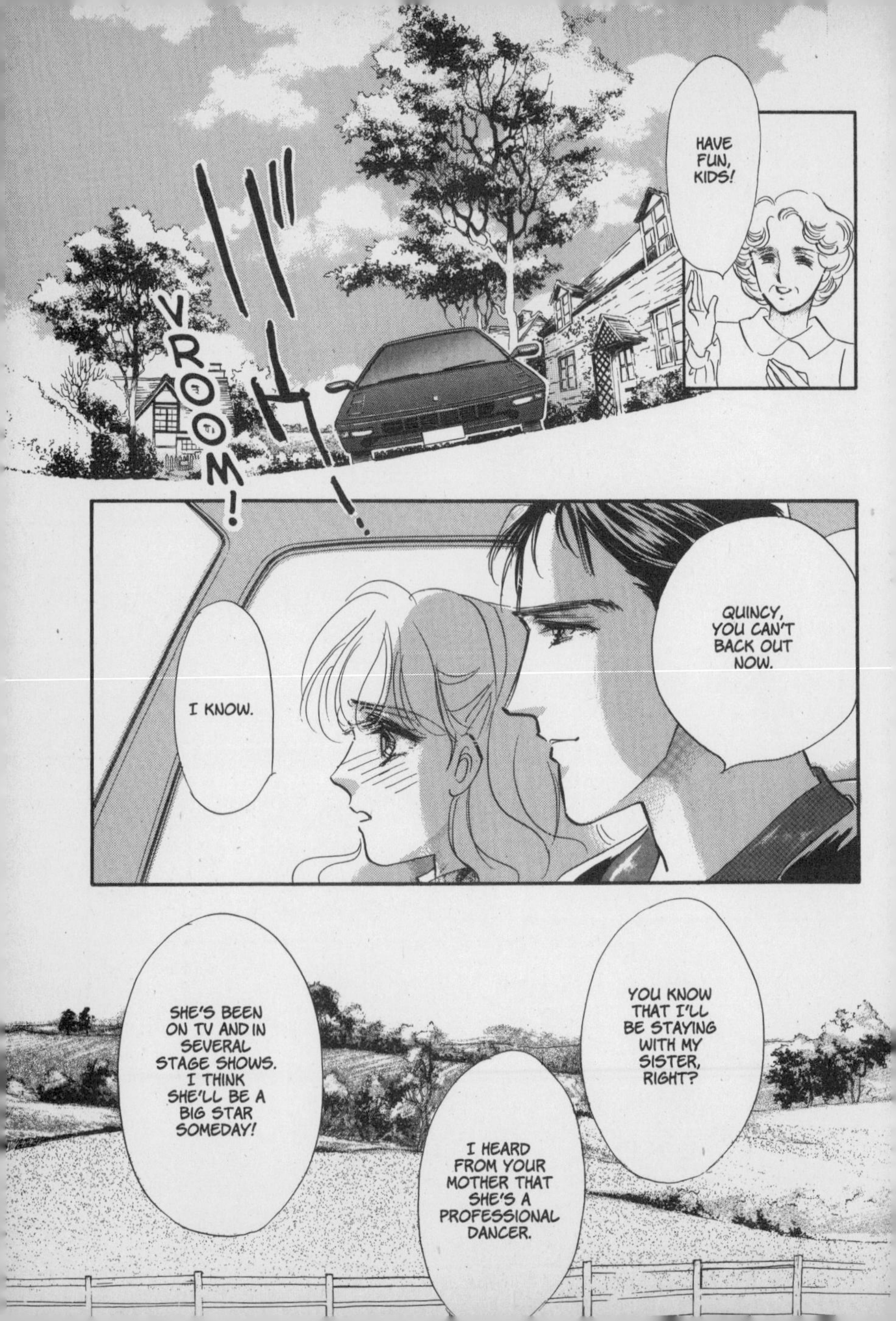
HAVE FUN, KIDS!
VROOM!
QUINCY, YOU CAN'T BACK OUT NOW.
I KNOW.
YOU KNOW THAT I'LL BE STAYING WITH MY SISTER, RIGHT?
I HEARD FROM YOUR MOTHER THAT SHE'S A PROFESSIONAL DANCER.
SHE'S BEEN ON TV AND IN SEVERAL STAGE SHOWS. I THINK SHE'LL BE A BIG STAR SOMEDAY!

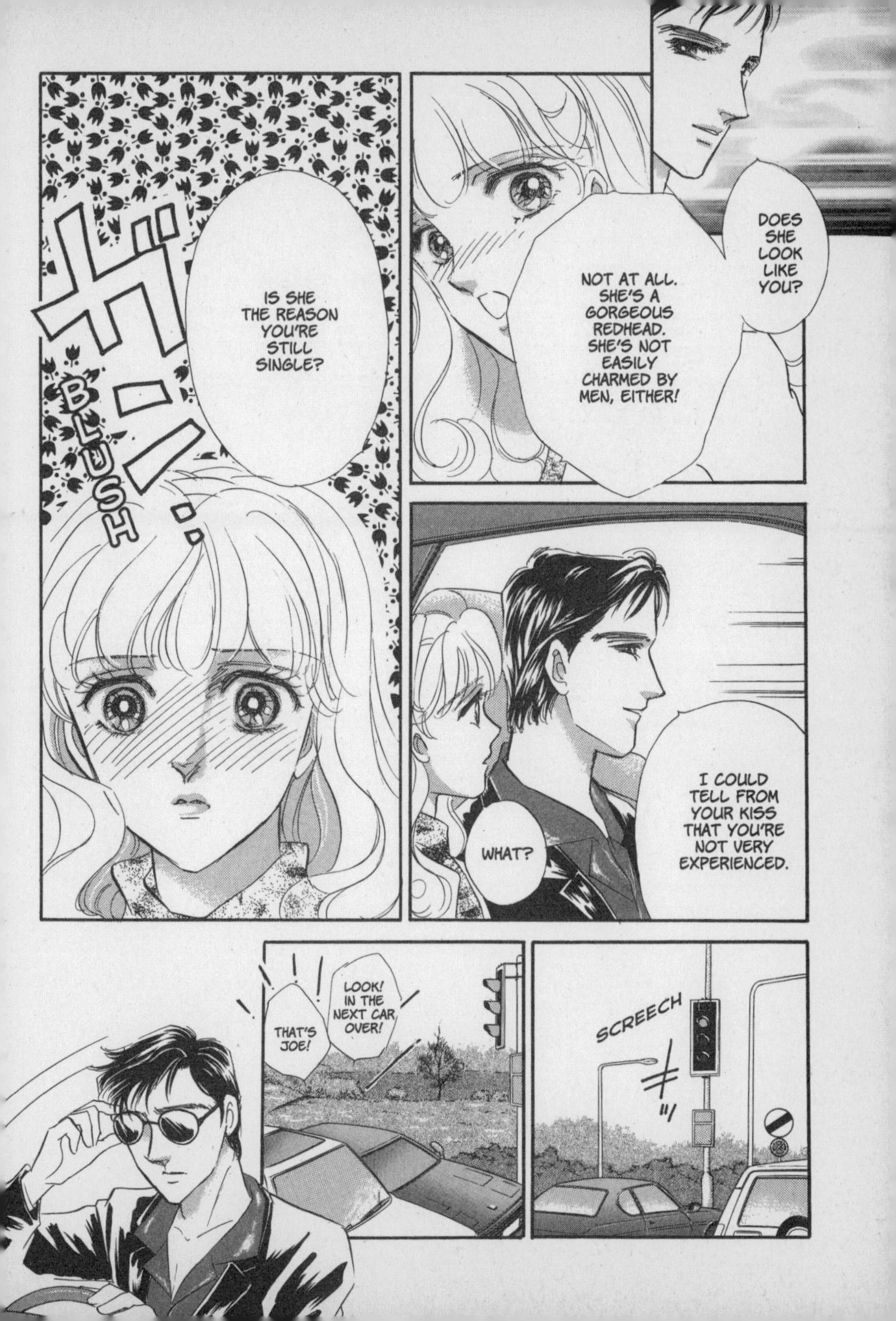
DOES SHE LOOK LIKE YOU?
NOT AT ALL. SHE'S A GORGEOUS REDHEAD. SHE'S NOT EASILY CHARMED BY MEN, EITHER!
IS SHE THE REASON YOU'RE STILL SINGLE?
BLUSH
I COULD TELL FROM YOUR KISS THAT YOU'RE NOT VERY EXPERIENCED.
WHAT?
SCREECH
LOOK! IN THE NEXT CAR OVER!
THAT'S JOE!

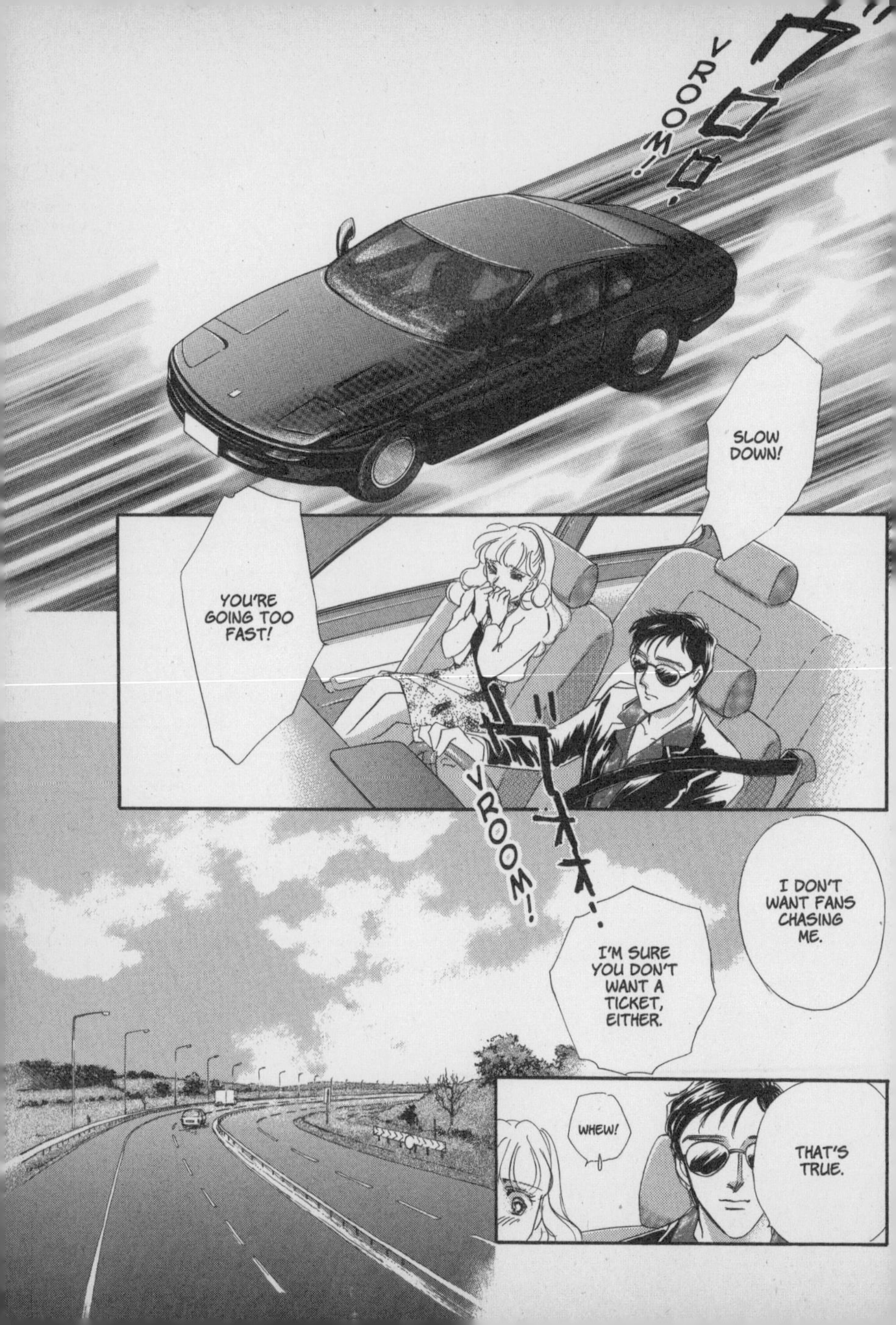
VROOM!
SLOW DOWN!
YOU'RE GOING TOO FAST!
VROOM!
I DON'T WANT FANS CHASING ME.
I'M SURE YOU DON'T WANT A TICKET, EITHER.
THAT'S TRUE.
WHEW!

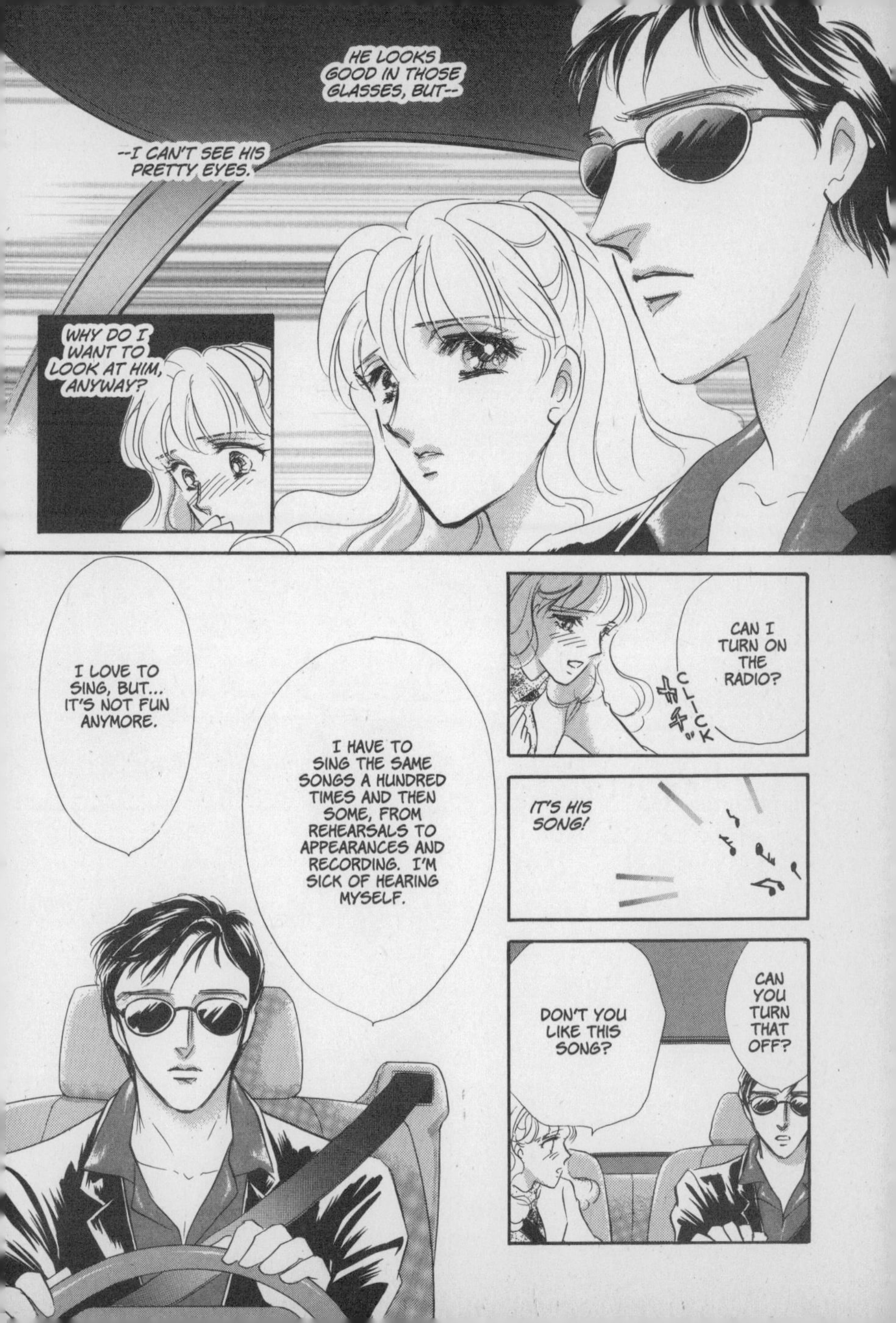
HE LOOKS GOOD IN THOSE GLASSES, BUT--
--I CAN'T SEE HIS PRETTY EYES.
WHY DO I WANT TO LOOK AT HIM, ANYWAY?
CAN I TURN ON THE RADIO?
CLICK
IT'S HIS SONG!
CAN YOU TURN THAT OFF?
DON'T YOU LIKE THIS SONG?
I LOVE TO SING, BUT... IT'S NOT FUN ANYMORE.
I HAVE TO SING THE SAME SONGS A HUNDRED TIMES AND THEN SOME, FROM REHEARSALS TO APPEARANCES AND RECORDING. I'M SICK OF HEARING MYSELF.

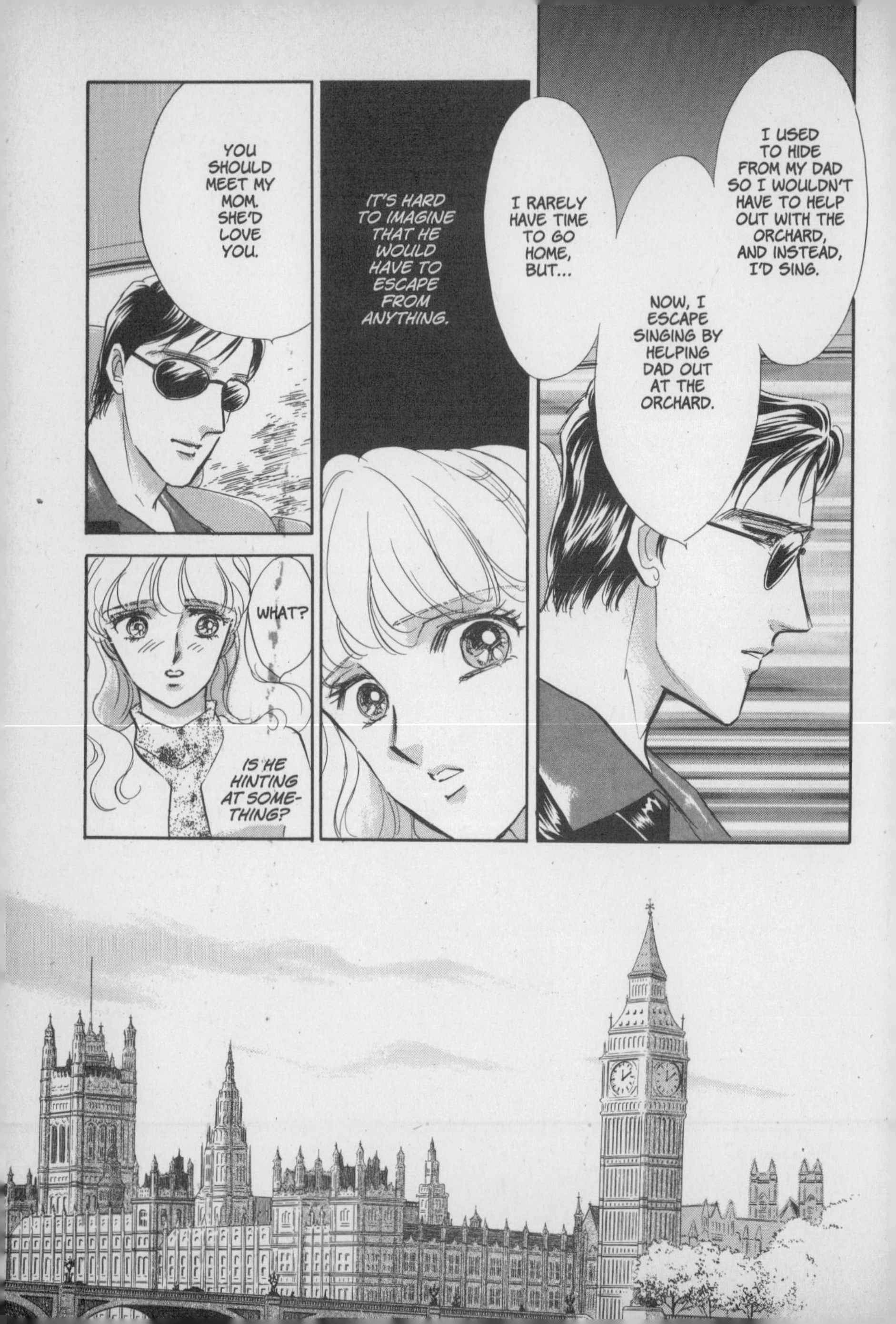

I USED TO HIDE FROM MY DAD SO I WOULDN'T HAVE TO HELP OUT WITH THE ORCHARD, AND INSTEAD, I'D SING.
I RARELY HAVE TIME TO GO HOME, BUT...
NOW, I ESCAPE SINGING BY HELPING DAD OUT AT THE ORCHARD.
IT'S HARD TO IMAGINE THAT HE WOULD HAVE TO ESCAPE FROM ANYTHING.
YOU SHOULD MEET MY MOM. SHE'D LOVE YOU.
WHAT?
IS HE HINTING AT SOME-THING?

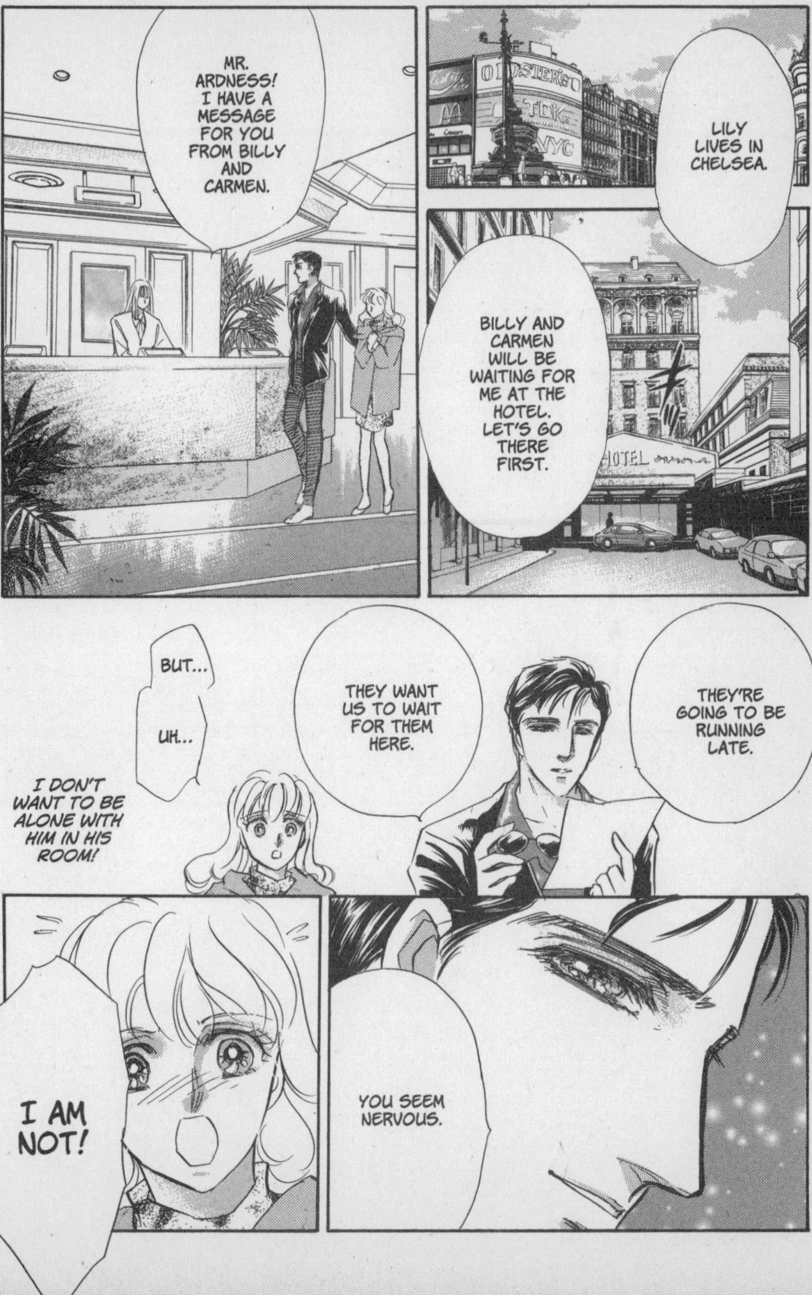
LILY LIVES IN CHELSEA.
TDK
NYC
BILLY AND CARMEN WILL BE WAITING FOR ME AT THE HOTEL. LET'S GO THERE FIRST.
HOTEL
MR. ARDNESS! I HAVE A MESSAGE FOR YOU FROM BILLY AND CARMEN.
THEY'RE GOING TO BE RUNNING LATE.
THEY WANT US TO WAIT FOR THEM HERE.
BUT...
UH...
I DON'T WANT TO BE ALONE WITH HIM IN HIS ROOM!
YOU SEEM NERVOUS.
I AM NOT!

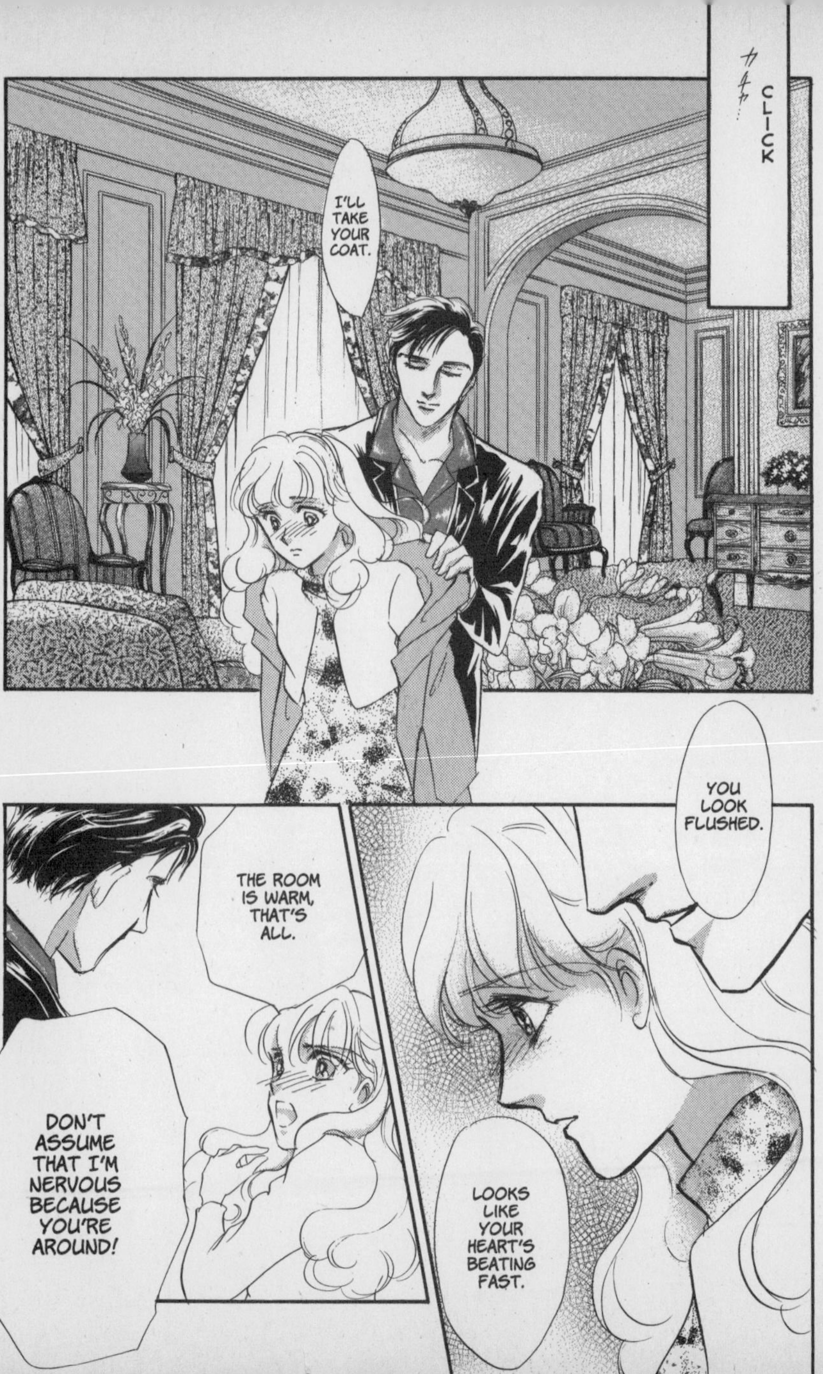

CLICK
カチャ…
I'LL TAKE YOUR COAT.
YOU LOOK FLUSHED.
LOOKS LIKE YOUR HEART'S BEATING FAST.
THE ROOM IS WARM, THAT'S ALL.
DON'T ASSUME THAT I'M NERVOUS BECAUSE YOU'RE AROUND!

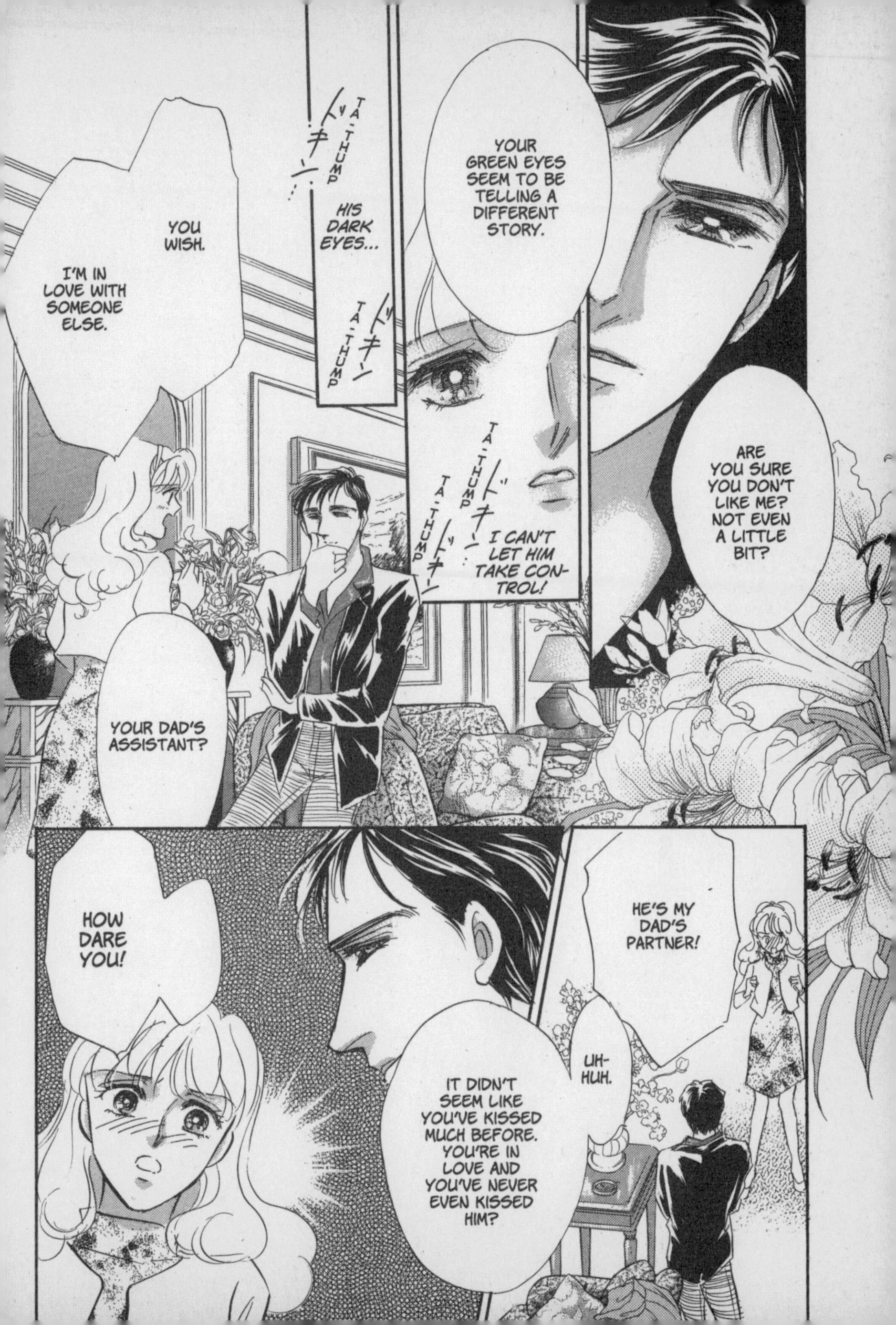

YOUR GREEN EYES SEEM TO BE TELLING A DIFFERENT STORY.
ARE YOU SURE YOU DON'T LIKE ME? NOT EVEN A LITTLE BIT?
TA-THUMP
HIS DARK EYES...
TA-THUMP
TA-THUMP
TA-THUMP
I CAN'T LET HIM TAKE CON-TROL!
YOU WISH.
I'M IN LOVE WITH SOMEONE ELSE.
YOUR DAD'S ASSISTANT?
HE'S MY DAD'S PARTNER!
UH-HUH.
IT DIDN'T SEEM LIKE YOU'VE KISSED MUCH BEFORE. YOU'RE IN LOVE AND YOU'VE NEVER EVEN KISSED HIM?
HOW DARE YOU!

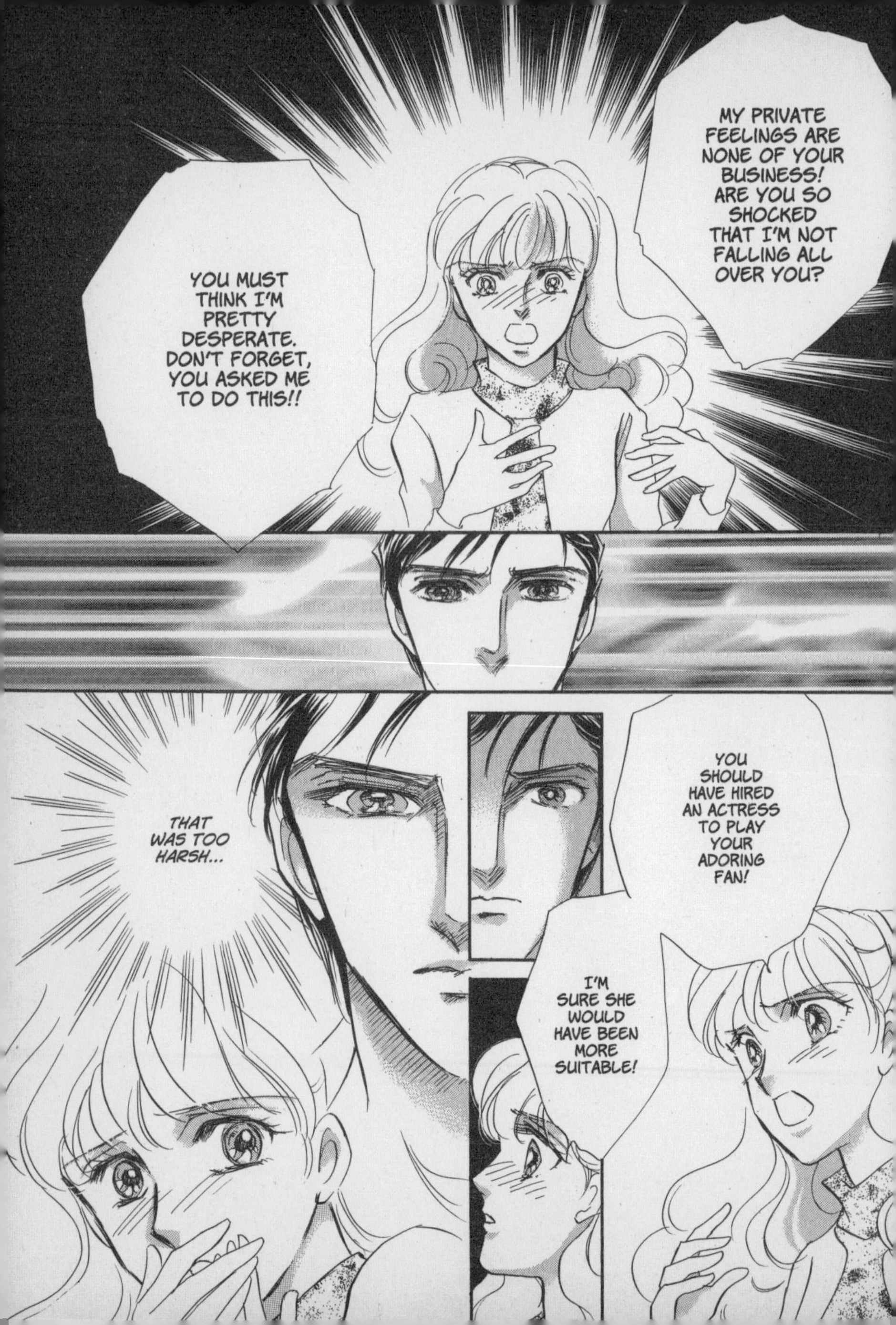
MY PRIVATE FEELINGS ARE NONE OF YOUR BUSINESS! ARE YOU SO SHOCKED THAT I'M NOT FALLING ALL OVER YOU?
YOU MUST THINK I'M PRETTY DESPERATE. DON'T FORGET, YOU ASKED ME TO DO THIS!!
YOU SHOULD HAVE HIRED AN ACTRESS TO PLAY YOUR ADORING FAN!
I'M SURE SHE WOULD HAVE BEEN MORE SUITABLE!
THAT WAS TOO HARSH...

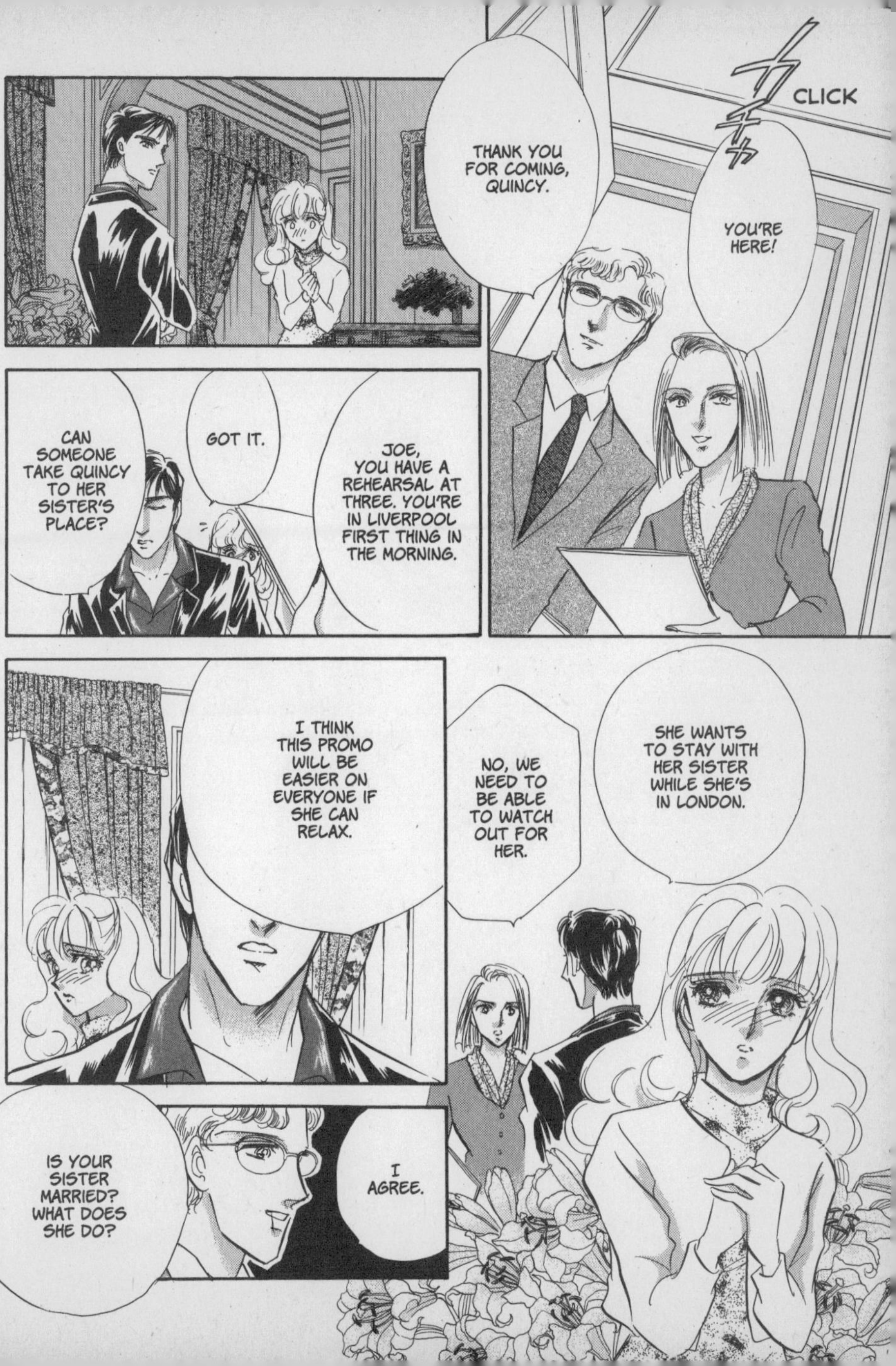
CLICK
YOU'RE HERE!
THANK YOU FOR COMING, QUINCY.
JOE, YOU HAVE A REHEARSAL AT THREE. YOU'RE IN LIVERPOOL FIRST THING IN THE MORNING.
GOT IT.
CAN SOMEONE TAKE QUINCY TO HER SISTER'S PLACE?
SHE WANTS TO STAY WITH HER SISTER WHILE SHE'S IN LONDON.
NO, WE NEED TO BE ABLE TO WATCH OUT FOR HER.
I THINK THIS PROMO WILL BE EASIER ON EVERYONE IF SHE CAN RELAX.
I AGREE.
IS YOUR SISTER MARRIED? WHAT DOES SHE DO?

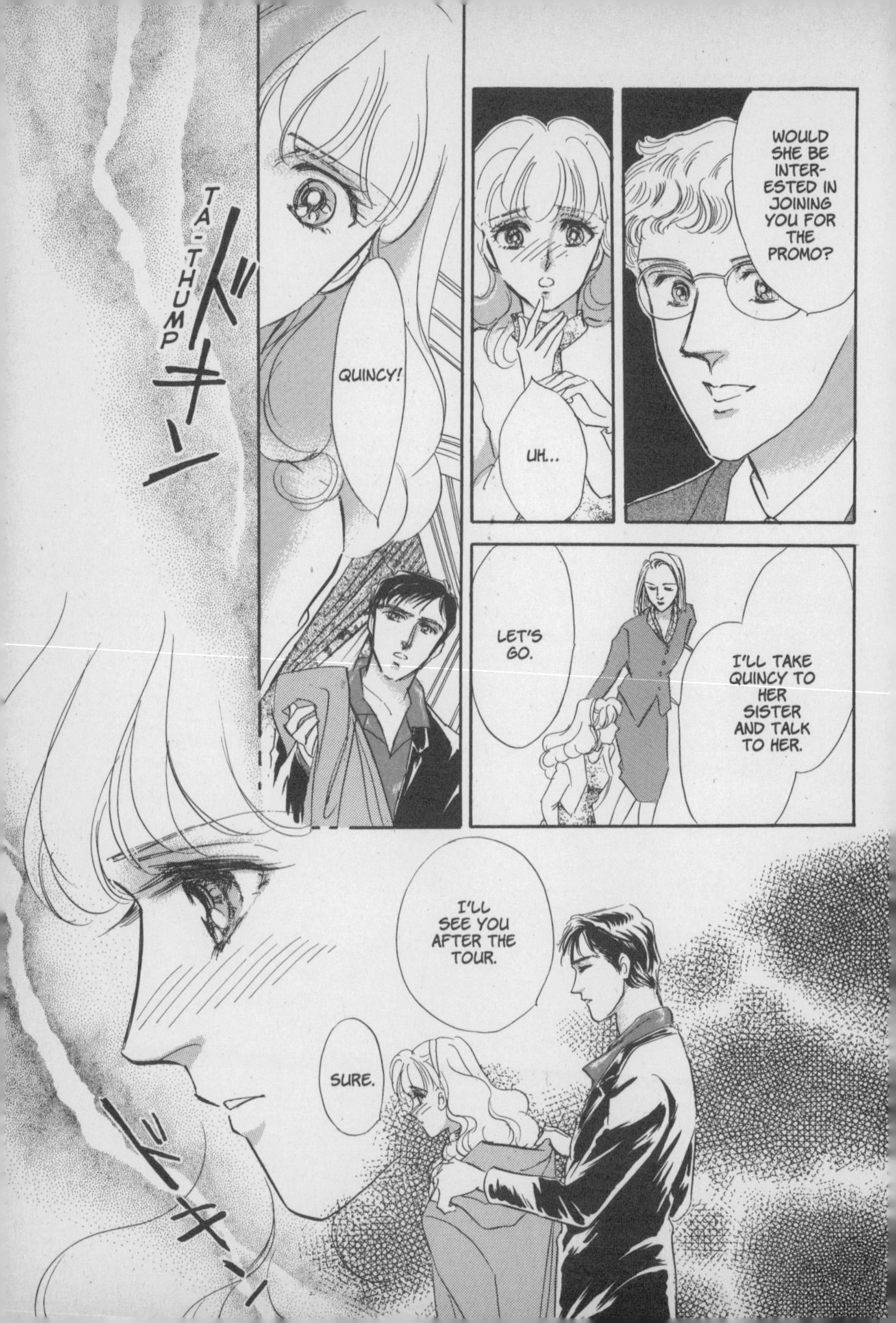
WOULD SHE BE INTER-ESTED IN JOINING YOU FOR THE PROMO?
UH...
I'LL TAKE QUINCY TO HER SISTER AND TALK TO HER.
LET'S GO.
QUINCY!
TA-THUMP
I'LL SEE YOU AFTER THE TOUR.
SURE.

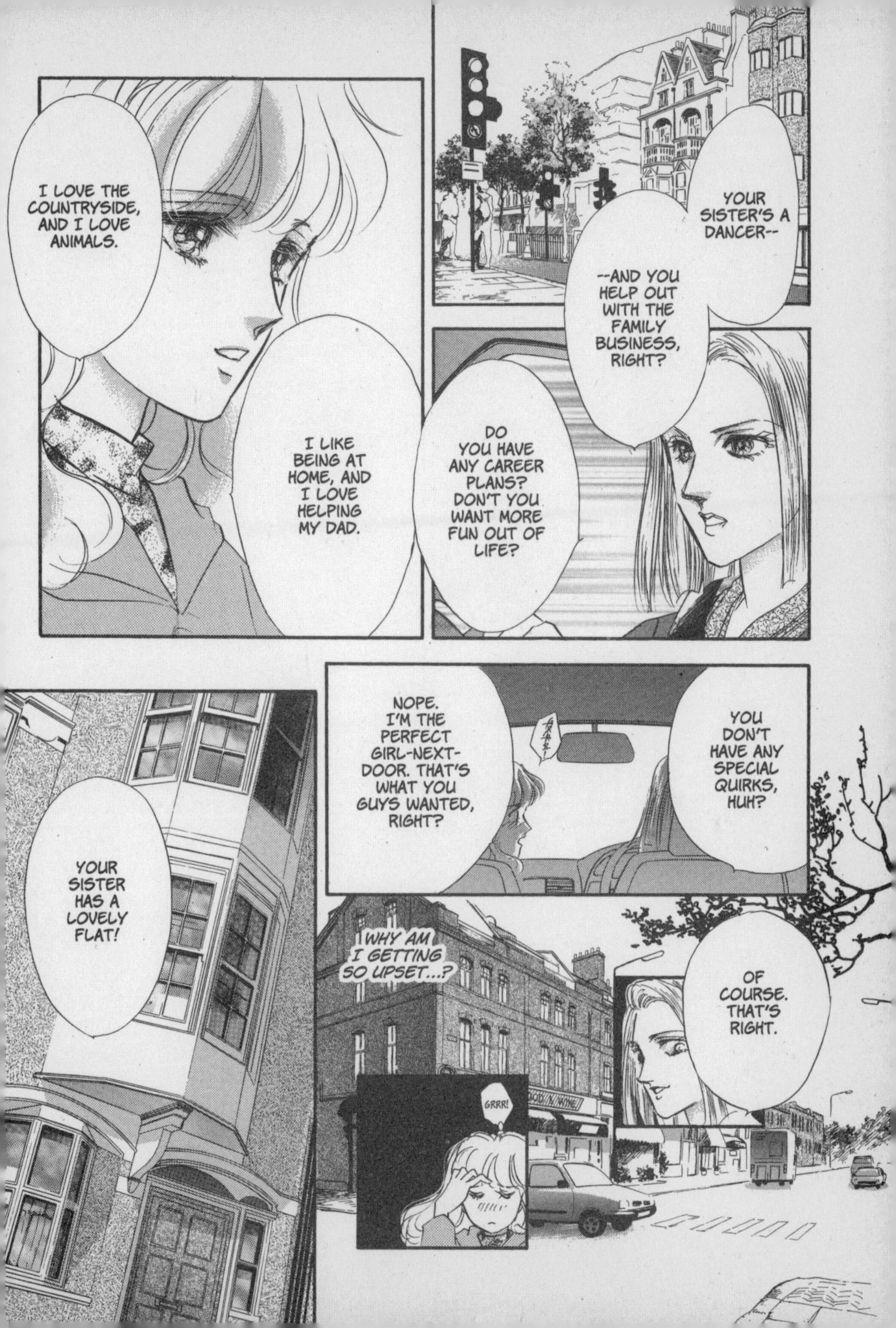
YOUR SISTER'S A DANCER--
--AND YOU HELP OUT WITH THE FAMILY BUSINESS, RIGHT?
DO YOU HAVE ANY CAREER PLANS? DON'T YOU WANT MORE FUN OUT OF LIFE?
I LIKE BEING AT HOME, AND I LOVE HELPING MY DAD.
I LOVE THE COUNTRYSIDE, AND I LOVE ANIMALS.
YOU DON'T HAVE ANY SPECIAL QUIRKS, HUH?
NOPE. I'M THE PERFECT GIRL-NEXT-DOOR. THAT'S WHAT YOU GUYS WANTED, RIGHT?
OF COURSE. THAT'S RIGHT.
WHY AM I GETTING SO UPSET...?
GRRR!
YOUR SISTER HAS A LOVELY FLAT!

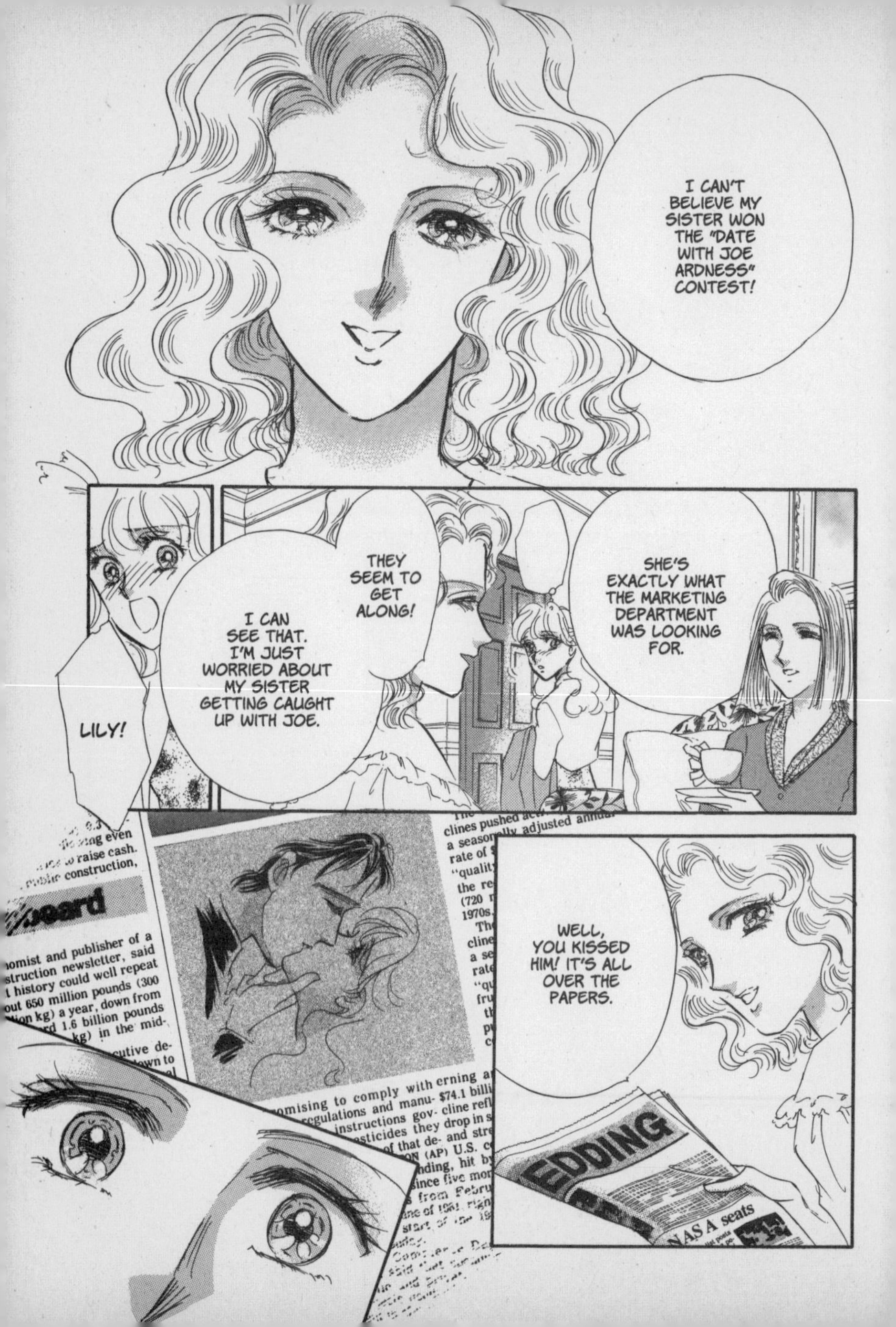
I CAN'T BELIEVE MY SISTER WON THE "DATE WITH JOE ARDNESS" CONTEST!
SHE'S EXACTLY WHAT THE MARKETING DEPARTMENT WAS LOOKING FOR.
THEY SEEM TO GET ALONG!
I CAN SEE THAT. I'M JUST WORRIED ABOUT MY SISTER GETTING CAUGHT UP WITH JOE.
LILY!
WELL, YOU KISSED HIM! IT'S ALL OVER THE PAPERS.
EDDING
NASA seats

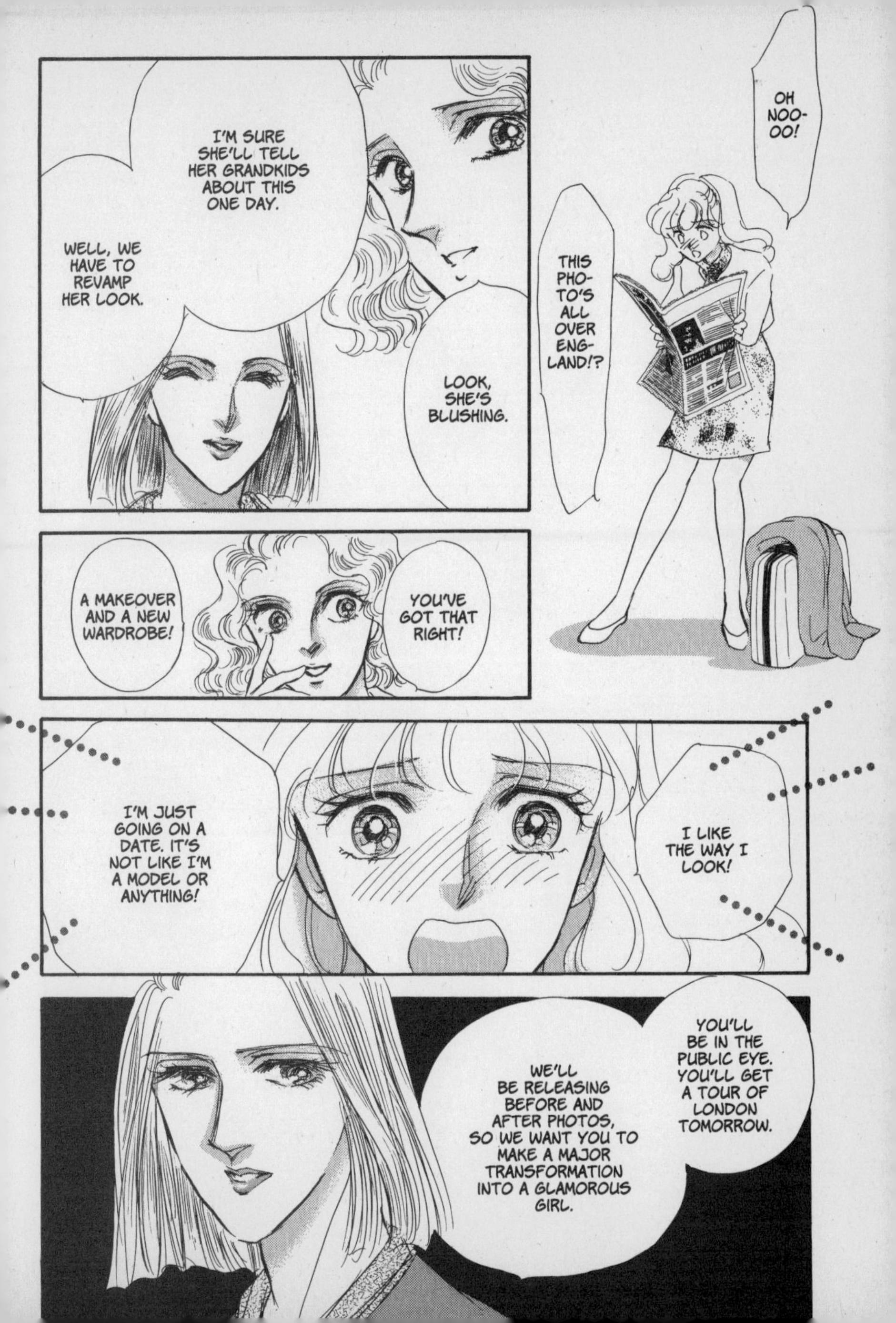
OH NOO-OO!
THIS PHO-TO'S ALL OVER ENG-LAND!?
LOOK, SHE'S BLUSHING.
I'M SURE SHE'LL TELL HER GRANDKIDS ABOUT THIS ONE DAY.
WELL, WE HAVE TO REVAMP HER LOOK.
YOU'VE GOT THAT RIGHT!
A MAKEOVER AND A NEW WARDROBE!
I LIKE THE WAY I LOOK!
I'M JUST GOING ON A DATE. IT'S NOT LIKE I'M A MODEL OR ANYTHING!
YOU'LL BE IN THE PUBLIC EYE. YOU'LL GET A TOUR OF LONDON TOMORROW.
WE'LL BE RELEASING BEFORE AND AFTER PHOTOS, SO WE WANT YOU TO MAKE A MAJOR TRANSFORMATION INTO A GLAMOROUS GIRL.

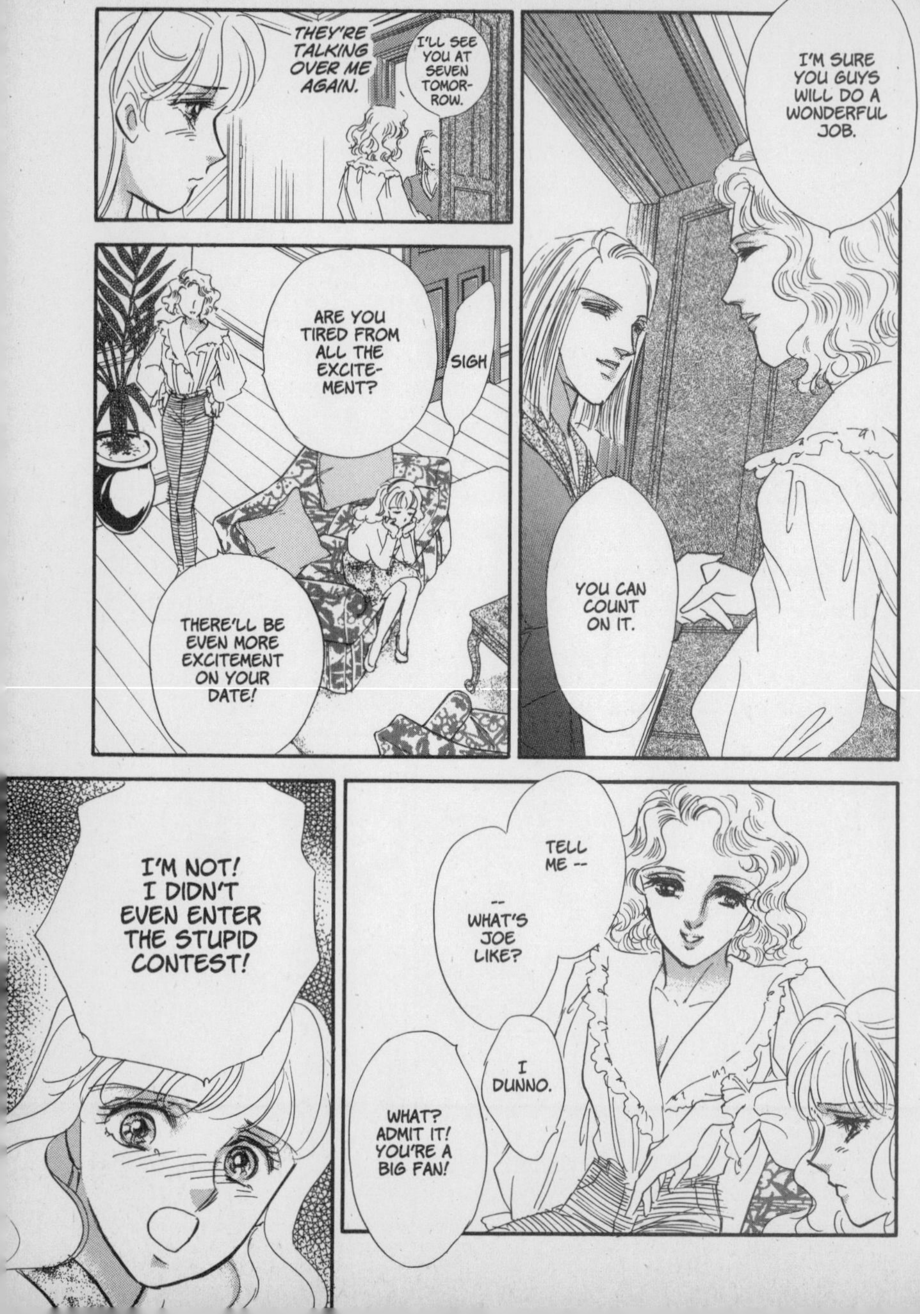
I'M SURE YOU GUYS WILL DO A WONDERFUL JOB.
YOU CAN COUNT ON IT.
I'LL SEE YOU AT SEVEN TOMOR-ROW.
THEY'RE TALKING OVER ME AGAIN.
SIGH
ARE YOU TIRED FROM ALL THE EXCITE-MENT?
THERE'LL BE EVEN MORE EXCITEMENT ON YOUR DATE!
TELL ME --
-- WHAT'S JOE LIKE?
I DUNNO.
WHAT? ADMIT IT! YOU'RE A BIG FAN!
I'M NOT! I DIDN'T EVEN ENTER THE STUPID CONTEST!

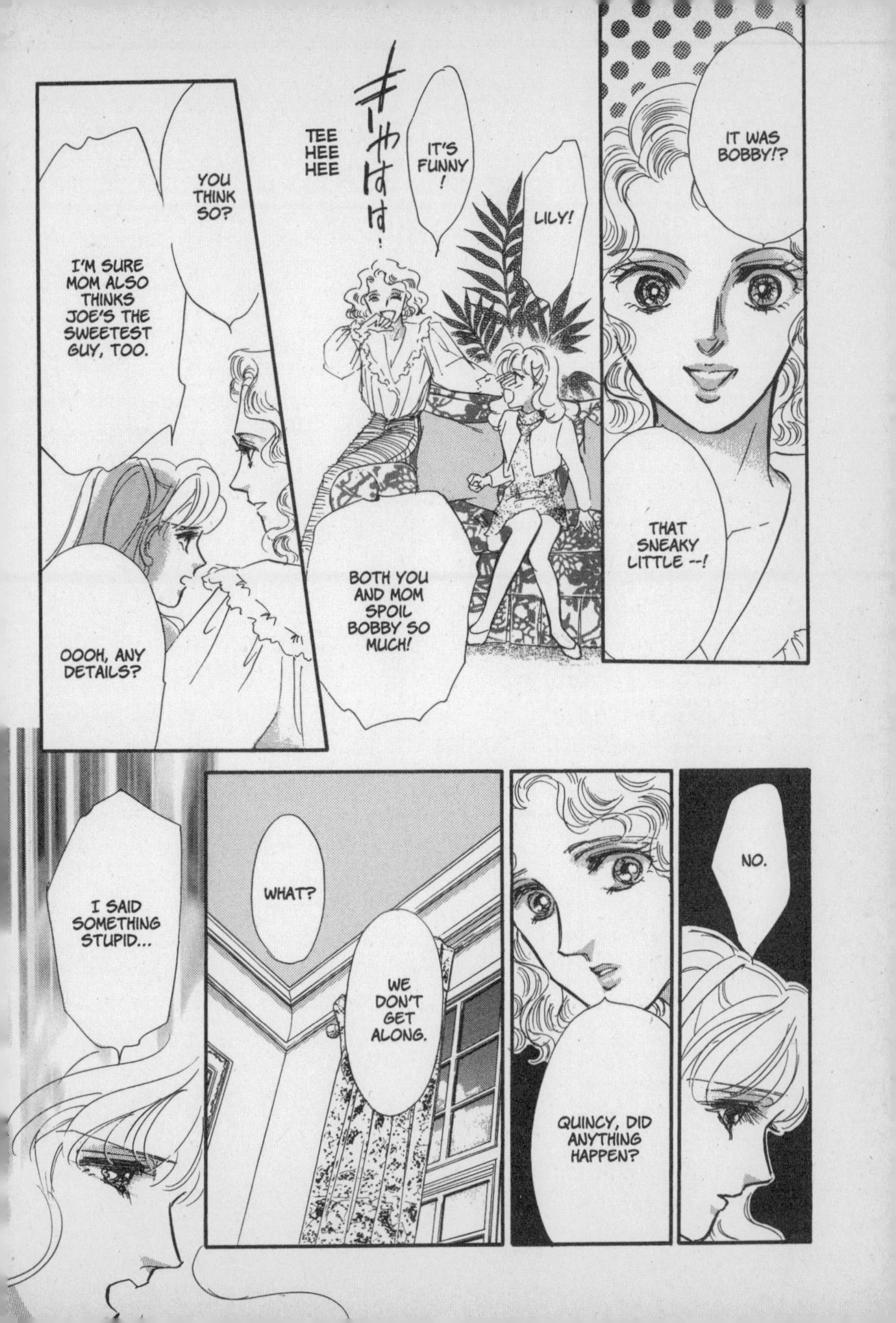
IT WAS BOBBY!?
THAT SNEAKY LITTLE --!
LILY!
IT'S FUNNY!
キャはは!
TEE HEE HEE
BOTH YOU AND MOM SPOIL BOBBY SO MUCH!
YOU THINK SO?
I'M SURE MOM ALSO THINKS JOE'S THE SWEETEST GUY, TOO.
OOOH, ANY DETAILS?
NO.
QUINCY, DID ANYTHING HAPPEN?
WHAT?
WE DON'T GET ALONG.
I SAID SOMETHING STUPID...

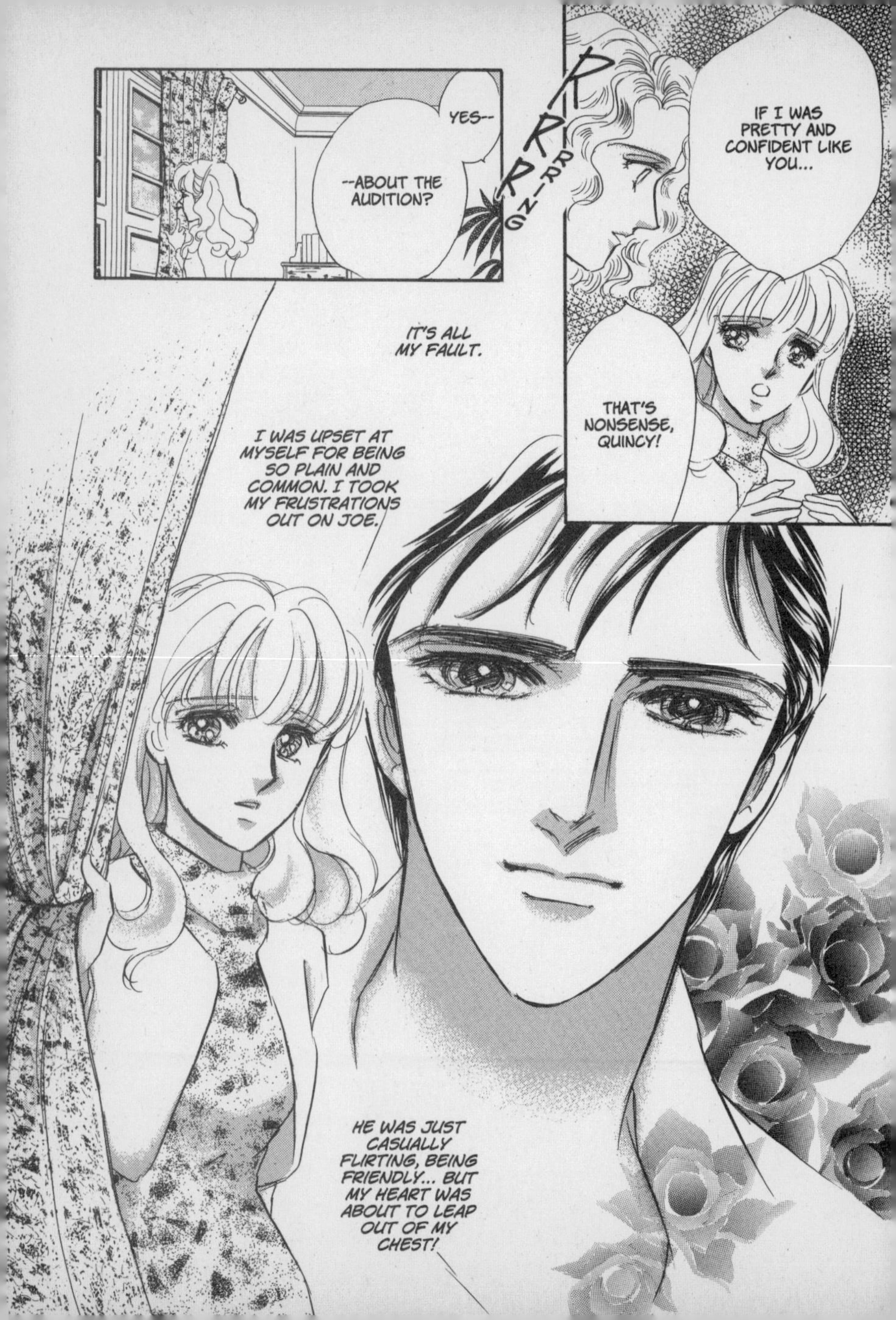
IF I WAS PRETTY AND CONFIDENT LIKE YOU...
THAT'S NONSENSE, QUINCY!
RRRRRRING
YES--
--ABOUT THE AUDITION?
IT'S ALL MY FAULT.
I WAS UPSET AT MYSELF FOR BEING SO PLAIN AND COMMON. I TOOK MY FRUSTRATIONS OUT ON JOE.
HE WAS JUST CASUALLY FLIRTING, BEING FRIENDLY... BUT MY HEART WAS ABOUT TO LEAP OUT OF MY CHEST!

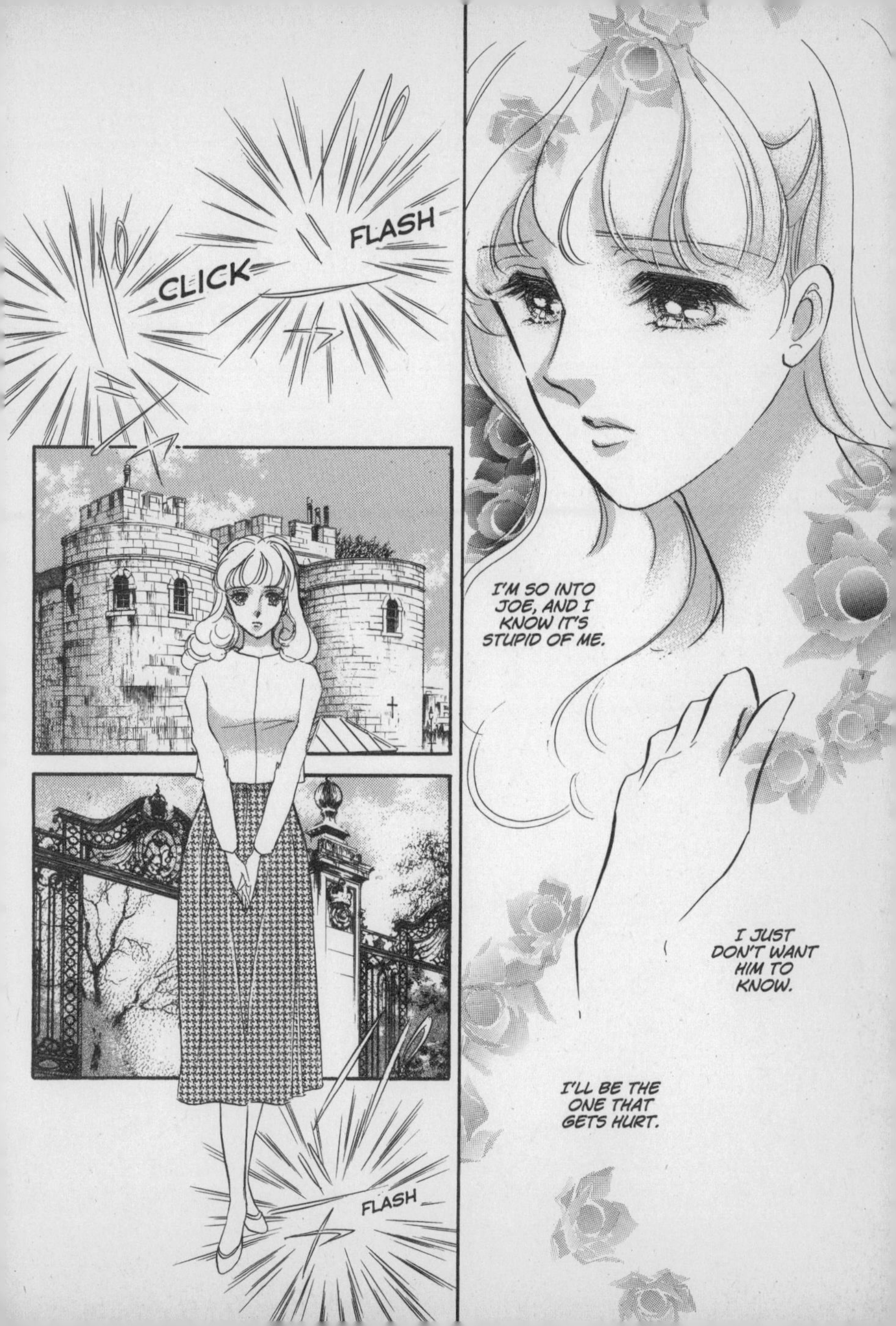
I'M SO INTO JOE, AND I KNOW IT'S STUPID OF ME.
I JUST DON'T WANT HIM TO KNOW.
I'LL BE THE ONE THAT GETS HURT.
FLASH
CLICK
FLASH

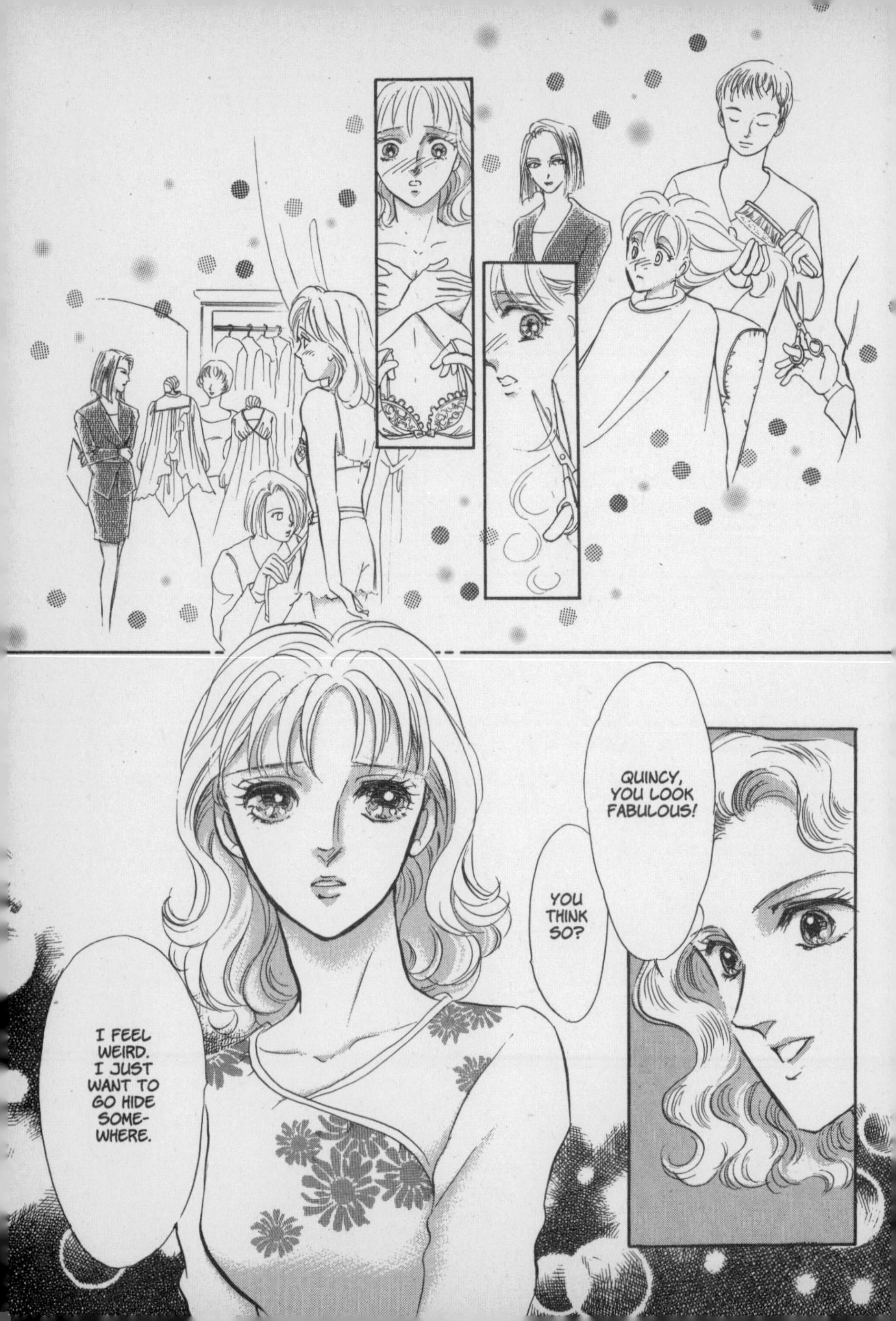
QUINCY, YOU LOOK FABULOUS!
YOU THINK SO?
I FEEL WEIRD. I JUST WANT TO GO HIDE SOME-WHERE.

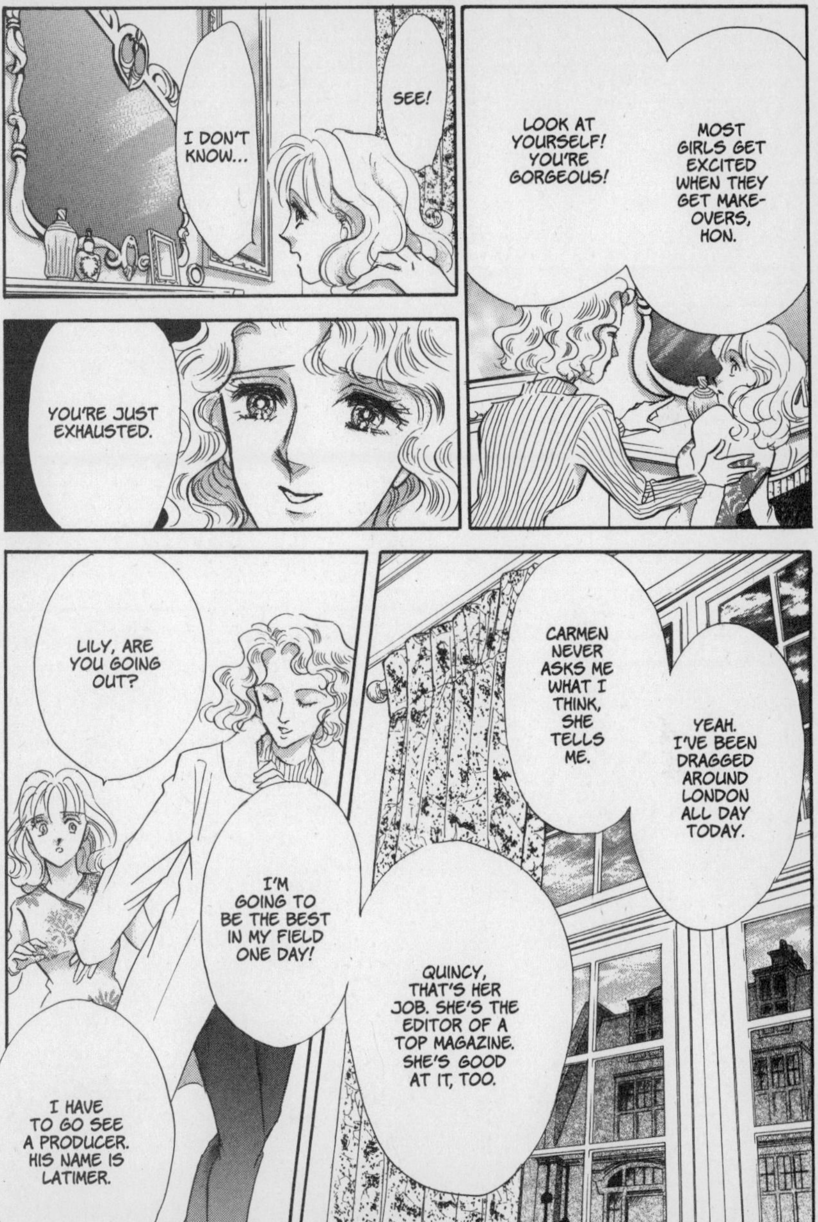
MOST GIRLS GET EXCITED WHEN THEY GET MAKE-OVERS, HON.
LOOK AT YOURSELF! YOU'RE GORGEOUS!
SEE!
I DON'T KNOW...
YOU'RE JUST EXHAUSTED.
YEAH. I'VE BEEN DRAGGED AROUND LONDON ALL DAY TODAY.
CARMEN NEVER ASKS ME WHAT I THINK, SHE TELLS ME.
QUINCY, THAT'S HER JOB. SHE'S THE EDITOR OF A TOP MAGAZINE. SHE'S GOOD AT IT, TOO.
I'M GOING TO BE THE BEST IN MY FIELD ONE DAY!
LILY, ARE YOU GOING OUT?
I HAVE TO GO SEE A PRODUCER. HIS NAME IS LATIMER.

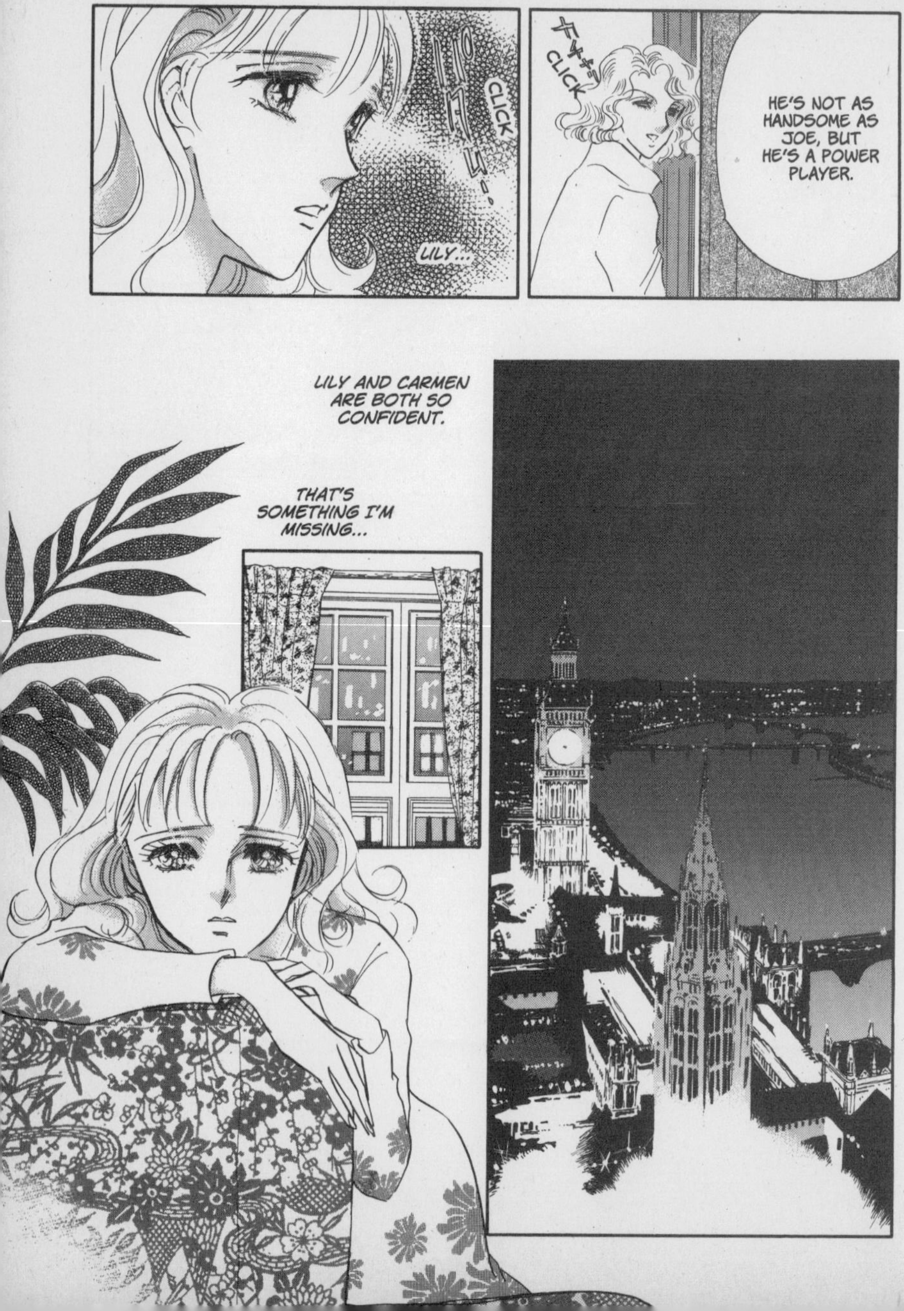
CLICK
HE'S NOT AS HANDSOME AS JOE, BUT HE'S A POWER PLAYER.
CLICK
LILY...
LILY AND CARMEN ARE BOTH SO CONFIDENT.
THAT'S SOMETHING I'M MISSING...

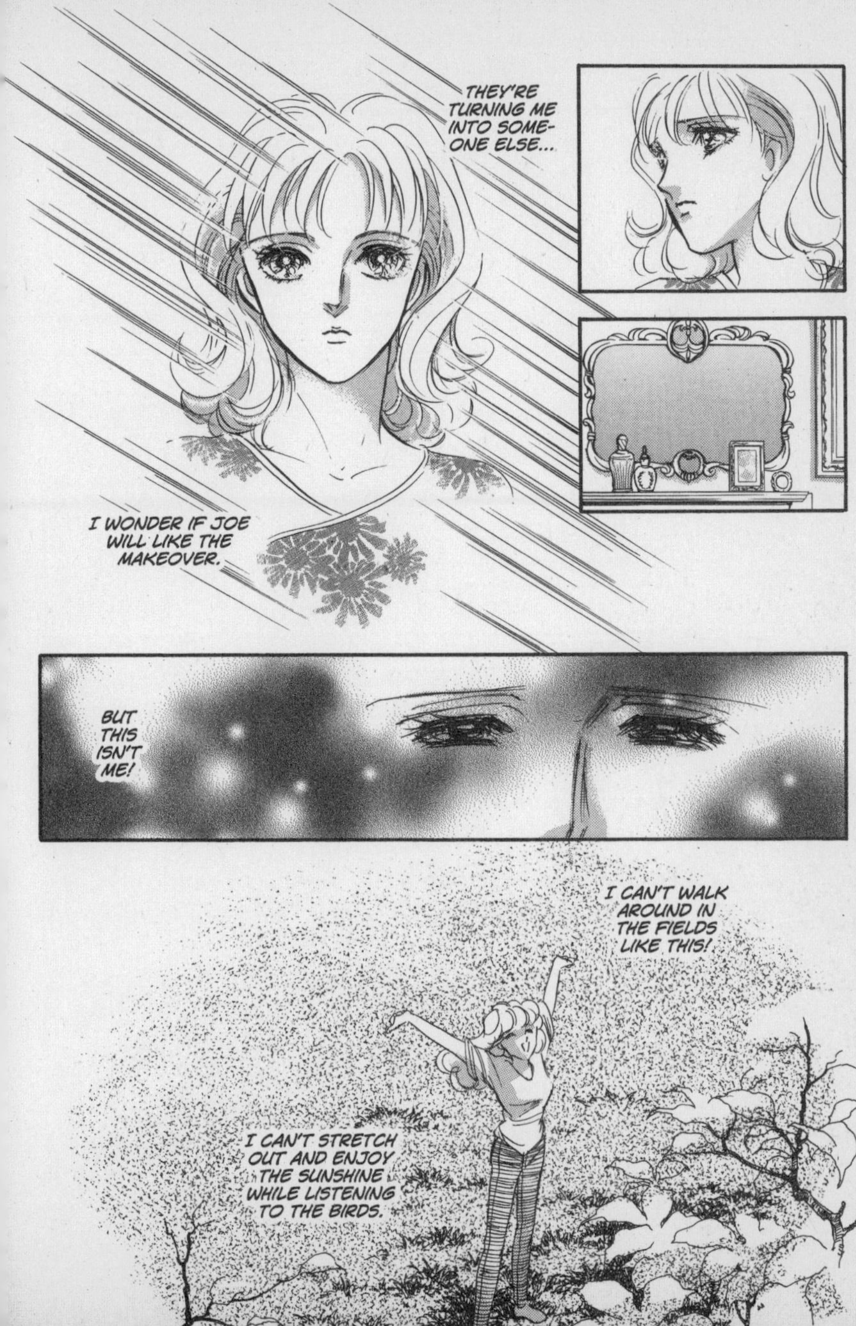
THEY'RE TURNING ME INTO SOME-ONE ELSE...
I WONDER IF JOE WILL LIKE THE MAKEOVER.
BUT THIS ISN'T ME!
I CAN'T WALK AROUND IN THE FIELDS LIKE THIS!
I CAN'T STRETCH OUT AND ENJOY THE SUNSHINE WHILE LISTENING TO THE BIRDS.

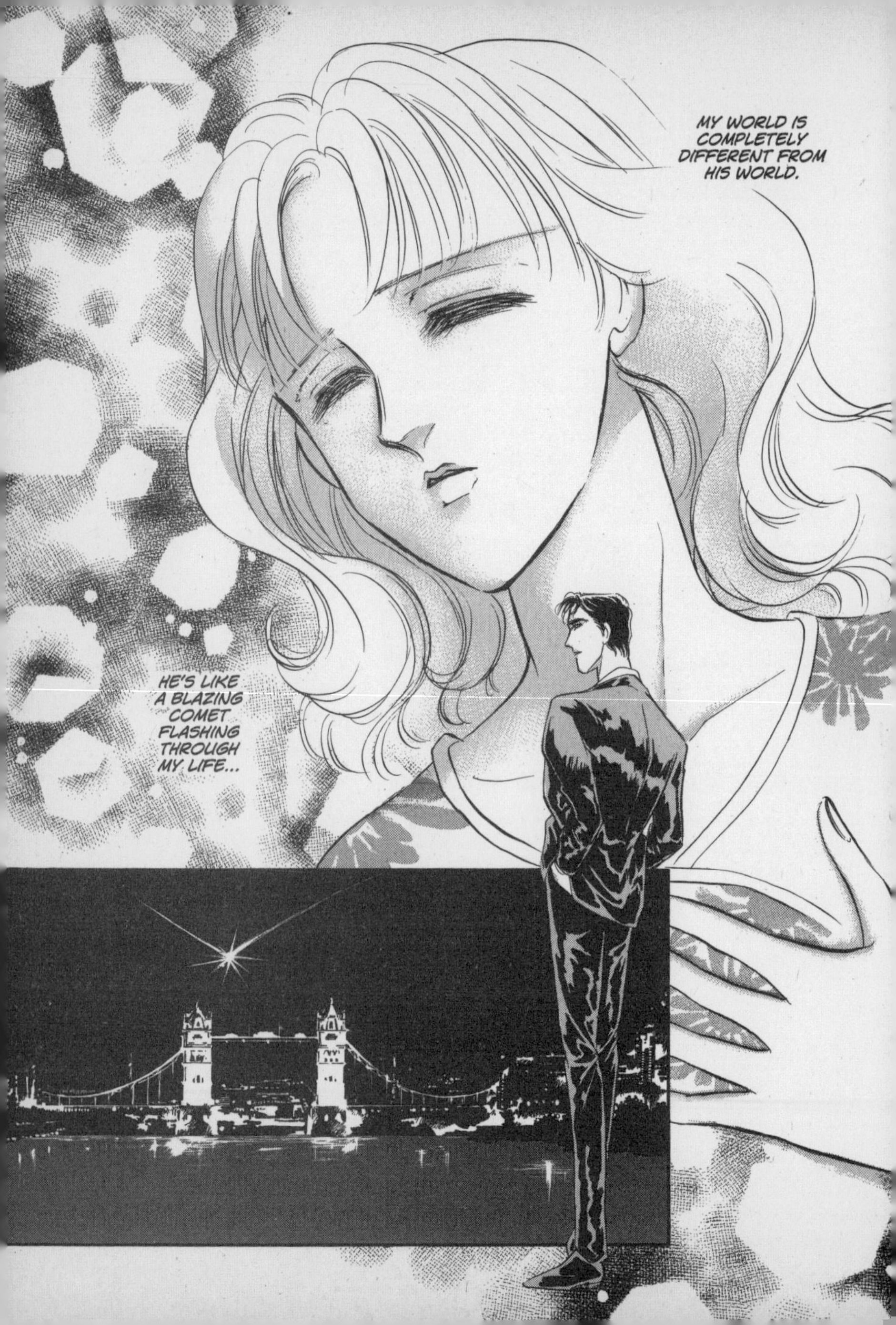
MY WORLD IS COMPLETELY DIFFERENT FROM HIS WORLD.
HE'S LIKE A BLAZING COMET FLASHING THROUGH MY LIFE...

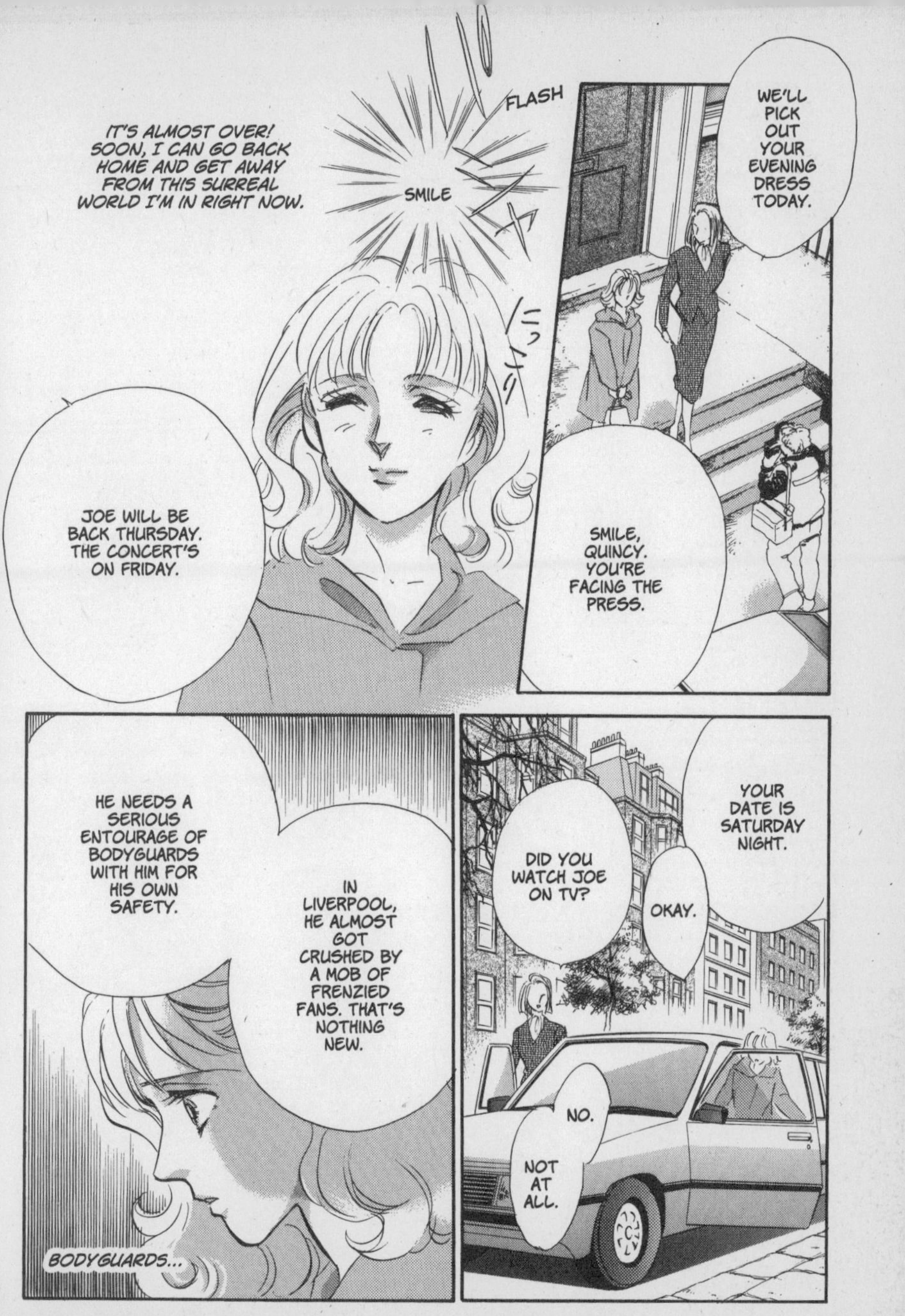
WE'LL PICK OUT YOUR EVENING DRESS TODAY.
SMILE, QUINCY. YOU'RE FACING THE PRESS.
FLASH
SMILE
IT'S ALMOST OVER! SOON, I CAN GO BACK HOME AND GET AWAY FROM THIS SURREAL WORLD I'M IN RIGHT NOW.
JOE WILL BE BACK THURSDAY. THE CONCERT'S ON FRIDAY.
YOUR DATE IS SATURDAY NIGHT.
OKAY.
DID YOU WATCH JOE ON TV?
NO.
NOT AT ALL.
IN LIVERPOOL, HE ALMOST GOT CRUSHED BY A MOB OF FRENZIED FANS. THAT'S NOTHING NEW.
HE NEEDS A SERIOUS ENTOURAGE OF BODYGUARDS WITH HIM FOR HIS OWN SAFETY.
BODYGUARDS...

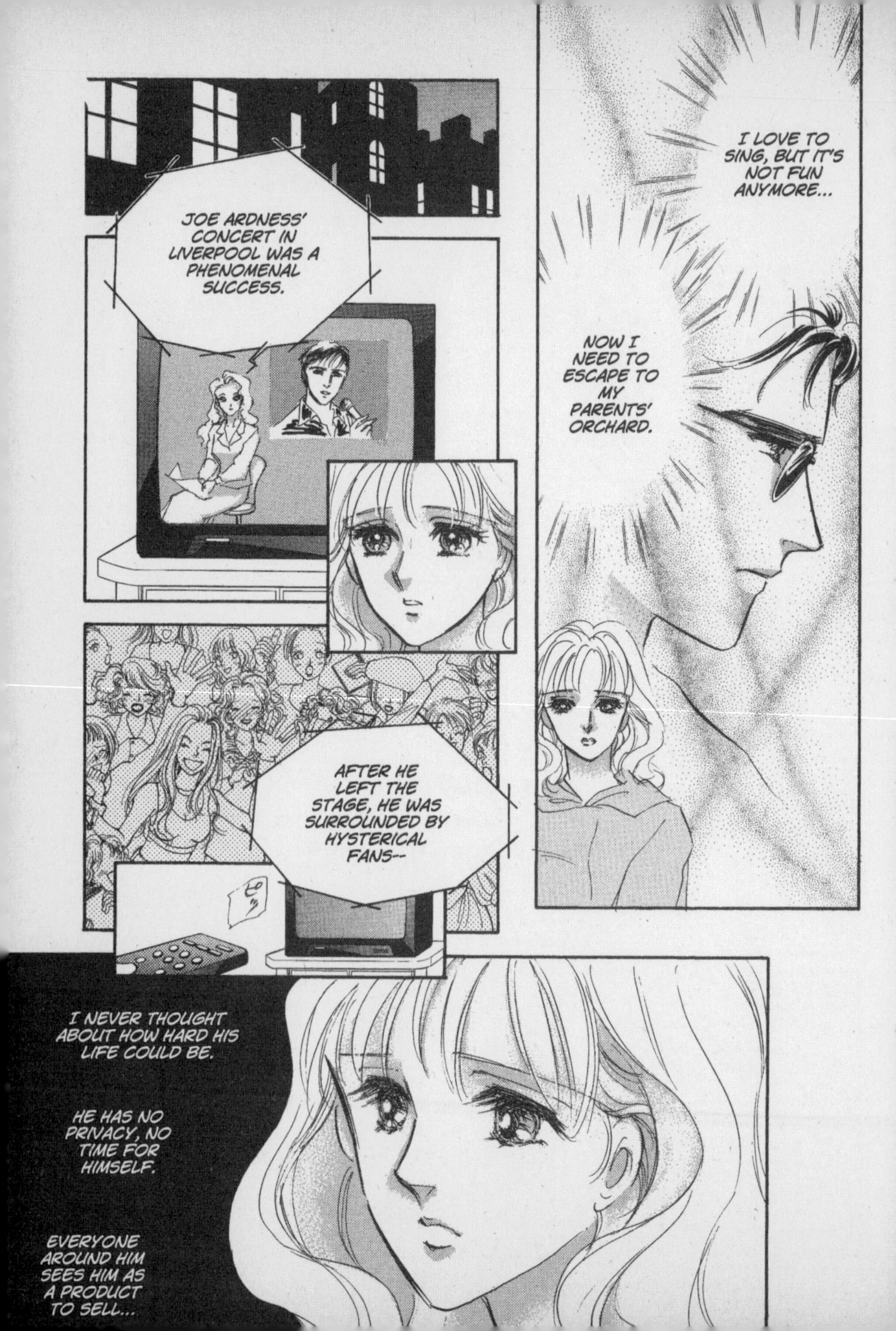
I LOVE TO SING, BUT IT'S NOT FUN ANYMORE...
NOW I NEED TO ESCAPE TO MY PARENTS' ORCHARD.
JOE ARDNESS' CONCERT IN LIVERPOOL WAS A PHENOMENAL SUCCESS.
AFTER HE LEFT THE STAGE, HE WAS SURROUNDED BY HYSTERICAL FANS--
I NEVER THOUGHT ABOUT HOW HARD HIS LIFE COULD BE.
HE HAS NO PRIVACY, NO TIME FOR HIMSELF.
EVERYONE AROUND HIM SEES HIM AS A PRODUCT TO SELL...

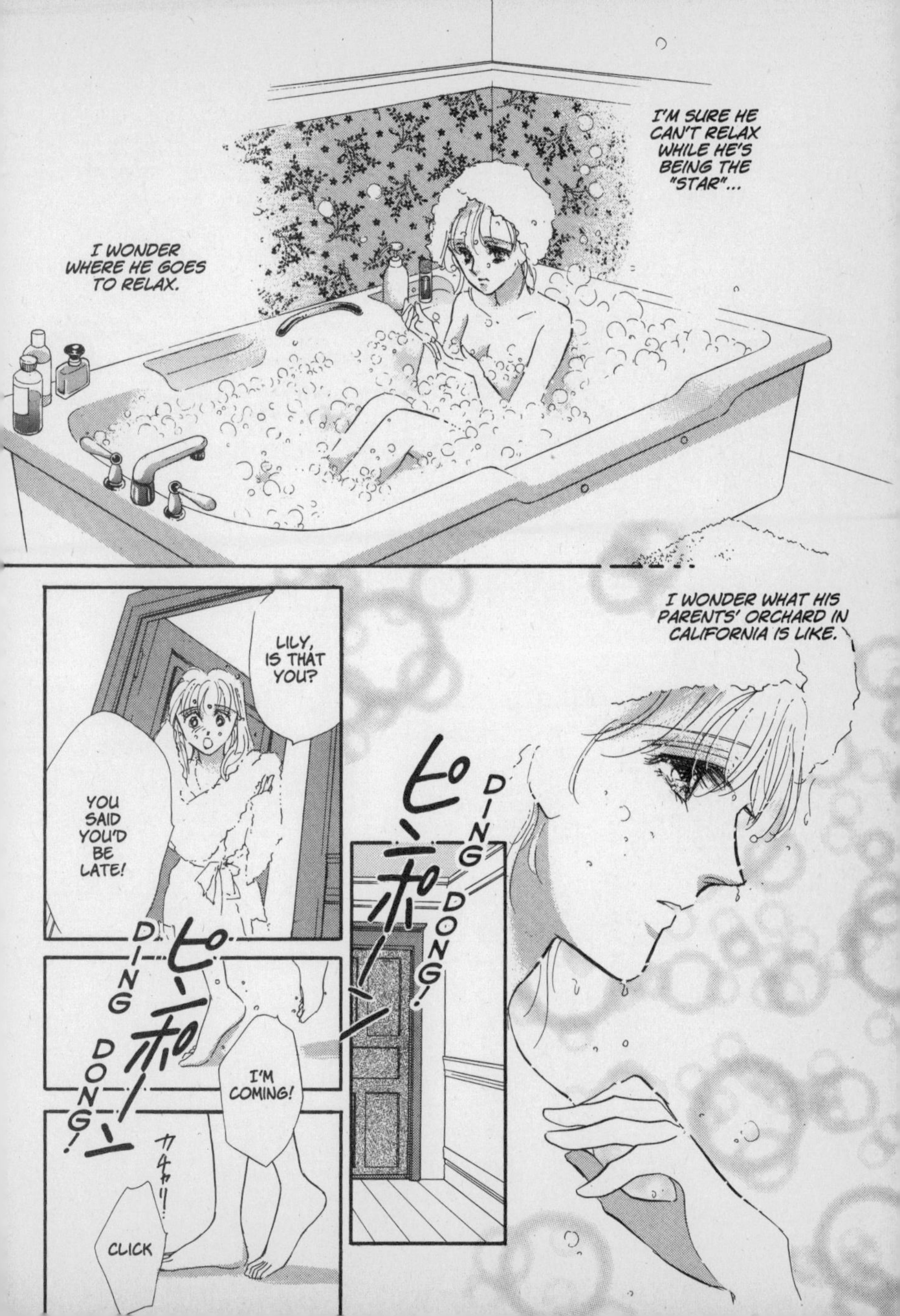
I'M SURE HE CAN'T RELAX WHILE HE'S BEING THE "STAR"...
I WONDER WHERE HE GOES TO RELAX.
I WONDER WHAT HIS PARENTS' ORCHARD IN CALIFORNIA IS LIKE.
ピンポーン
DING DONG!
LILY, IS THAT YOU?
YOU SAID YOU'D BE LATE!
ピンポーン
DING DONG!
I'M COMING!
カチャリ
CLICK

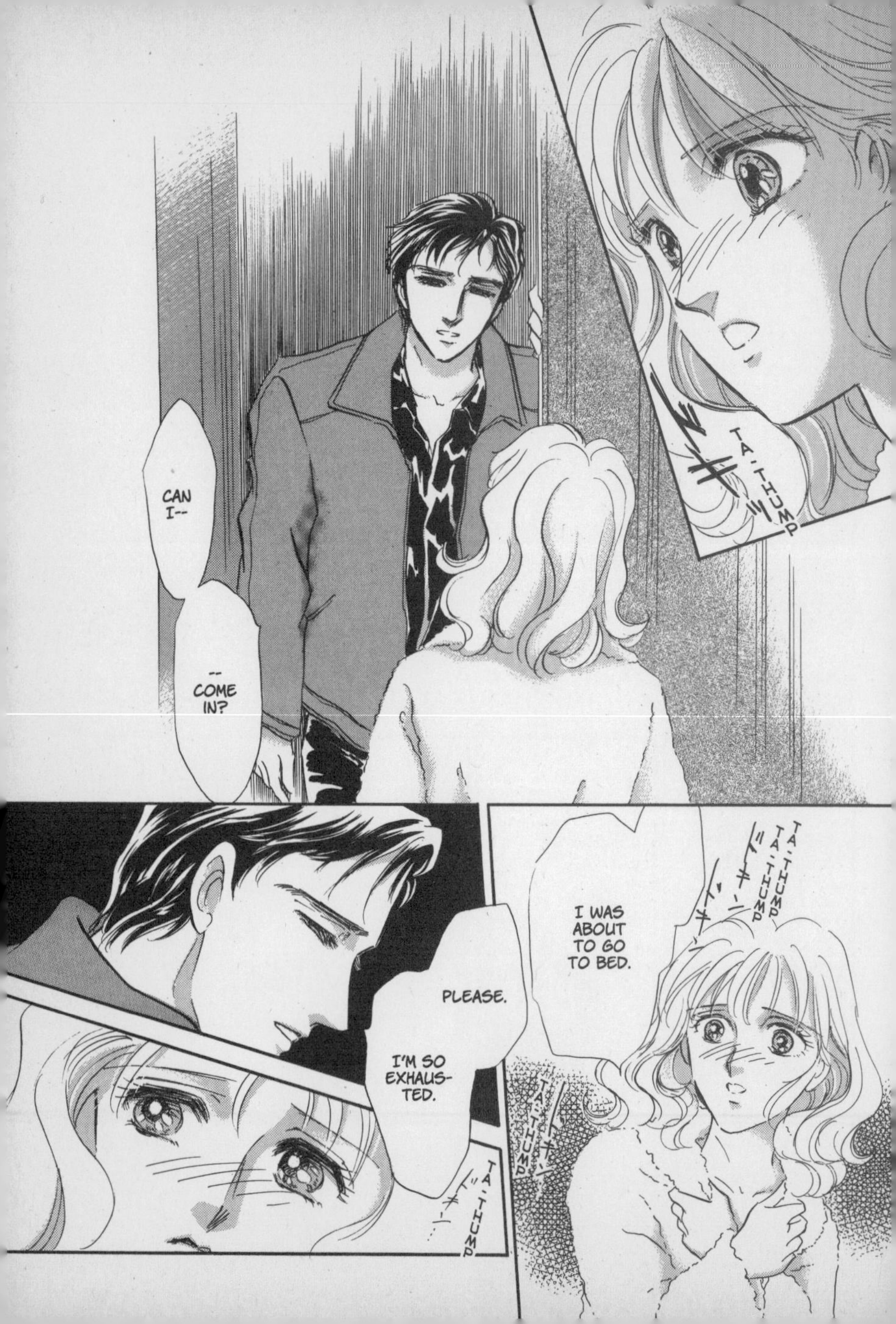
TA-THUMP
CAN I--
--COME IN?
TA-THUMP
TA-THUMP
I WAS ABOUT TO GO TO BED.
TA-THUMP
PLEASE.
I'M SO EXHAUS-TED.
TA-THUMP

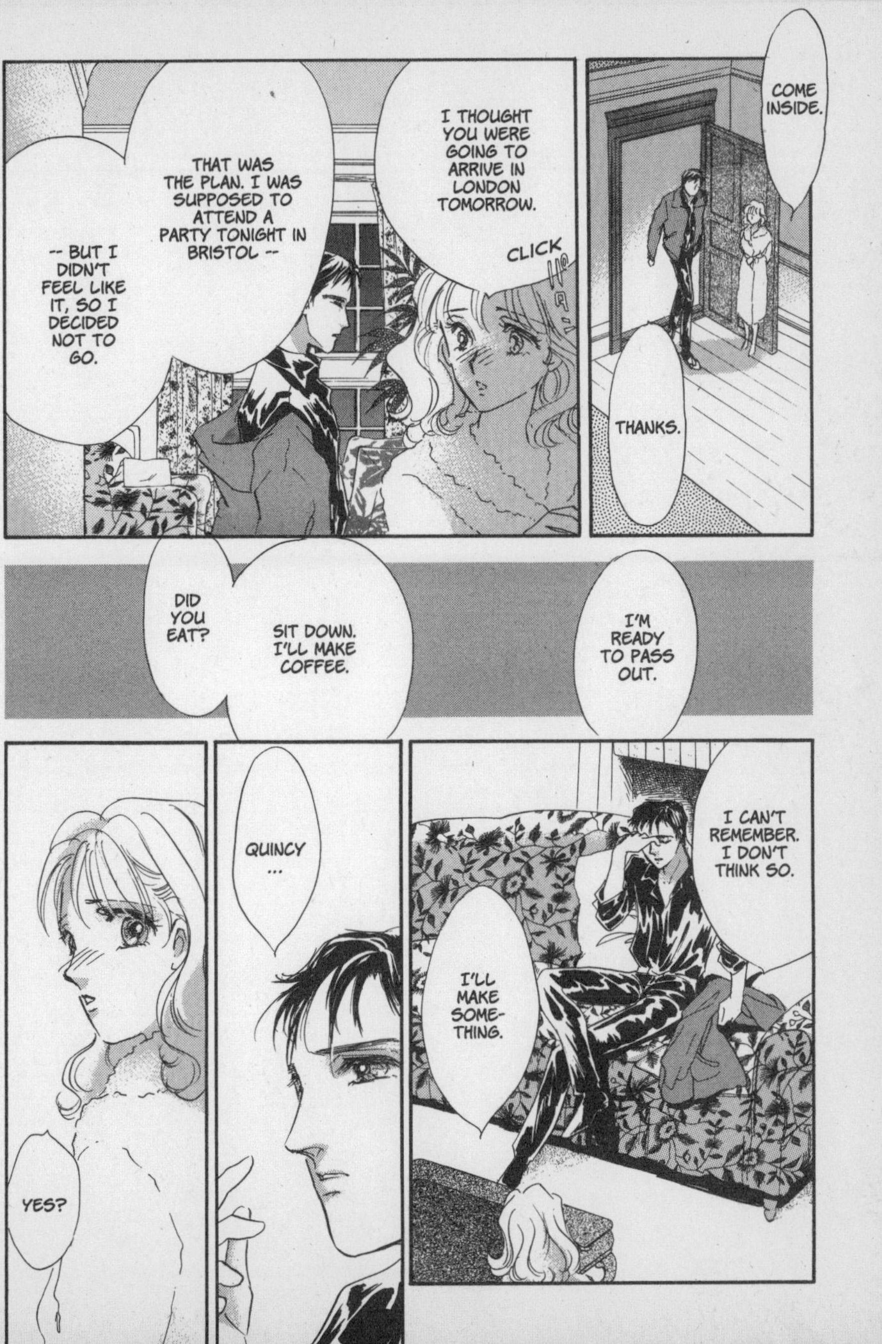
COME INSIDE.
THANKS.
I THOUGHT YOU WERE GOING TO ARRIVE IN LONDON TOMORROW.
CLICK
THAT WAS THE PLAN. I WAS SUPPOSED TO ATTEND A PARTY TONIGHT IN BRISTOL --
-- BUT I DIDN'T FEEL LIKE IT, SO I DECIDED NOT TO GO.
I'M READY TO PASS OUT.
SIT DOWN. I'LL MAKE COFFEE.
DID YOU EAT?
I CAN'T REMEMBER. I DON'T THINK SO.
I'LL MAKE SOME-THING.
QUINCY ...
YES?

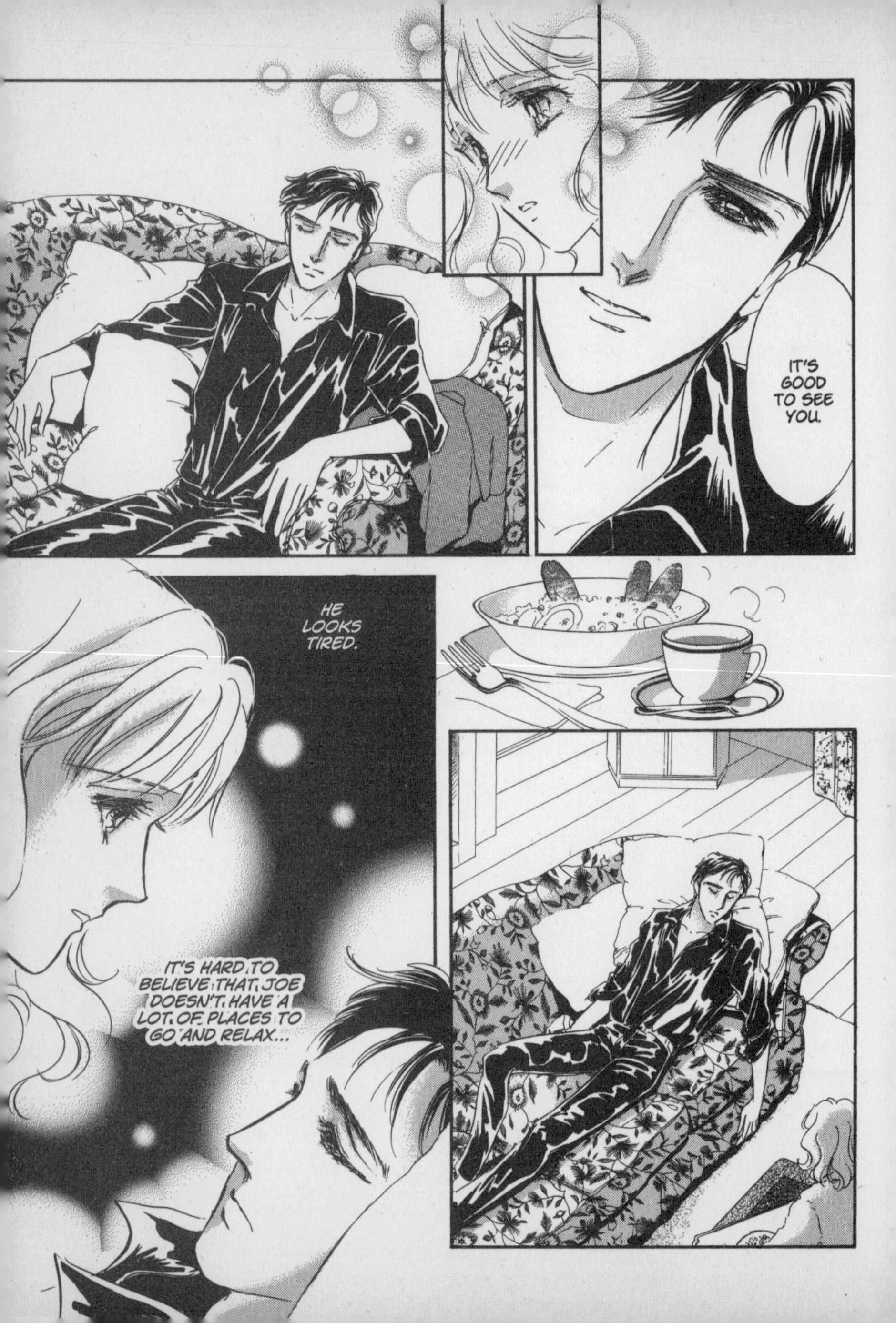
IT'S GOOD TO SEE YOU.
HE LOOKS TIRED.
IT'S HARD TO BELIEVE THAT JOE DOESN'T HAVE A LOT OF PLACES TO GO AND RELAX...

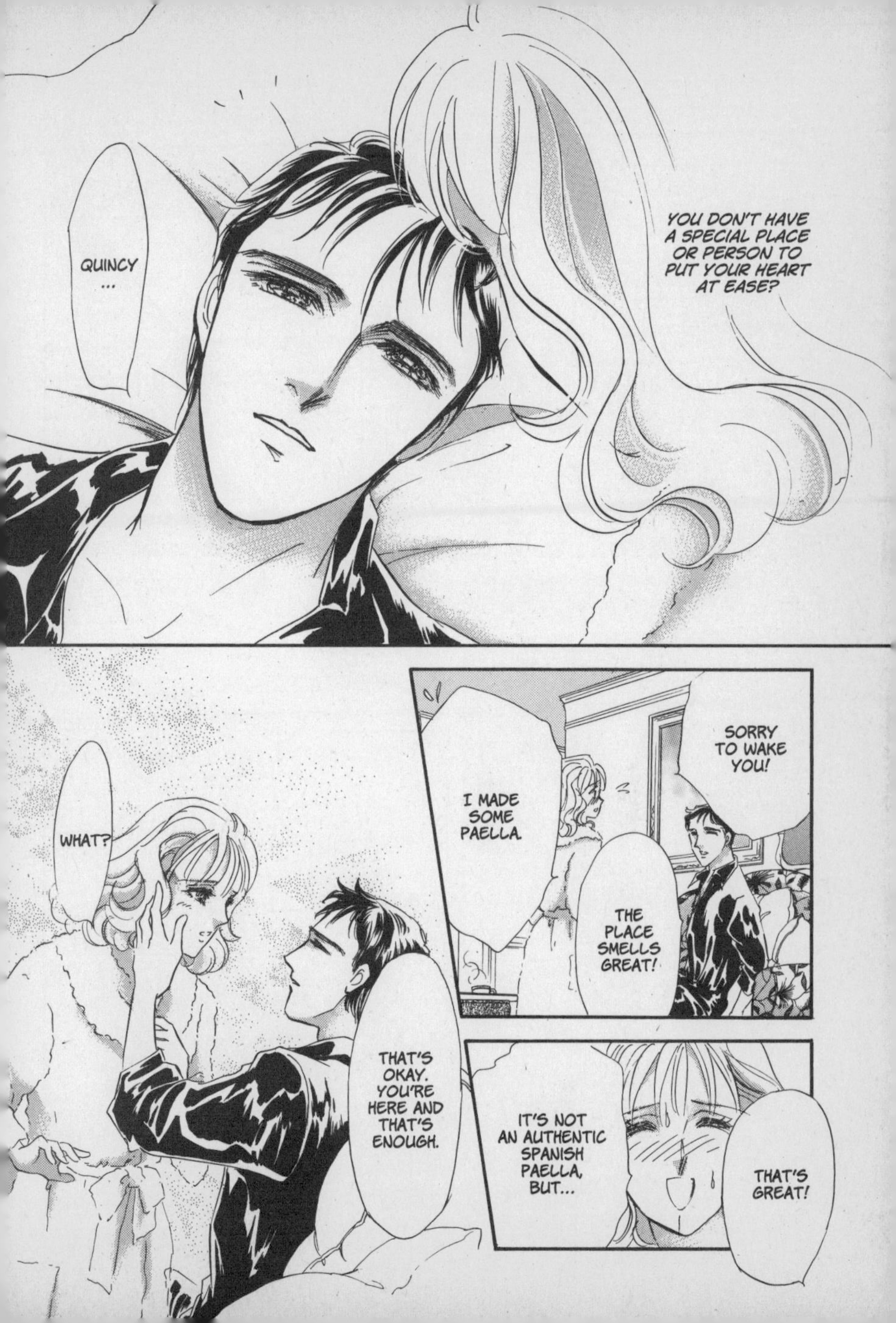
YOU DON'T HAVE A SPECIAL PLACE OR PERSON TO PUT YOUR HEART AT EASE?
QUINCY ...
SORRY TO WAKE YOU!
I MADE SOME PAELLA.
THE PLACE SMELLS GREAT!
IT'S NOT AN AUTHENTIC SPANISH PAELLA, BUT...
THAT'S GREAT!
WHAT?
THAT'S OKAY. YOU'RE HERE AND THAT'S ENOUGH.

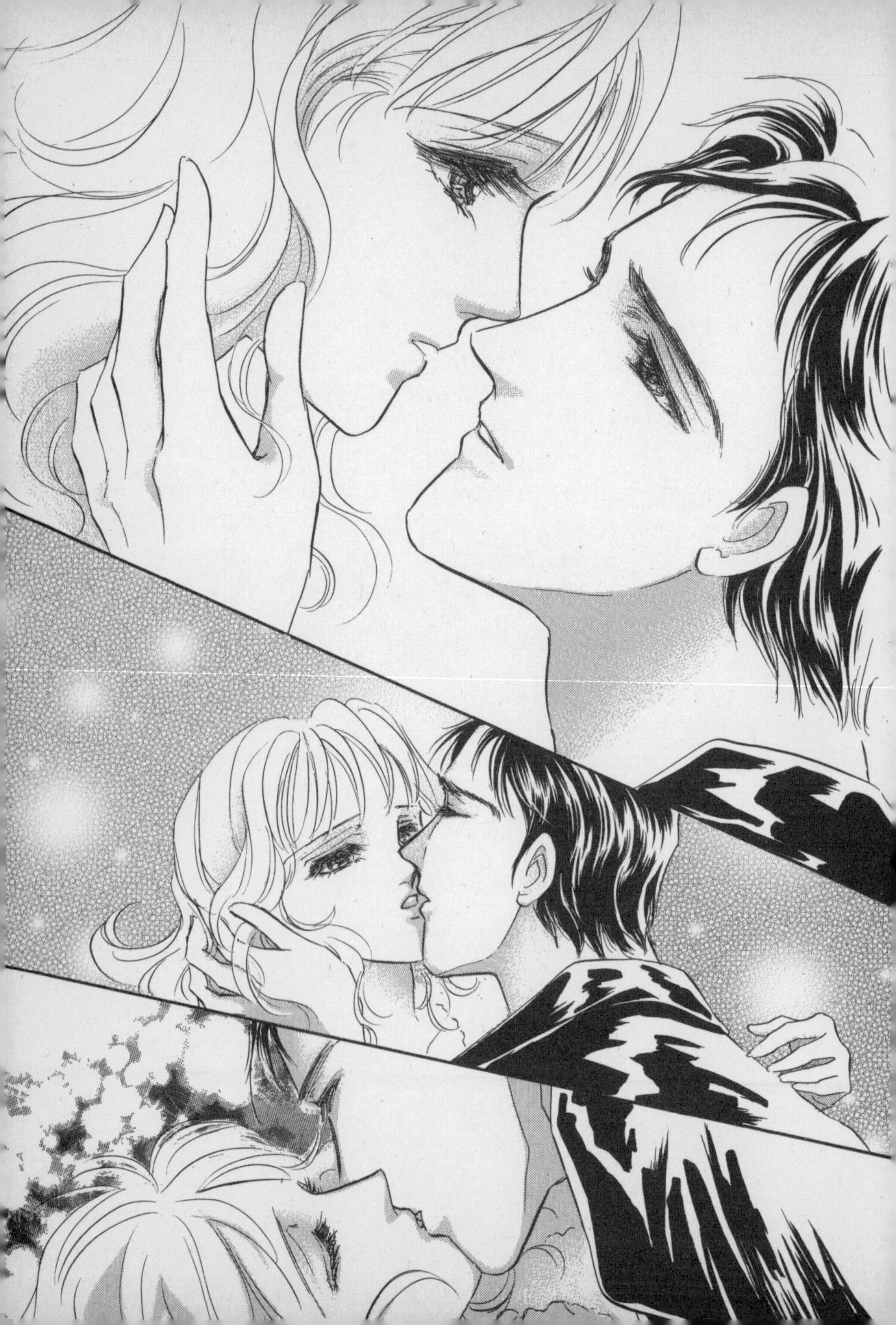

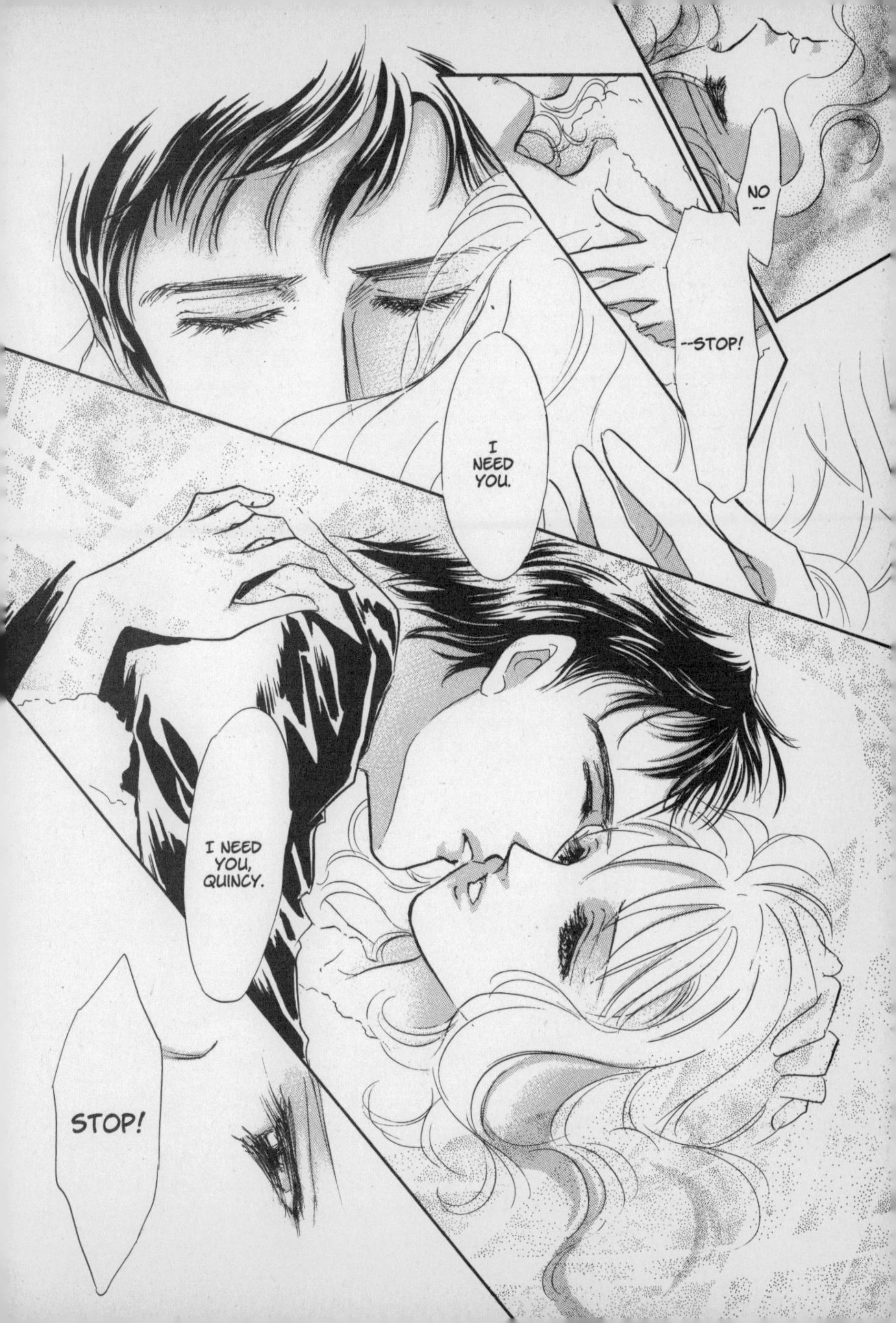
NO --
--STOP!
I NEED YOU.
I NEED YOU, QUINCY.
STOP!

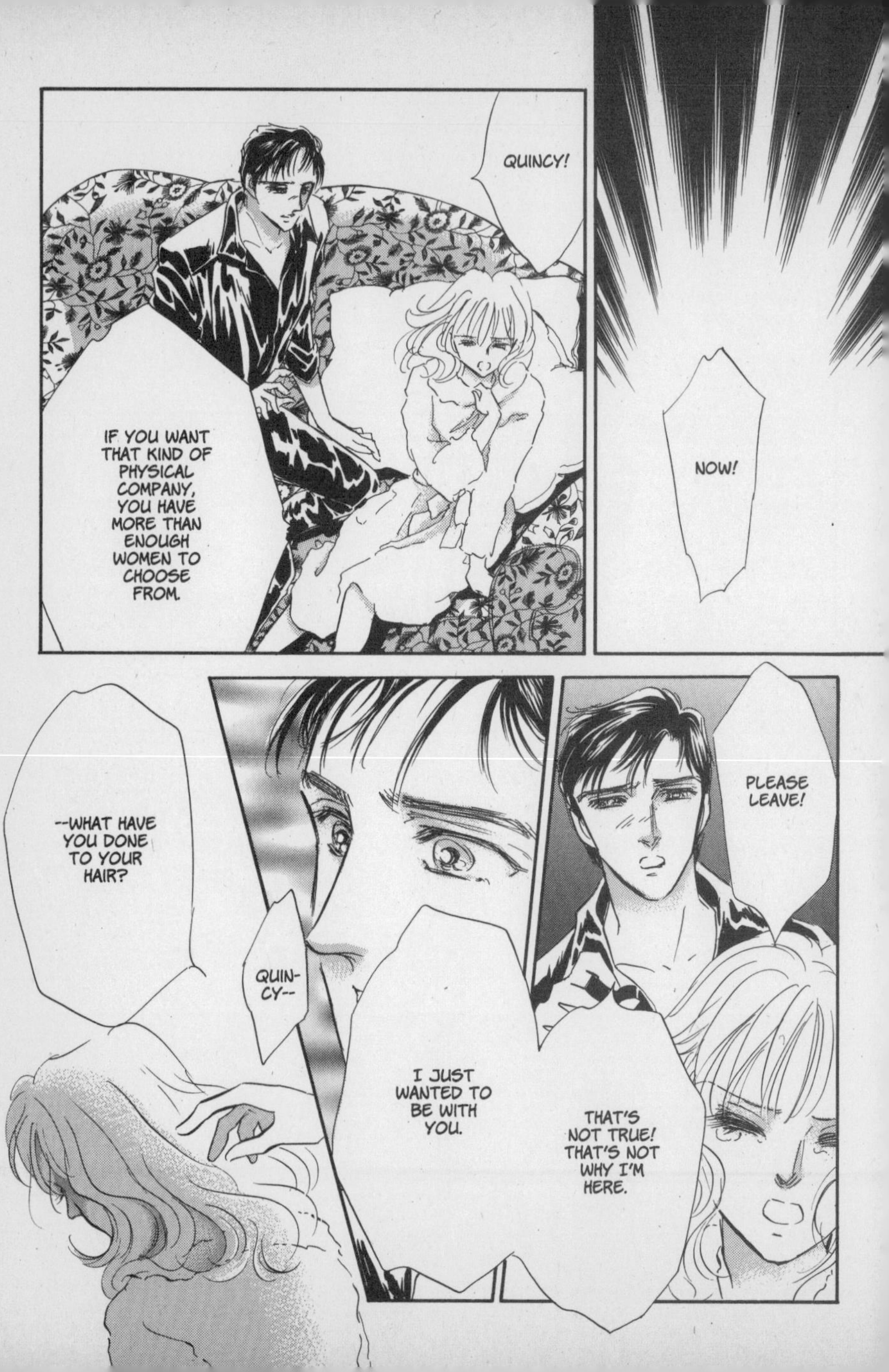
NOW!
QUINCY!
IF YOU WANT THAT KIND OF PHYSICAL COMPANY, YOU HAVE MORE THAN ENOUGH WOMEN TO CHOOSE FROM.
PLEASE LEAVE!
THAT'S NOT TRUE! THAT'S NOT WHY I'M HERE.
I JUST WANTED TO BE WITH YOU.
QUIN-CY--
--WHAT HAVE YOU DONE TO YOUR HAIR?

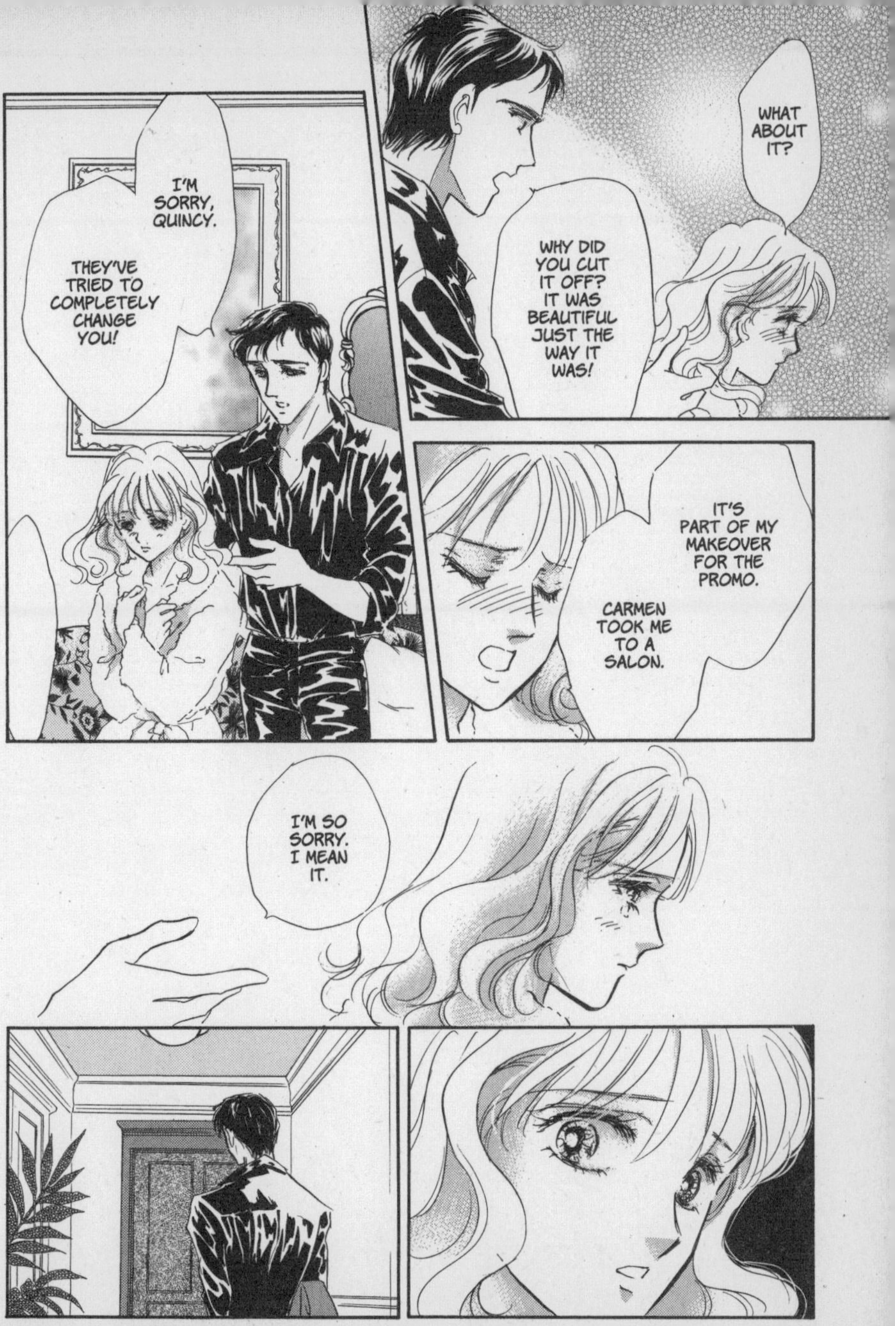
WHAT ABOUT IT?
WHY DID YOU CUT IT OFF? IT WAS BEAUTIFUL JUST THE WAY IT WAS!
IT'S PART OF MY MAKEOVER FOR THE PROMO.
CARMEN TOOK ME TO A SALON.
I'M SORRY, QUINCY.
THEY'VE TRIED TO COMPLETELY CHANGE YOU!
I'M SO SORRY. I MEAN IT.

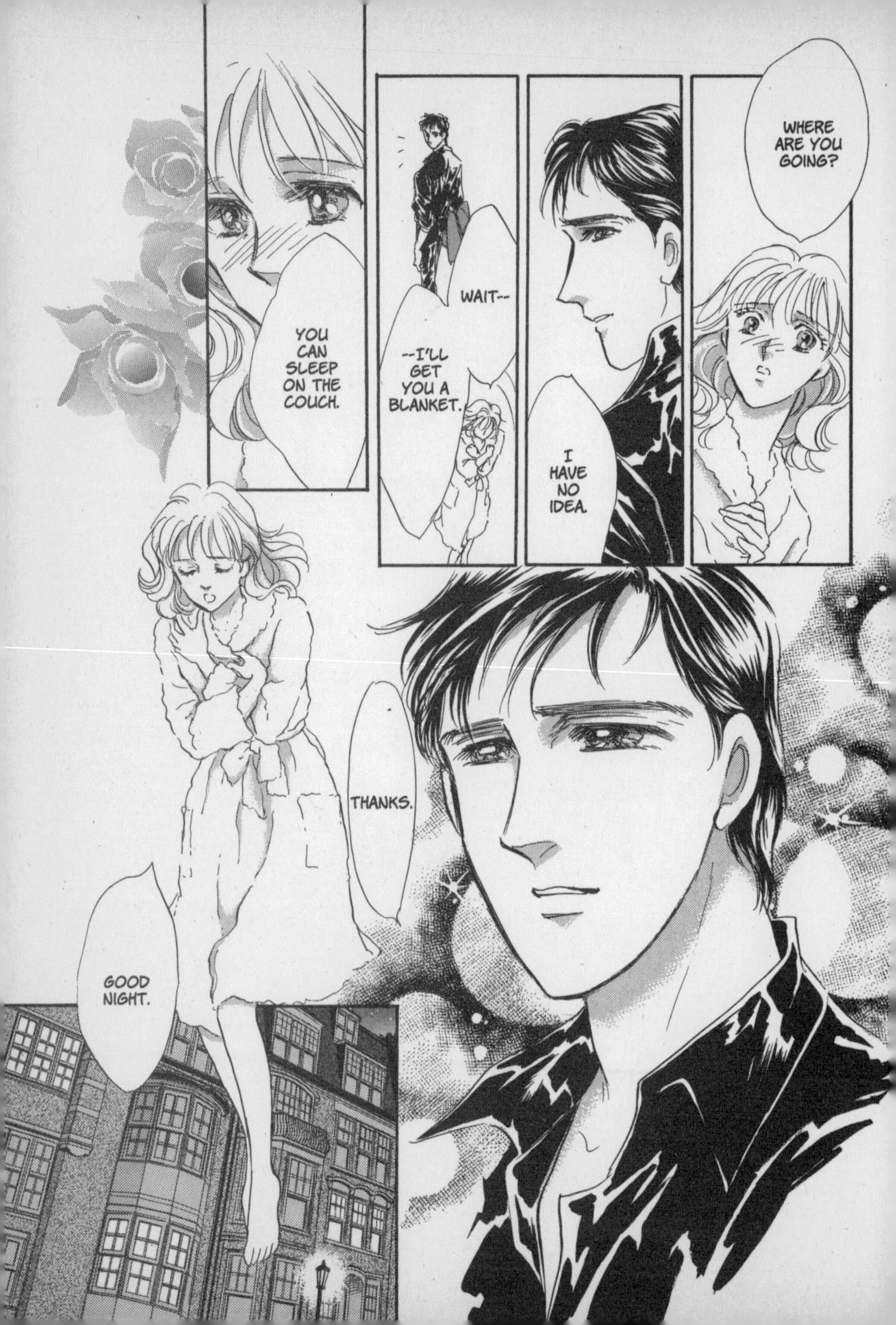
WHERE ARE YOU GOING?
I HAVE NO IDEA.
WAIT--
--I'LL GET YOU A BLANKET.
YOU CAN SLEEP ON THE COUCH.
THANKS.
GOOD NIGHT.

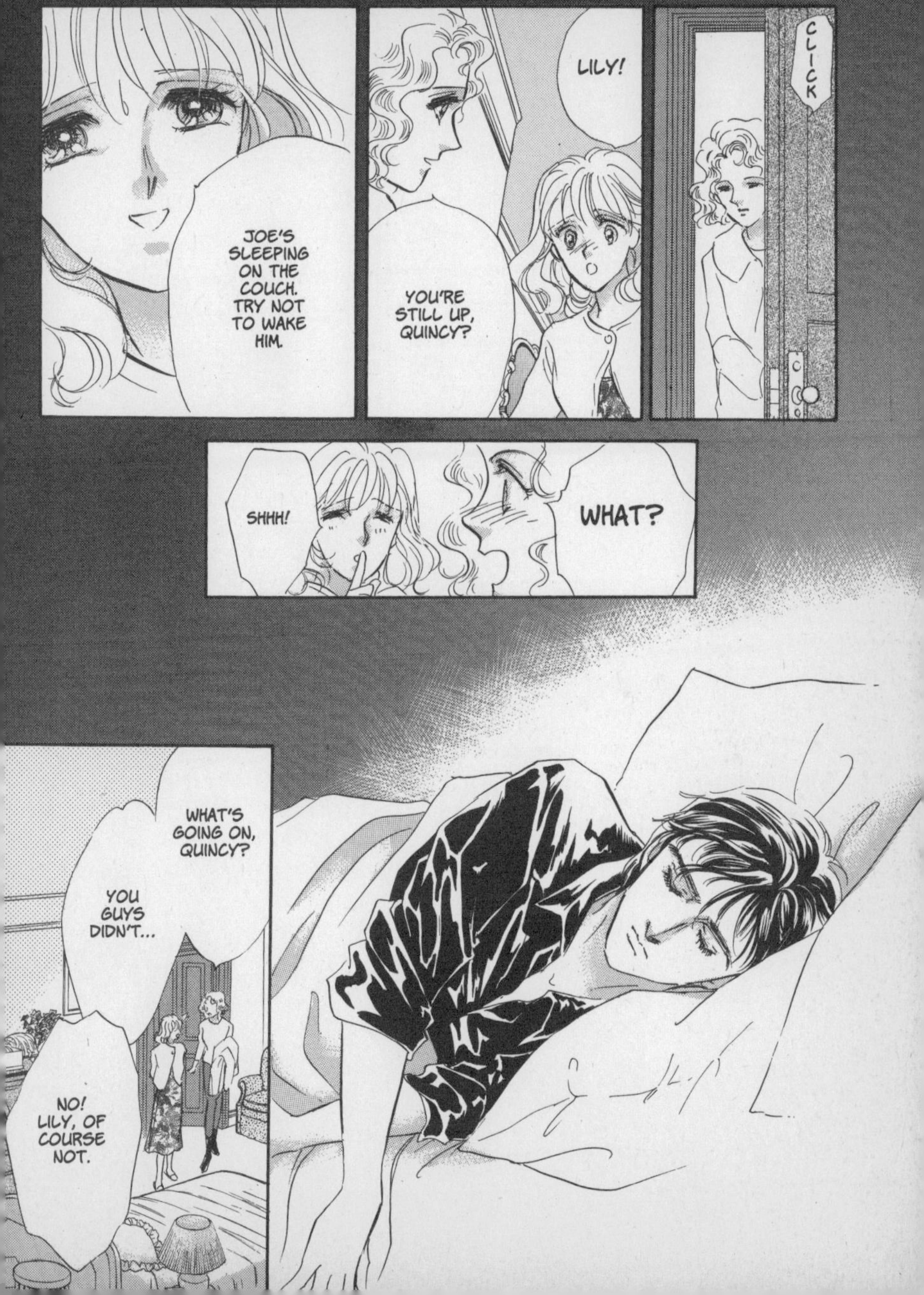
CLICK
LILY!
YOU'RE STILL UP, QUINCY?
JOE'S SLEEPING ON THE COUCH. TRY NOT TO WAKE HIM.
WHAT?
SHHH!
WHAT'S GOING ON, QUINCY?
YOU GUYS DIDN'T...
NO! LILY, OF COURSE NOT.

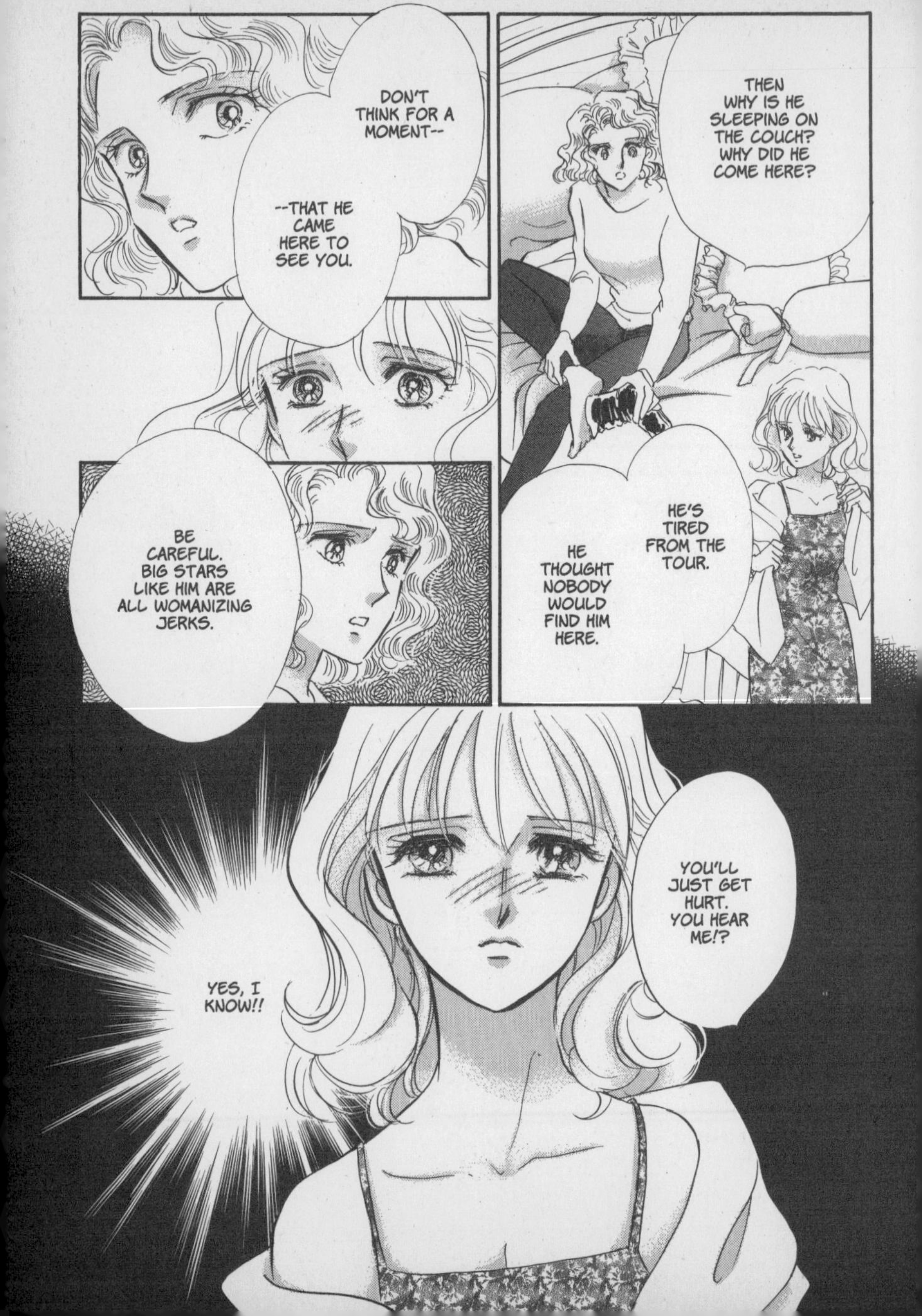
THEN WHY IS HE SLEEPING ON THE COUCH? WHY DID HE COME HERE?
HE'S TIRED FROM THE TOUR.
HE THOUGHT NOBODY WOULD FIND HIM HERE.
DON'T THINK FOR A MOMENT--
--THAT HE CAME HERE TO SEE YOU.
BE CAREFUL. BIG STARS LIKE HIM ARE ALL WOMANIZING JERKS.
YOU'LL JUST GET HURT. YOU HEAR ME!?
YES, I KNOW!!

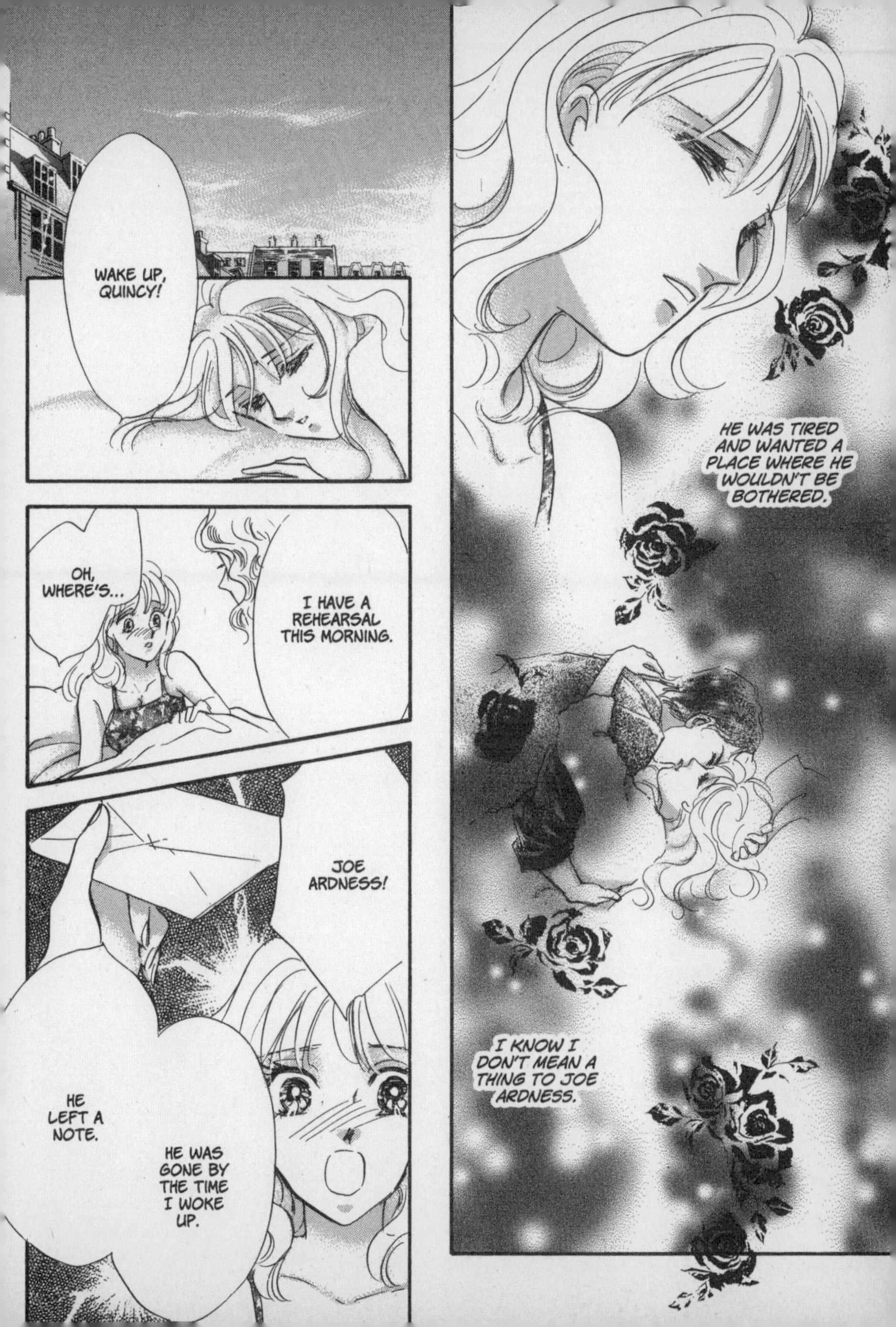
HE WAS TIRED AND WANTED A PLACE WHERE HE WOULDN'T BE BOTHERED.
I KNOW I DON'T MEAN A THING TO JOE ARDNESS.
WAKE UP, QUINCY!
I HAVE A REHEARSAL THIS MORNING.
OH, WHERE'S...
JOE ARDNESS!
HE WAS GONE BY THE TIME I WOKE UP.
HE LEFT A NOTE.

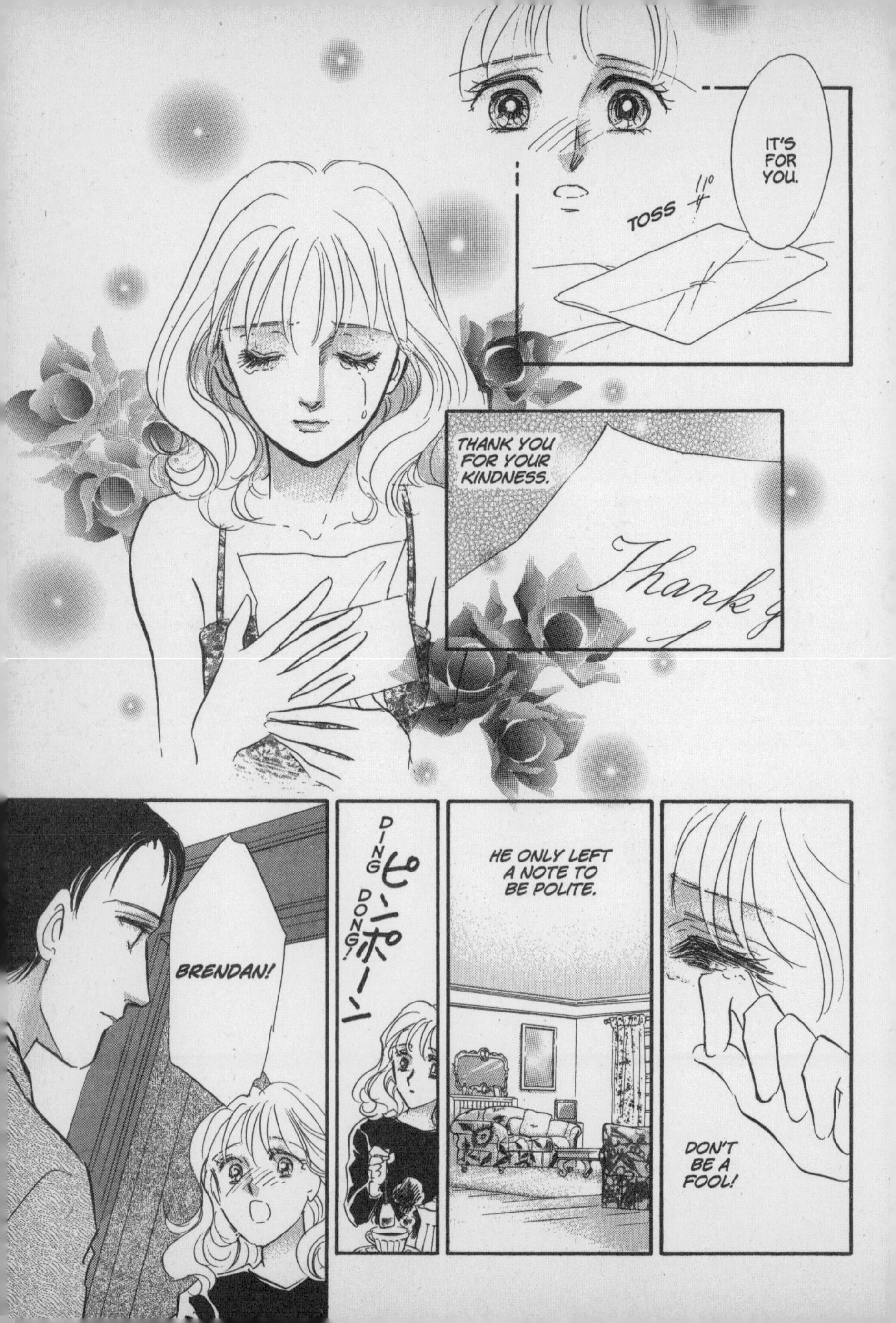
IT'S FOR YOU.
TOSS
THANK YOU FOR YOUR KINDNESS.
Thank
DON'T BE A FOOL!
HE ONLY LEFT A NOTE TO BE POLITE.
DING DONG!
ピンポーン
BRENDAN!

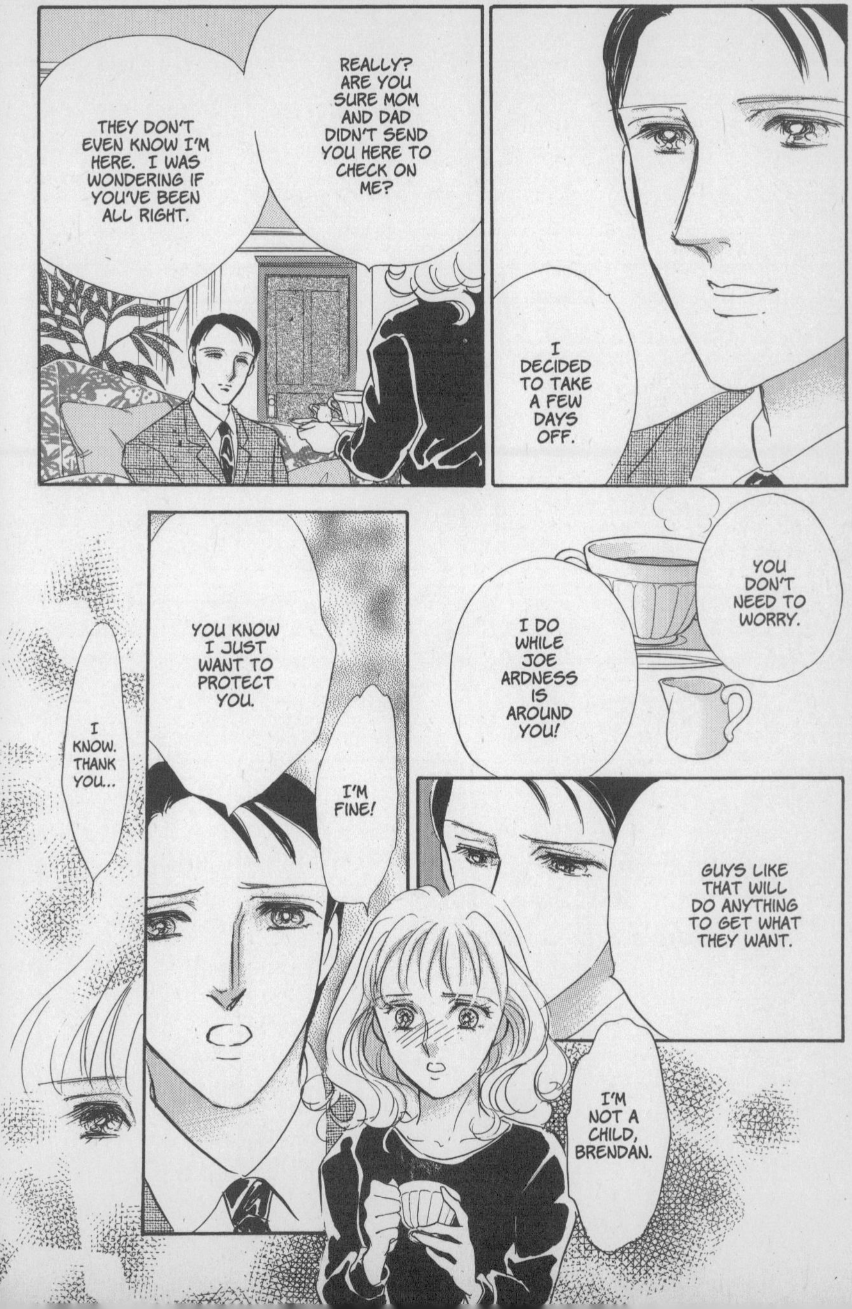
I DECIDED TO TAKE A FEW DAYS OFF.
REALLY? ARE YOU SURE MOM AND DAD DIDN'T SEND YOU HERE TO CHECK ON ME?
THEY DON'T EVEN KNOW I'M HERE. I WAS WONDERING IF YOU'VE BEEN ALL RIGHT.
YOU DON'T NEED TO WORRY.
I DO WHILE JOE ARDNESS IS AROUND YOU!
GUYS LIKE THAT WILL DO ANYTHING TO GET WHAT THEY WANT.
I'M NOT A CHILD, BRENDAN.
I'M FINE!
YOU KNOW I JUST WANT TO PROTECT YOU.
I KNOW. THANK YOU...

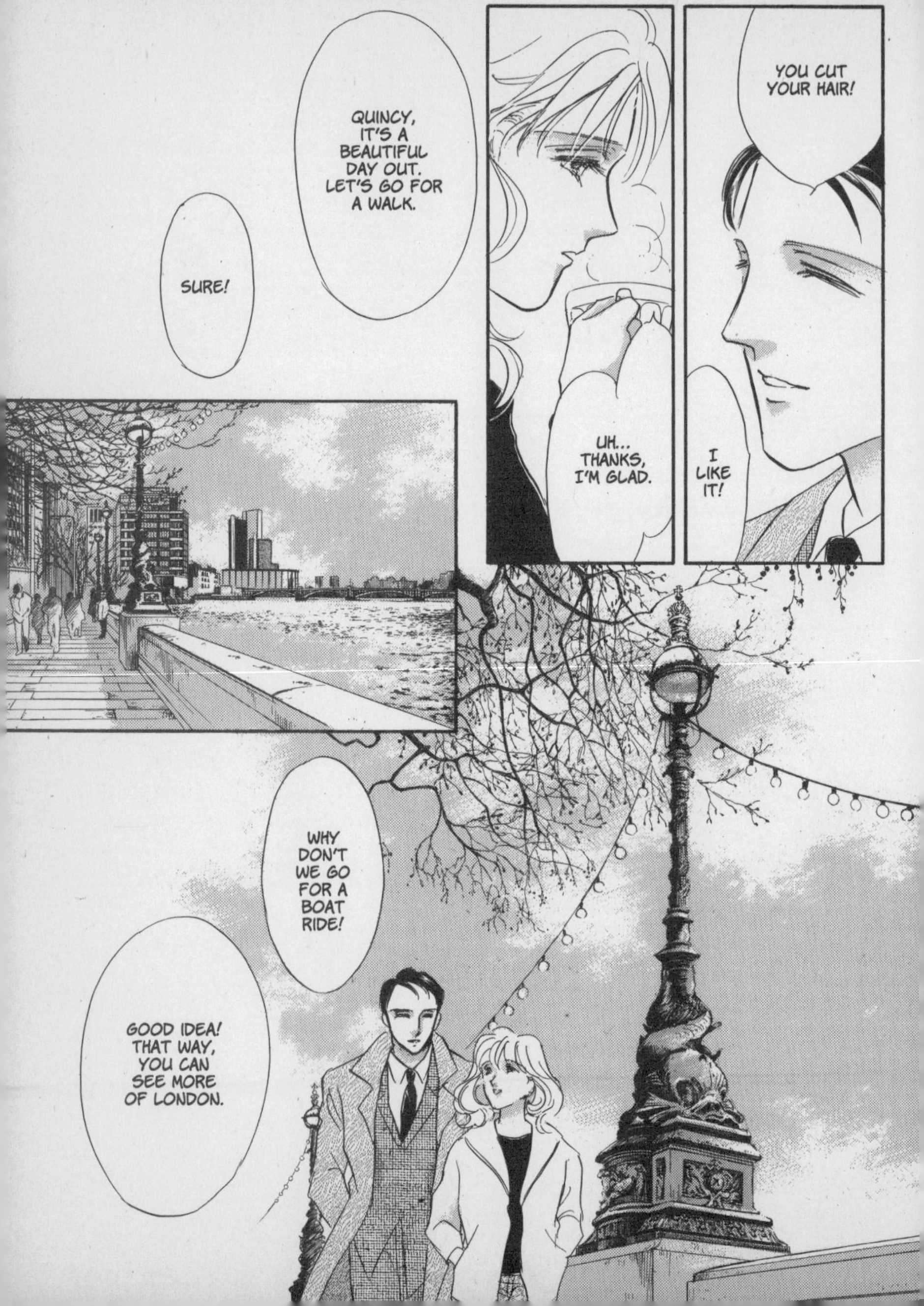
YOU CUT YOUR HAIR!
I LIKE IT!
UH... THANKS, I'M GLAD.
QUINCY, IT'S A BEAUTIFUL DAY OUT. LET'S GO FOR A WALK.
SURE!
WHY DON'T WE GO FOR A BOAT RIDE!
GOOD IDEA! THAT WAY, YOU CAN SEE MORE OF LONDON.

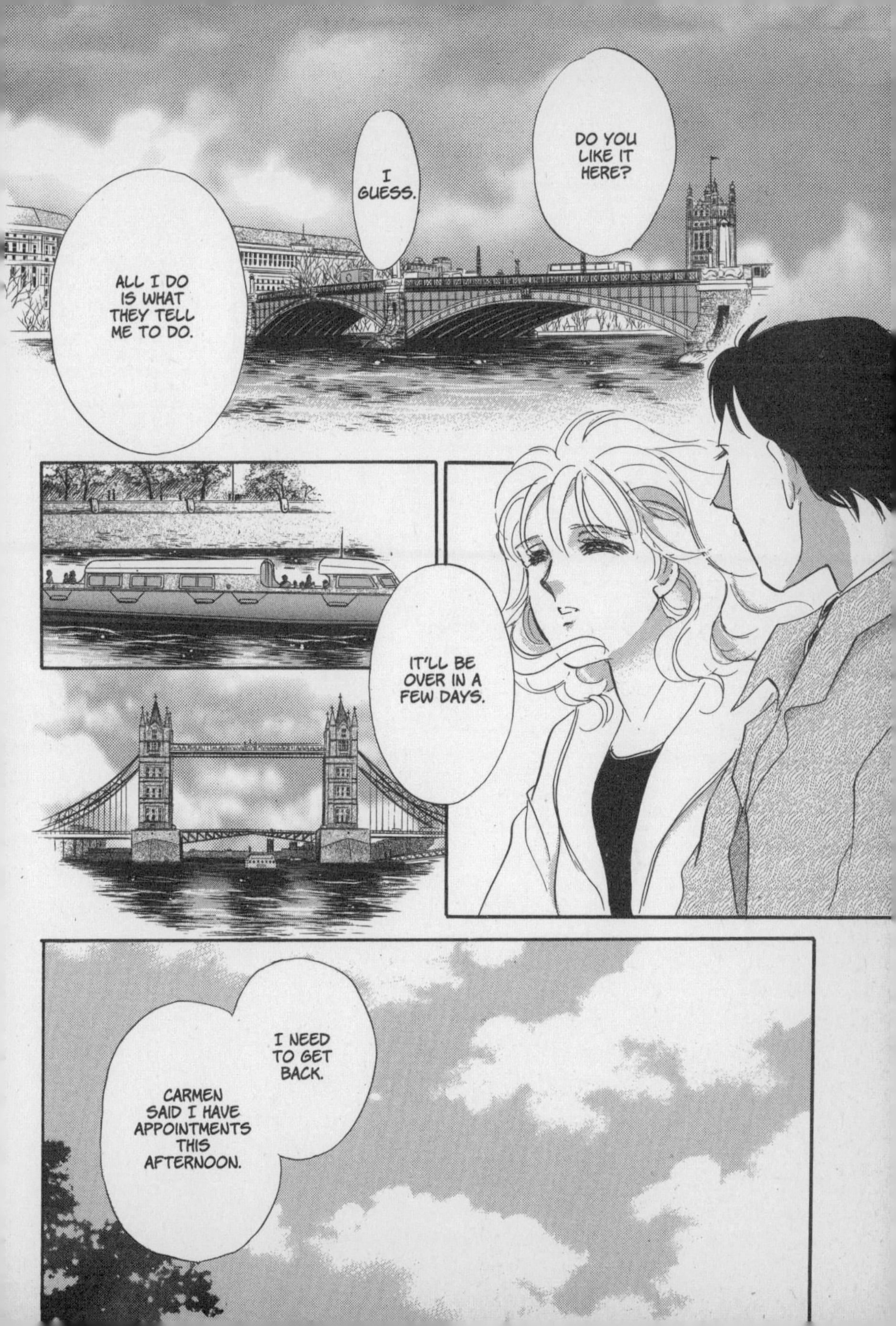
DO YOU LIKE IT HERE?
I GUESS.
ALL I DO IS WHAT THEY TELL ME TO DO.
IT'LL BE OVER IN A FEW DAYS.
I NEED TO GET BACK.
CARMEN SAID I HAVE APPOINTMENTS THIS AFTERNOON.

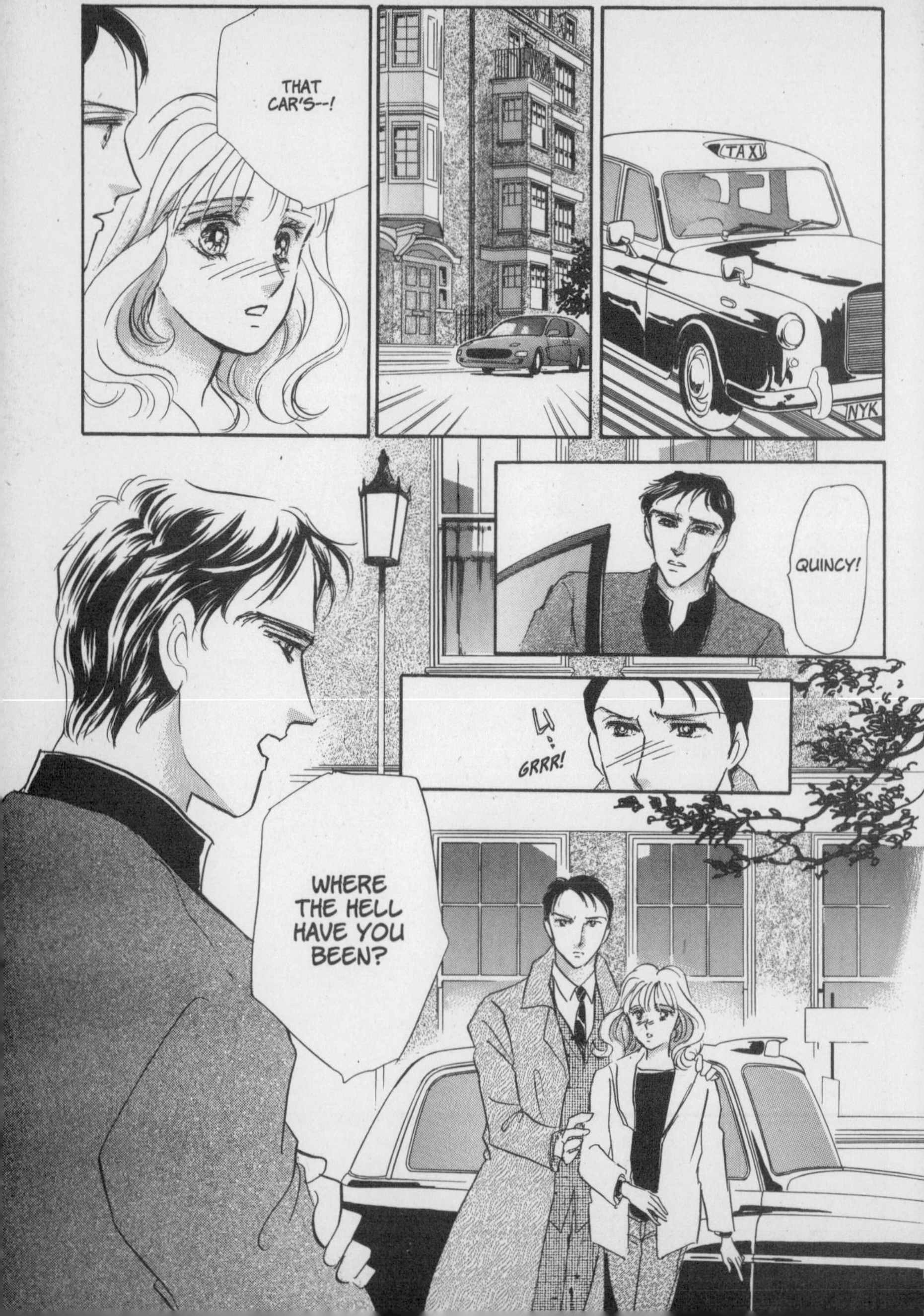
THAT CAR'S--!
QUINCY!
GRRR!
WHERE THE HELL HAVE YOU BEEN?

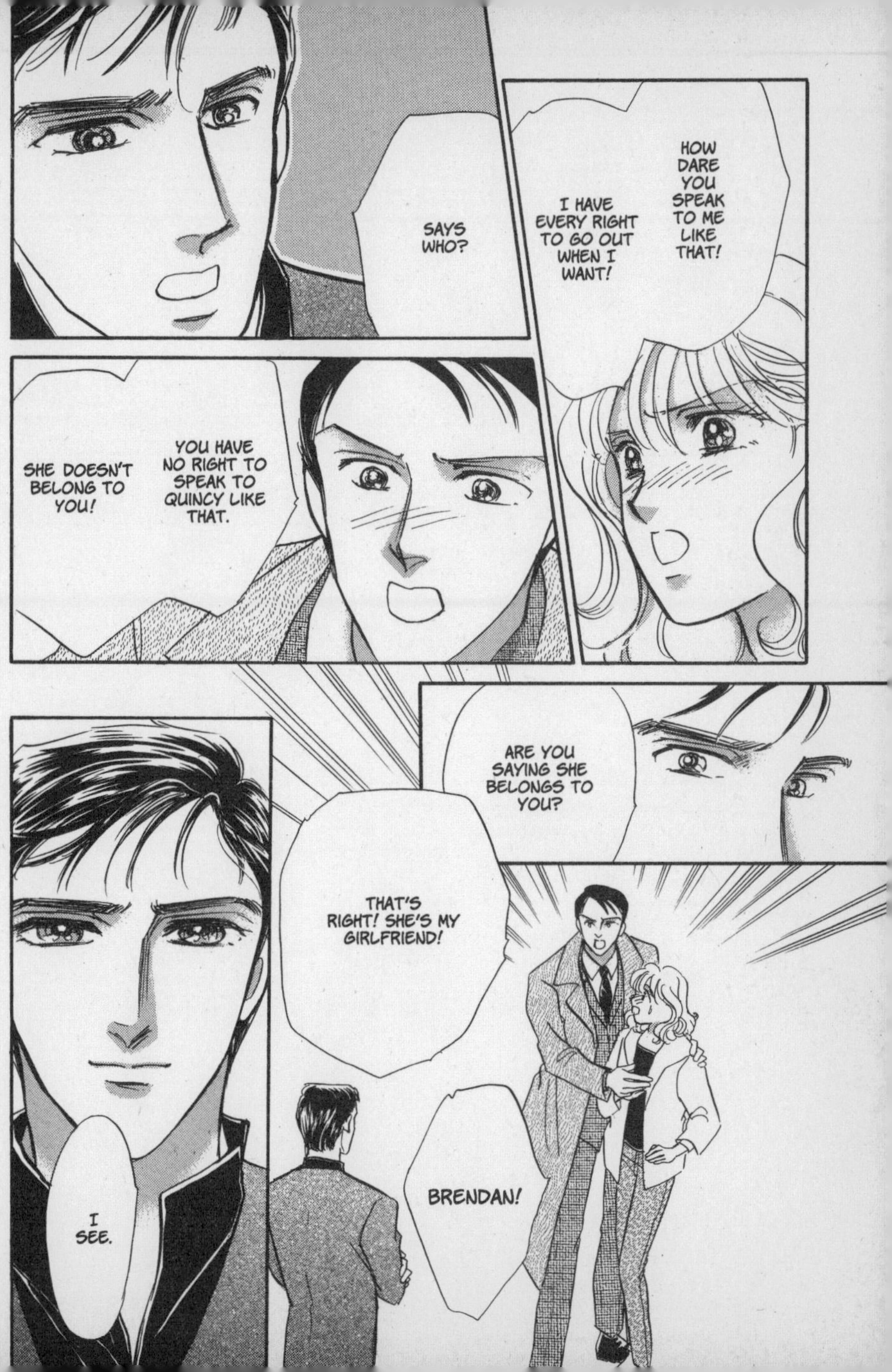
HOW DARE YOU SPEAK TO ME LIKE THAT!
I HAVE EVERY RIGHT TO GO OUT WHEN I WANT!
SAYS WHO?
YOU HAVE NO RIGHT TO SPEAK TO QUINCY LIKE THAT.
SHE DOESN'T BELONG TO YOU!
ARE YOU SAYING SHE BELONGS TO YOU?
THAT'S RIGHT! SHE'S MY GIRLFRIEND!
BRENDAN!
I SEE.

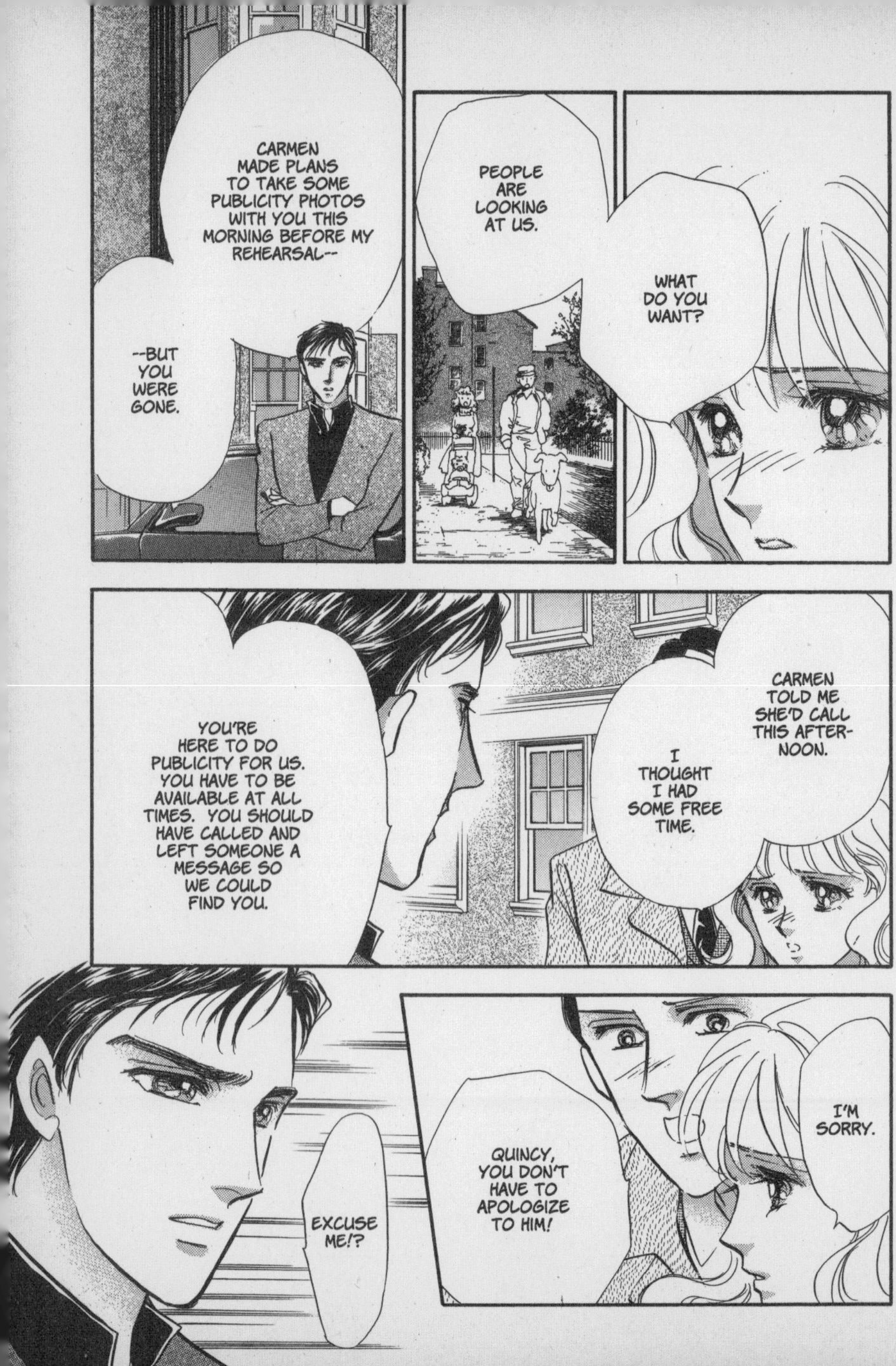
WHAT DO YOU WANT?
PEOPLE ARE LOOKING AT US.
CARMEN MADE PLANS TO TAKE SOME PUBLICITY PHOTOS WITH YOU THIS MORNING BEFORE MY REHEARSAL--
--BUT YOU WERE GONE.
CARMEN TOLD ME SHE'D CALL THIS AFTER-NOON.
I THOUGHT I HAD SOME FREE TIME.
YOU'RE HERE TO DO PUBLICITY FOR US. YOU HAVE TO BE AVAILABLE AT ALL TIMES. YOU SHOULD HAVE CALLED AND LEFT SOMEONE A MESSAGE SO WE COULD FIND YOU.
I'M SORRY.
QUINCY, YOU DON'T HAVE TO APOLOGIZE TO HIM!
EXCUSE ME!?

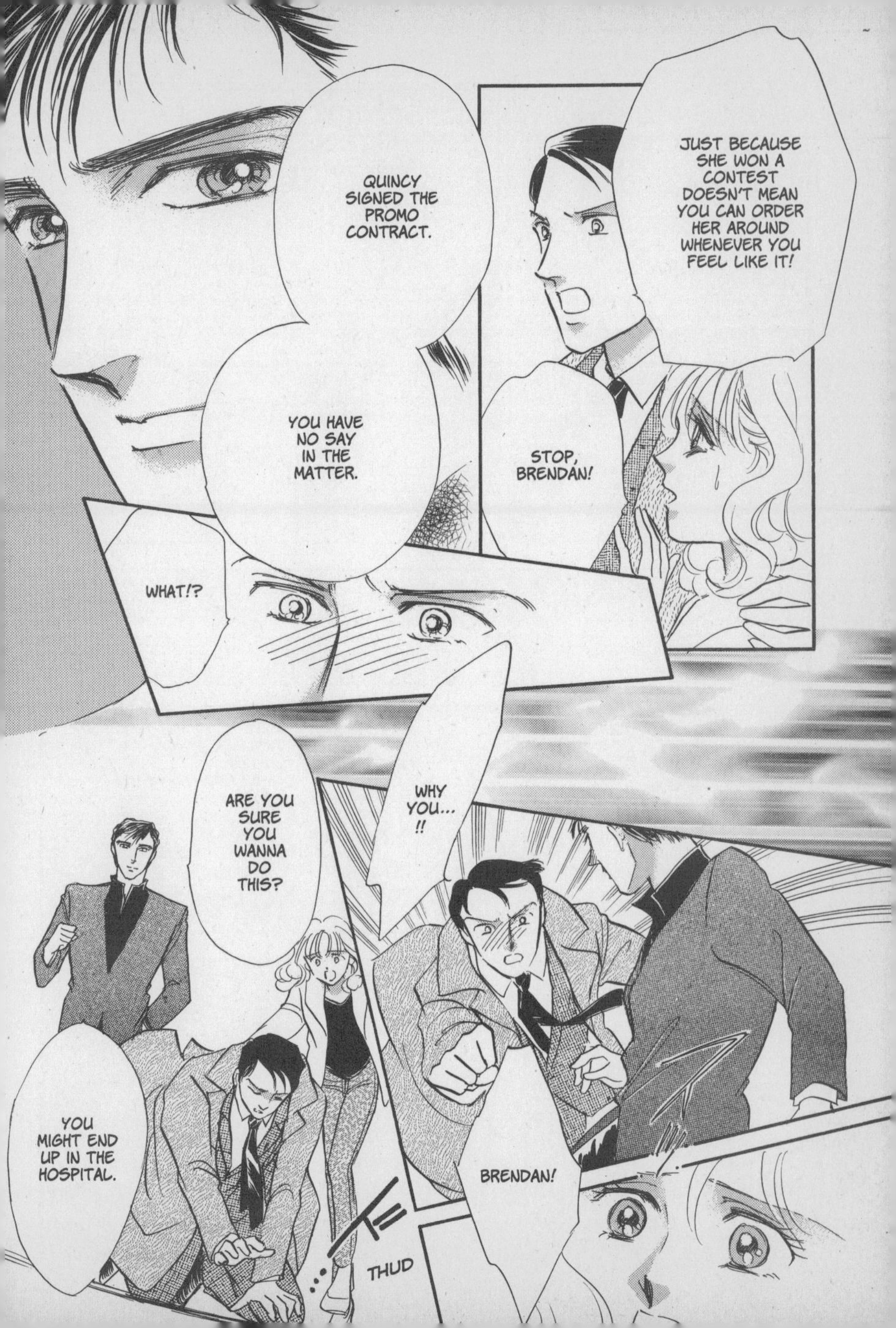
JUST BECAUSE SHE WON A CONTEST DOESN'T MEAN YOU CAN ORDER HER AROUND WHENEVER YOU FEEL LIKE IT!
STOP, BRENDAN!
QUINCY SIGNED THE PROMO CONTRACT.
YOU HAVE NO SAY IN THE MATTER.
WHAT!?
WHY YOU... !!
ARE YOU SURE YOU WANNA DO THIS?
YOU MIGHT END UP IN THE HOSPITAL.
THUD
BRENDAN!

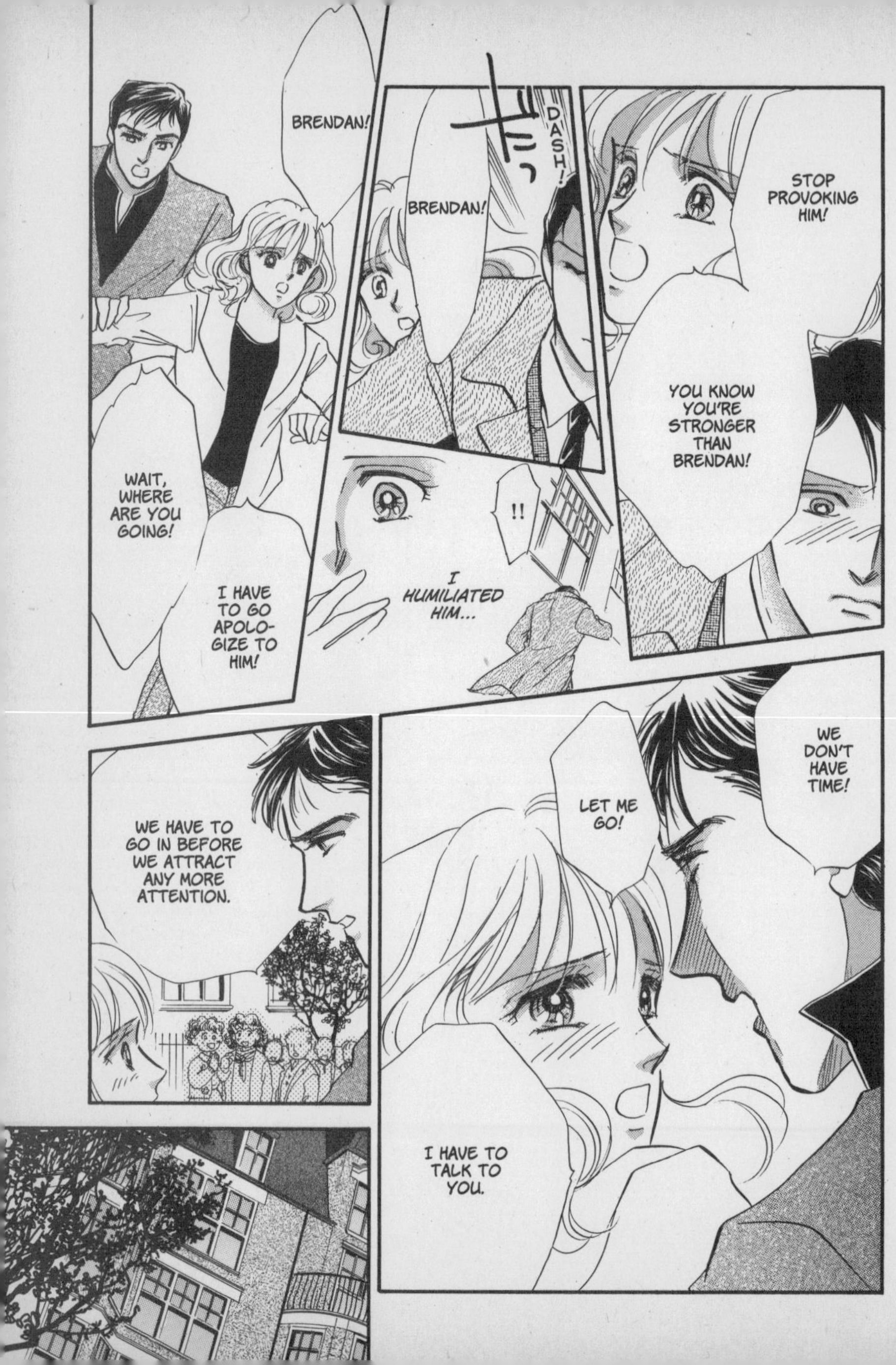
STOP PROVOKING HIM!
YOU KNOW YOU'RE STRONGER THAN BRENDAN!
DASH!
BRENDAN!
!!
I HUMILIATED HIM...
BRENDAN!
WAIT, WHERE ARE YOU GOING!
I HAVE TO GO APOLOGIZE TO HIM!
WE DON'T HAVE TIME!
LET ME GO!
I HAVE TO TALK TO YOU.
WE HAVE TO GO IN BEFORE WE ATTRACT ANY MORE ATTENTION.

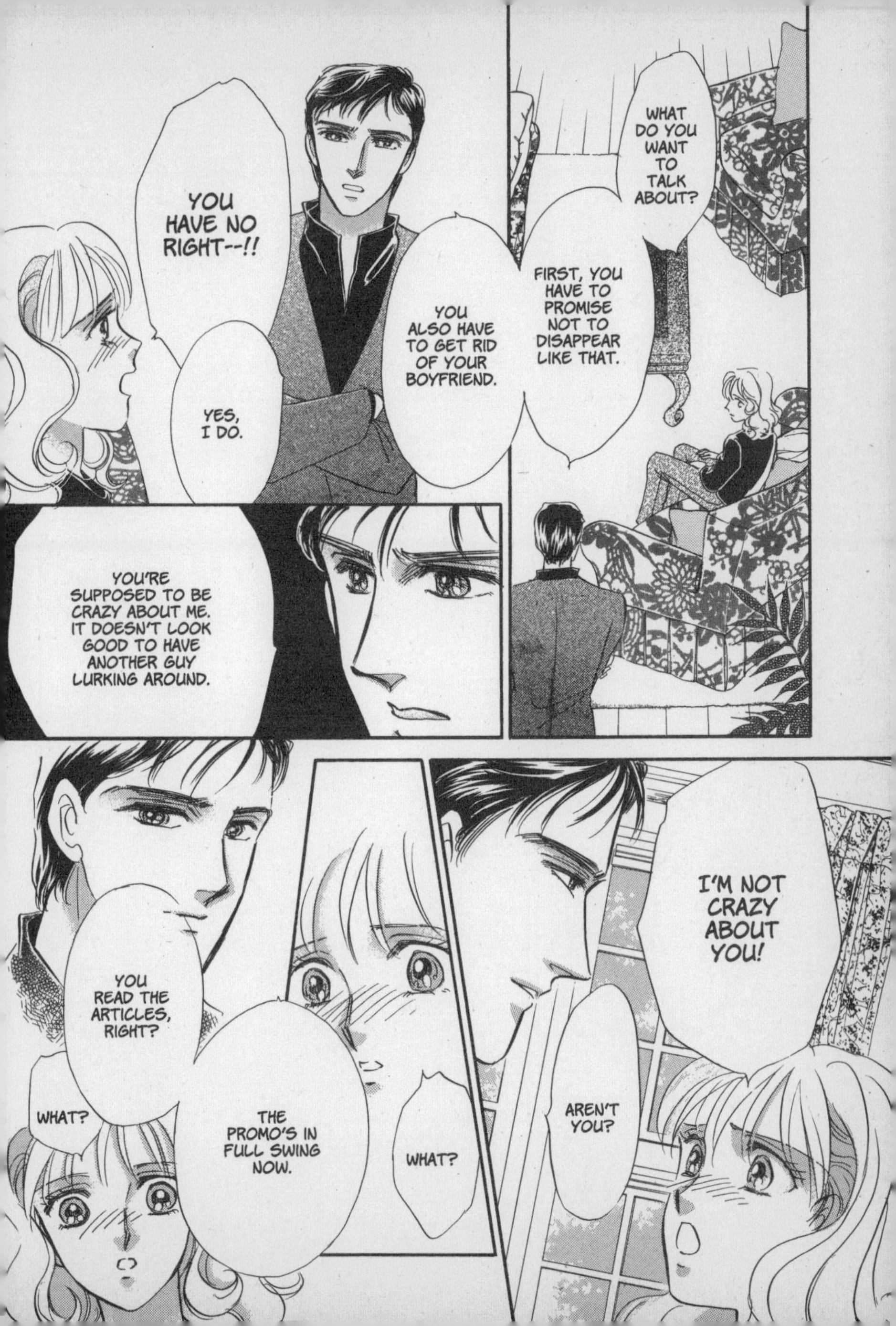
WHAT DO YOU WANT TO TALK ABOUT?
FIRST, YOU HAVE TO PROMISE NOT TO DISAPPEAR LIKE THAT.
YOU ALSO HAVE TO GET RID OF YOUR BOYFRIEND.
YOU HAVE NO RIGHT--!!
YES, I DO.
YOU'RE SUPPOSED TO BE CRAZY ABOUT ME. IT DOESN'T LOOK GOOD TO HAVE ANOTHER GUY LURKING AROUND.
I'M NOT CRAZY ABOUT YOU!
AREN'T YOU?
WHAT?
YOU READ THE ARTICLES, RIGHT?
THE PROMO'S IN FULL SWING NOW.
WHAT?

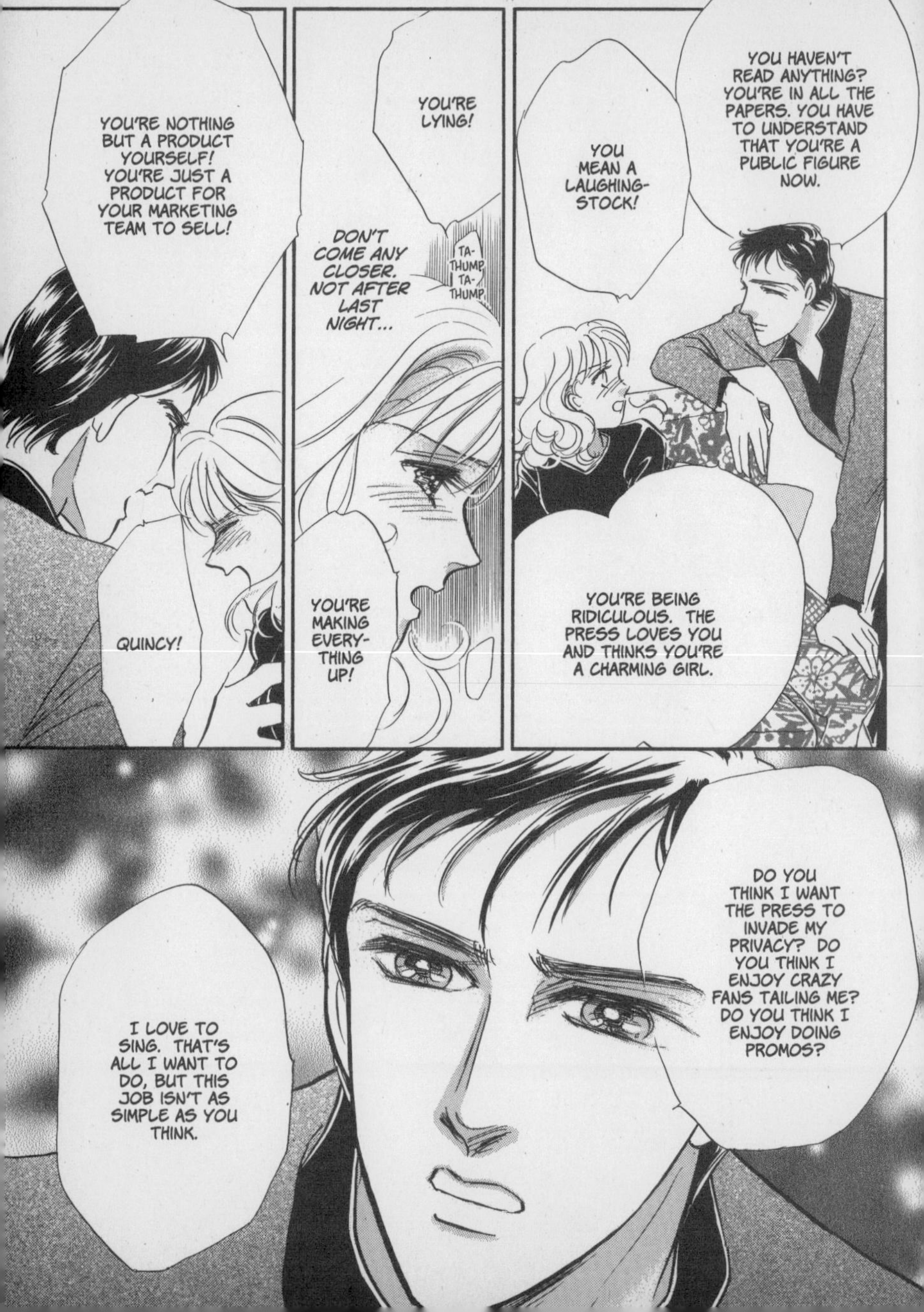
YOU HAVEN'T READ ANYTHING? YOU'RE IN ALL THE PAPERS. YOU HAVE TO UNDERSTAND THAT YOU'RE A PUBLIC FIGURE NOW.
YOU MEAN A LAUGHING-STOCK!
YOU'RE BEING RIDICULOUS. THE PRESS LOVES YOU AND THINKS YOU'RE A CHARMING GIRL.
YOU'RE LYING!
DON'T COME ANY CLOSER. NOT AFTER LAST NIGHT...
TA-THUMP TA-THUMP
YOU'RE MAKING EVERY-THING UP!
YOU'RE NOTHING BUT A PRODUCT YOURSELF! YOU'RE JUST A PRODUCT FOR YOUR MARKETING TEAM TO SELL!
QUINCY!
DO YOU THINK I WANT THE PRESS TO INVADE MY PRIVACY? DO YOU THINK I ENJOY CRAZY FANS TAILING ME? DO YOU THINK I ENJOY DOING PROMOS?
I LOVE TO SING. THAT'S ALL I WANT TO DO, BUT THIS JOB ISN'T AS SIMPLE AS YOU THINK.

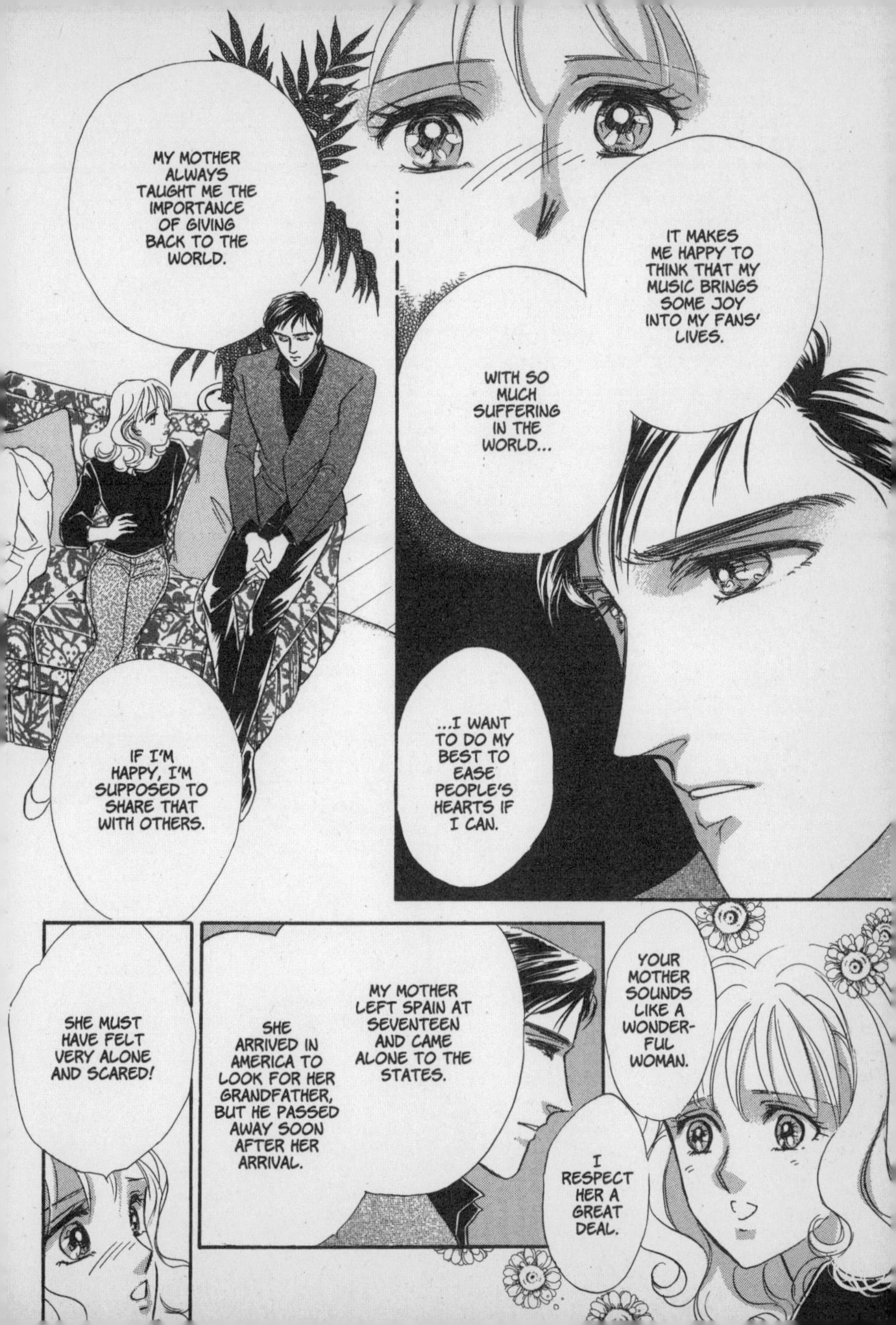
IT MAKES ME HAPPY TO THINK THAT MY MUSIC BRINGS SOME JOY INTO MY FANS' LIVES.
WITH SO MUCH SUFFERING IN THE WORLD...
...I WANT TO DO MY BEST TO EASE PEOPLE'S HEARTS IF I CAN.
MY MOTHER ALWAYS TAUGHT ME THE IMPORTANCE OF GIVING BACK TO THE WORLD.
IF I'M HAPPY, I'M SUPPOSED TO SHARE THAT WITH OTHERS.
YOUR MOTHER SOUNDS LIKE A WONDER-FUL WOMAN.
I RESPECT HER A GREAT DEAL.
MY MOTHER LEFT SPAIN AT SEVENTEEN AND CAME ALONE TO THE STATES.
SHE ARRIVED IN AMERICA TO LOOK FOR HER GRANDFATHER, BUT HE PASSED AWAY SOON AFTER HER ARRIVAL.
SHE MUST HAVE FELT VERY ALONE AND SCARED!

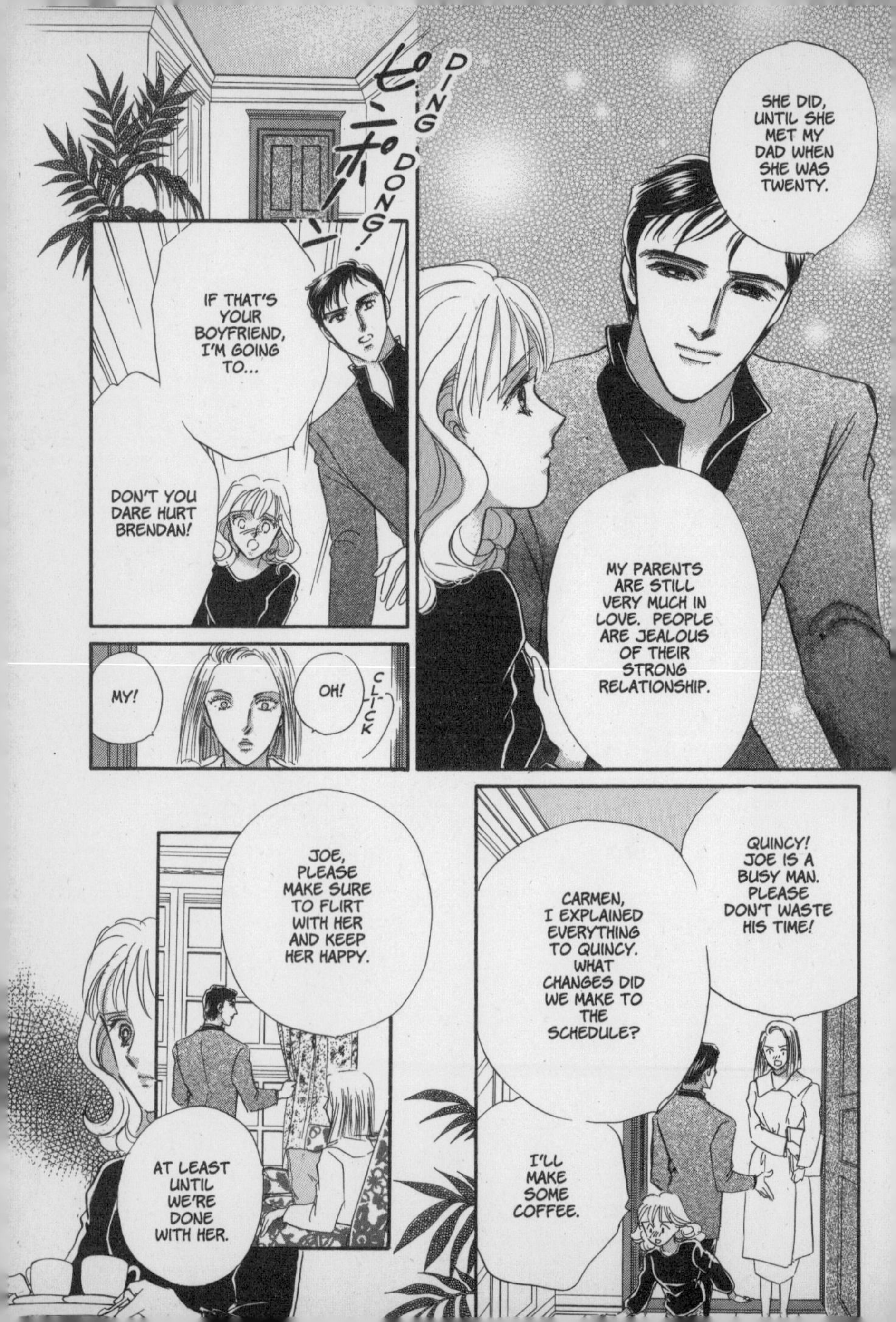
SHE DID, UNTIL SHE MET MY DAD WHEN SHE WAS TWENTY.
MY PARENTS ARE STILL VERY MUCH IN LOVE. PEOPLE ARE JEALOUS OF THEIR STRONG RELATIONSHIP.
DING DONG!
IF THAT'S YOUR BOYFRIEND, I'M GOING TO...
DON'T YOU DARE HURT BRENDAN!
CLICK
OH!
MY!
QUINCY! JOE IS A BUSY MAN. PLEASE DON'T WASTE HIS TIME!
CARMEN, I EXPLAINED EVERYTHING TO QUINCY. WHAT CHANGES DID WE MAKE TO THE SCHEDULE?
I'LL MAKE SOME COFFEE.
JOE, PLEASE MAKE SURE TO FLIRT WITH HER AND KEEP HER HAPPY.
AT LEAST UNTIL WE'RE DONE WITH HER.

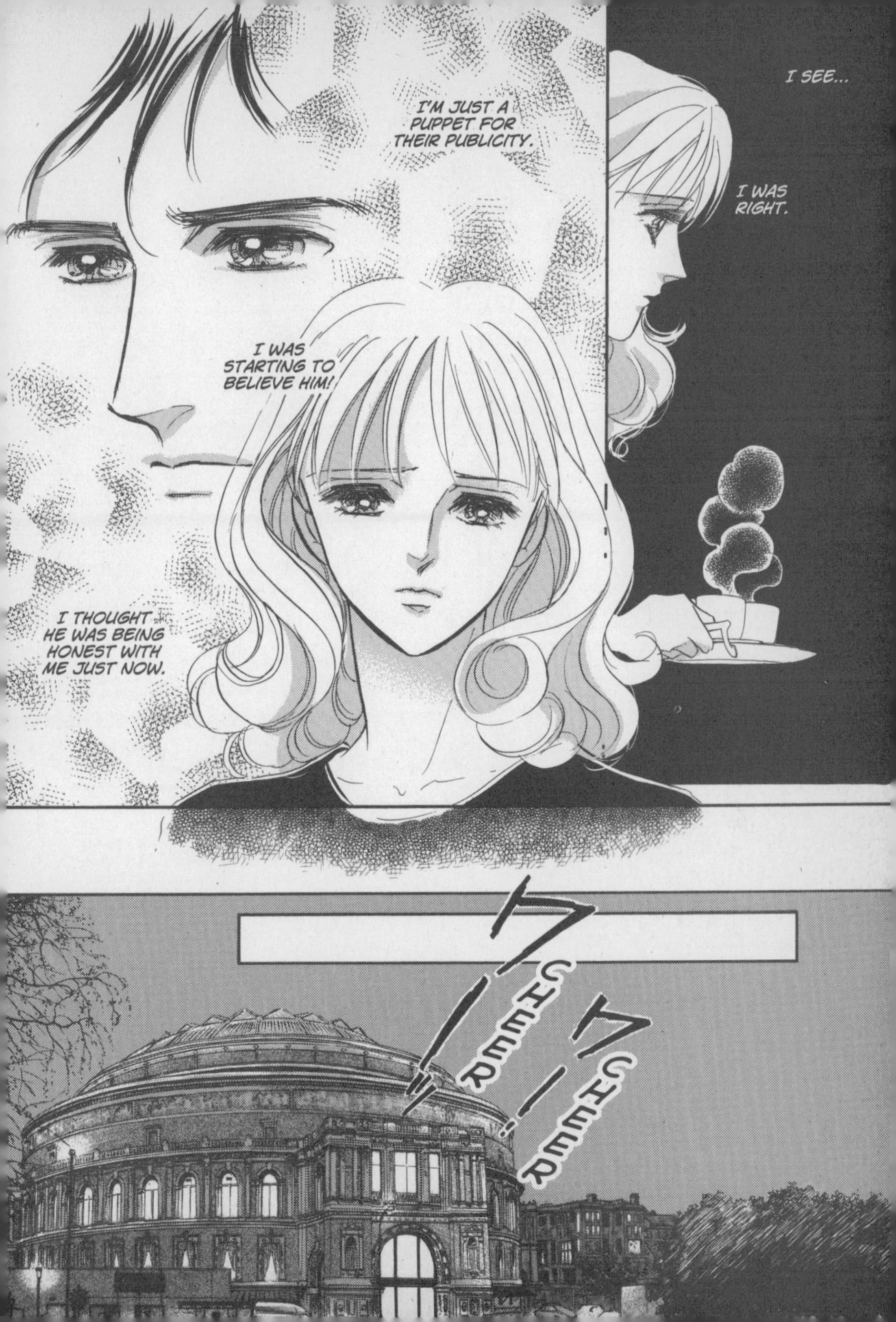
I SEE...
I WAS RIGHT.
I'M JUST A PUPPET FOR THEIR PUBLICITY.
I WAS STARTING TO BELIEVE HIM!
I THOUGHT HE WAS BEING HONEST WITH ME JUST NOW.
CHEER
CHEER!

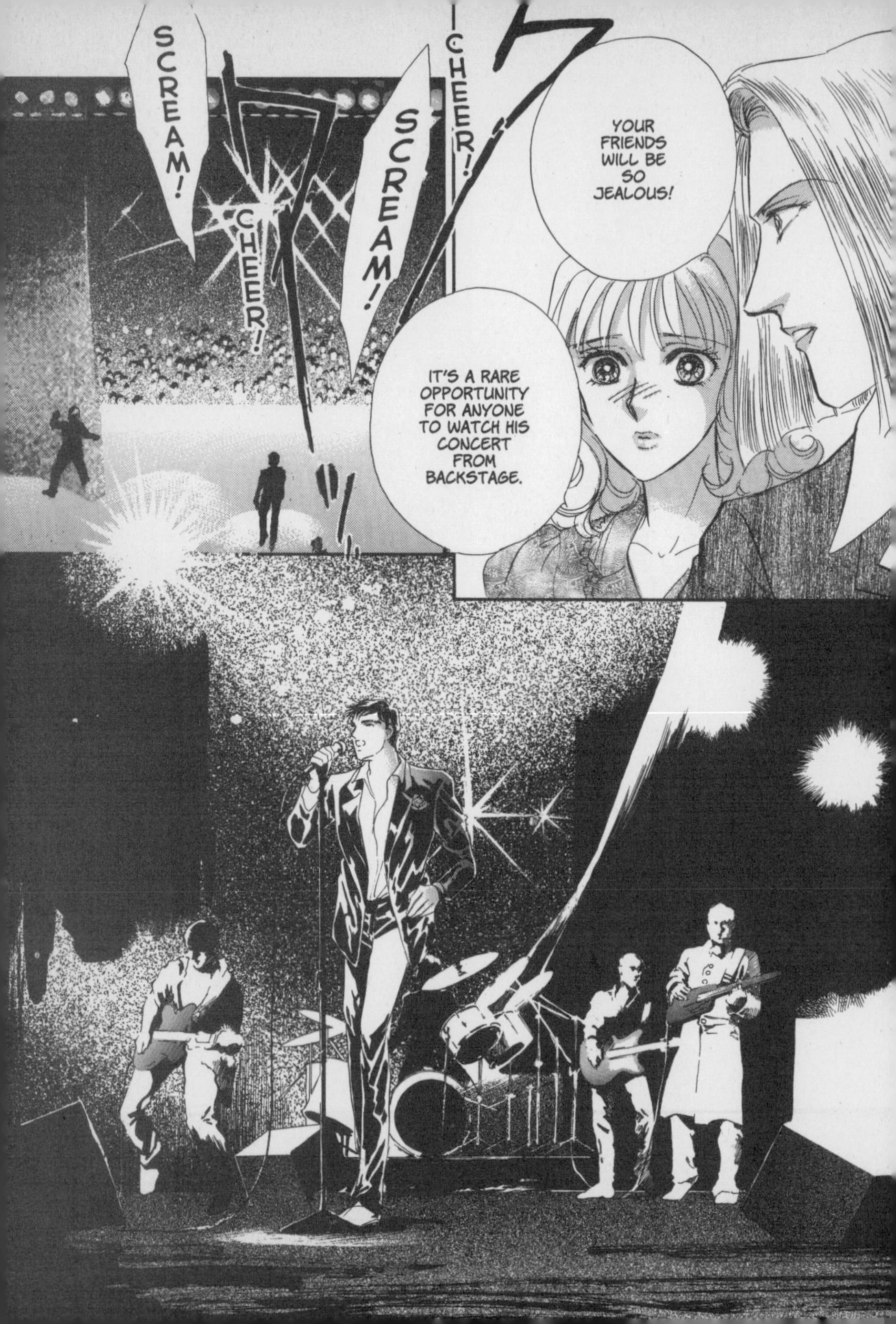
YOUR FRIENDS WILL BE SO JEALOUS!
IT'S A RARE OPPORTUNITY FOR ANYONE TO WATCH HIS CONCERT FROM BACKSTAGE.
CHEER!
SCREAM!
CHEER!
SCREAM!

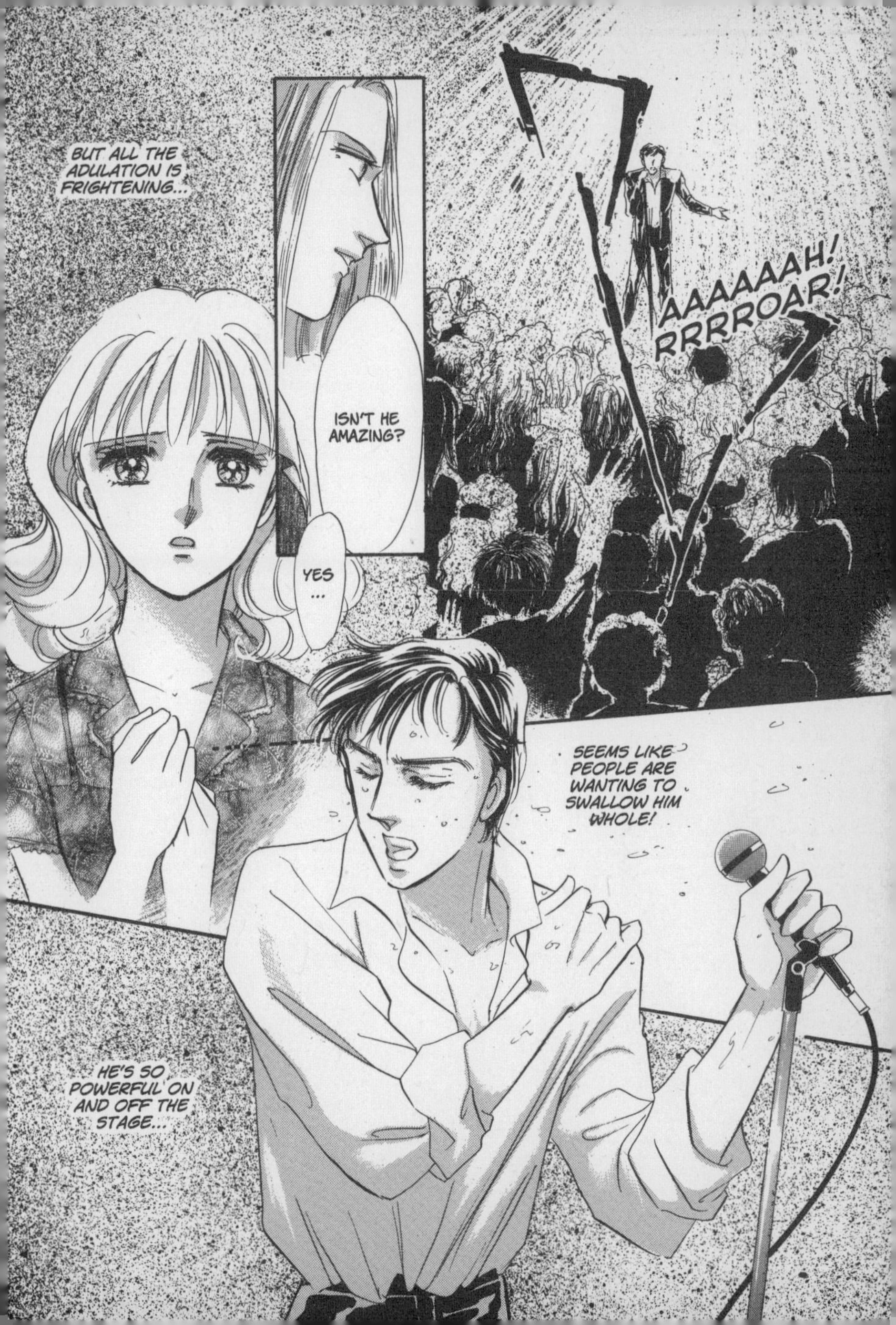

AAAAAAH! RRRROAR!
ISN'T HE AMAZING?
YES ...
BUT ALL THE ADULATION IS FRIGHTENING...
SEEMS LIKE PEOPLE ARE WANTING TO SWALLOW HIM WHOLE!
HE'S SO POWERFUL ON AND OFF THE STAGE...

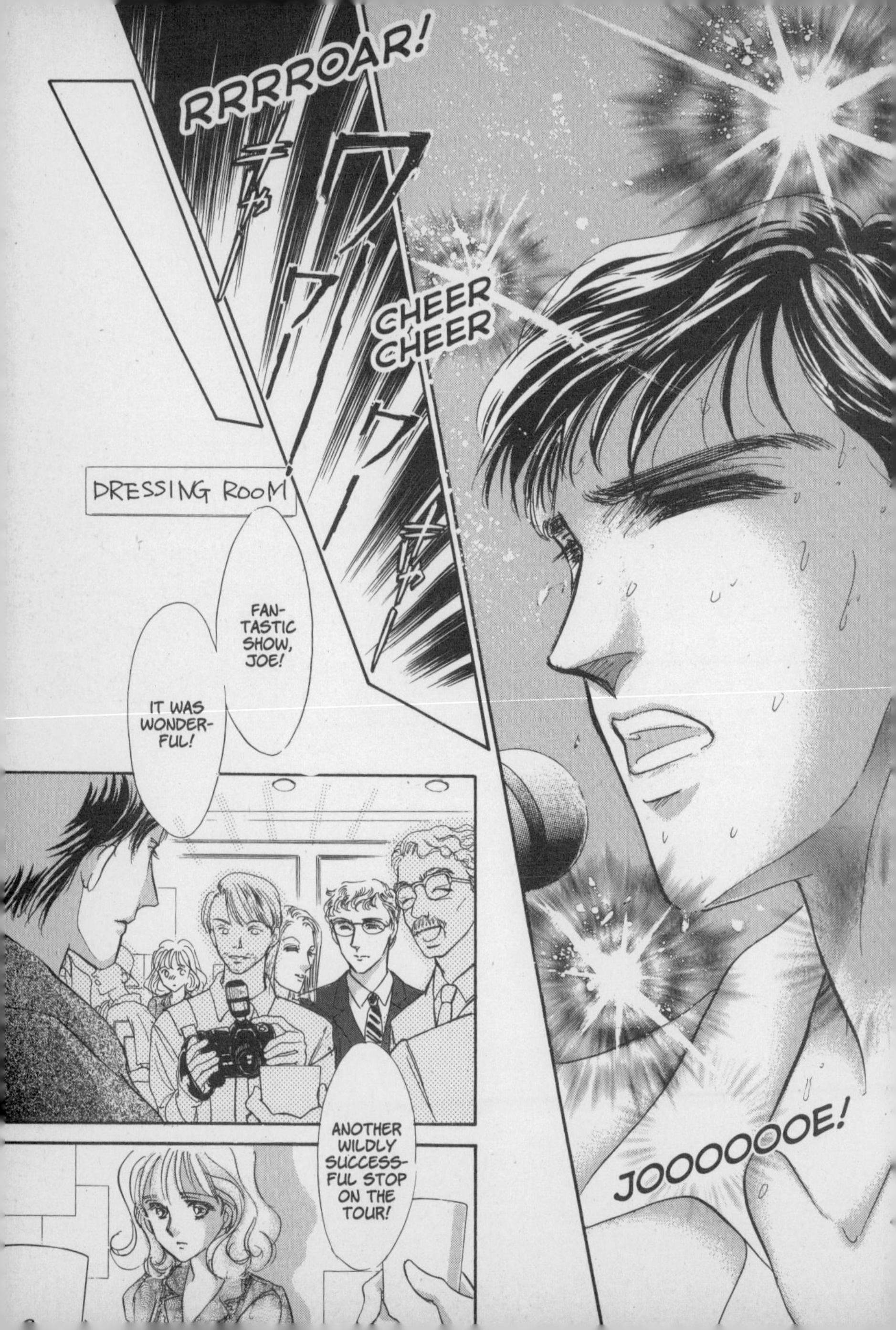
RRRROAR!
CHEER CHEER
JOOOOOOE!
DRESSING ROOM
FAN-TASTIC SHOW, JOE!
IT WAS WONDER-FUL!
ANOTHER WILDLY SUCCESS-FUL STOP ON THE TOUR!

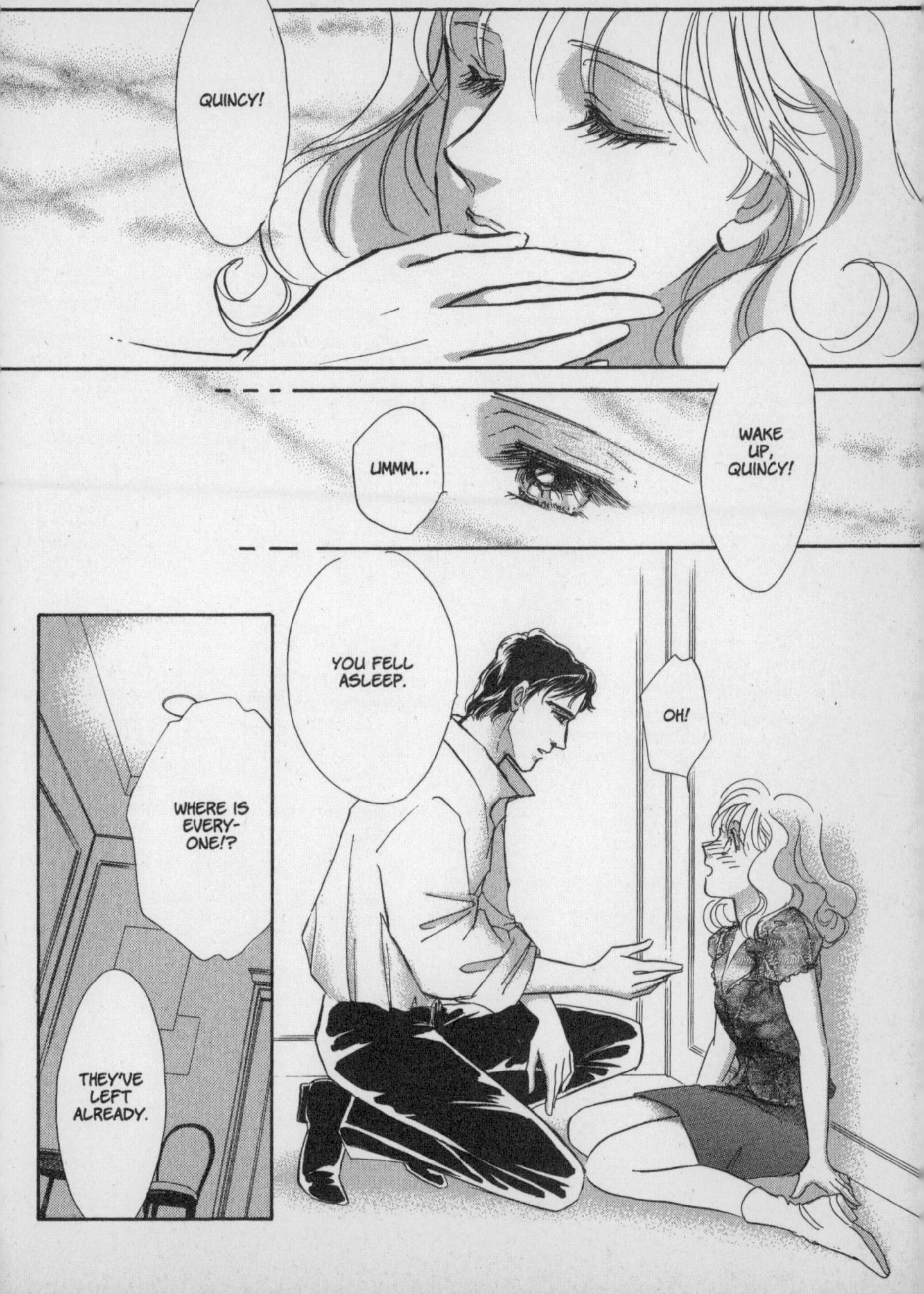
QUINCY!
WAKE UP, QUINCY!
UMMM...
OH!
YOU FELL ASLEEP.
WHERE IS EVERY-ONE!?
THEY'VE LEFT ALREADY.

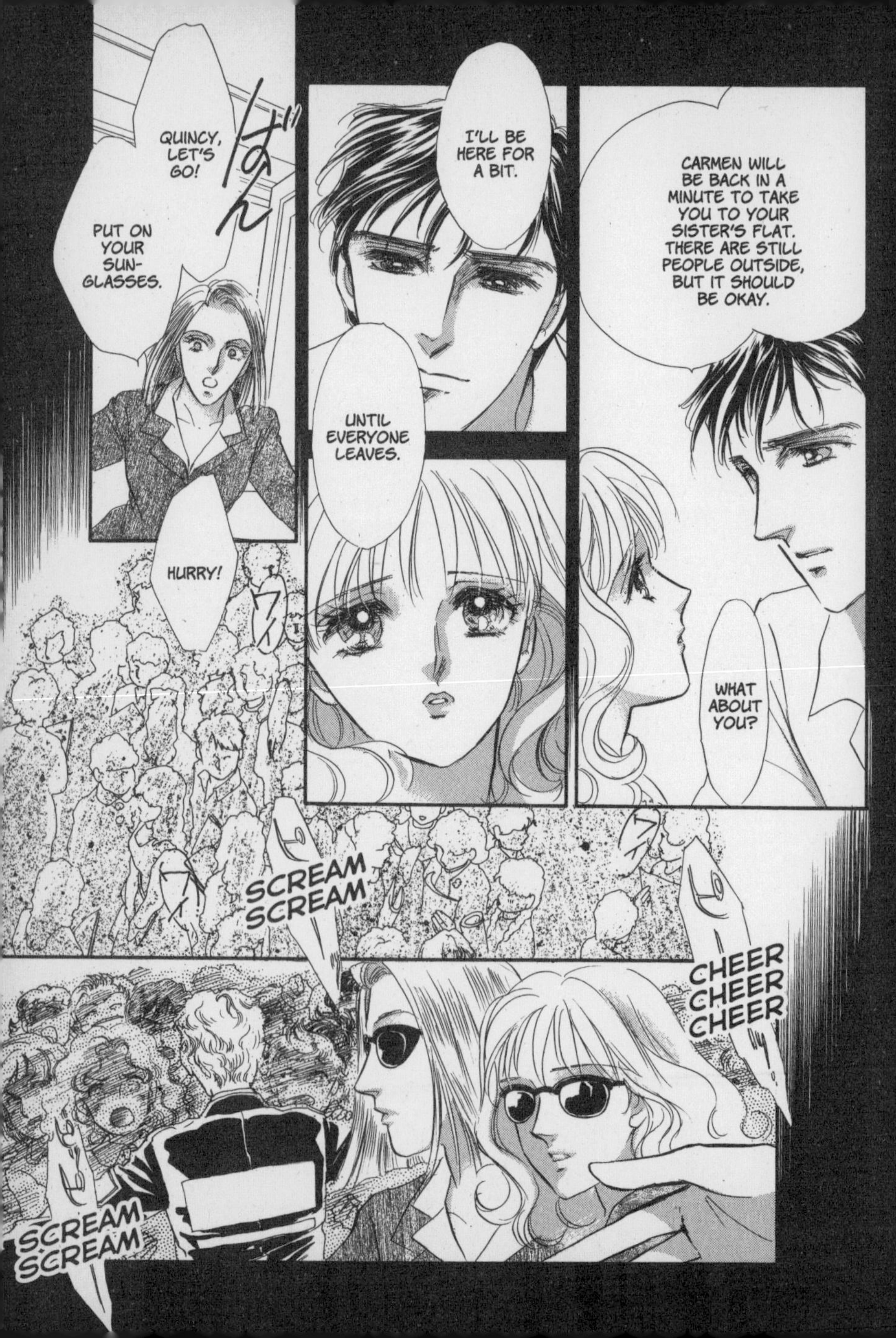
CARMEN WILL BE BACK IN A MINUTE TO TAKE YOU TO YOUR SISTER'S FLAT. THERE ARE STILL PEOPLE OUTSIDE, BUT IT SHOULD BE OKAY.
WHAT ABOUT YOU?
I'LL BE HERE FOR A BIT.
UNTIL EVERYONE LEAVES.
ばん
QUINCY, LET'S GO!
PUT ON YOUR SUN-GLASSES.
HURRY!
SCREAM SCREAM
CHEER CHEER CHEER
SCREAM SCREAM

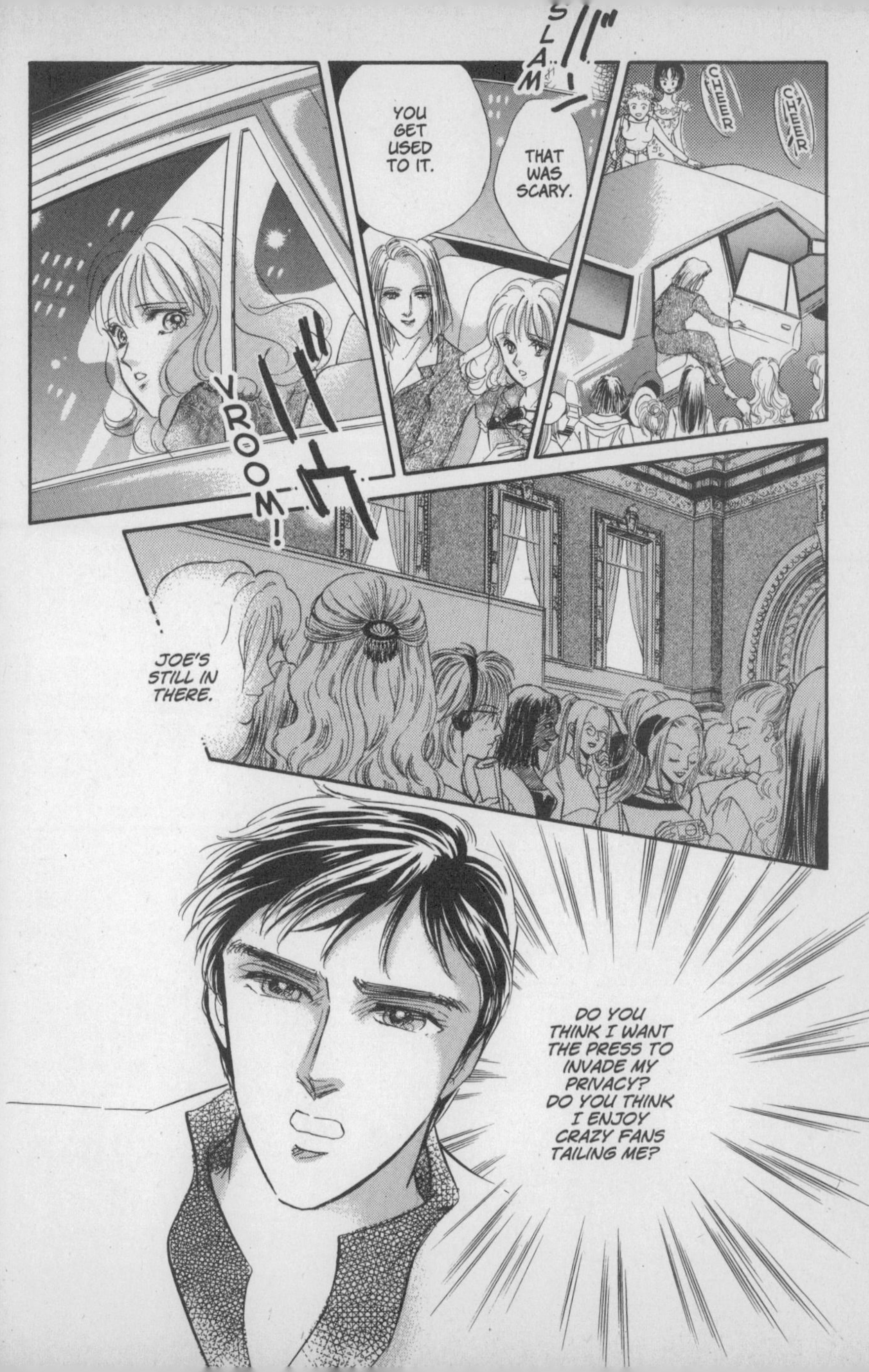
CHEER
CHEER
SLAM!
THAT WAS SCARY.
YOU GET USED TO IT.
VROOM!
JOE'S STILL IN THERE.
DO YOU THINK I WANT THE PRESS TO INVADE MY PRIVACY? DO YOU THINK I ENJOY CRAZY FANS TAILING ME?

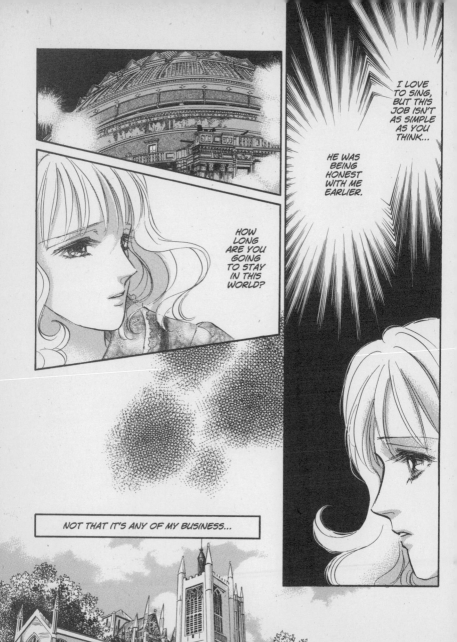

I LOVE TO SING, BUT THIS JOB ISN'T AS SIMPLE AS YOU THINK...

HE WAS BEING HONEST WITH ME EARLIER.

HOW LONG ARE YOU GOING TO STAY IN THIS WORLD?

NOT THAT IT'S ANY OF MY BUSINESS...

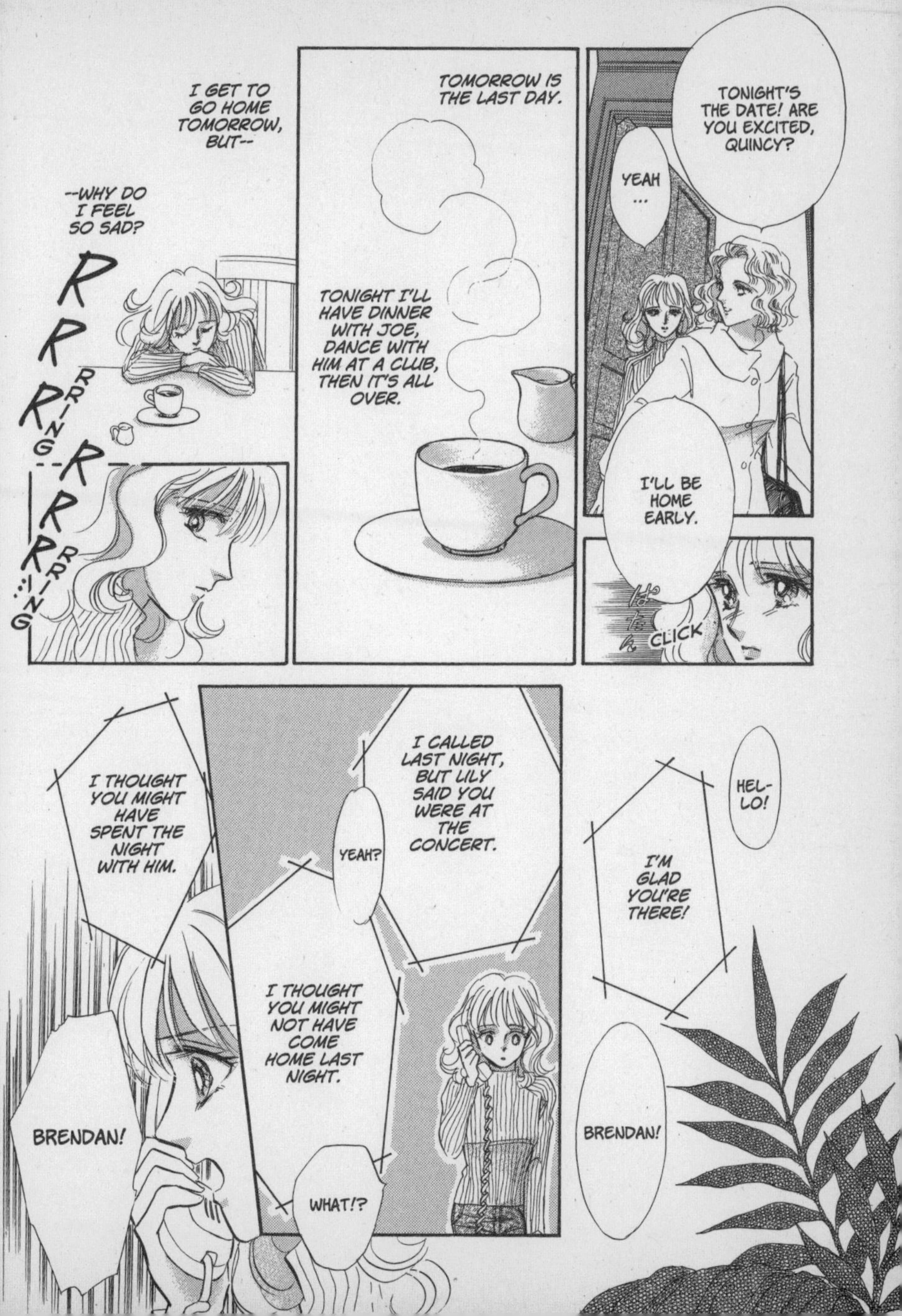
TONIGHT'S THE DATE! ARE YOU EXCITED, QUINCY?
YEAH ...
I'LL BE HOME EARLY.
CLICK
TOMORROW IS THE LAST DAY.
TONIGHT I'LL HAVE DINNER WITH JOE, DANCE WITH HIM AT A CLUB, THEN IT'S ALL OVER.
I GET TO GO HOME TOMORROW, BUT--
--WHY DO I FEEL SO SAD?
RRRRING
RRRRING
HEL-LO!
I'M GLAD YOU'RE THERE!
BRENDAN!
I CALLED LAST NIGHT, BUT LILY SAID YOU WERE AT THE CONCERT.
YEAH?
I THOUGHT YOU MIGHT NOT HAVE COME HOME LAST NIGHT.
WHAT!?
I THOUGHT YOU MIGHT HAVE SPENT THE NIGHT WITH HIM.
BRENDAN!

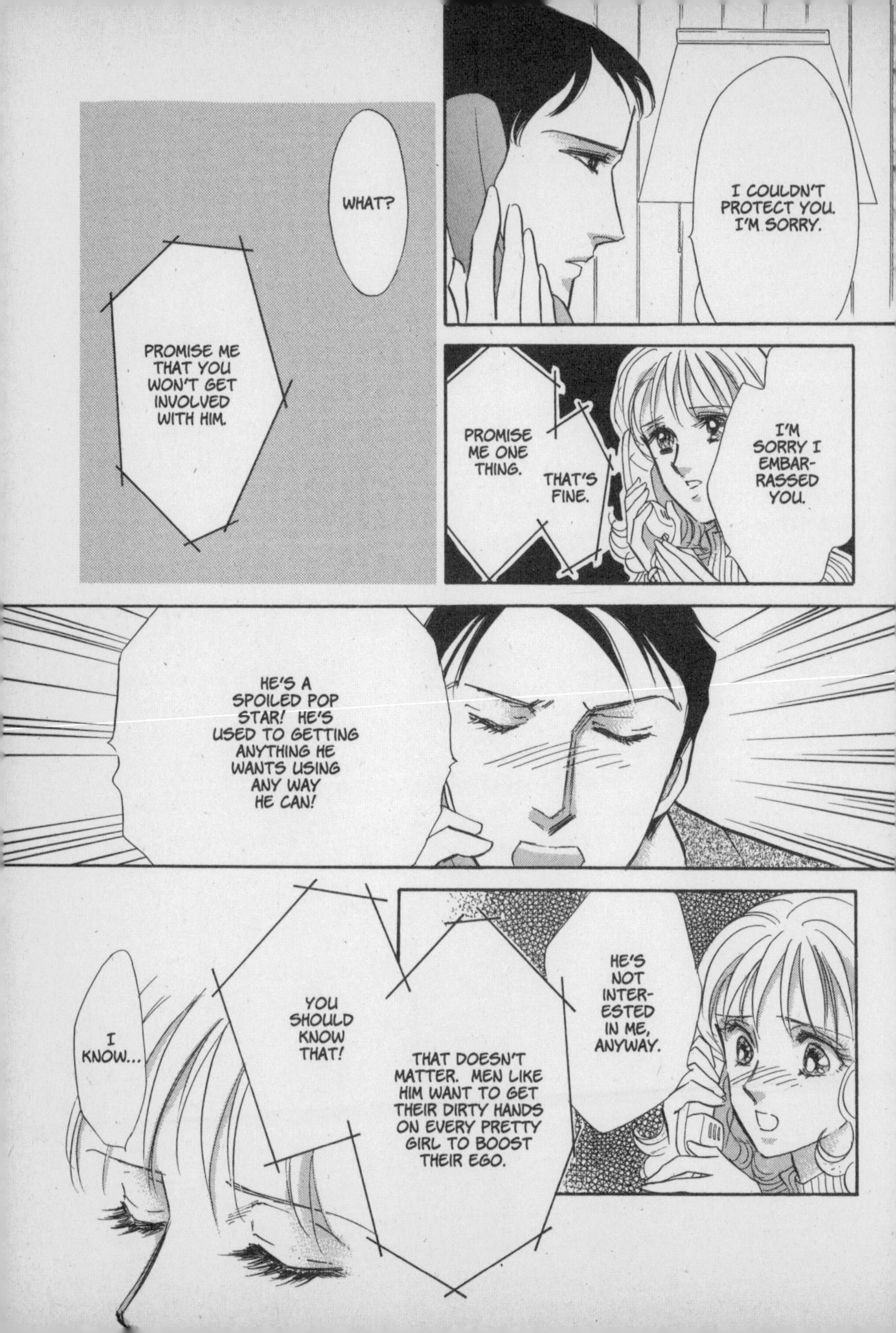
I COULDN'T PROTECT YOU. I'M SORRY.
I'M SORRY I EMBARRASSED YOU.
THAT'S FINE.
PROMISE ME ONE THING.
WHAT?
PROMISE ME THAT YOU WON'T GET INVOLVED WITH HIM.
HE'S A SPOILED POP STAR! HE'S USED TO GETTING ANYTHING HE WANTS USING ANY WAY HE CAN!
HE'S NOT INTERESTED IN ME, ANYWAY.
THAT DOESN'T MATTER. MEN LIKE HIM WANT TO GET THEIR DIRTY HANDS ON EVERY PRETTY GIRL TO BOOST THEIR EGO.
YOU SHOULD KNOW THAT!
I KNOW...

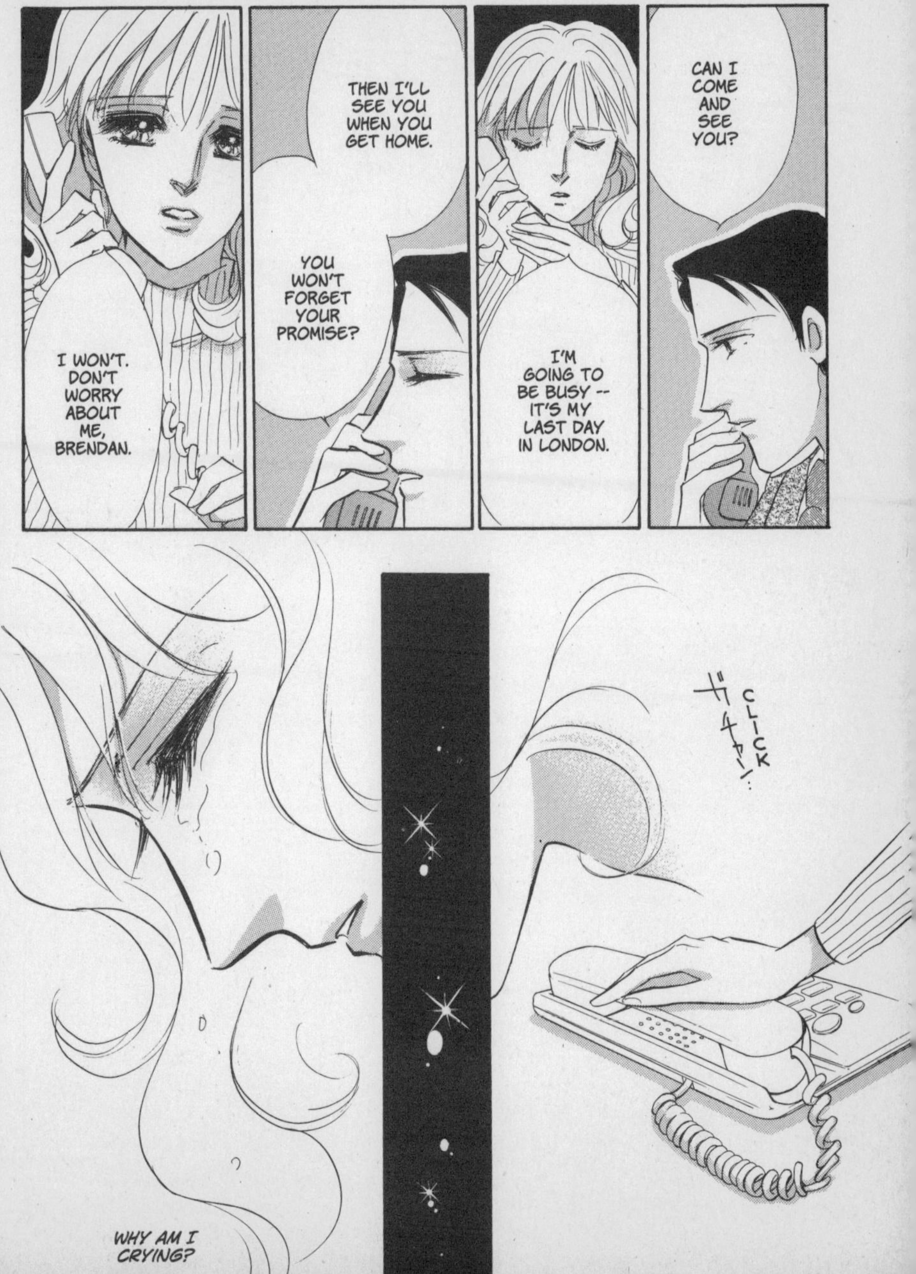
CAN I COME AND SEE YOU?
I'M GOING TO BE BUSY -- IT'S MY LAST DAY IN LONDON.
THEN I'LL SEE YOU WHEN YOU GET HOME.
YOU WON'T FORGET YOUR PROMISE?
I WON'T. DON'T WORRY ABOUT ME, BRENDAN.
CLICK
WHY AM I CRYING?

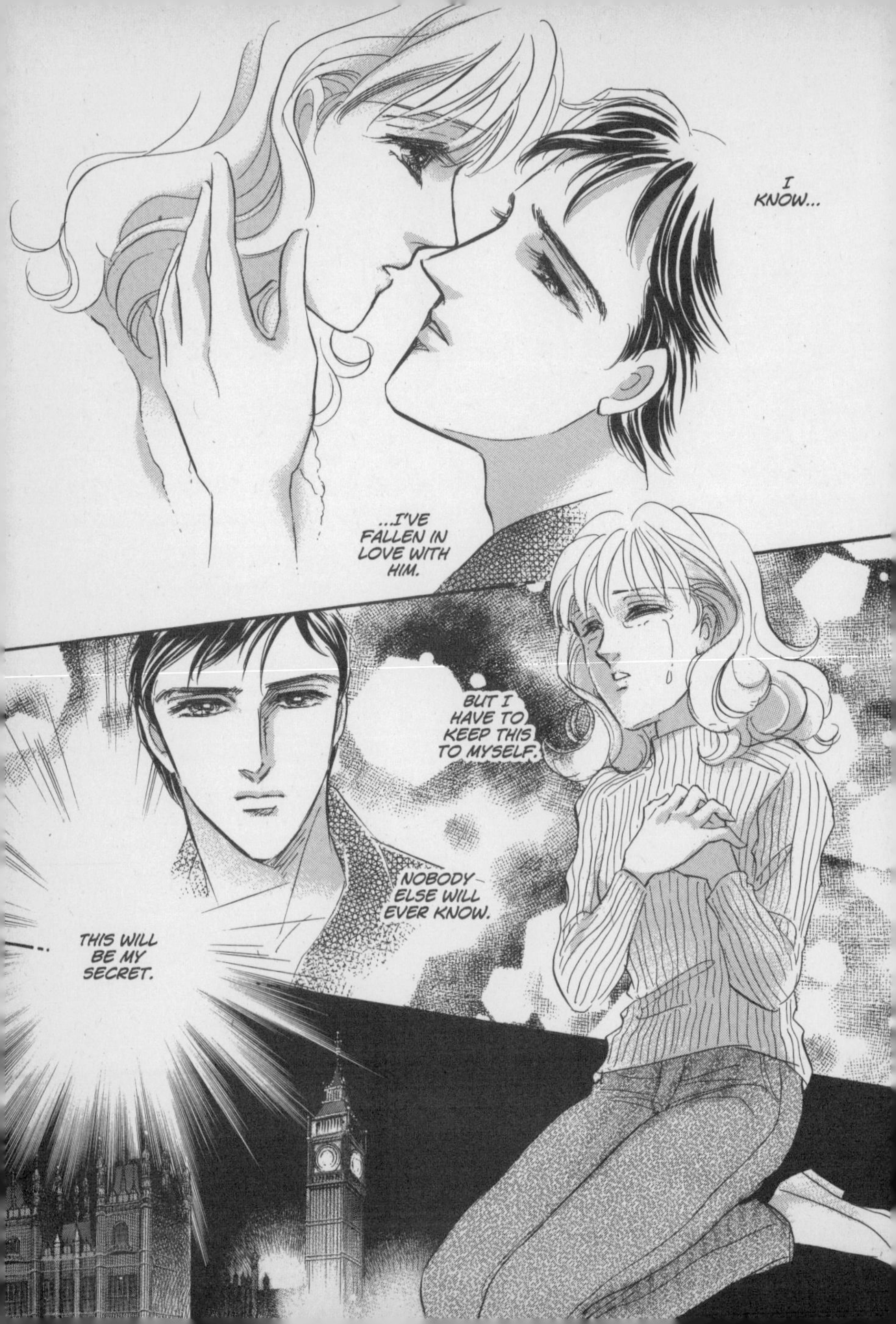
I KNOW...
...I'VE FALLEN IN LOVE WITH HIM.
BUT I HAVE TO KEEP THIS TO MYSELF.
NOBODY ELSE WILL EVER KNOW.
THIS WILL BE MY SECRET.

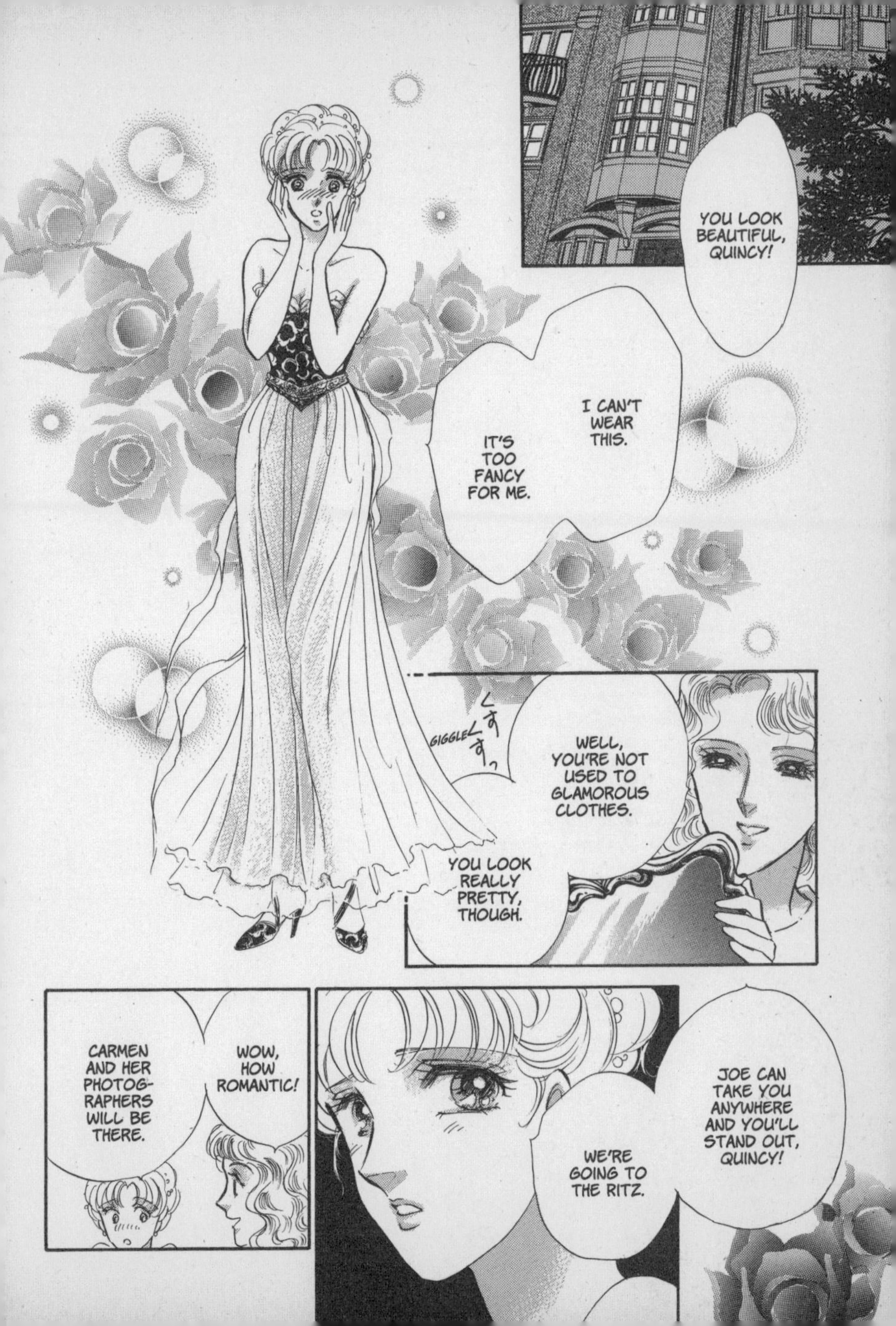
YOU LOOK BEAUTIFUL, QUINCY!
I CAN'T WEAR THIS.
IT'S TOO FANCY FOR ME.
くすくすっ
GIGGLE
WELL, YOU'RE NOT USED TO GLAMOROUS CLOTHES.
YOU LOOK REALLY PRETTY, THOUGH.
JOE CAN TAKE YOU ANYWHERE AND YOU'LL STAND OUT, QUINCY!
WE'RE GOING TO THE RITZ.
WOW, HOW ROMANTIC!
CARMEN AND HER PHOTOGRAPHERS WILL BE THERE.

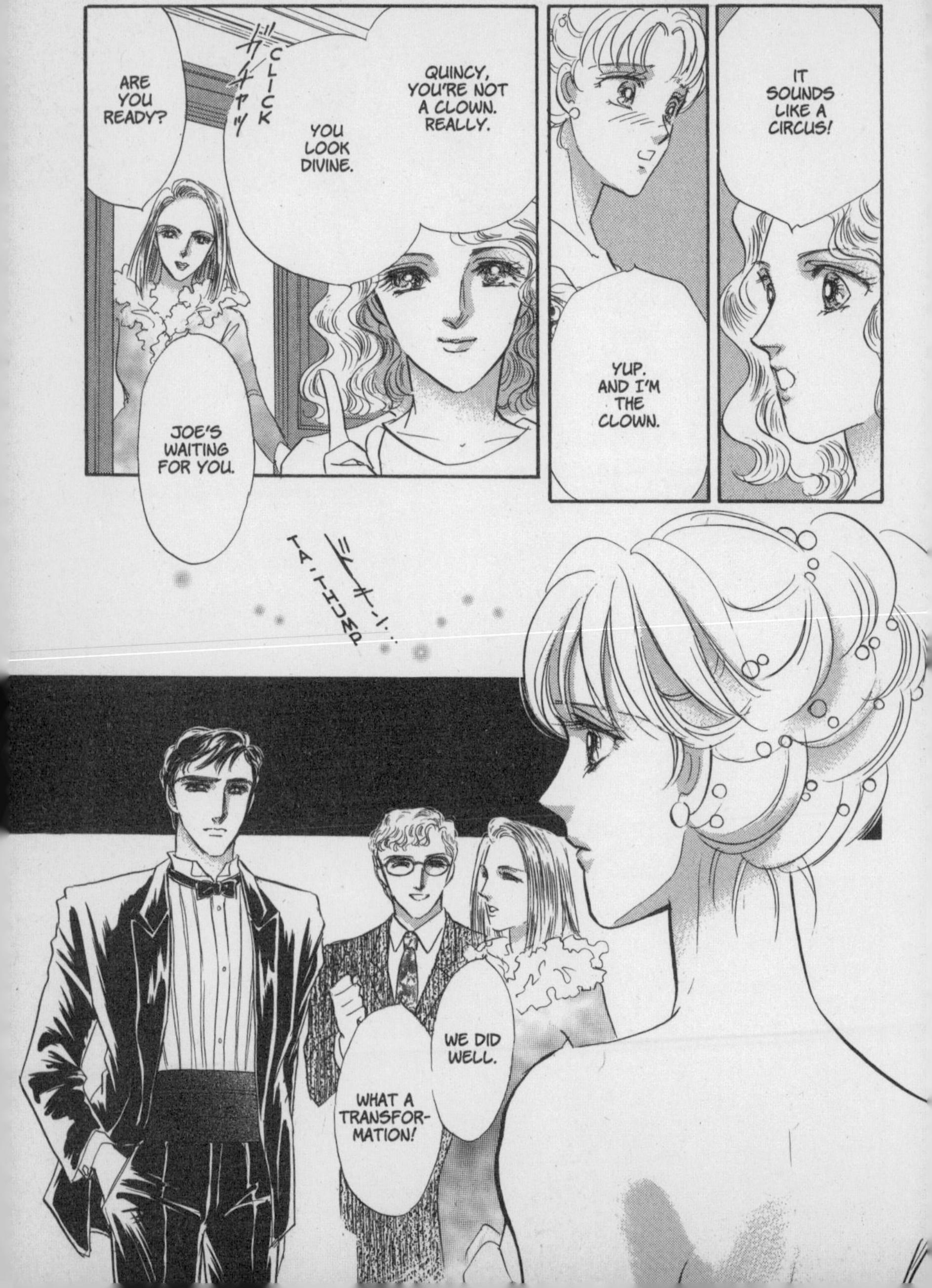
IT SOUNDS LIKE A CIRCUS!
YUP. AND I'M THE CLOWN.
QUINCY, YOU'RE NOT A CLOWN. REALLY.
YOU LOOK DIVINE.
CLICK
ARE YOU READY?
JOE'S WAITING FOR YOU.
TA-THUMP
WE DID WELL.
WHAT A TRANSFORMATION!

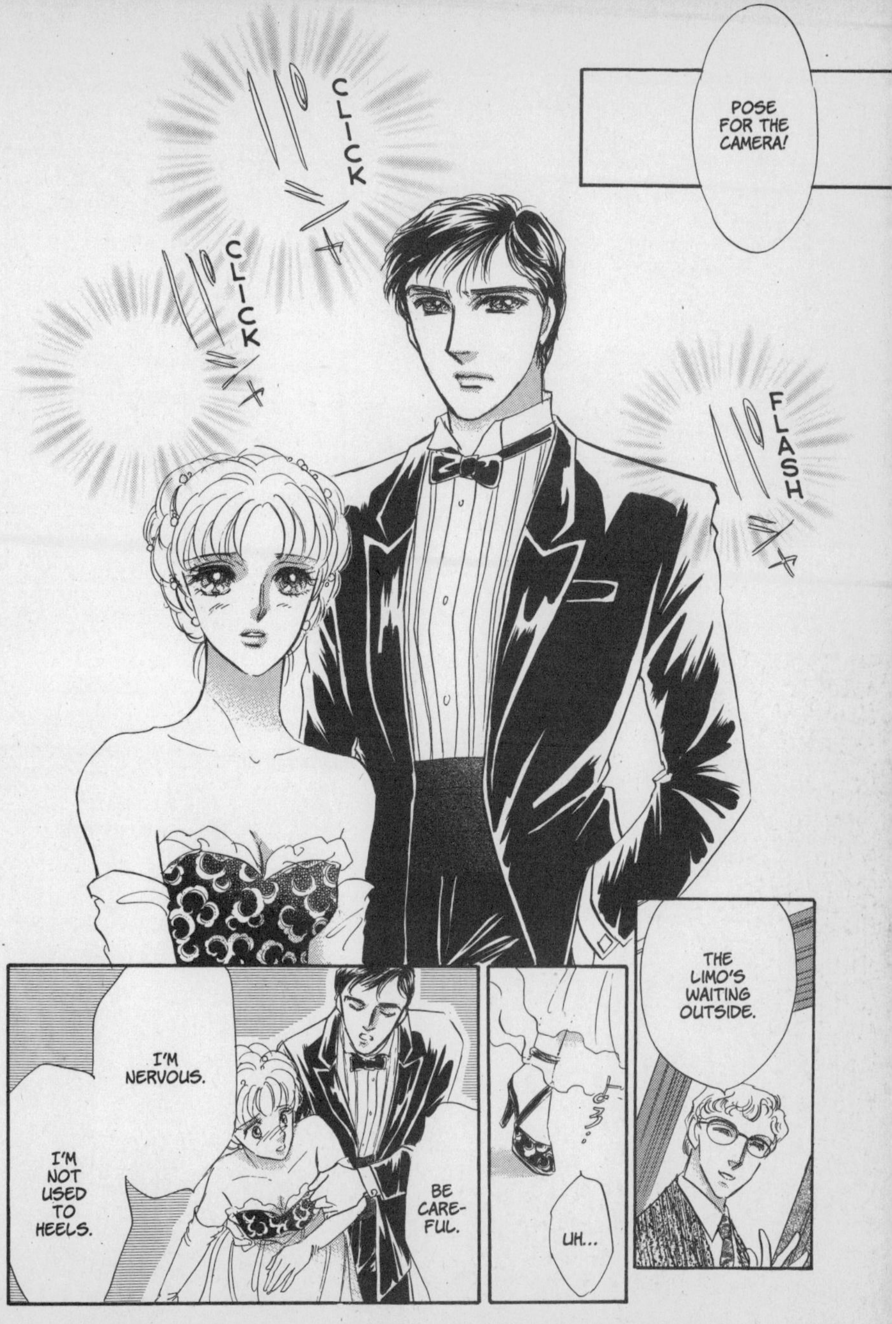
POSE FOR THE CAMERA!
FLASH
CLICK
CLICK
THE LIMO'S WAITING OUTSIDE.
UH...
BE CARE-FUL.
I'M NERVOUS.
I'M NOT USED TO HEELS.

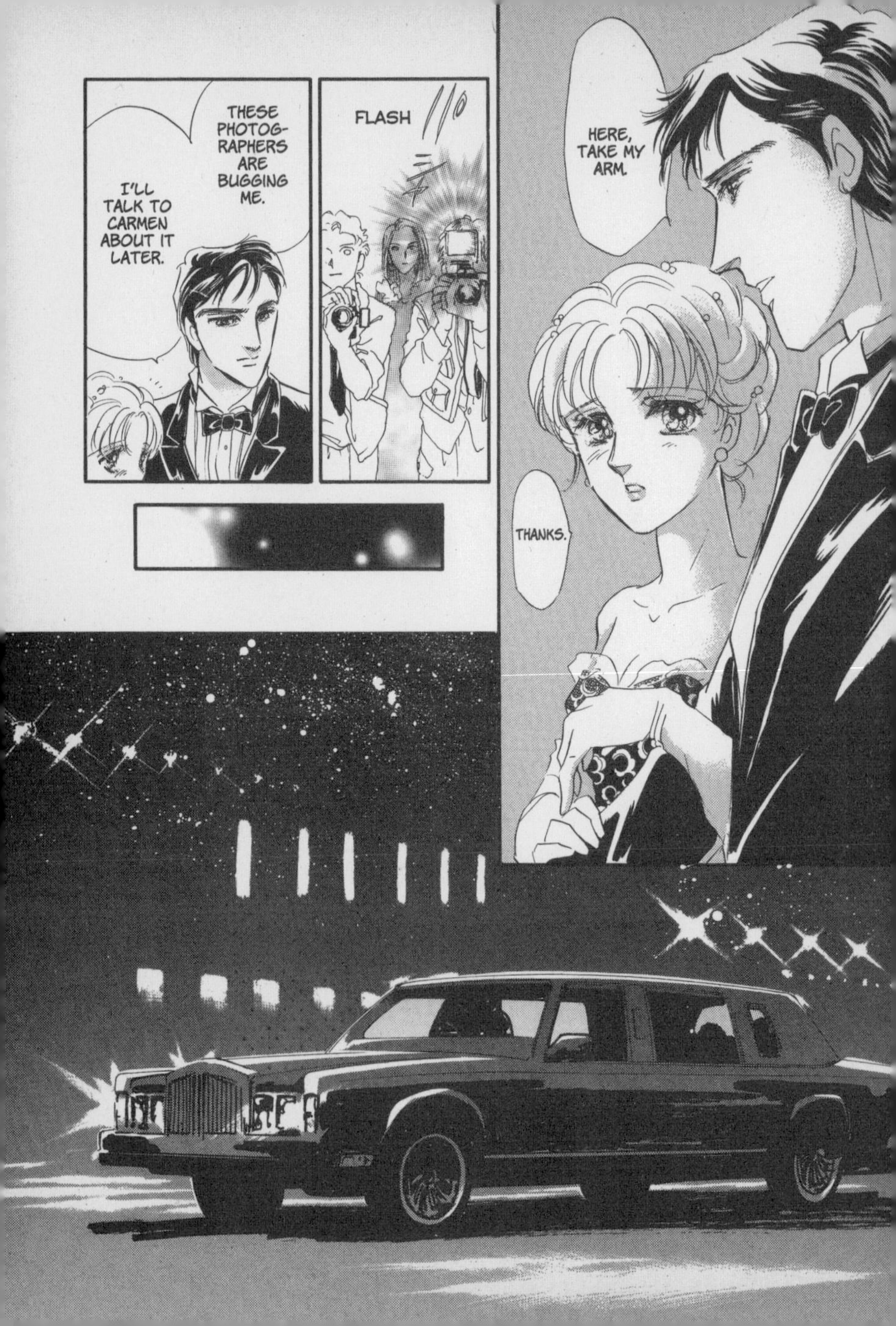
HERE, TAKE MY ARM.
THANKS.
FLASH
THESE PHOTOGRAPHERS ARE BUGGING ME.
I'LL TALK TO CARMEN ABOUT IT LATER.

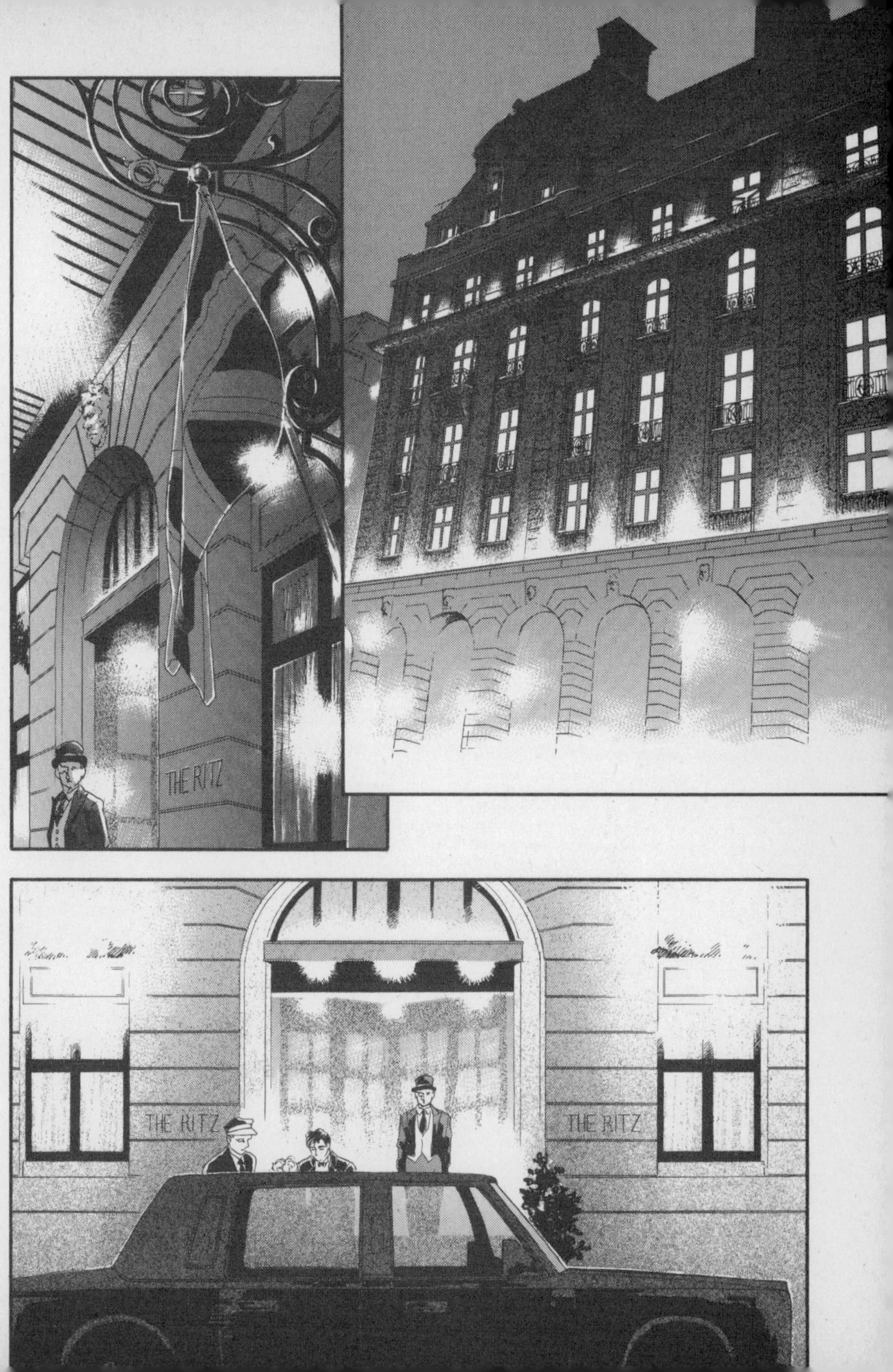
THE RITZ
THE RITZ
THE RITZ

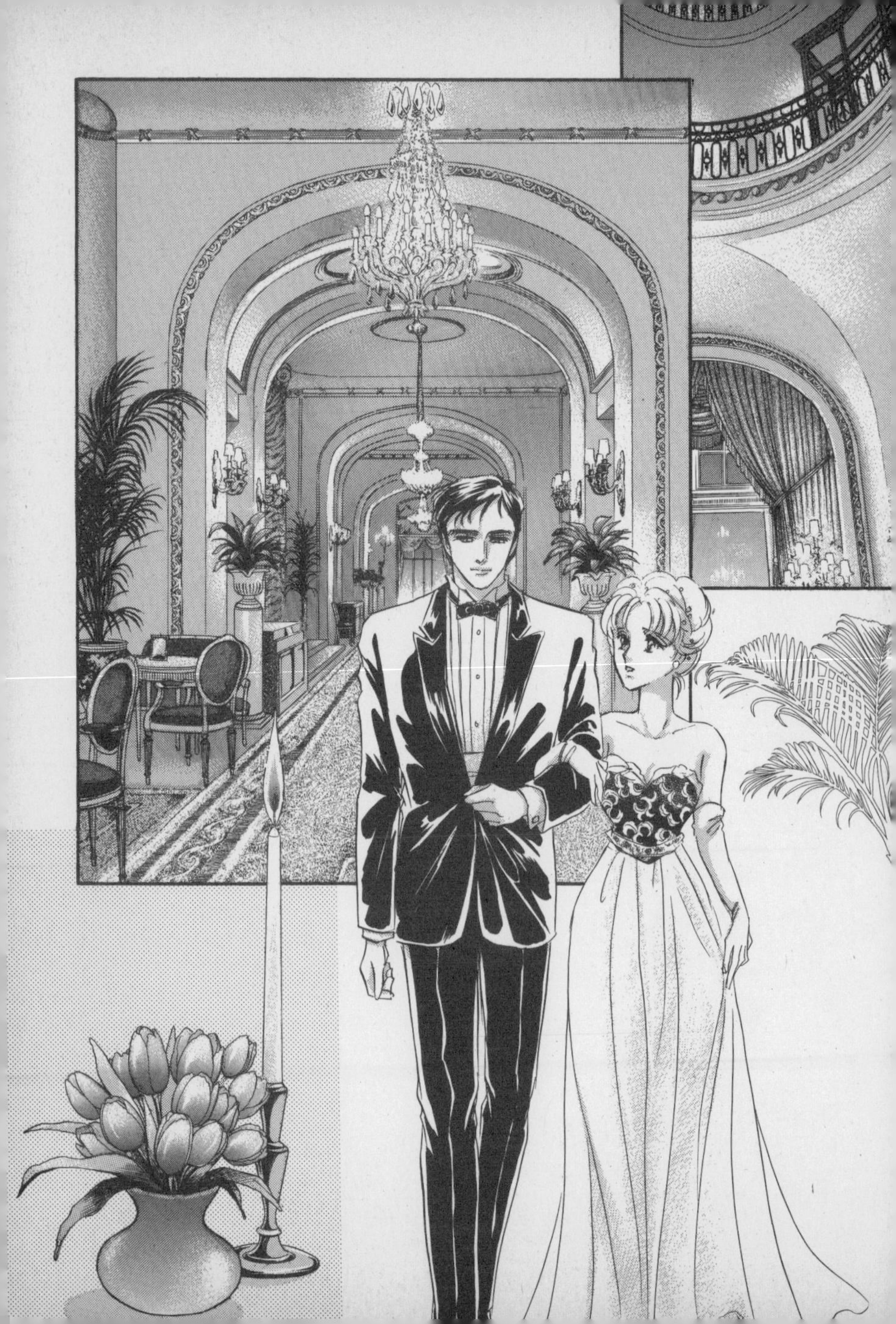

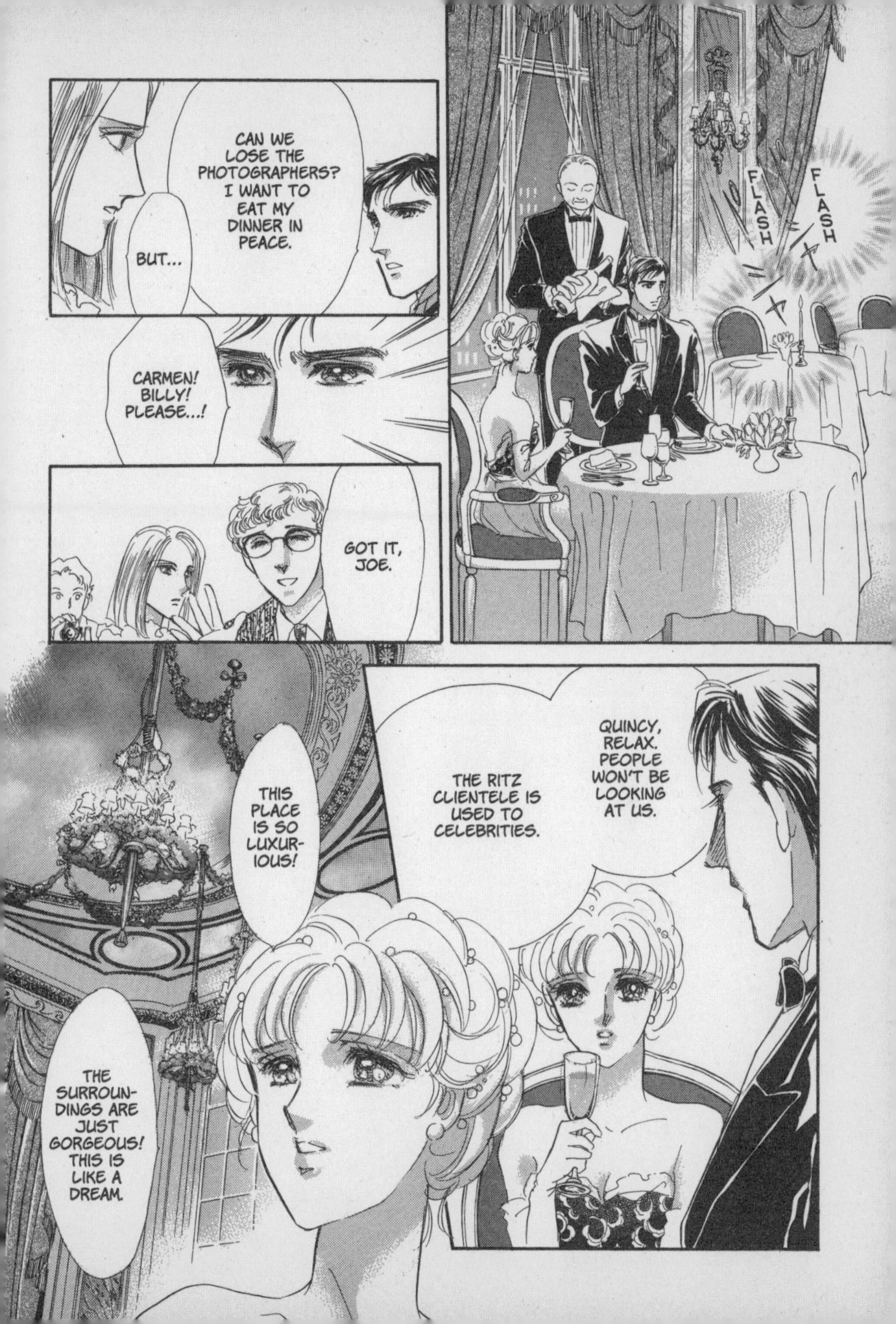
FLASH
FLASH
CAN WE LOSE THE PHOTOGRAPHERS? I WANT TO EAT MY DINNER IN PEACE.
BUT...
CARMEN! BILLY! PLEASE...!
GOT IT, JOE.
QUINCY, RELAX. PEOPLE WON'T BE LOOKING AT US.
THE RITZ CLIENTELE IS USED TO CELEBRITIES.
THIS PLACE IS SO LUXUR-IOUS!
THE SURROUN-DINGS ARE JUST GORGEOUS! THIS IS LIKE A DREAM.

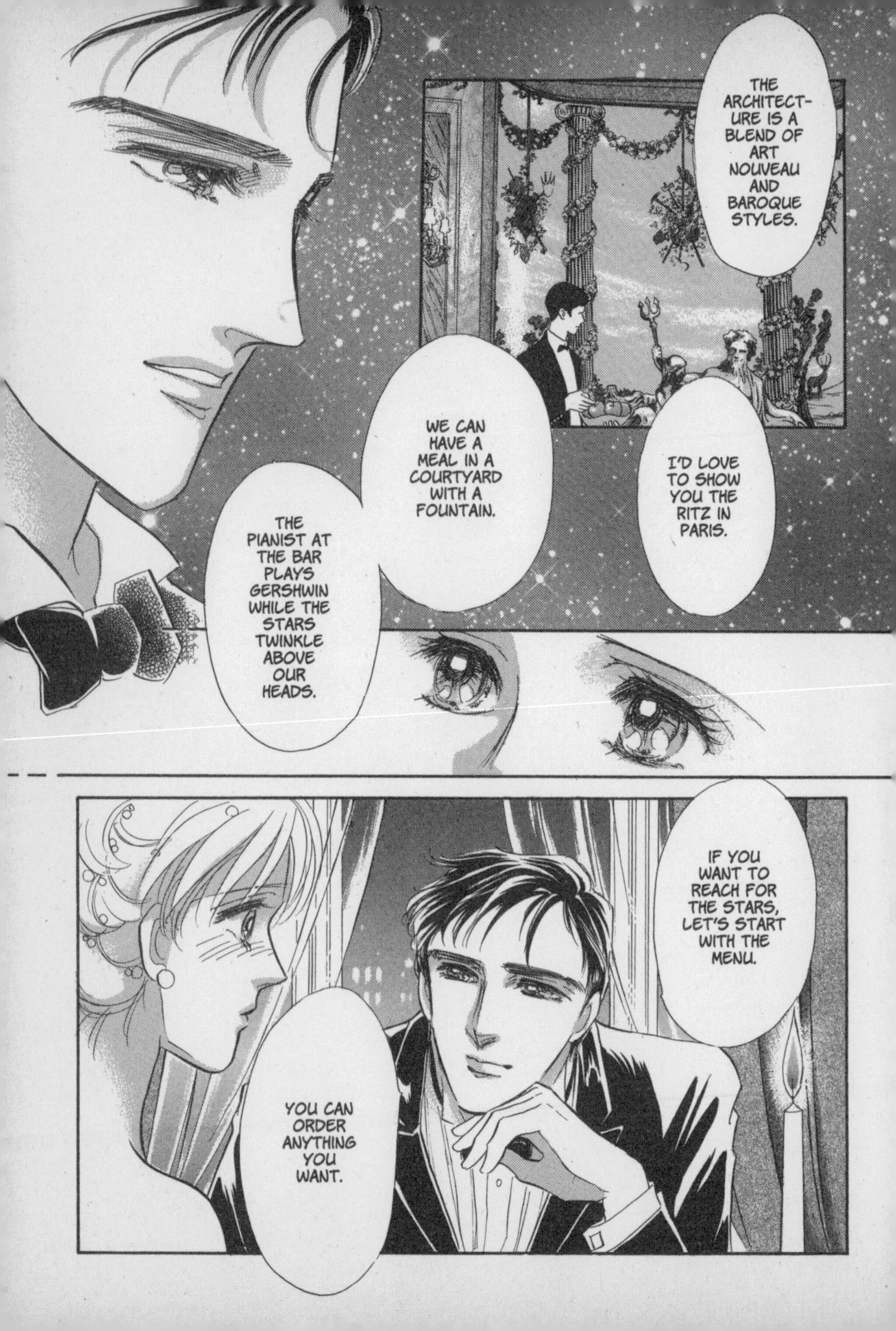
I'D LOVE TO SHOW YOU THE RITZ IN PARIS.
THE ARCHITECT-URE IS A BLEND OF ART NOUVEAU AND BAROQUE STYLES.
WE CAN HAVE A MEAL IN A COURTYARD WITH A FOUNTAIN.
THE PIANIST AT THE BAR PLAYS GERSHWIN WHILE THE STARS TWINKLE ABOVE OUR HEADS.
IF YOU WANT TO REACH FOR THE STARS, LET'S START WITH THE MENU.
YOU CAN ORDER ANYTHING YOU WANT.

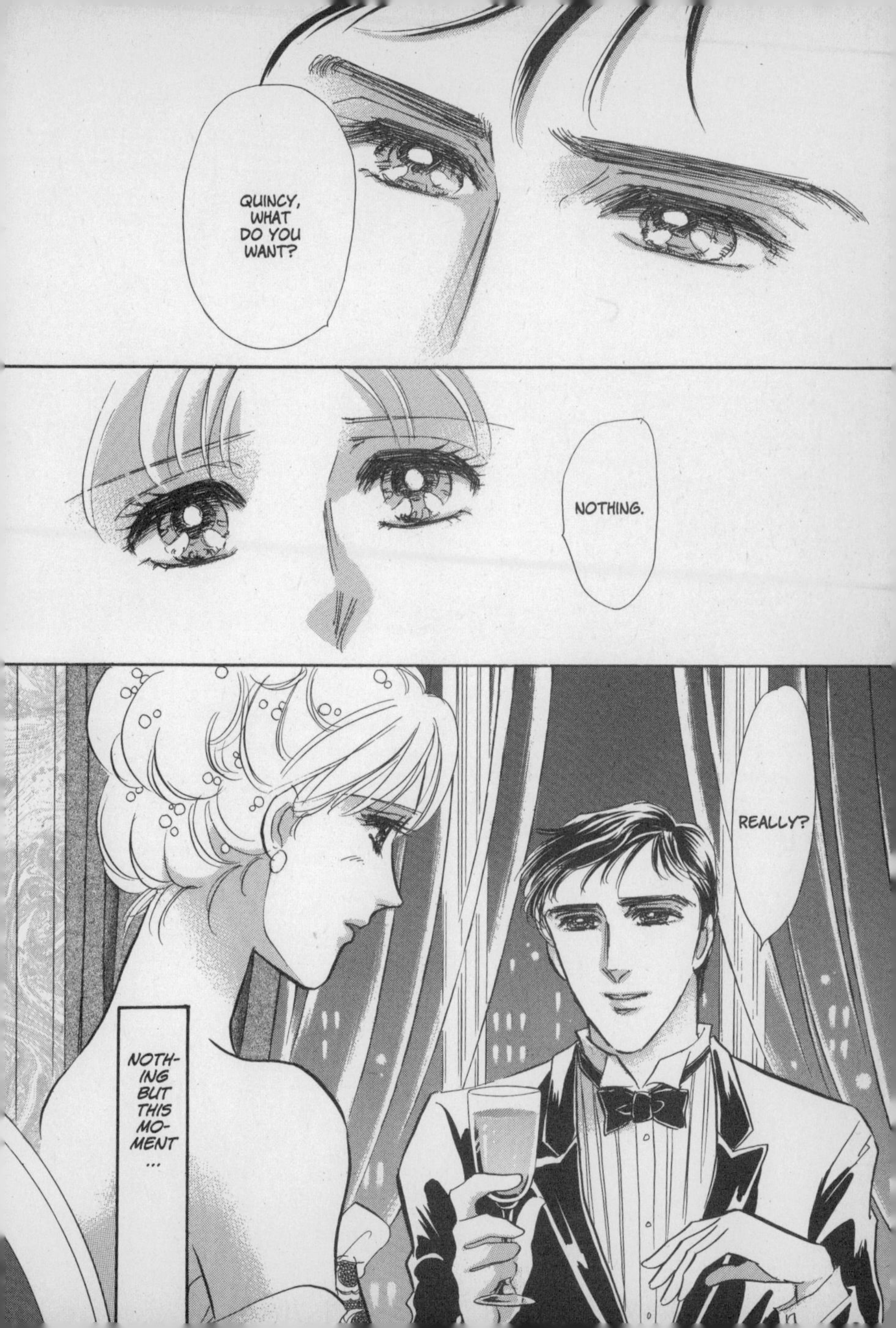
QUINCY, WHAT DO YOU WANT?
NOTHING.
REALLY?
NOTHING BUT THIS MOMENT...

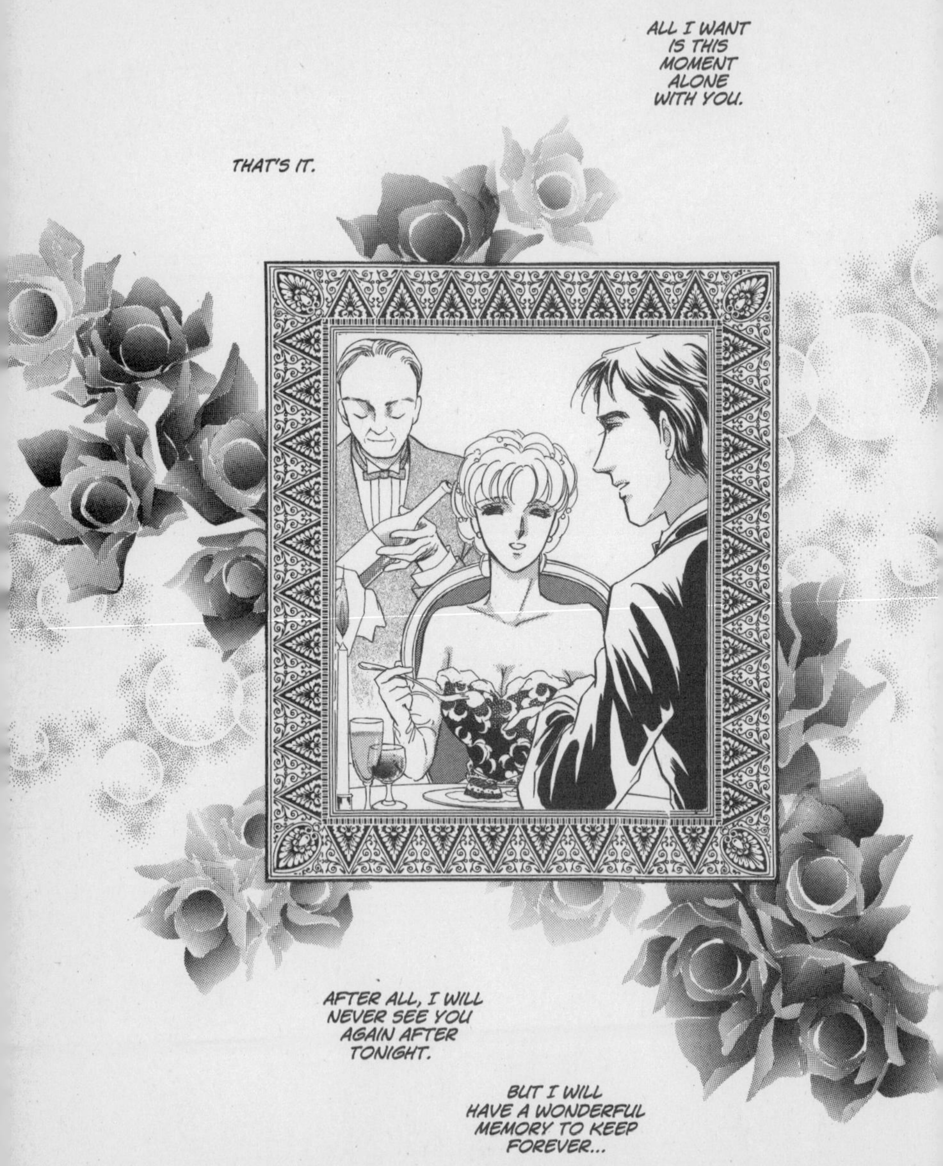
ALL I WANT IS THIS MOMENT ALONE WITH YOU.
THAT'S IT.
AFTER ALL, I WILL NEVER SEE YOU AGAIN AFTER TONIGHT.
BUT I WILL HAVE A WONDERFUL MEMORY TO KEEP FOREVER...

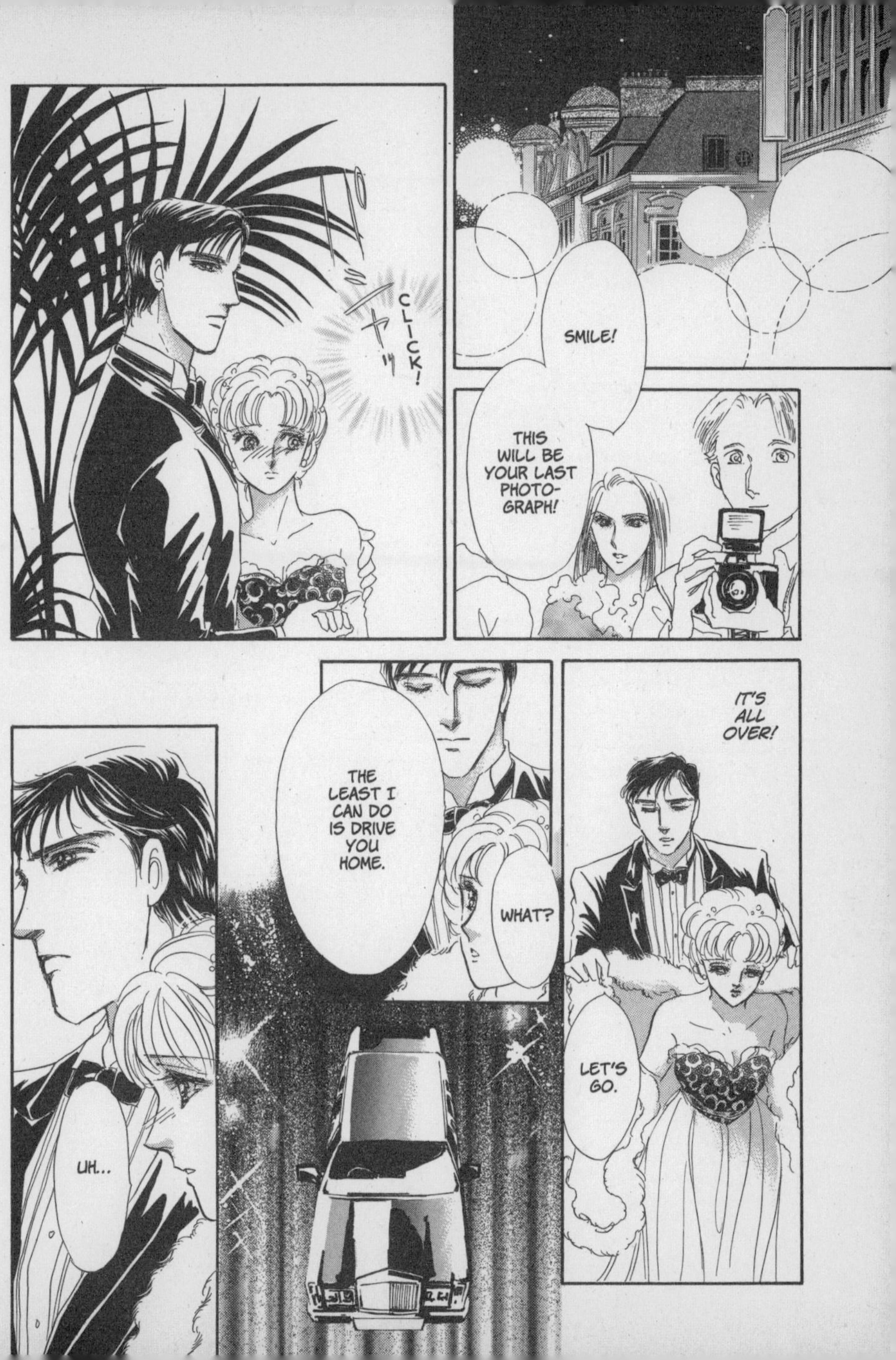
SMILE!
THIS WILL BE YOUR LAST PHOTOGRAPH!
CLICK!
IT'S ALL OVER!
LET'S GO.
THE LEAST I CAN DO IS DRIVE YOU HOME.
WHAT?
UH...

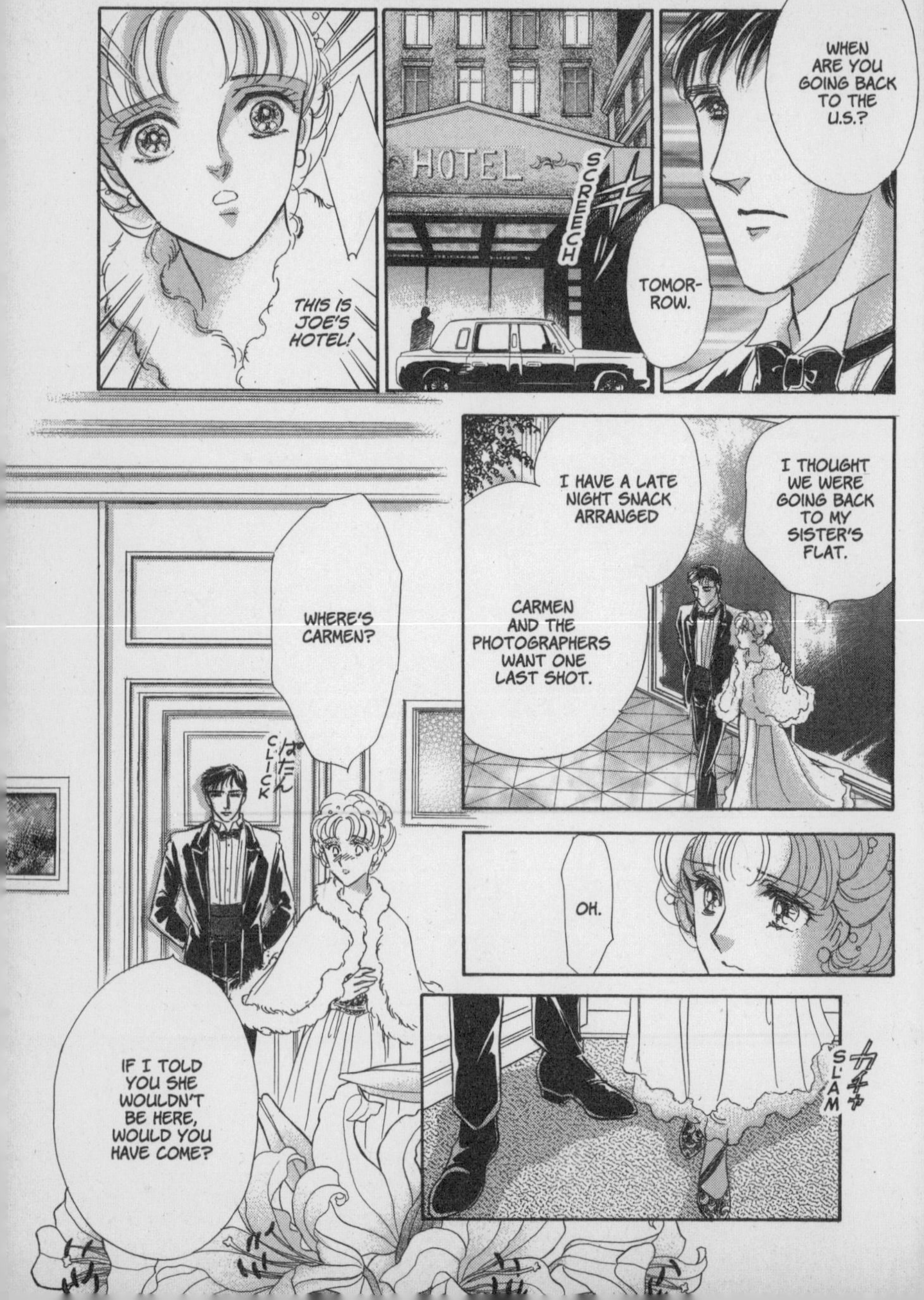
WHEN ARE YOU GOING BACK TO THE U.S.?
TOMOR-ROW.
SCREECH
HOTEL
THIS IS JOE'S HOTEL!
I THOUGHT WE WERE GOING BACK TO MY SISTER'S FLAT.
I HAVE A LATE NIGHT SNACK ARRANGED
CARMEN AND THE PHOTOGRAPHERS WANT ONE LAST SHOT.
OH.
SLAM
WHERE'S CARMEN?
CLICK
IF I TOLD YOU SHE WOULDN'T BE HERE, WOULD YOU HAVE COME?

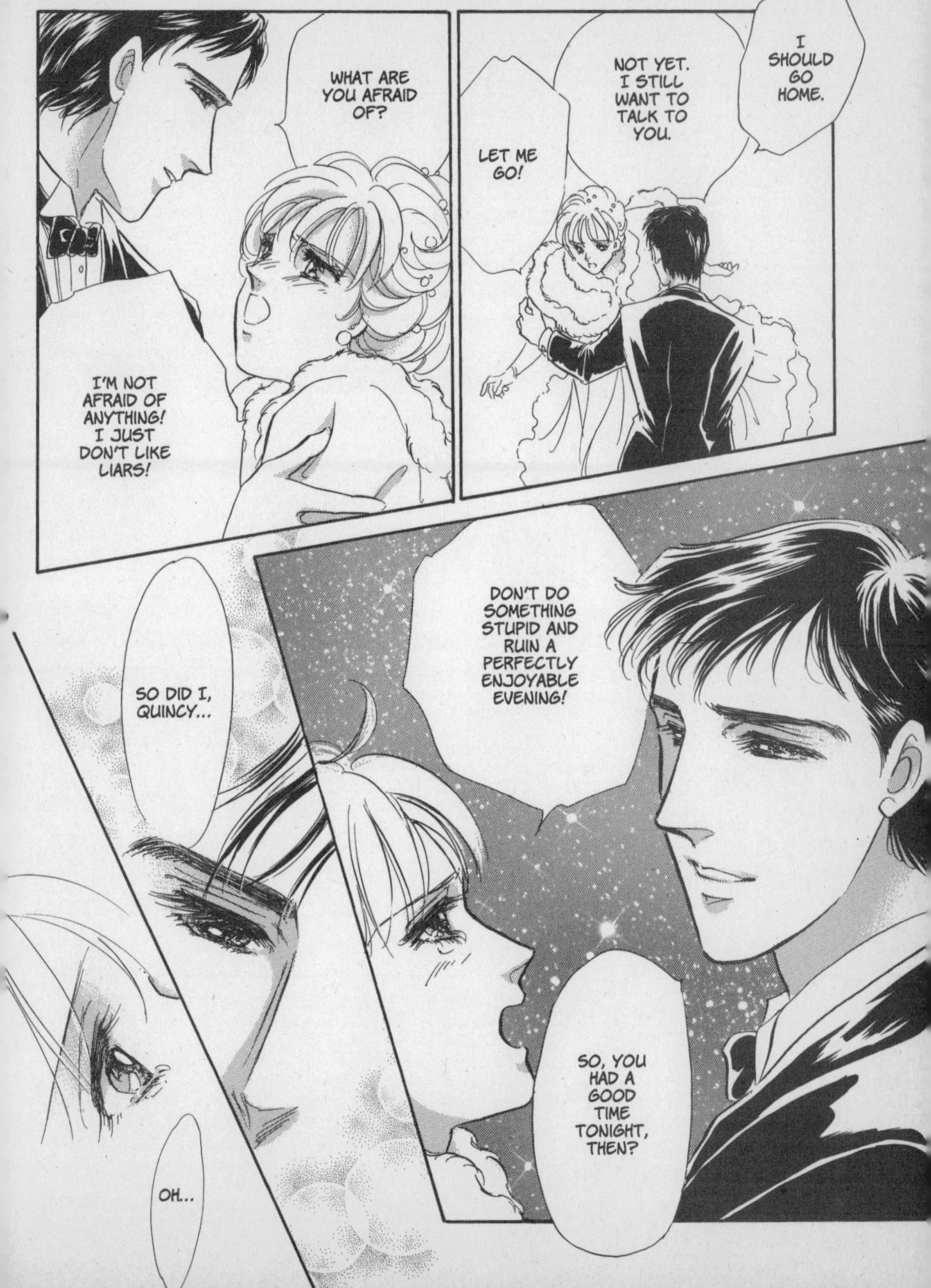
I SHOULD GO HOME.
NOT YET. I STILL WANT TO TALK TO YOU.
LET ME GO!
WHAT ARE YOU AFRAID OF?
I'M NOT AFRAID OF ANYTHING! I JUST DON'T LIKE LIARS!
DON'T DO SOMETHING STUPID AND RUIN A PERFECTLY ENJOYABLE EVENING!
SO, YOU HAD A GOOD TIME TONIGHT, THEN?
SO DID I, QUINCY...
OH...

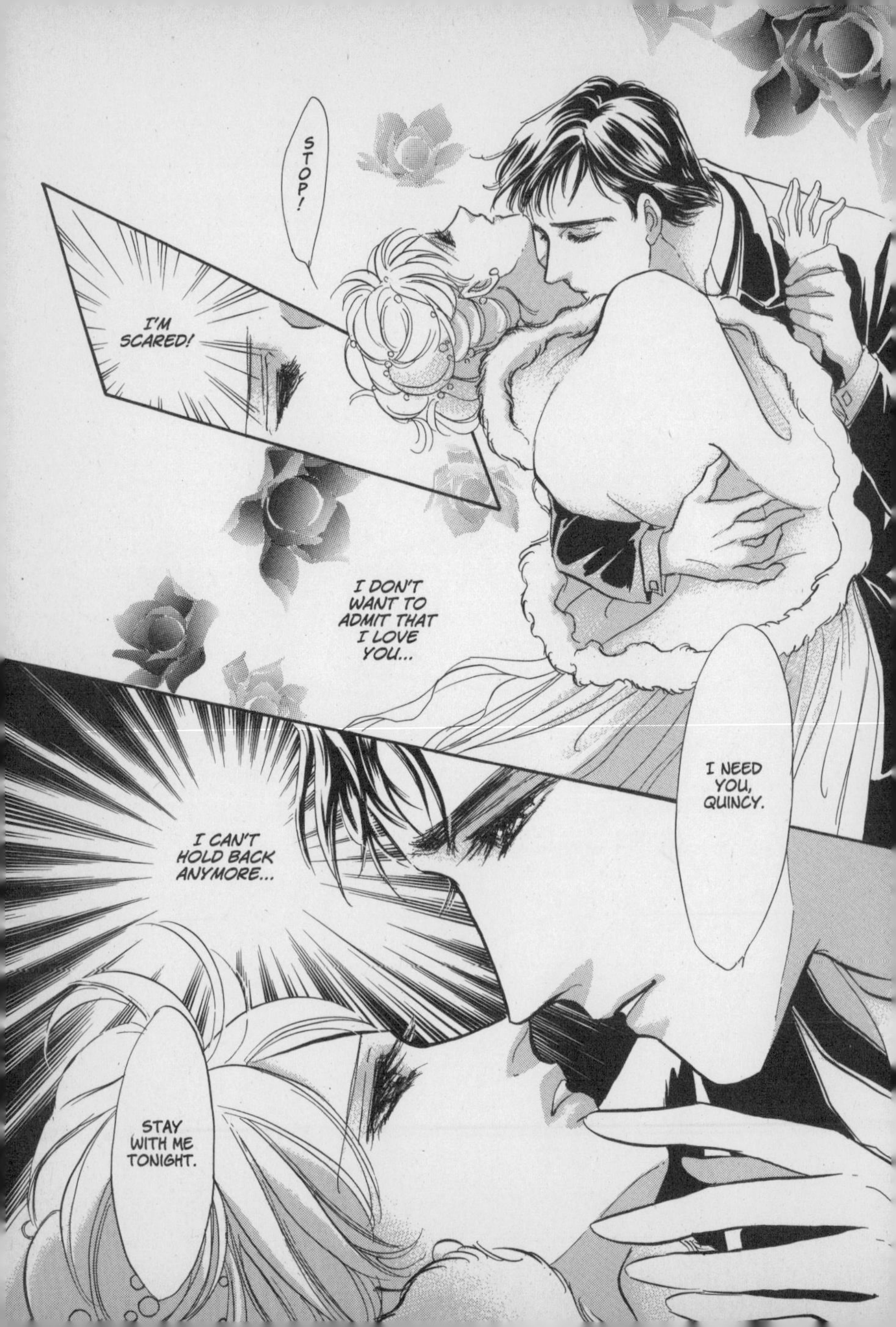
STOP!
I'M SCARED!
I DON'T WANT TO ADMIT THAT I LOVE YOU...
I NEED YOU, QUINCY.
I CAN'T HOLD BACK ANYMORE...
STAY WITH ME TONIGHT.

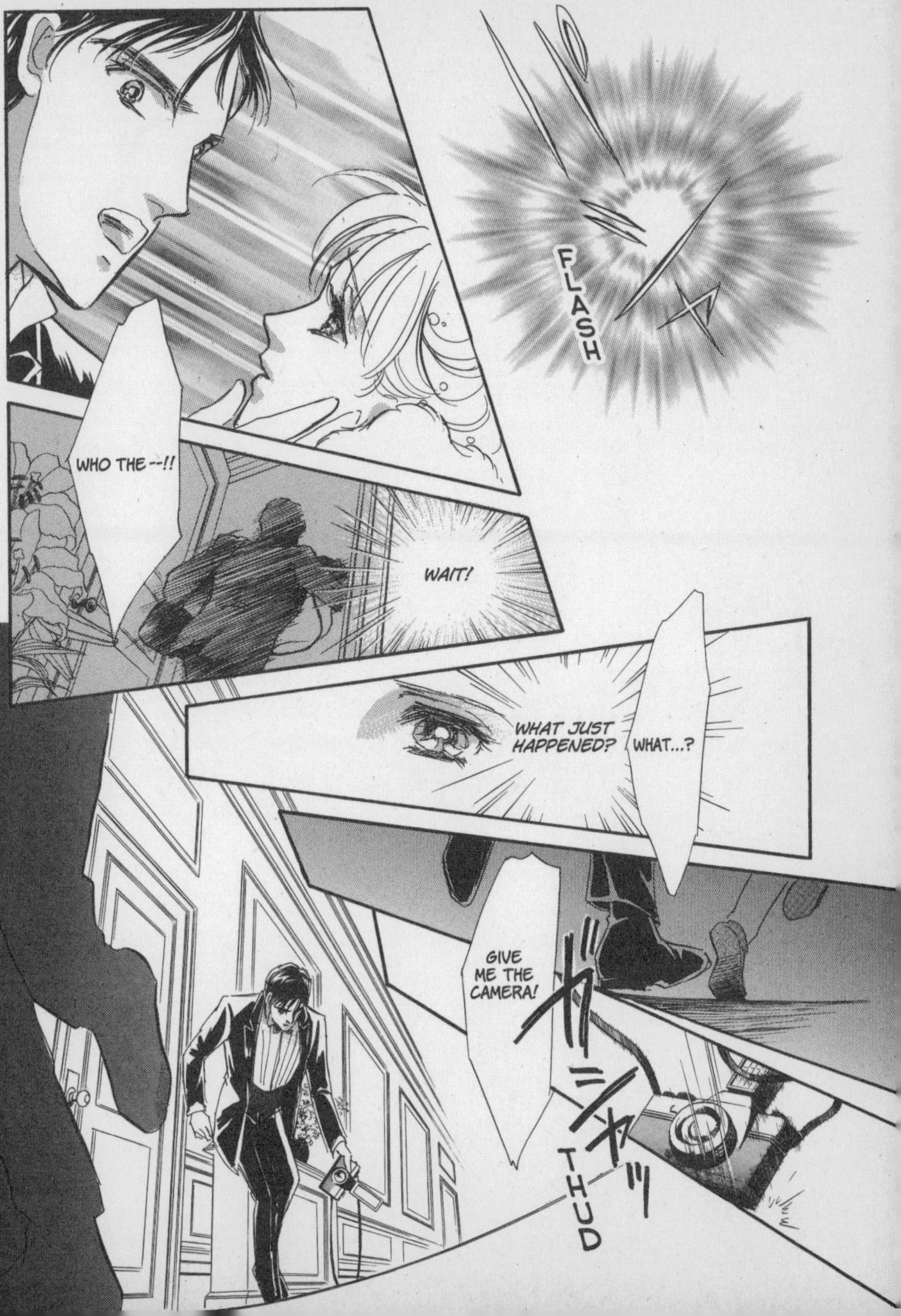
FLASH
WHO THE--!!
WAIT!
WHAT...?
WHAT JUST HAPPENED?
THUD
GIVE ME THE CAMERA!

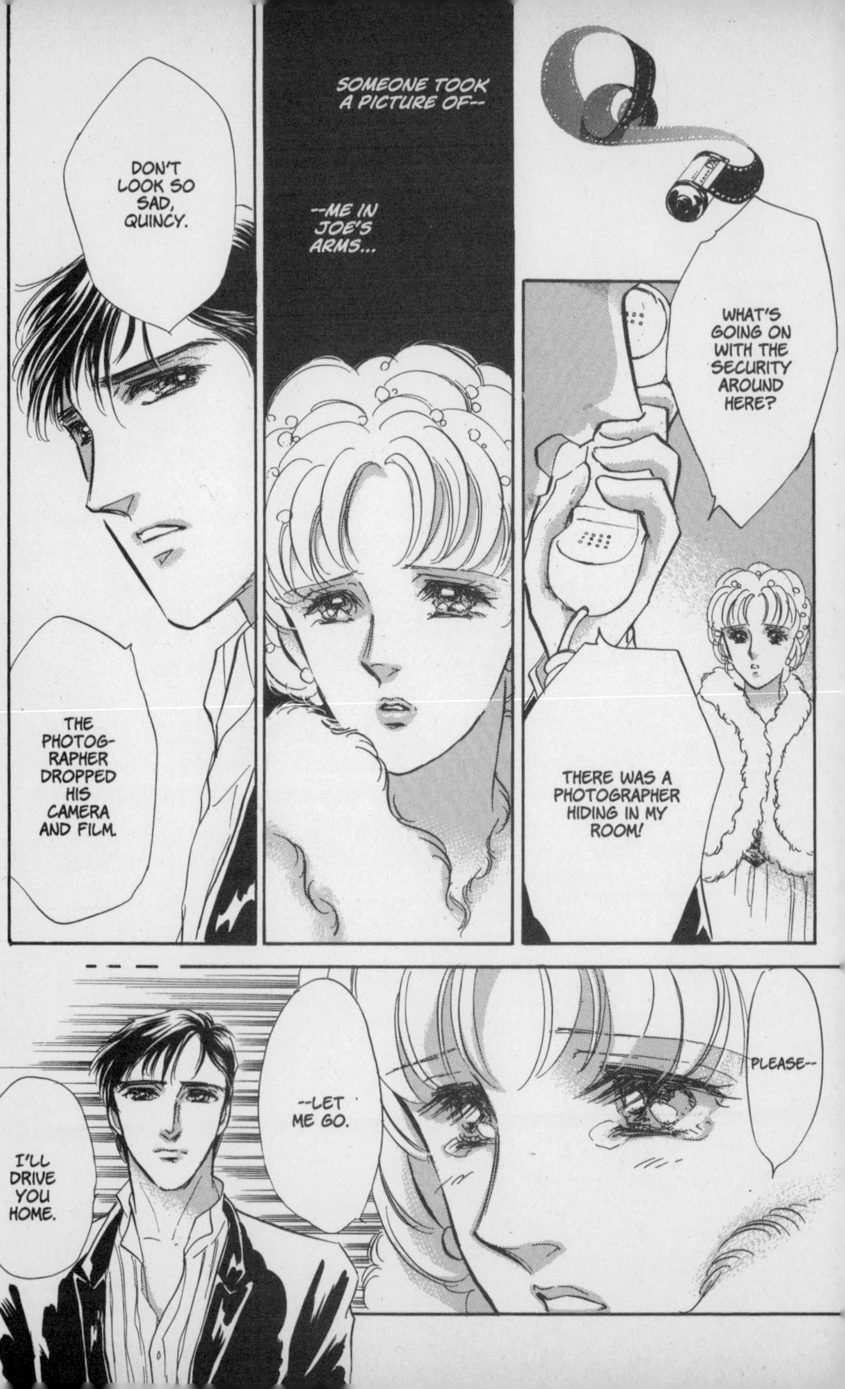
WHAT'S GOING ON WITH THE SECURITY AROUND HERE?
THERE WAS A PHOTOGRAPHER HIDING IN MY ROOM!
SOMEONE TOOK A PICTURE OF--
--ME IN JOE'S ARMS...
DON'T LOOK SO SAD, QUINCY.
THE PHOTOG-RAPHER DROPPED HIS CAMERA AND FILM.
PLEASE--
--LET ME GO.
I'LL DRIVE YOU HOME.

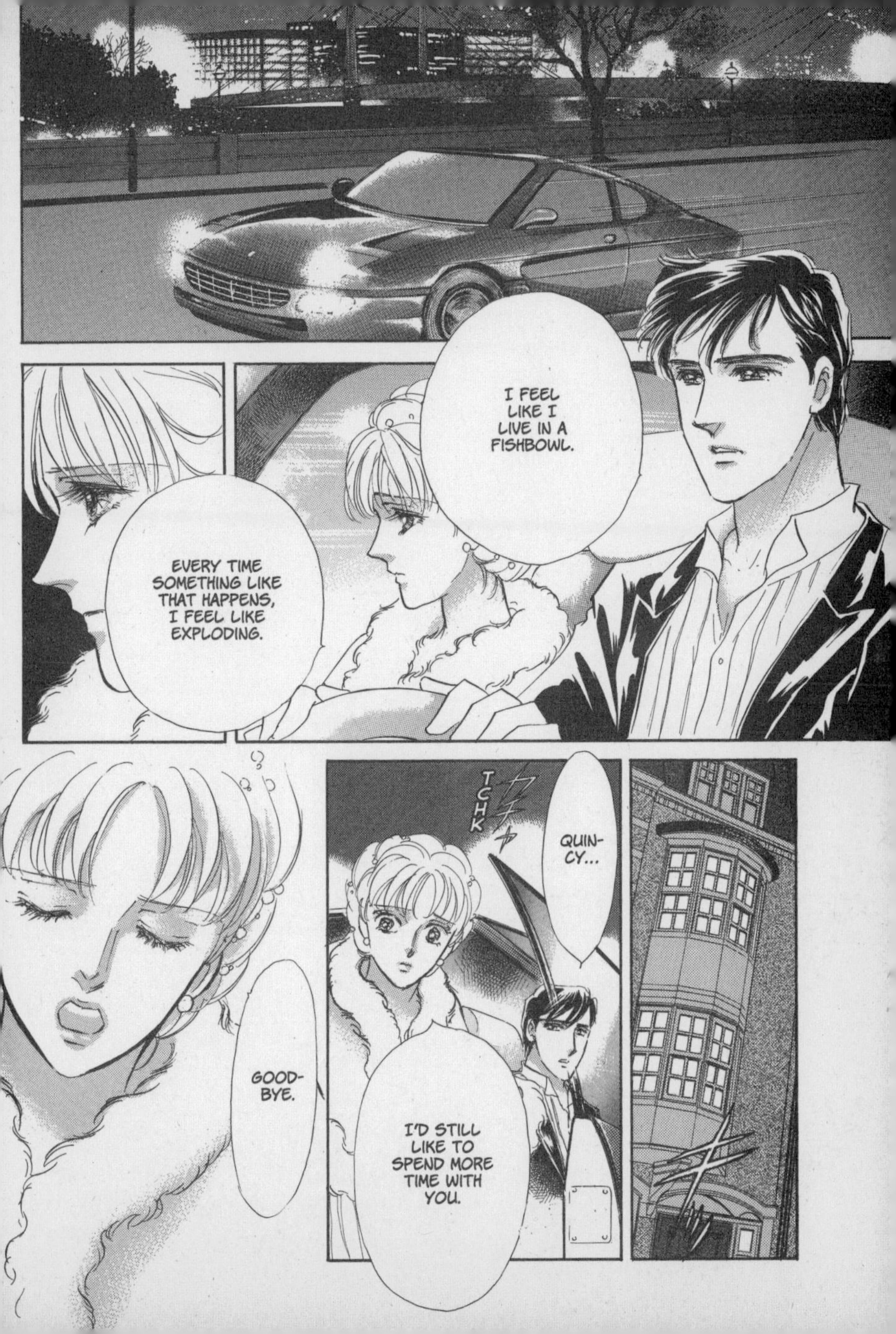
I FEEL LIKE I LIVE IN A FISHBOWL.
EVERY TIME SOMETHING LIKE THAT HAPPENS, I FEEL LIKE EXPLODING.
QUIN-CY...
TCHK
I'D STILL LIKE TO SPEND MORE TIME WITH YOU.
GOOD-BYE.

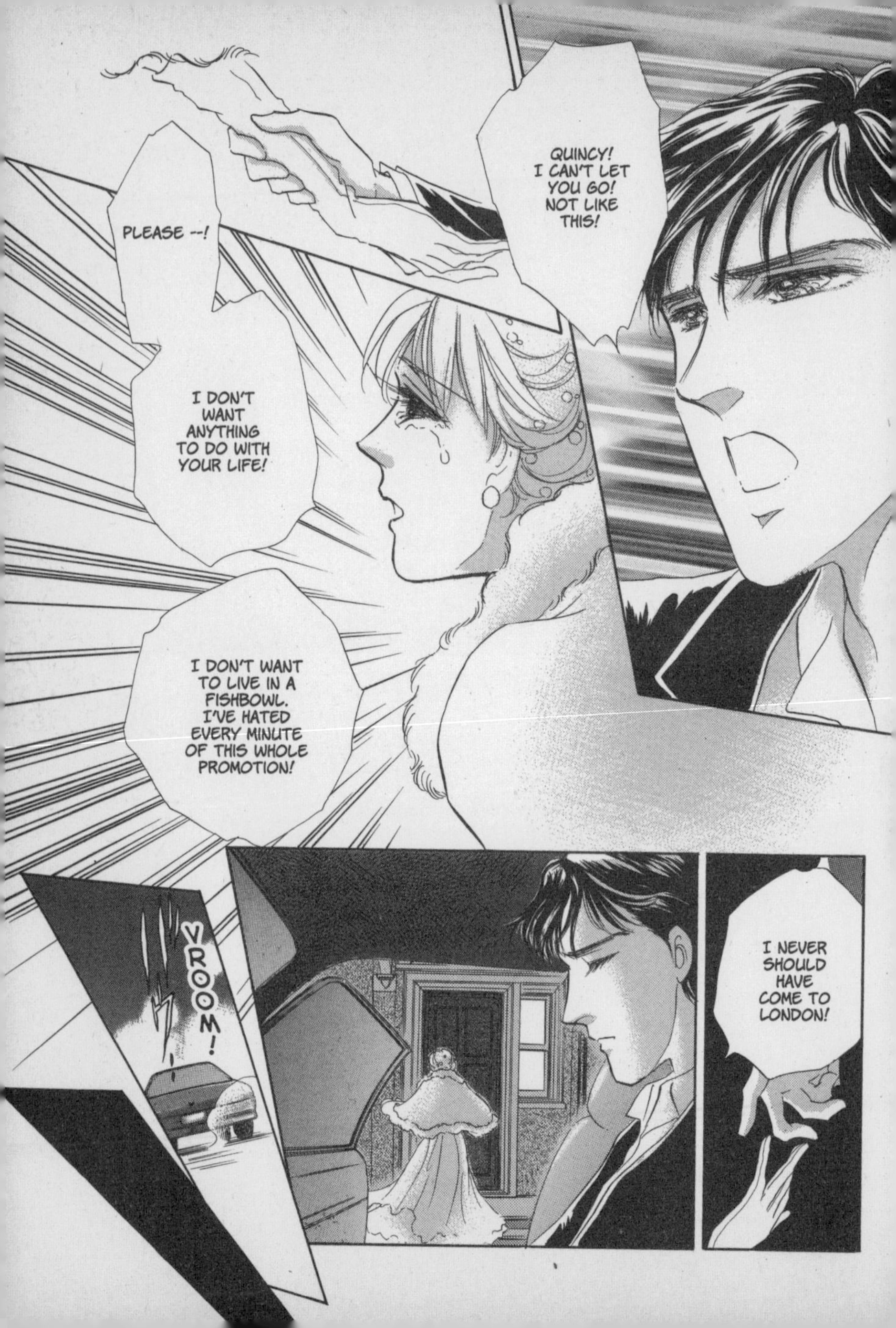
QUINCY! I CAN'T LET YOU GO! NOT LIKE THIS!
PLEASE --!
I DON'T WANT ANYTHING TO DO WITH YOUR LIFE!
I DON'T WANT TO LIVE IN A FISHBOWL. I'VE HATED EVERY MINUTE OF THIS WHOLE PROMOTION!
I NEVER SHOULD HAVE COME TO LONDON!
VROOM!

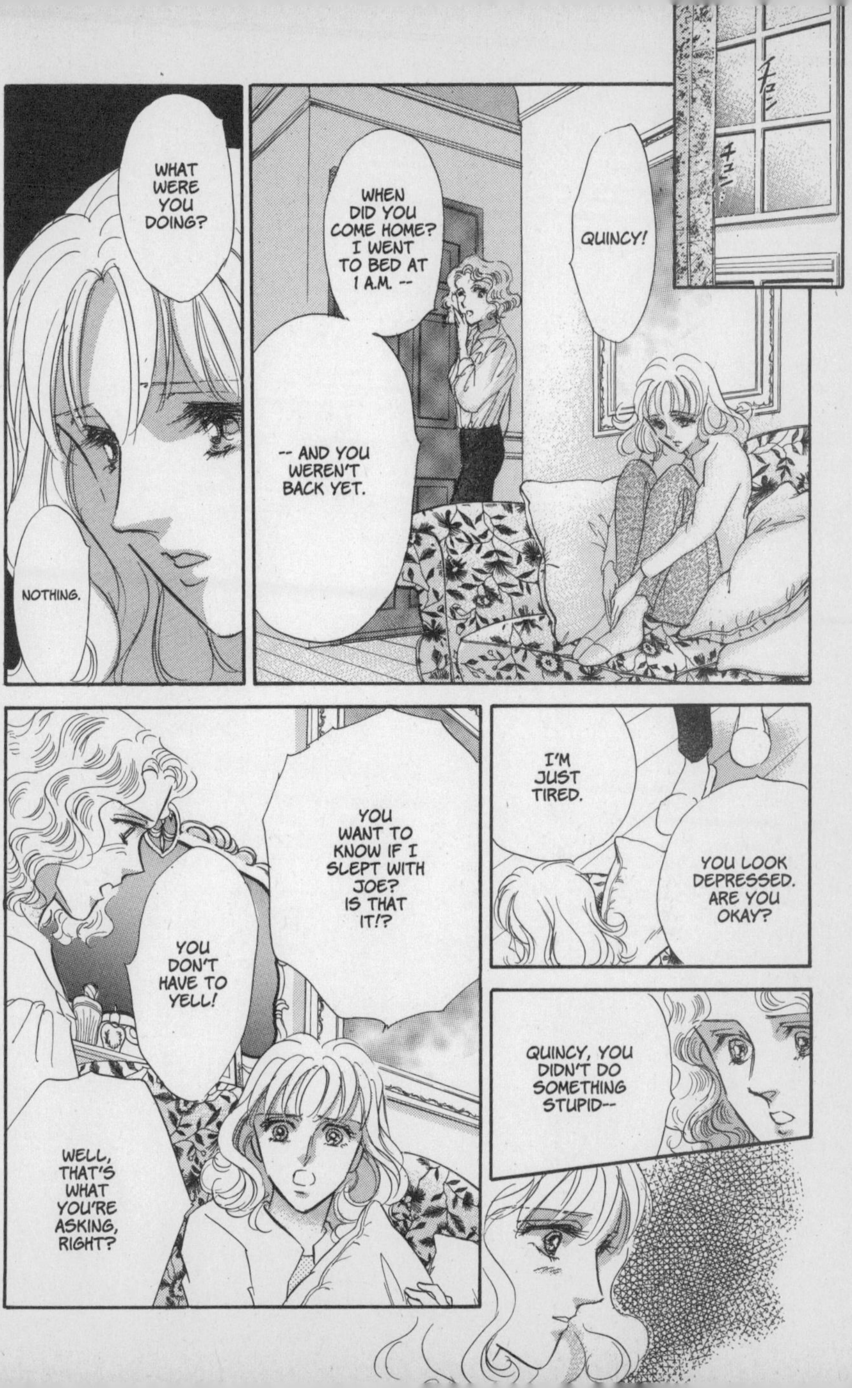
QUINCY!
WHEN DID YOU COME HOME? I WENT TO BED AT 1 A.M. --
-- AND YOU WEREN'T BACK YET.
WHAT WERE YOU DOING?
NOTHING.
YOU LOOK DEPRESSED. ARE YOU OKAY?
I'M JUST TIRED.
QUINCY, YOU DIDN'T DO SOMETHING STUPID--
YOU WANT TO KNOW IF I SLEPT WITH JOE? IS THAT IT!?
YOU DON'T HAVE TO YELL!
WELL, THAT'S WHAT YOU'RE ASKING, RIGHT?

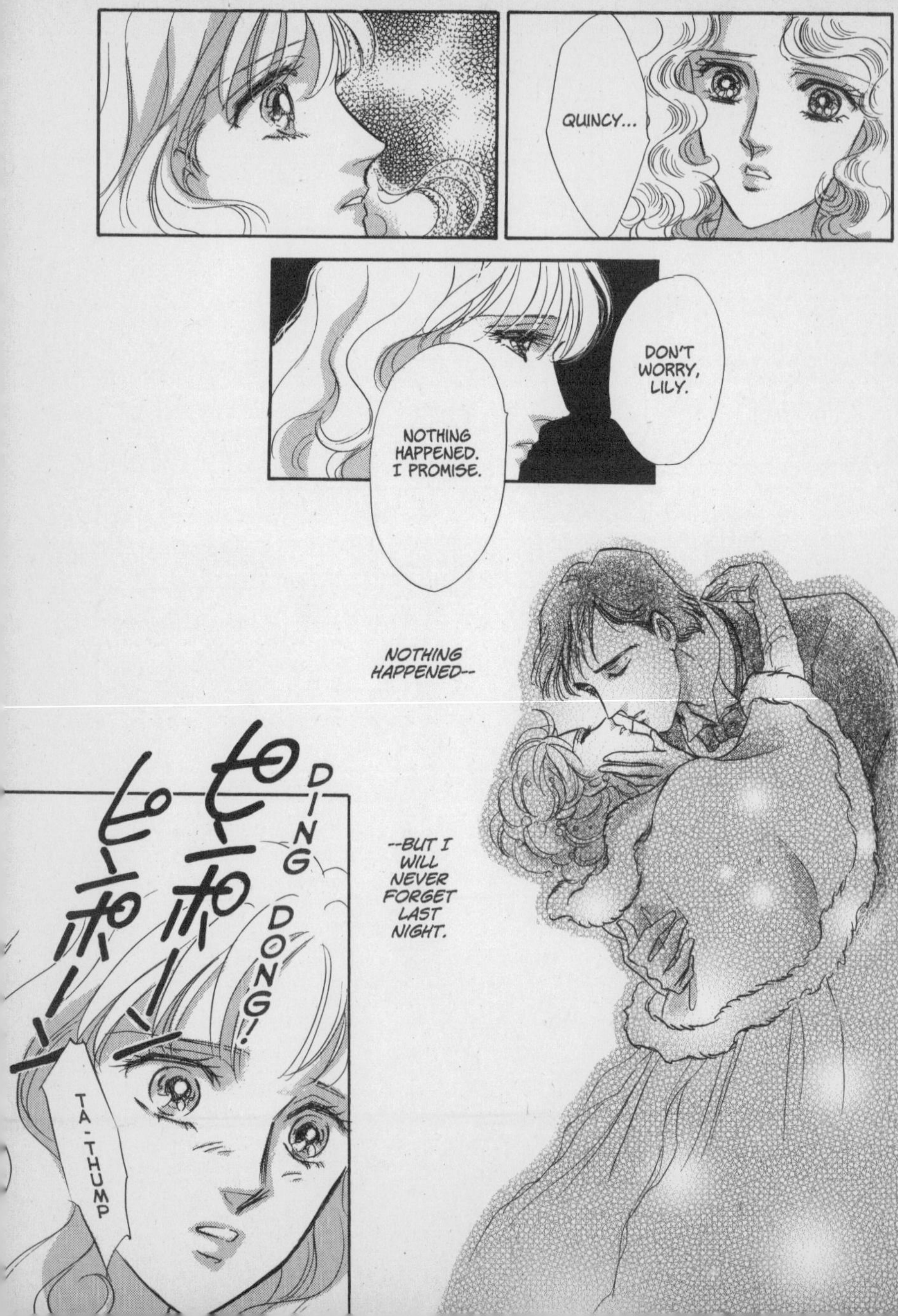
QUINCY...
DON'T WORRY, LILY.
NOTHING HAPPENED. I PROMISE.
NOTHING HAPPENED--
--BUT I WILL NEVER FORGET LAST NIGHT.
DING DONG!
TA-THUMP

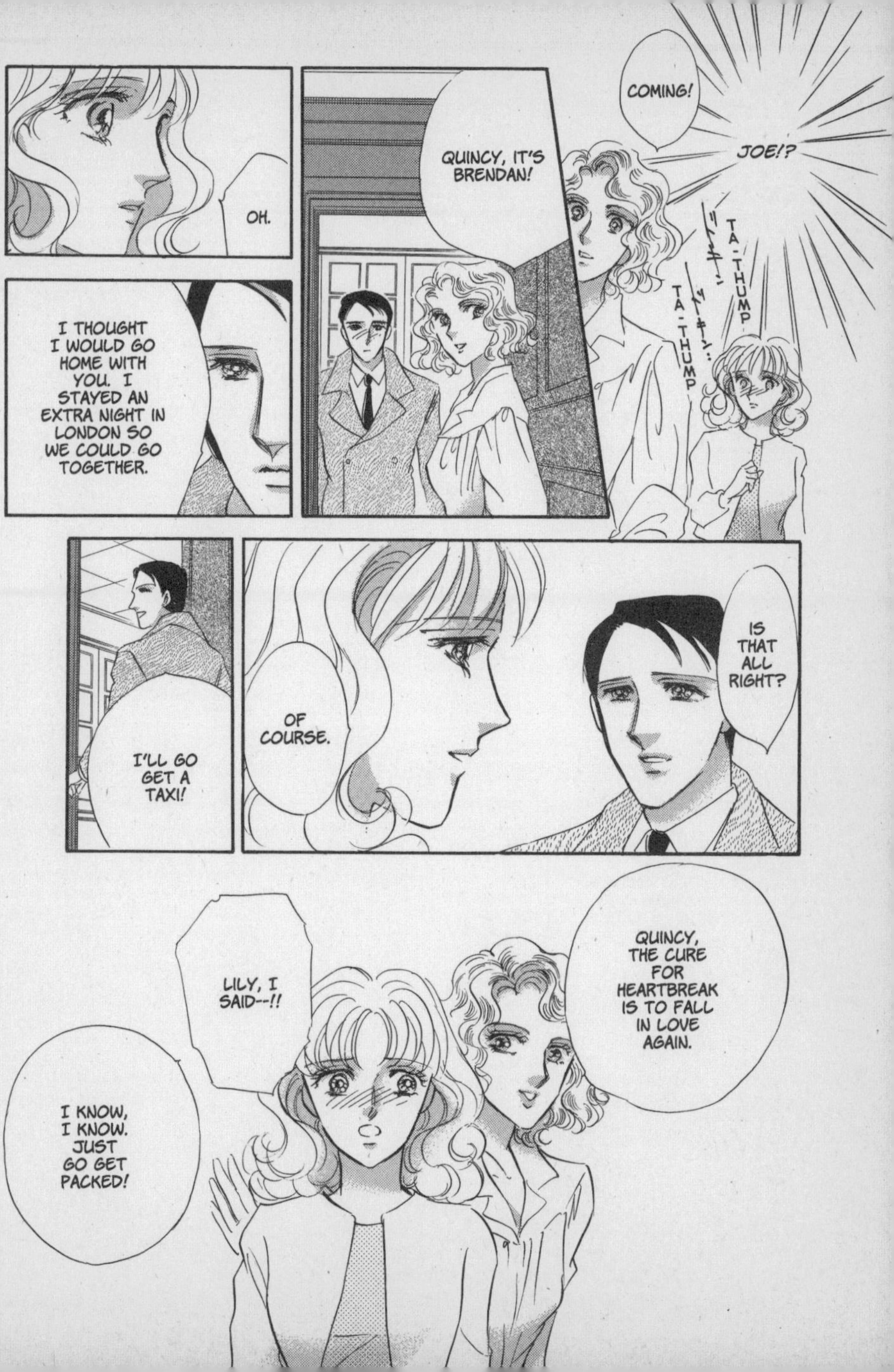
COMING!
JOE!?
TA-THUMP
TA-THUMP
QUINCY, IT'S BRENDAN!
OH.
I THOUGHT I WOULD GO HOME WITH YOU. I STAYED AN EXTRA NIGHT IN LONDON SO WE COULD GO TOGETHER.
IS THAT ALL RIGHT?
OF COURSE.
I'LL GO GET A TAXI!
QUINCY, THE CURE FOR HEARTBREAK IS TO FALL IN LOVE AGAIN.
LILY, I SAID--!!
I KNOW, I KNOW. JUST GO GET PACKED!

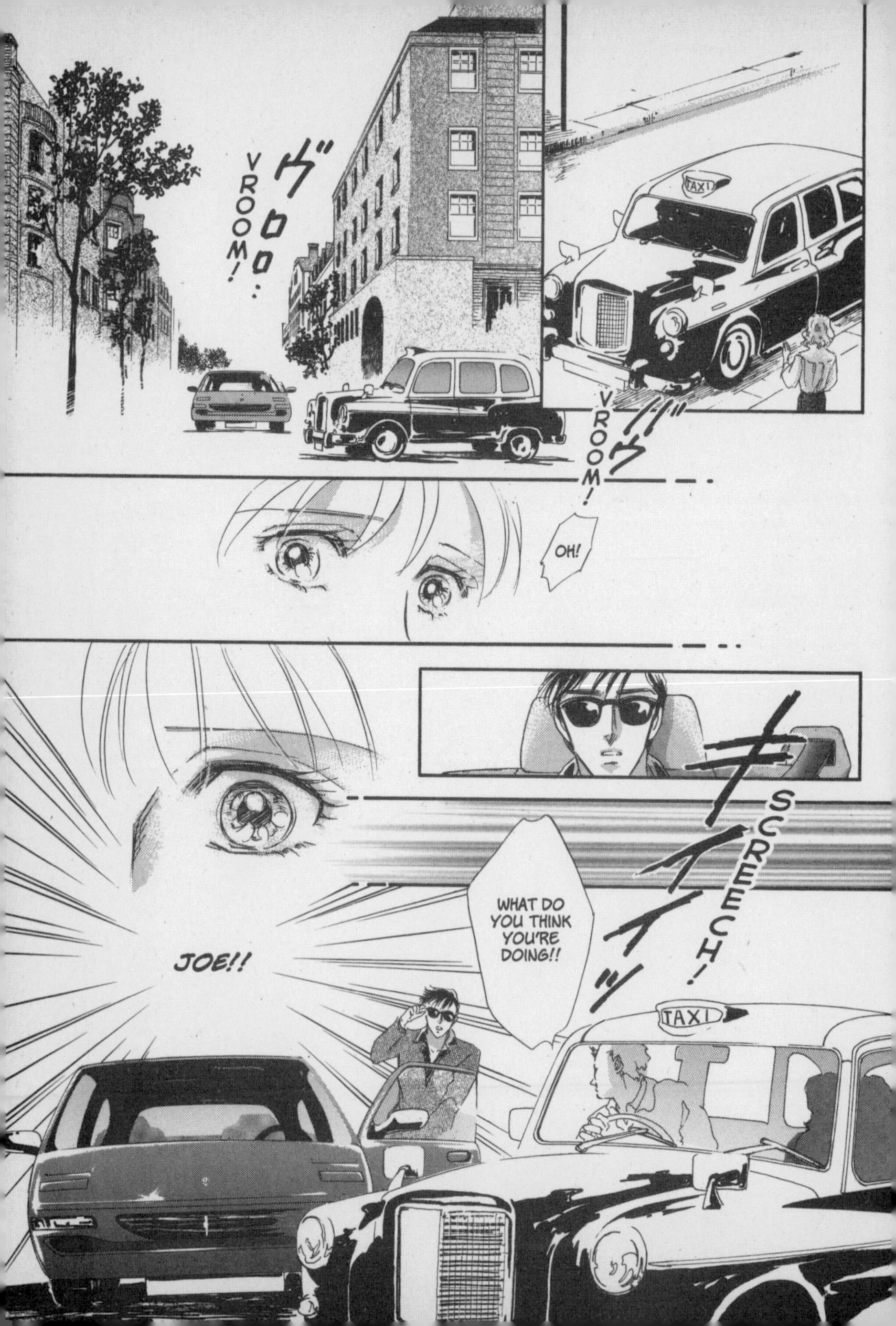
VROOM!
VROOM!
OH!
SCREECH!
WHAT DO YOU THINK YOU'RE DOING!!
JOE!!

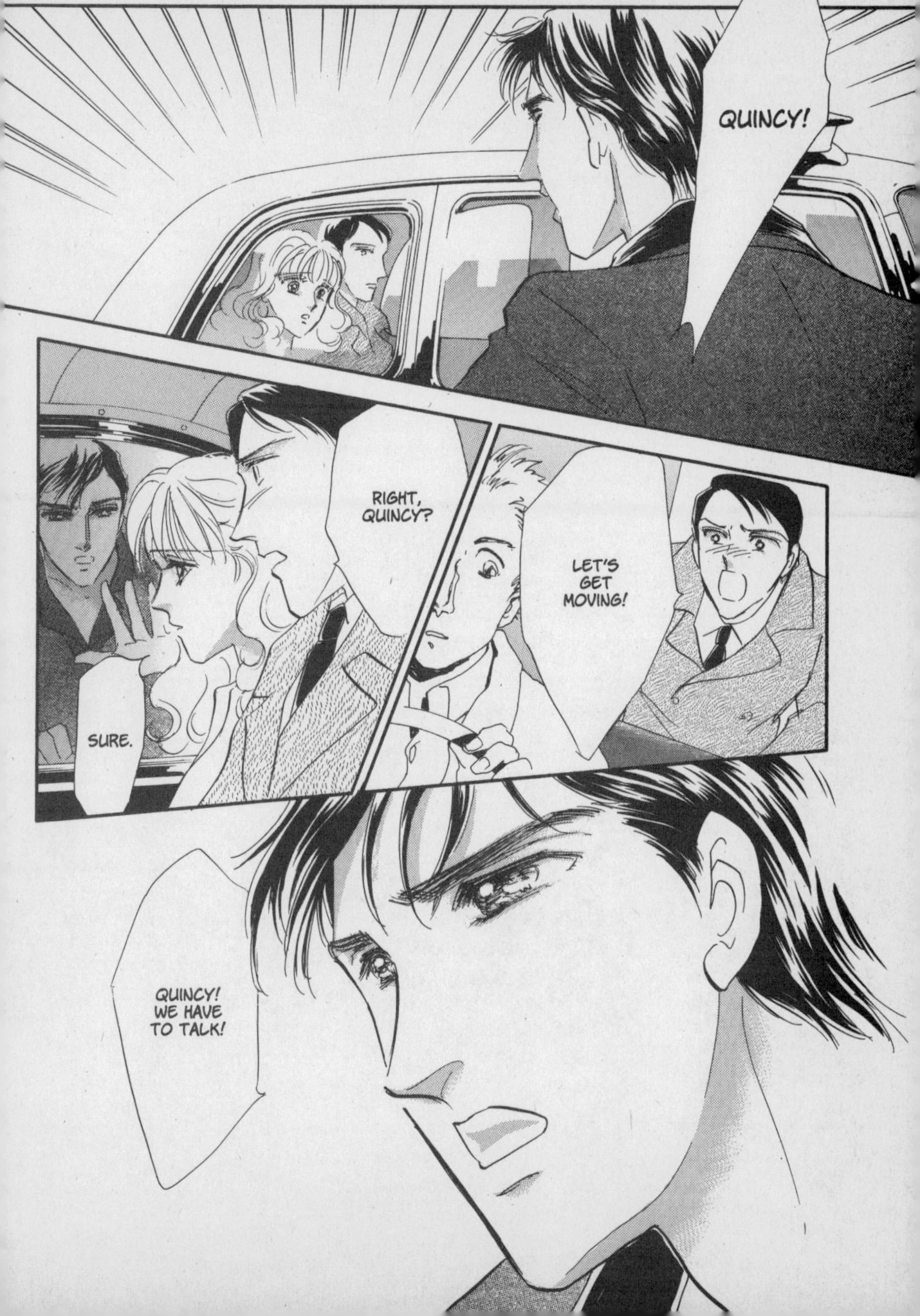
QUINCY!
LET'S GET MOVING!
RIGHT, QUINCY?
SURE.
QUINCY! WE HAVE TO TALK!

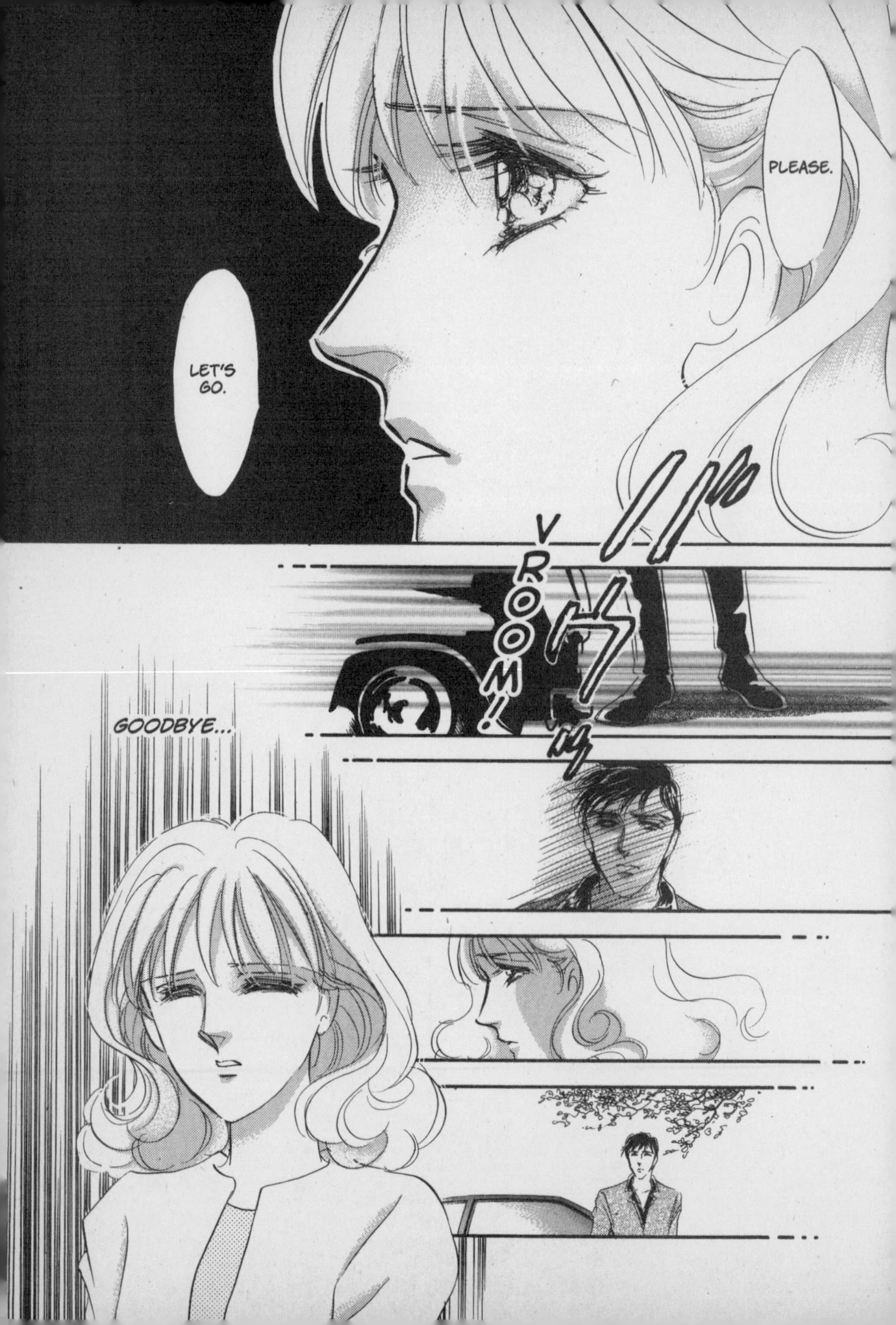
PLEASE.
LET'S GO.
VROOM!
GOODBYE...

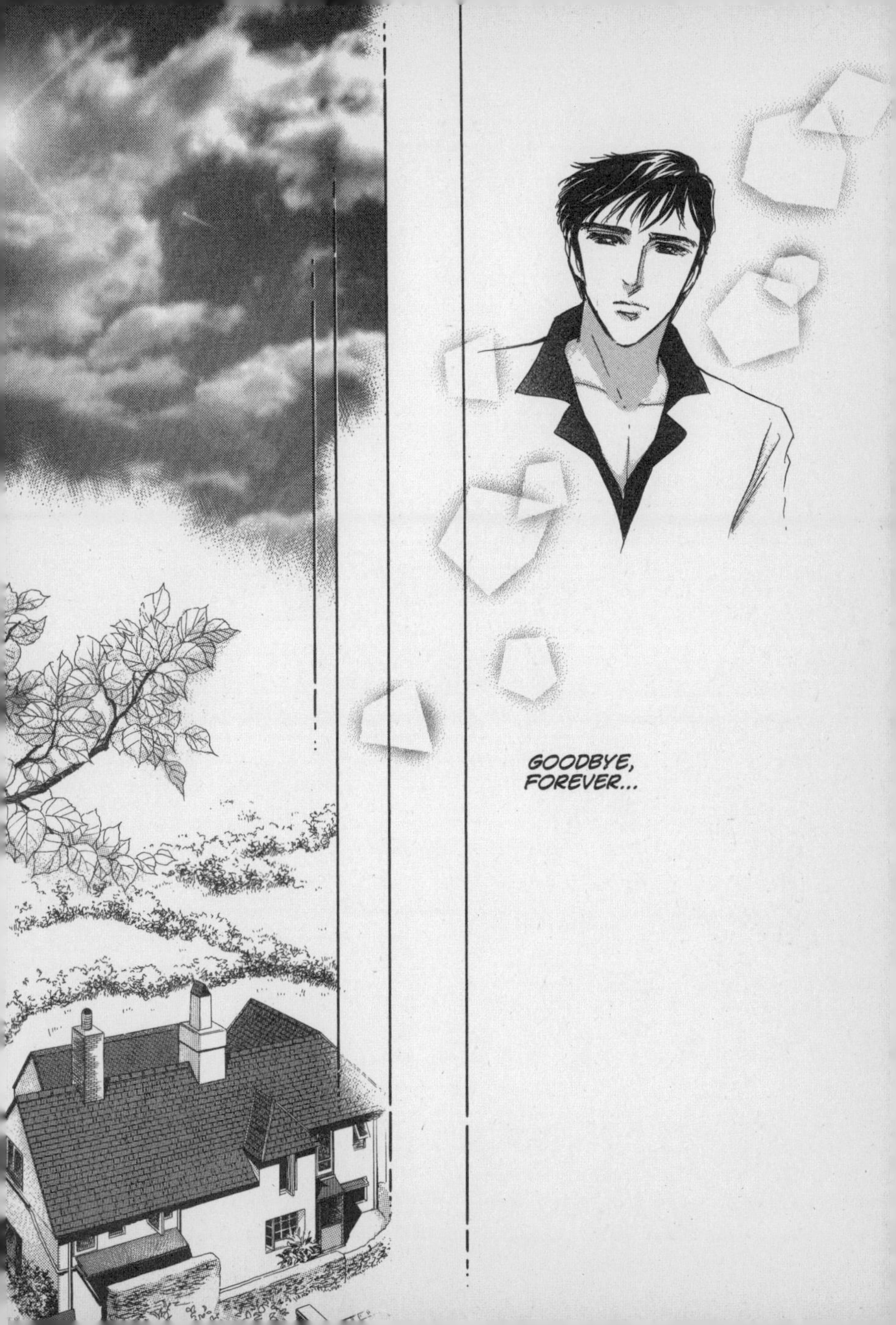
GOODBYE, FOREVER...

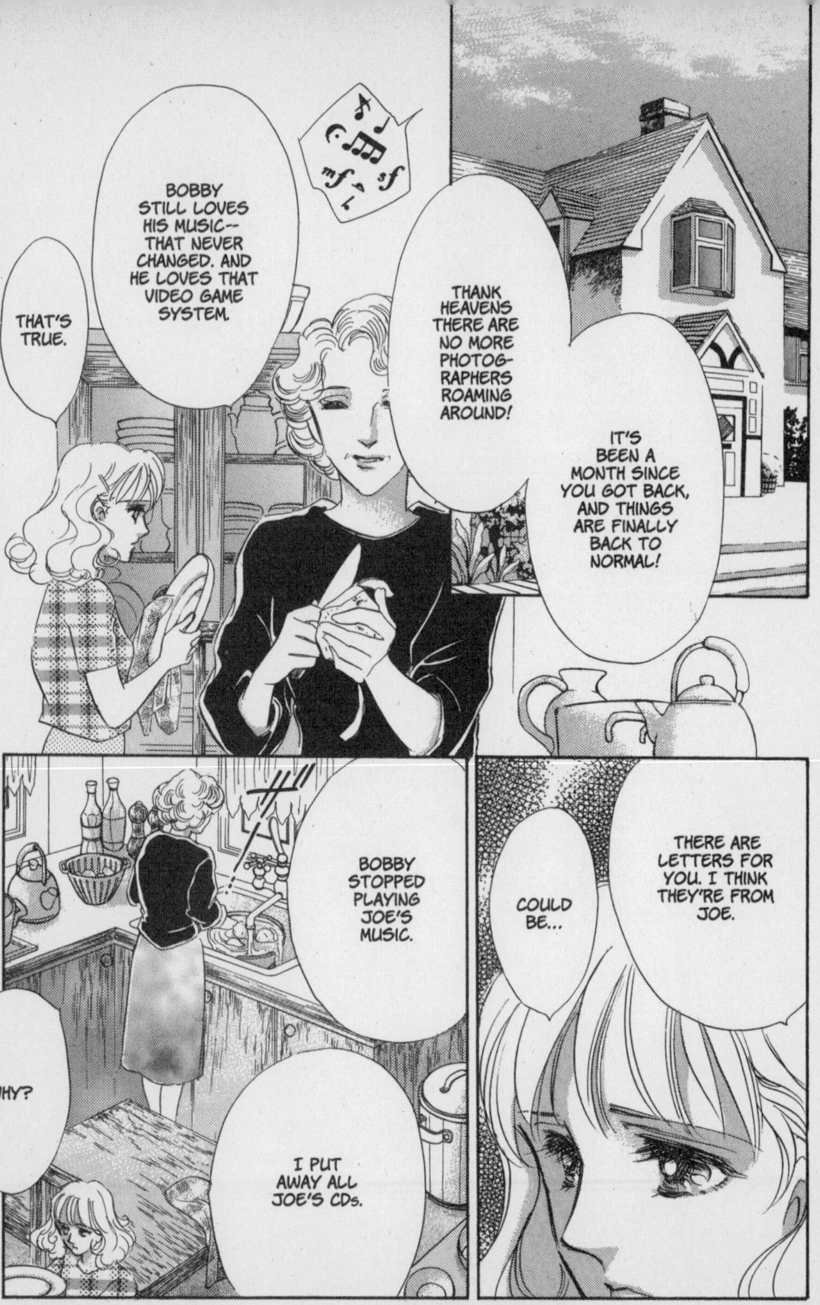
IT'S BEEN A MONTH SINCE YOU GOT BACK, AND THINGS ARE FINALLY BACK TO NORMAL!
THANK HEAVENS THERE ARE NO MORE PHOTOGRAPHERS ROAMING AROUND!
BOBBY STILL LOVES HIS MUSIC--THAT NEVER CHANGED. AND HE LOVES THAT VIDEO GAME SYSTEM.
THAT'S TRUE.
THERE ARE LETTERS FOR YOU. I THINK THEY'RE FROM JOE.
COULD BE...
BOBBY STOPPED PLAYING JOE'S MUSIC.
WHY?
I PUT AWAY ALL JOE'S CDs.

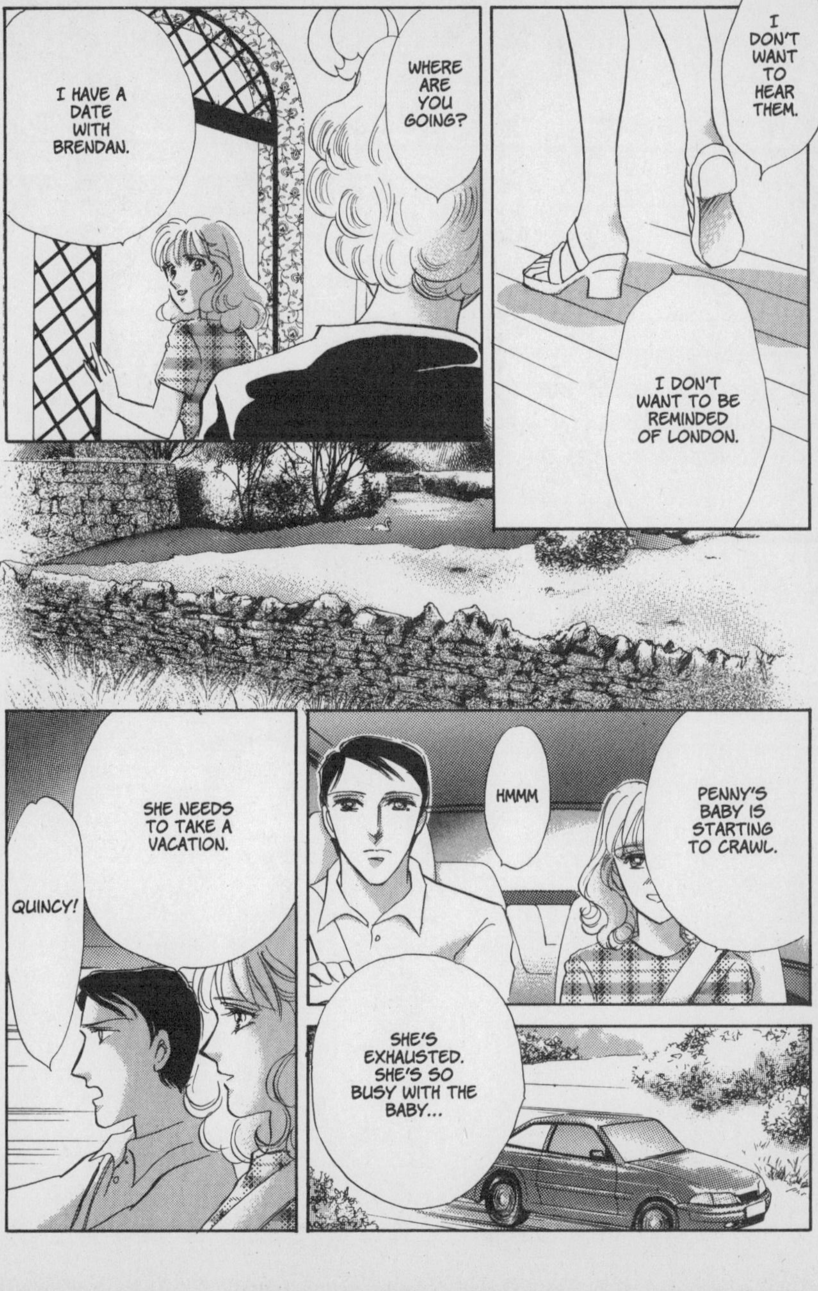
I DON'T WANT TO HEAR THEM.
I DON'T WANT TO BE REMINDED OF LONDON.
WHERE ARE YOU GOING?
I HAVE A DATE WITH BRENDAN.
PENNY'S BABY IS STARTING TO CRAWL.
HMMM
SHE'S EXHAUSTED. SHE'S SO BUSY WITH THE BABY...
SHE NEEDS TO TAKE A VACATION.
QUINCY!

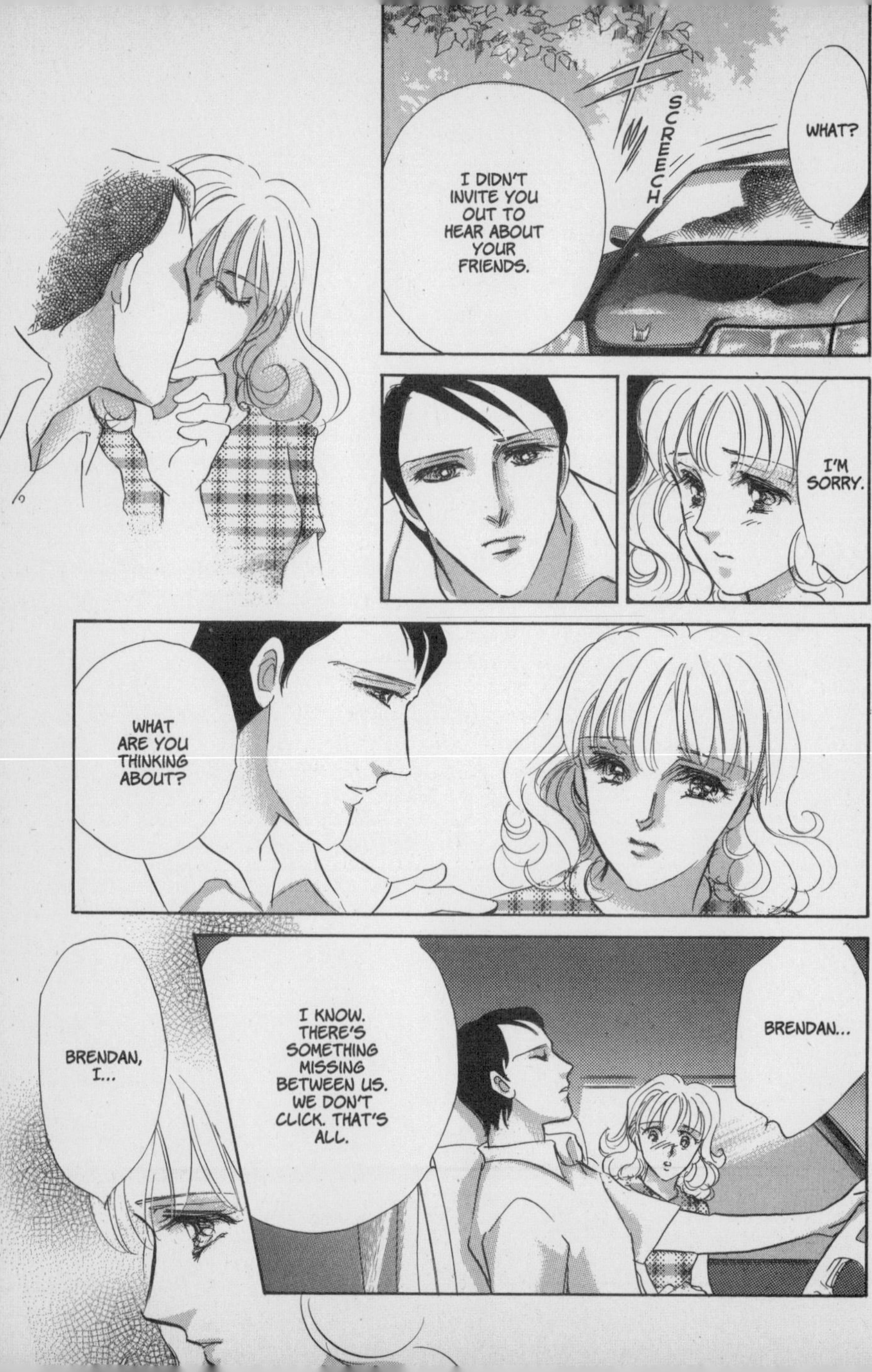
WHAT?
SCREECH
I DIDN'T INVITE YOU OUT TO HEAR ABOUT YOUR FRIENDS.
I'M SORRY.
WHAT ARE YOU THINKING ABOUT?
BRENDAN...
I KNOW. THERE'S SOMETHING MISSING BETWEEN US. WE DON'T CLICK. THAT'S ALL.
BRENDAN, I...

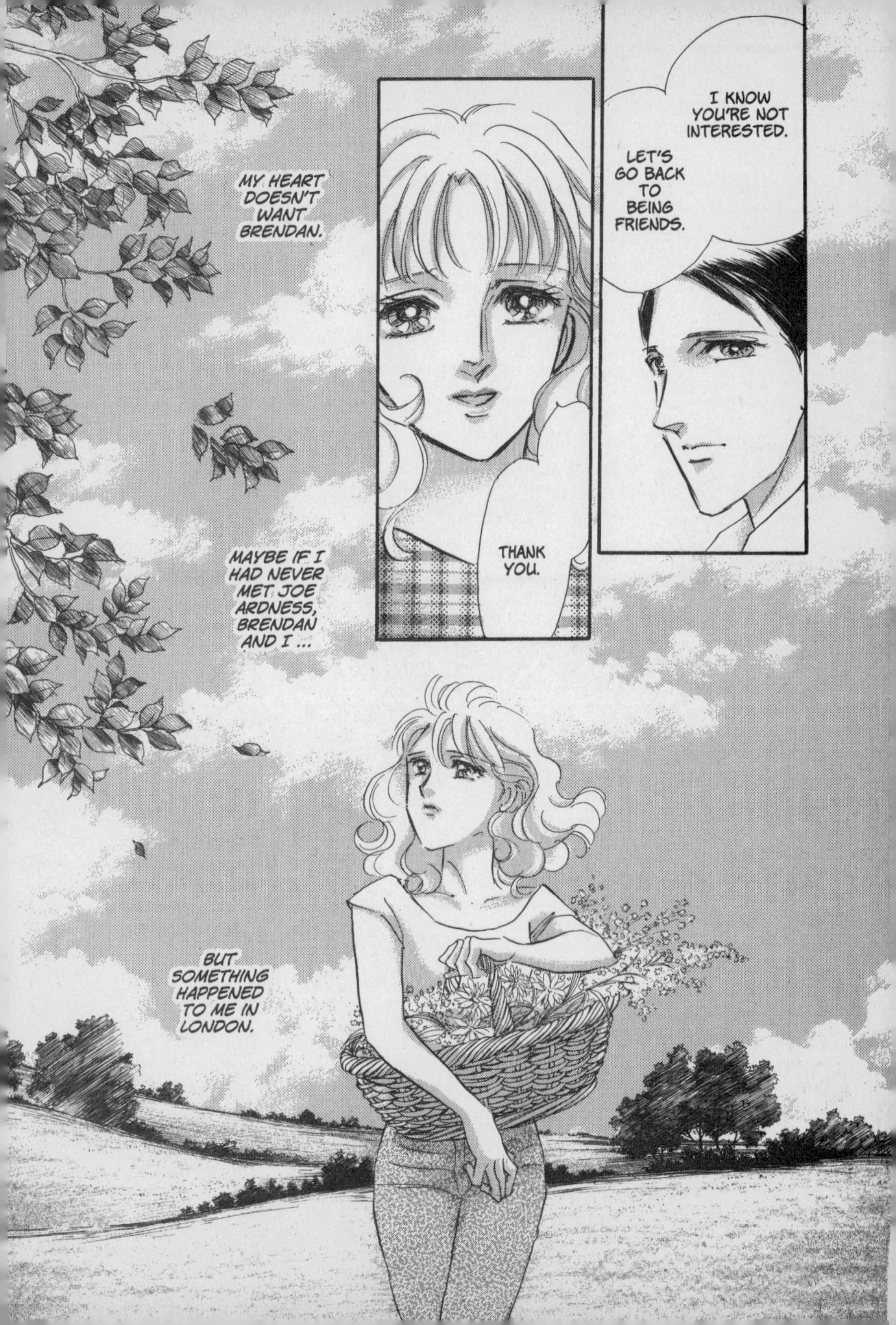
I KNOW YOU'RE NOT INTERESTED.
LET'S GO BACK TO BEING FRIENDS.
THANK YOU.
MY HEART DOESN'T WANT BRENDAN.
MAYBE IF I HAD NEVER MET JOE ARDNESS, BRENDAN AND I ...
BUT SOMETHING HAPPENED TO ME IN LONDON.

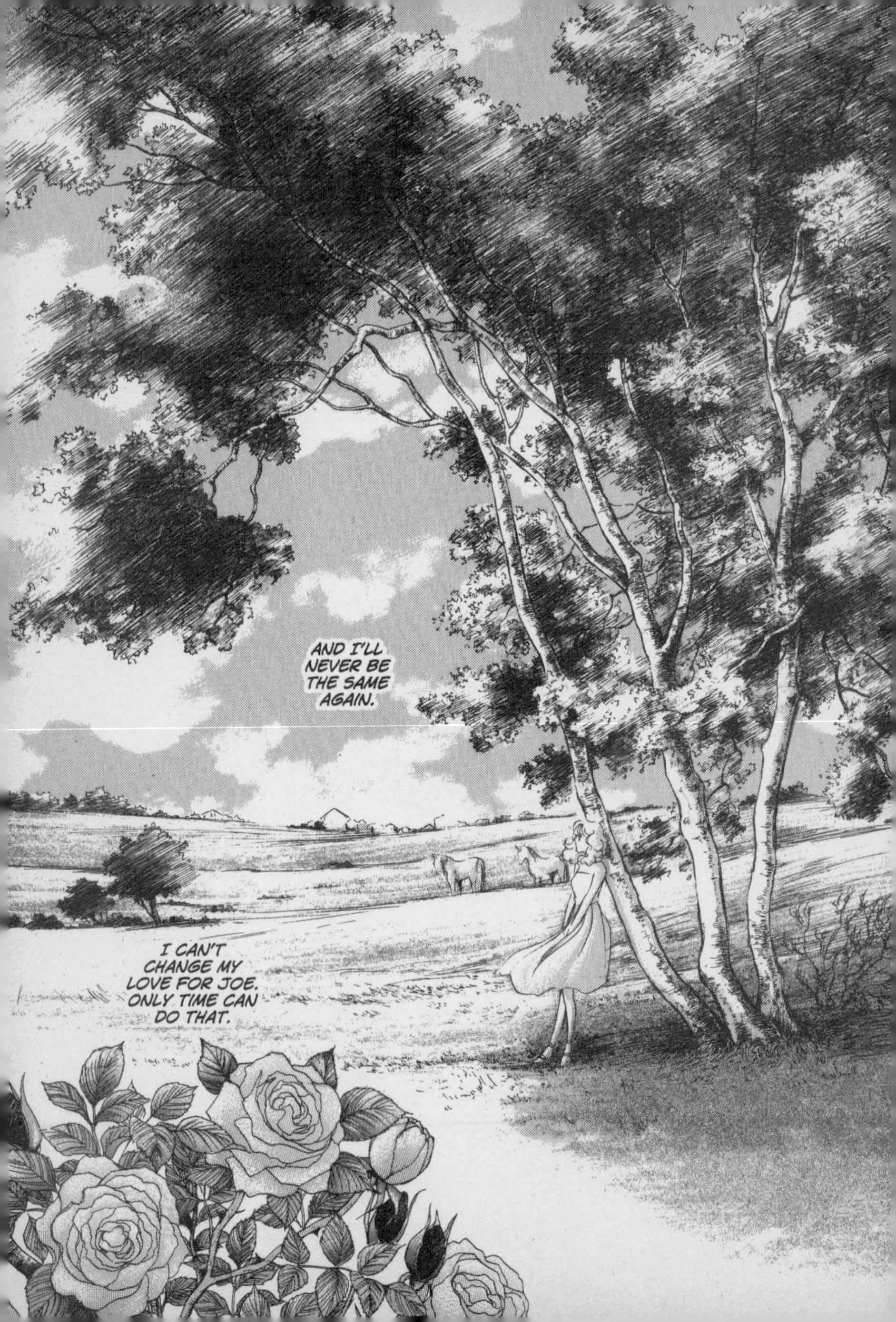
AND I'LL NEVER BE THE SAME AGAIN.
I CAN'T CHANGE MY LOVE FOR JOE. ONLY TIME CAN DO THAT.

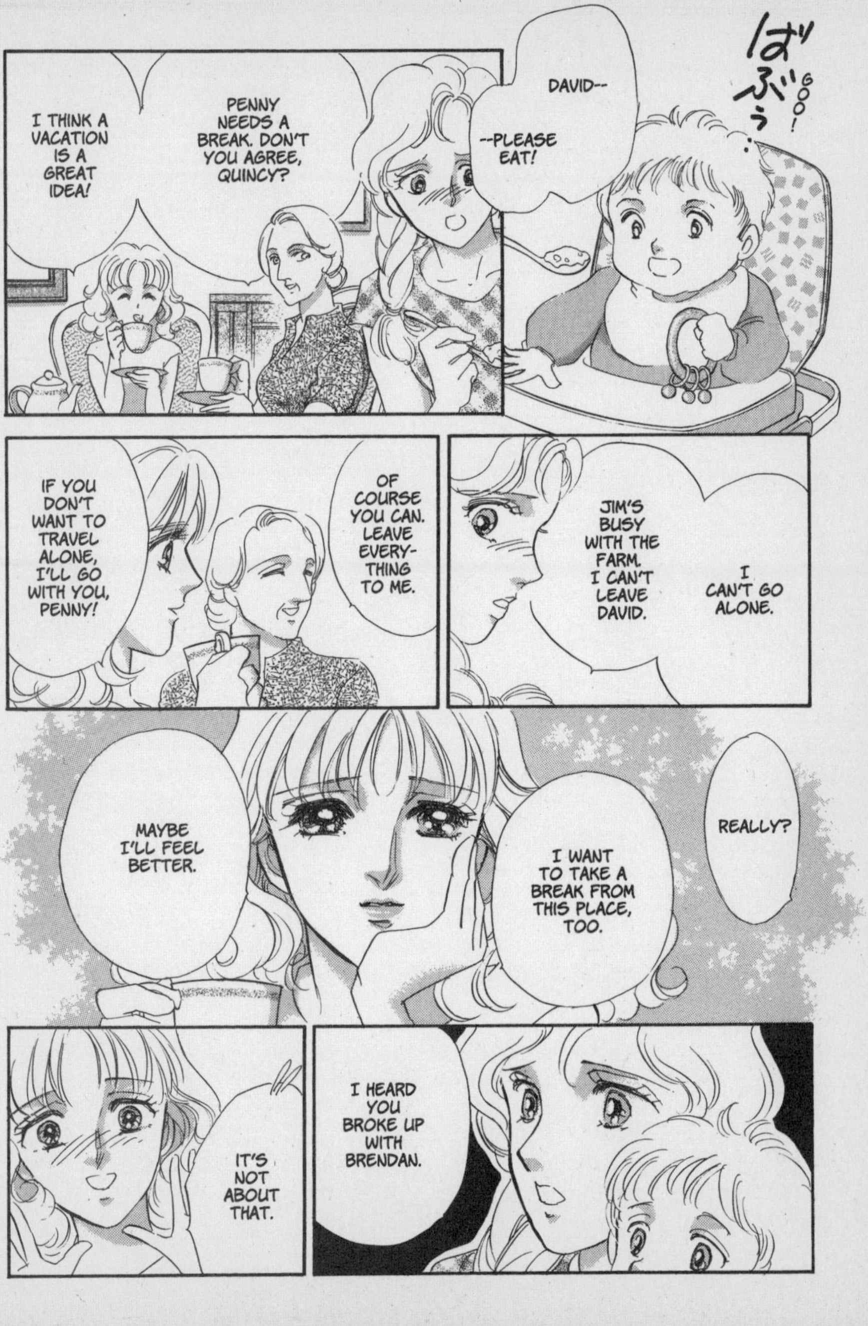

ばぶぅ
GOO!
DAVID--
--PLEASE EAT!
PENNY NEEDS A BREAK. DON'T YOU AGREE, QUINCY?
I THINK A VACATION IS A GREAT IDEA!
I CAN'T GO ALONE.
JIM'S BUSY WITH THE FARM. I CAN'T LEAVE DAVID.
OF COURSE YOU CAN. LEAVE EVERY-THING TO ME.
IF YOU DON'T WANT TO TRAVEL ALONE, I'LL GO WITH YOU, PENNY!
REALLY?
I WANT TO TAKE A BREAK FROM THIS PLACE, TOO.
MAYBE I'LL FEEL BETTER.
I HEARD YOU BROKE UP WITH BRENDAN.
IT'S NOT ABOUT THAT.

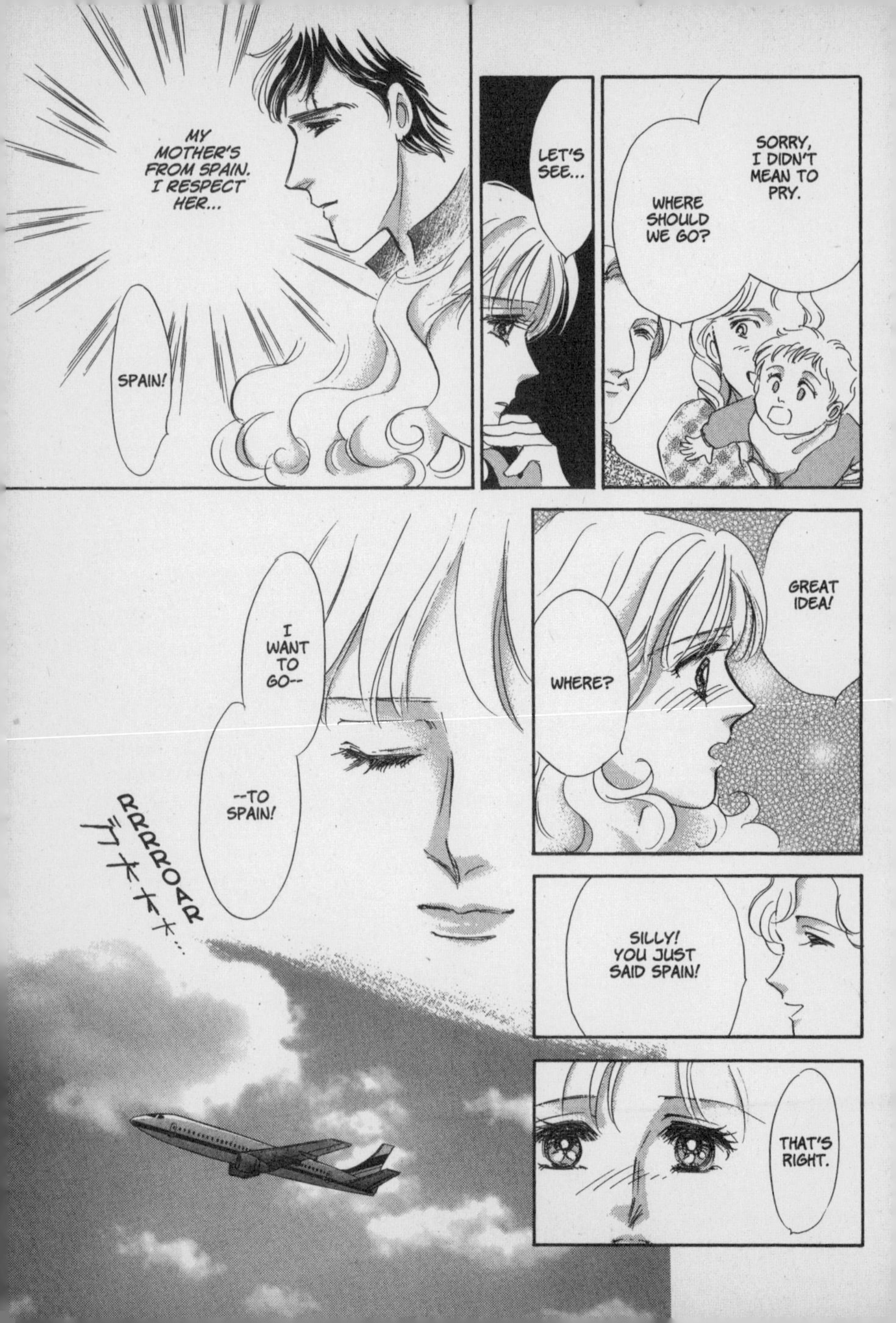
SORRY, I DIDN'T MEAN TO PRY.
WHERE SHOULD WE GO?
LET'S SEE...
MY MOTHER'S FROM SPAIN. I RESPECT HER...
SPAIN!
GREAT IDEA!
WHERE?
SILLY! YOU JUST SAID SPAIN!
THAT'S RIGHT.
I WANT TO GO--
--TO SPAIN!
RRRROAR

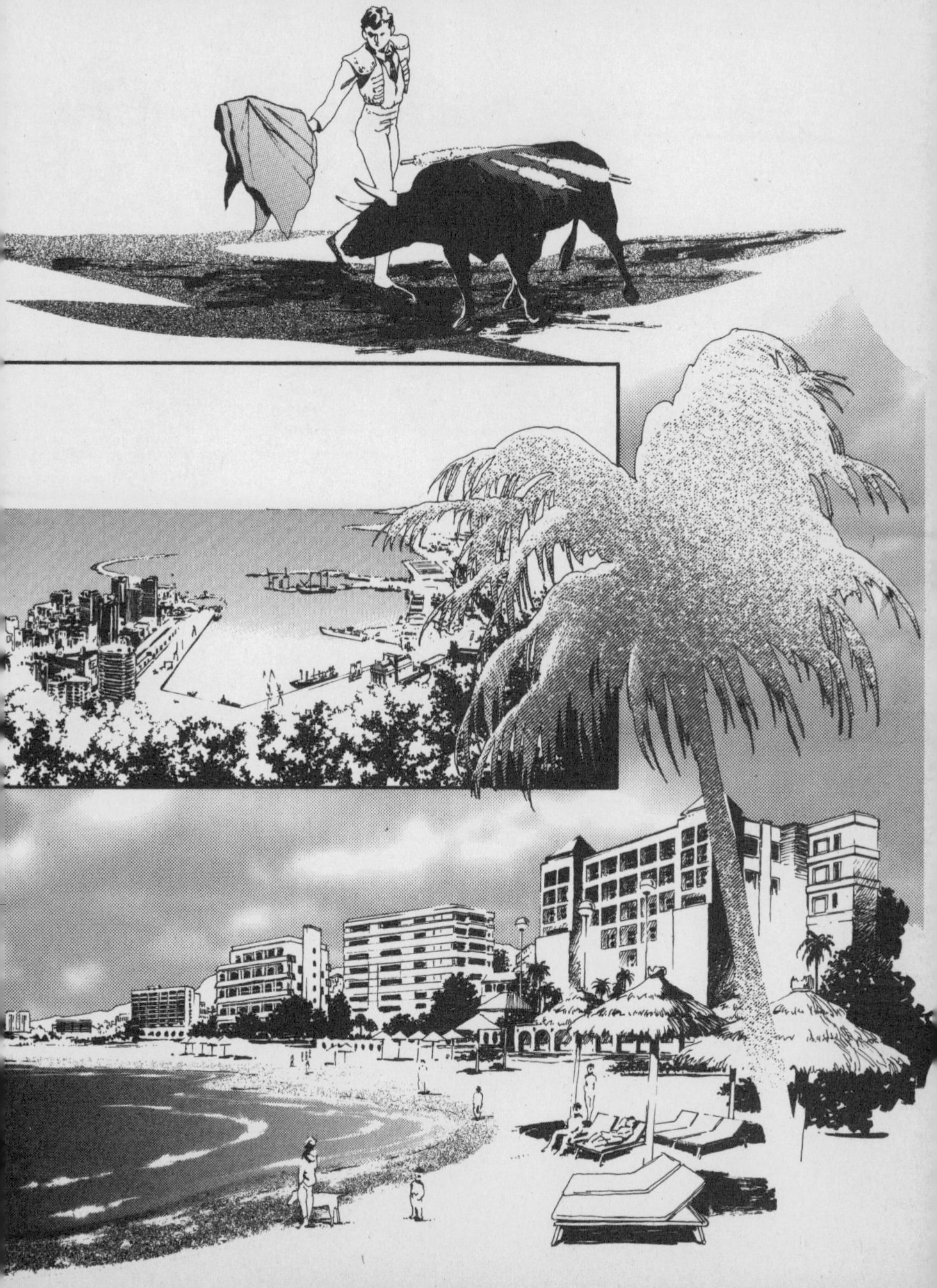

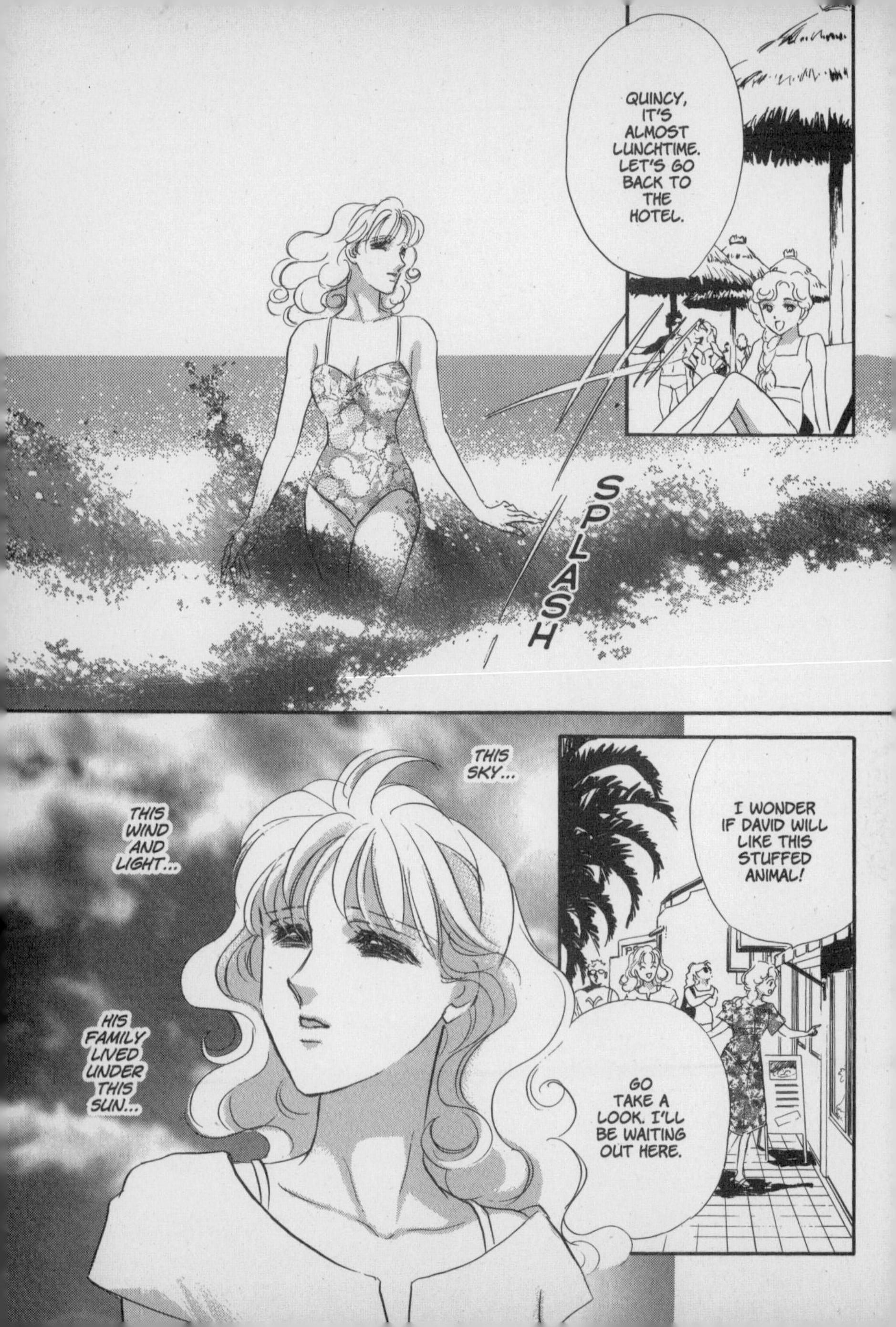
QUINCY, IT'S ALMOST LUNCHTIME. LET'S GO BACK TO THE HOTEL.
SPLASH
I WONDER IF DAVID WILL LIKE THIS STUFFED ANIMAL!
GO TAKE A LOOK. I'LL BE WAITING OUT HERE.
THIS SKY...
THIS WIND AND LIGHT...
HIS FAMILY LIVED UNDER THIS SUN...

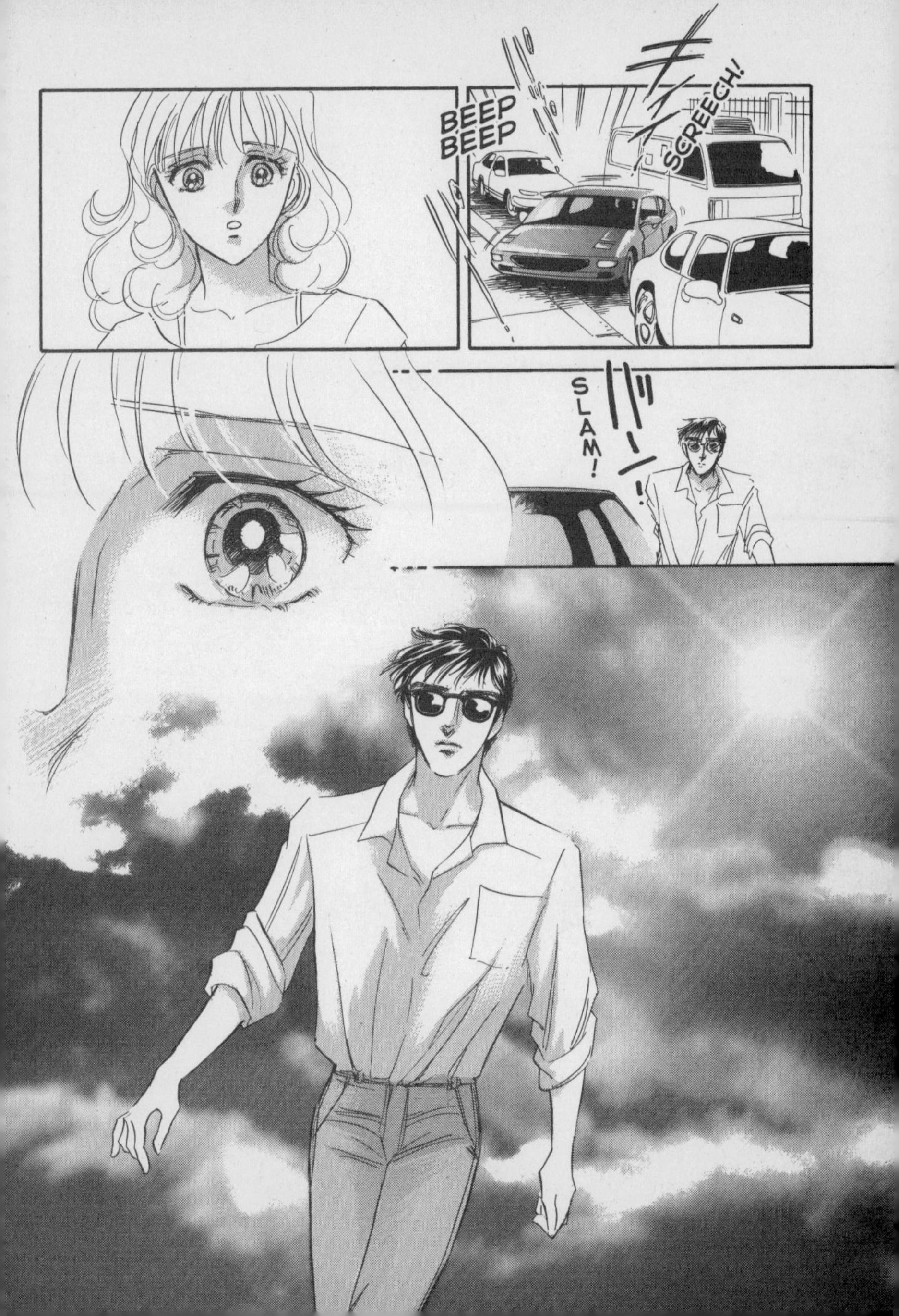
SCREECH!
BEEP BEEP
SLAM!

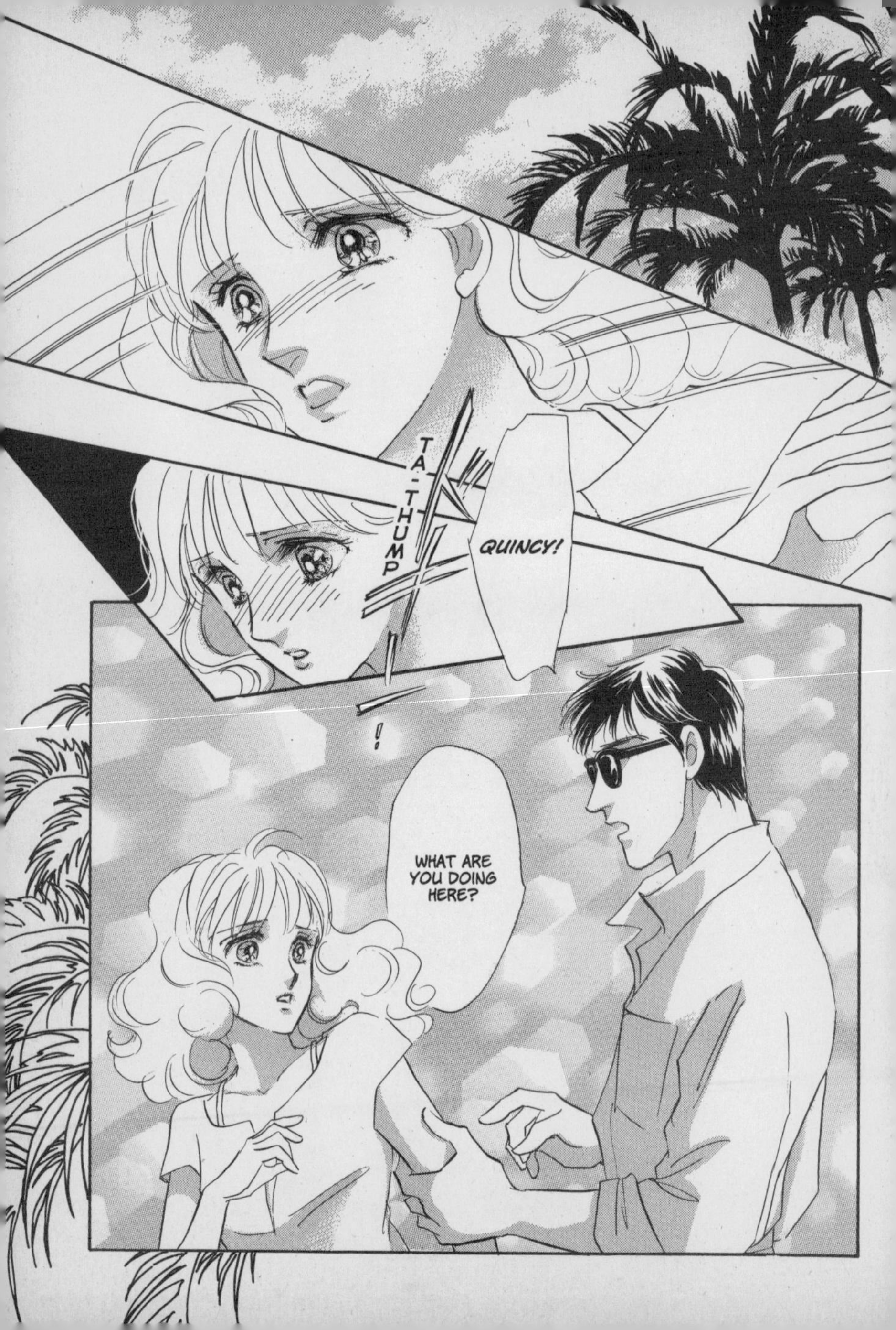
TA-THUMP
QUINCY!
!
WHAT ARE YOU DOING HERE?

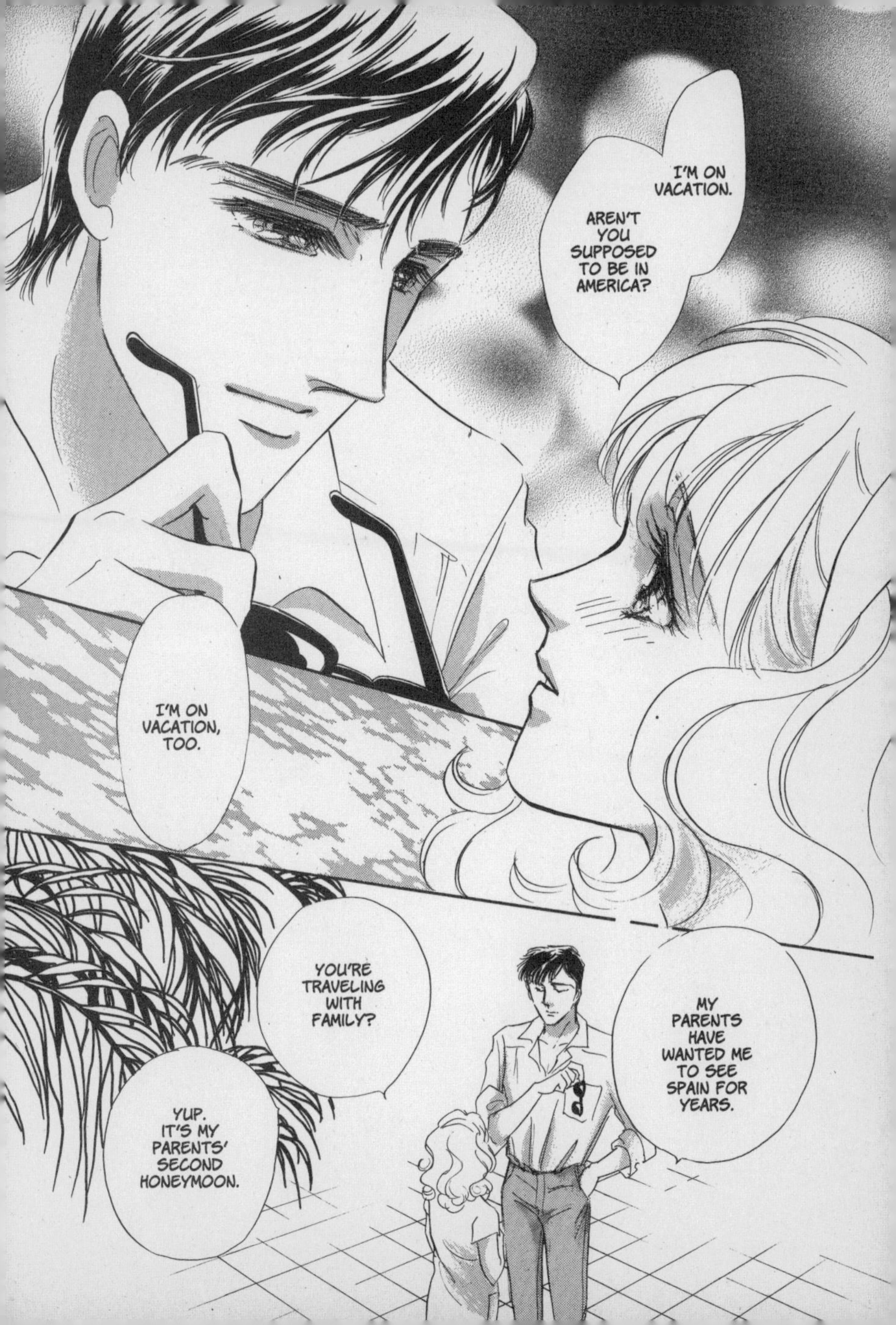
I'M ON VACATION.
AREN'T YOU SUPPOSED TO BE IN AMERICA?
I'M ON VACATION, TOO.
MY PARENTS HAVE WANTED ME TO SEE SPAIN FOR YEARS.
YOU'RE TRAVELING WITH FAMILY?
YUP. IT'S MY PARENTS' SECOND HONEYMOON.

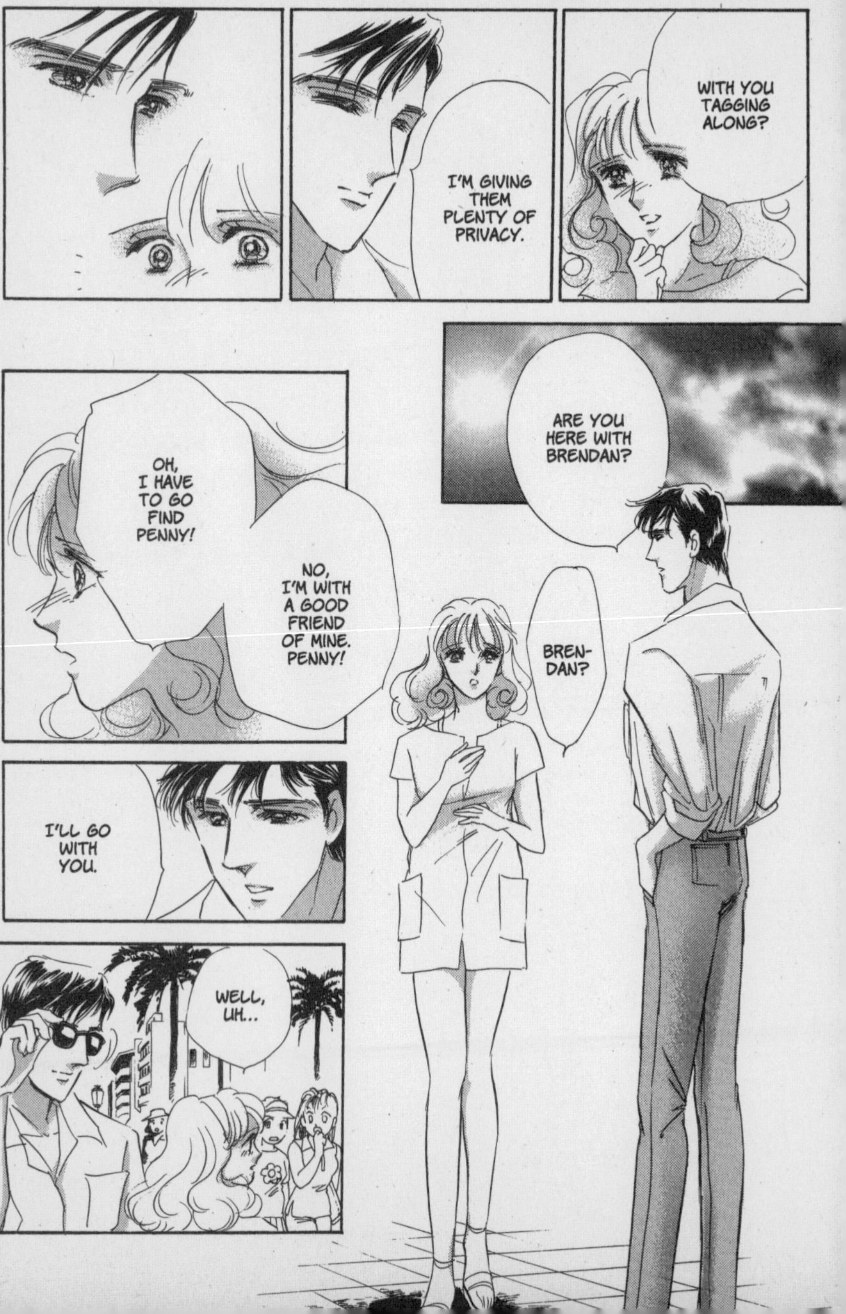
WITH YOU TAGGING ALONG?
I'M GIVING THEM PLENTY OF PRIVACY.
ARE YOU HERE WITH BRENDAN?
BREN-DAN?
NO, I'M WITH A GOOD FRIEND OF MINE. PENNY!
OH, I HAVE TO GO FIND PENNY!
I'LL GO WITH YOU.
WELL, UH...

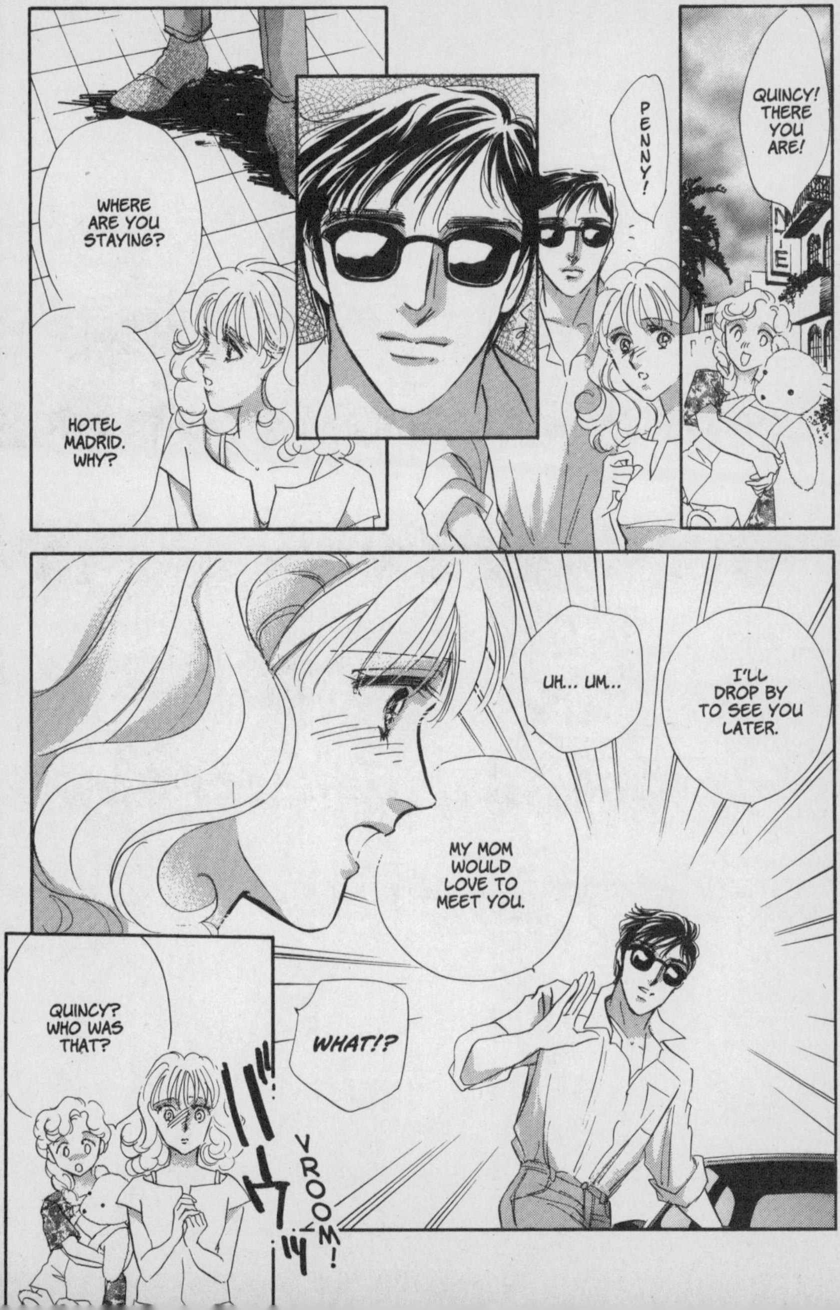
QUINCY! THERE YOU ARE!
PENNY!
WHERE ARE YOU STAYING?
HOTEL MADRID. WHY?
I'LL DROP BY TO SEE YOU LATER.
UH... UM..
MY MOM WOULD LOVE TO MEET YOU.
WHAT!?
VROOOM!
QUINCY? WHO WAS THAT?

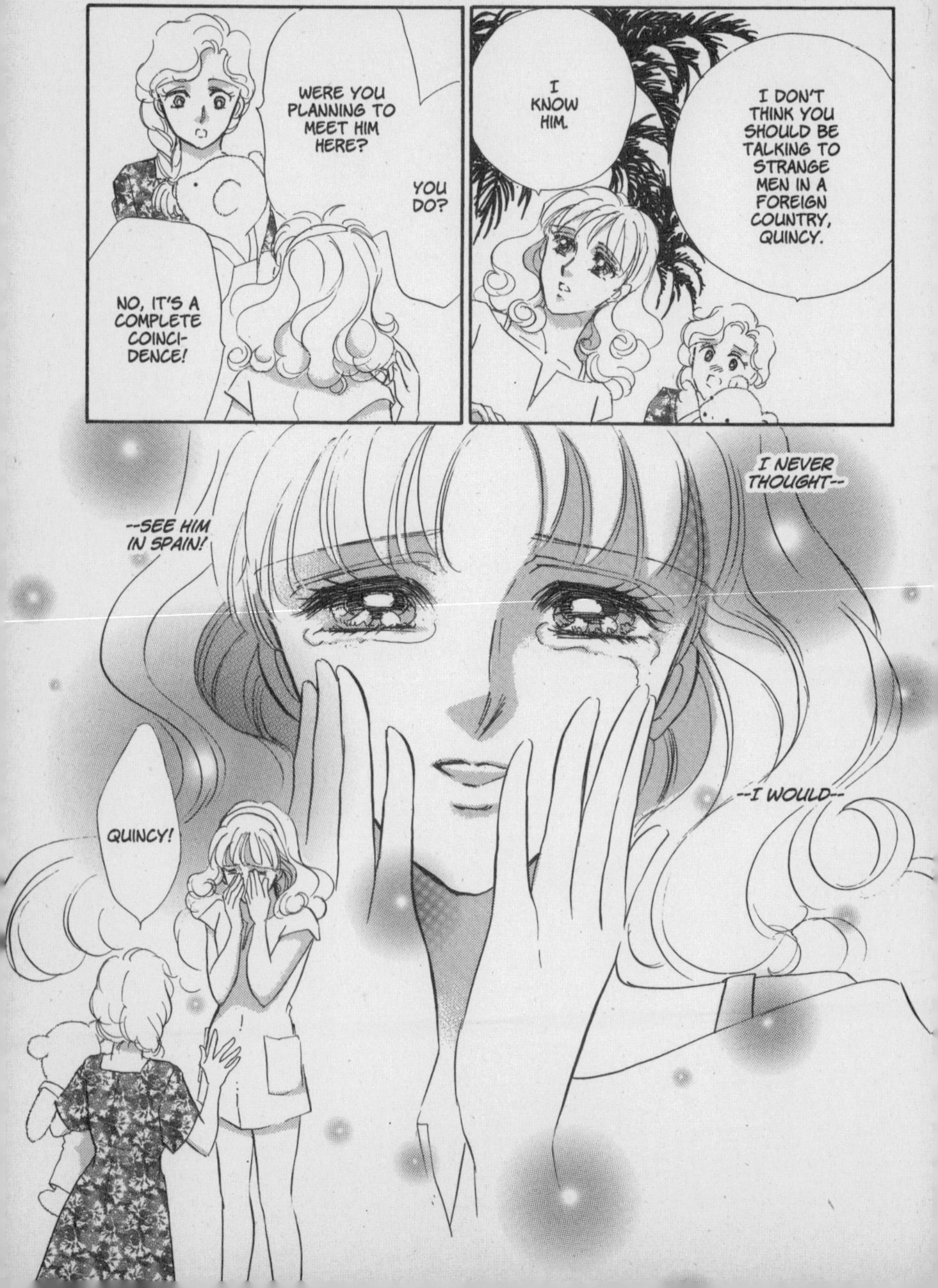
I DON'T THINK YOU SHOULD BE TALKING TO STRANGE MEN IN A FOREIGN COUNTRY, QUINCY.
I KNOW HIM.
YOU DO?
WERE YOU PLANNING TO MEET HIM HERE?
NO, IT'S A COMPLETE COINCI-DENCE!
I NEVER THOUGHT--
--I WOULD--
--SEE HIM IN SPAIN!
QUINCY!

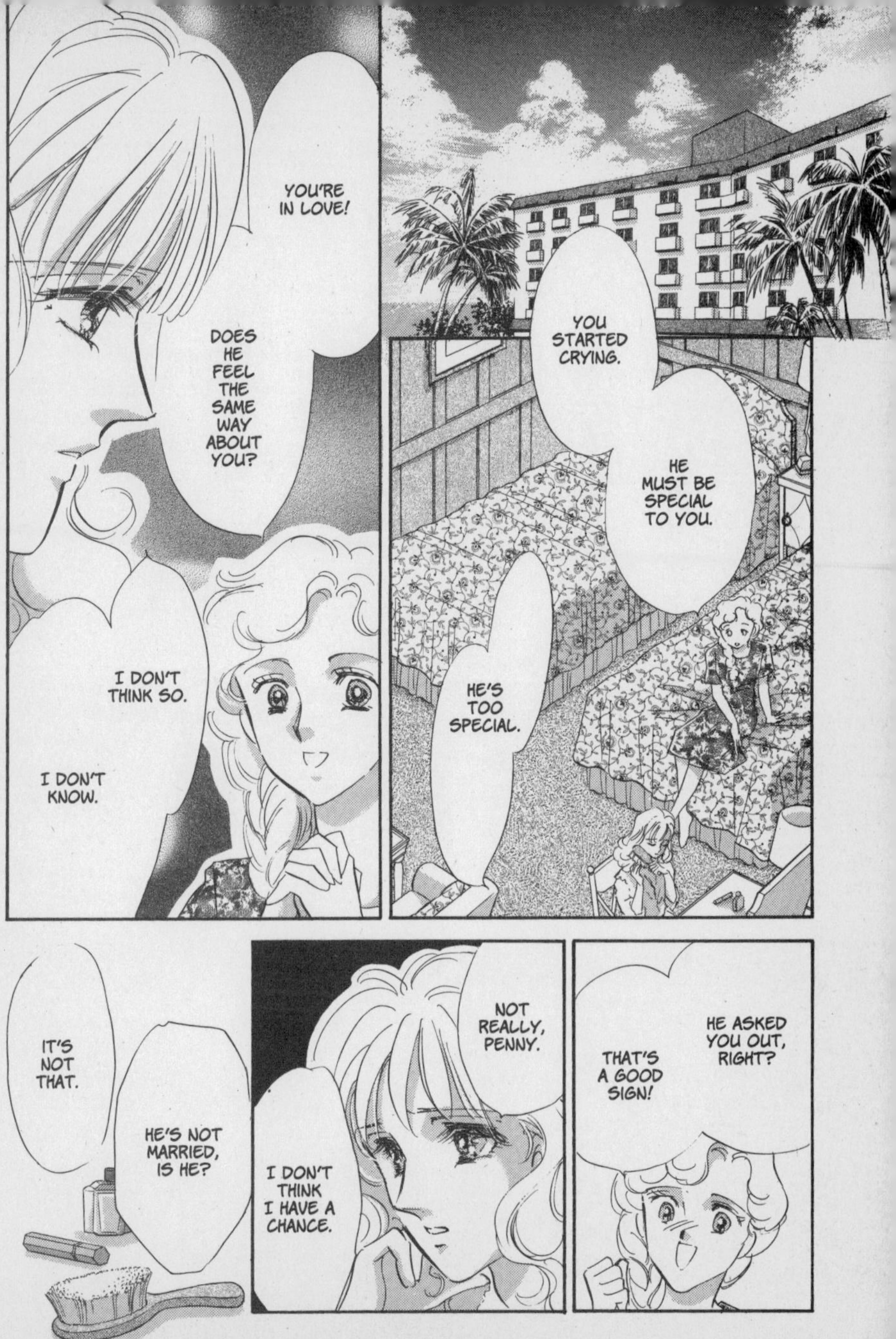
YOU STARTED CRYING.
HE MUST BE SPECIAL TO YOU.
HE'S TOO SPECIAL.
YOU'RE IN LOVE!
DOES HE FEEL THE SAME WAY ABOUT YOU?
I DON'T THINK SO.
I DON'T KNOW.
HE ASKED YOU OUT, RIGHT?
THAT'S A GOOD SIGN!
NOT REALLY, PENNY.
I DON'T THINK I HAVE A CHANCE.
HE'S NOT MARRIED, IS HE?
IT'S NOT THAT.

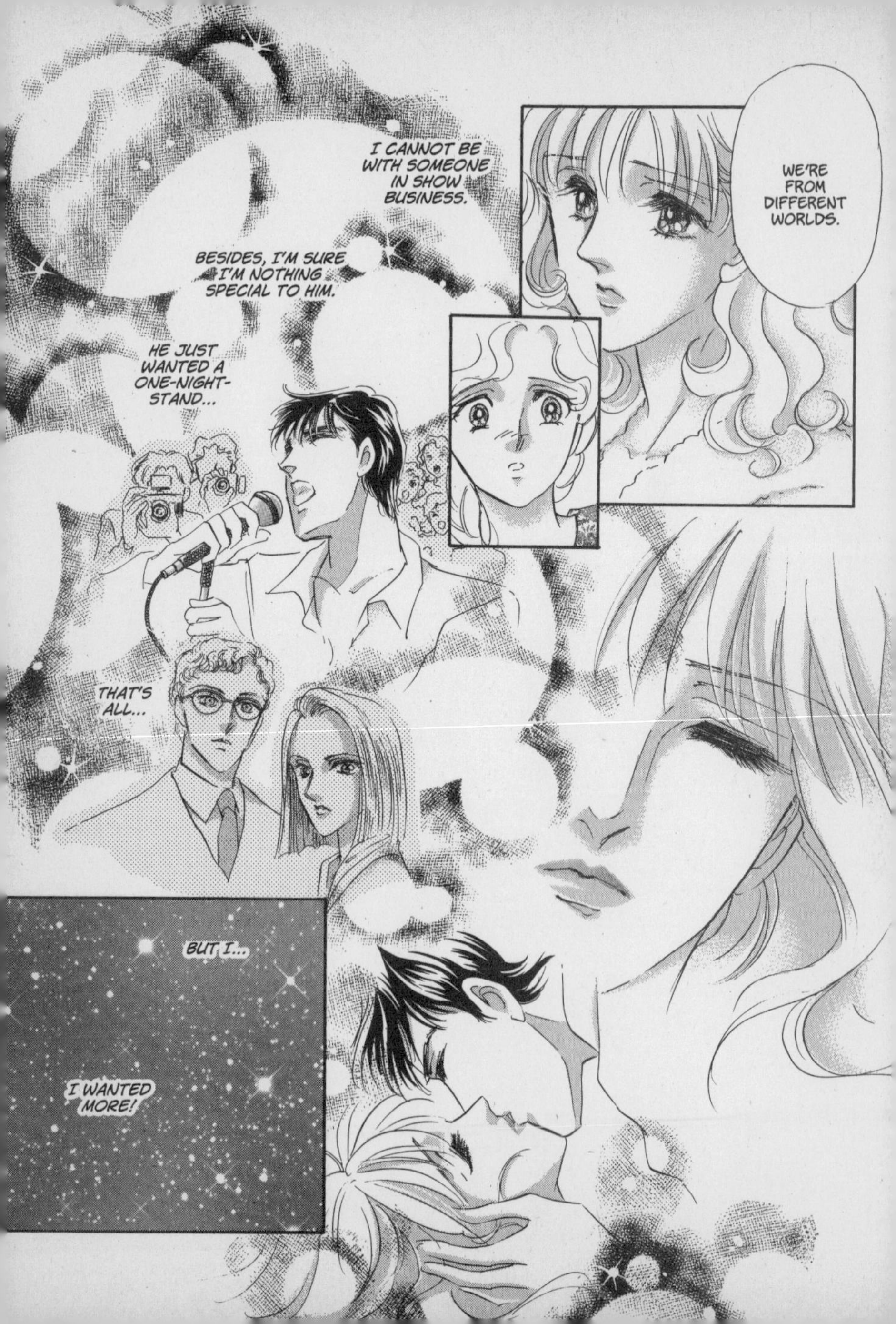
WE'RE FROM DIFFERENT WORLDS.
I CANNOT BE WITH SOMEONE IN SHOW BUSINESS.
BESIDES, I'M SURE I'M NOTHING SPECIAL TO HIM.
HE JUST WANTED A ONE-NIGHT-STAND...
THAT'S ALL...
BUT I...
I WANTED MORE!

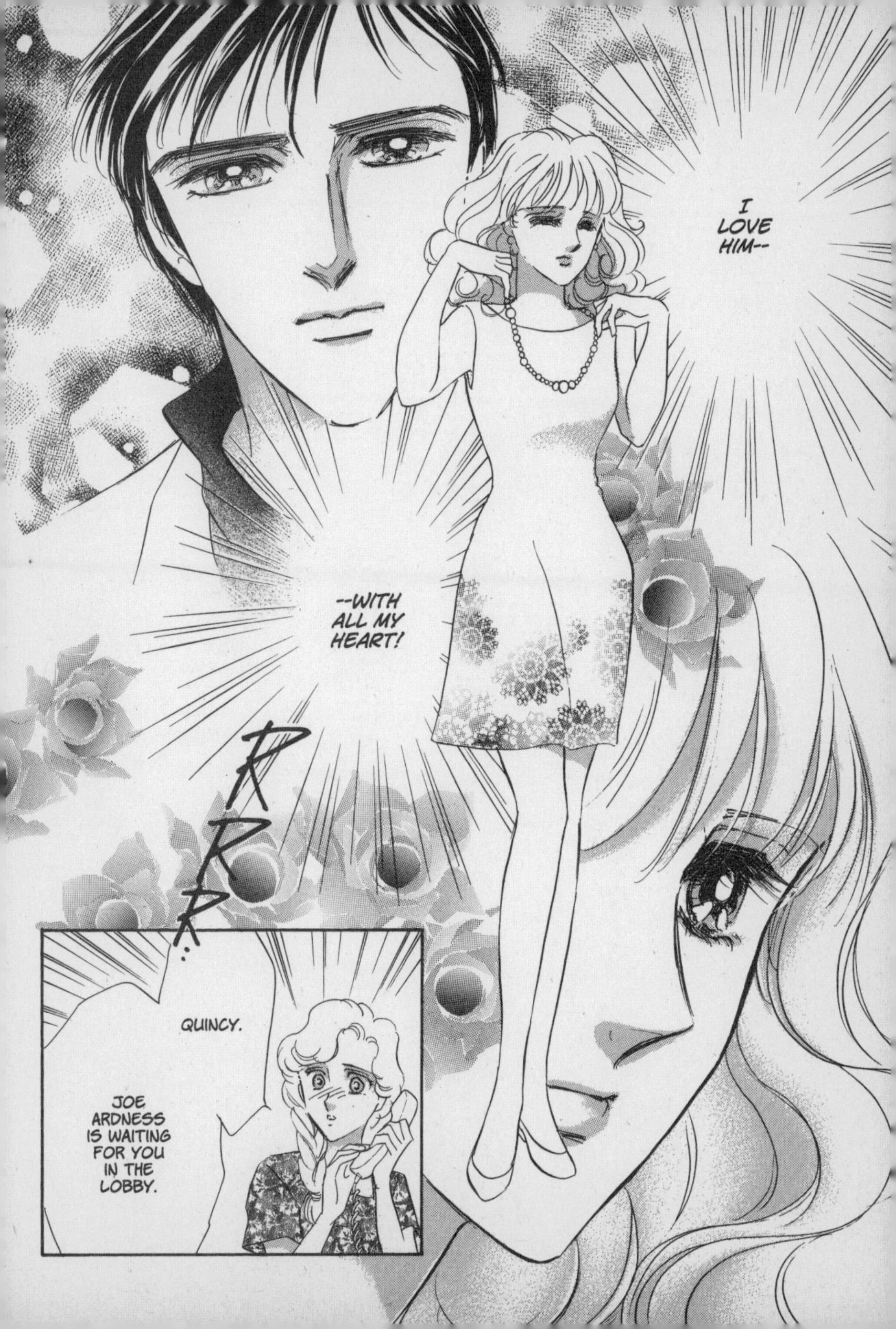
I LOVE HIM--
--WITH ALL MY HEART!
RRR..
QUINCY.
JOE ARDNESS IS WAITING FOR YOU IN THE LOBBY.

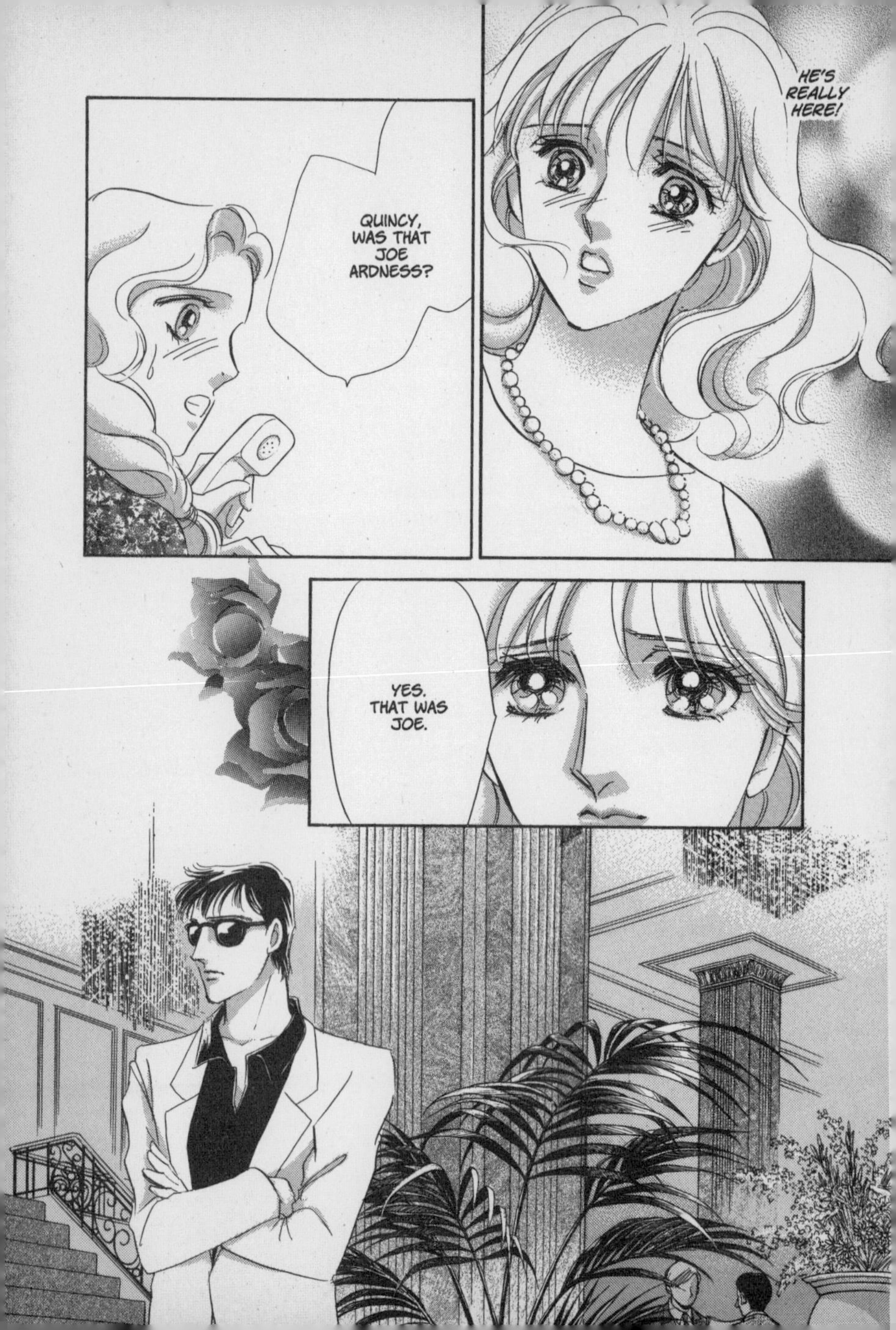
HE'S REALLY HERE!
QUINCY, WAS THAT JOE ARDNESS?
YES. THAT WAS JOE.

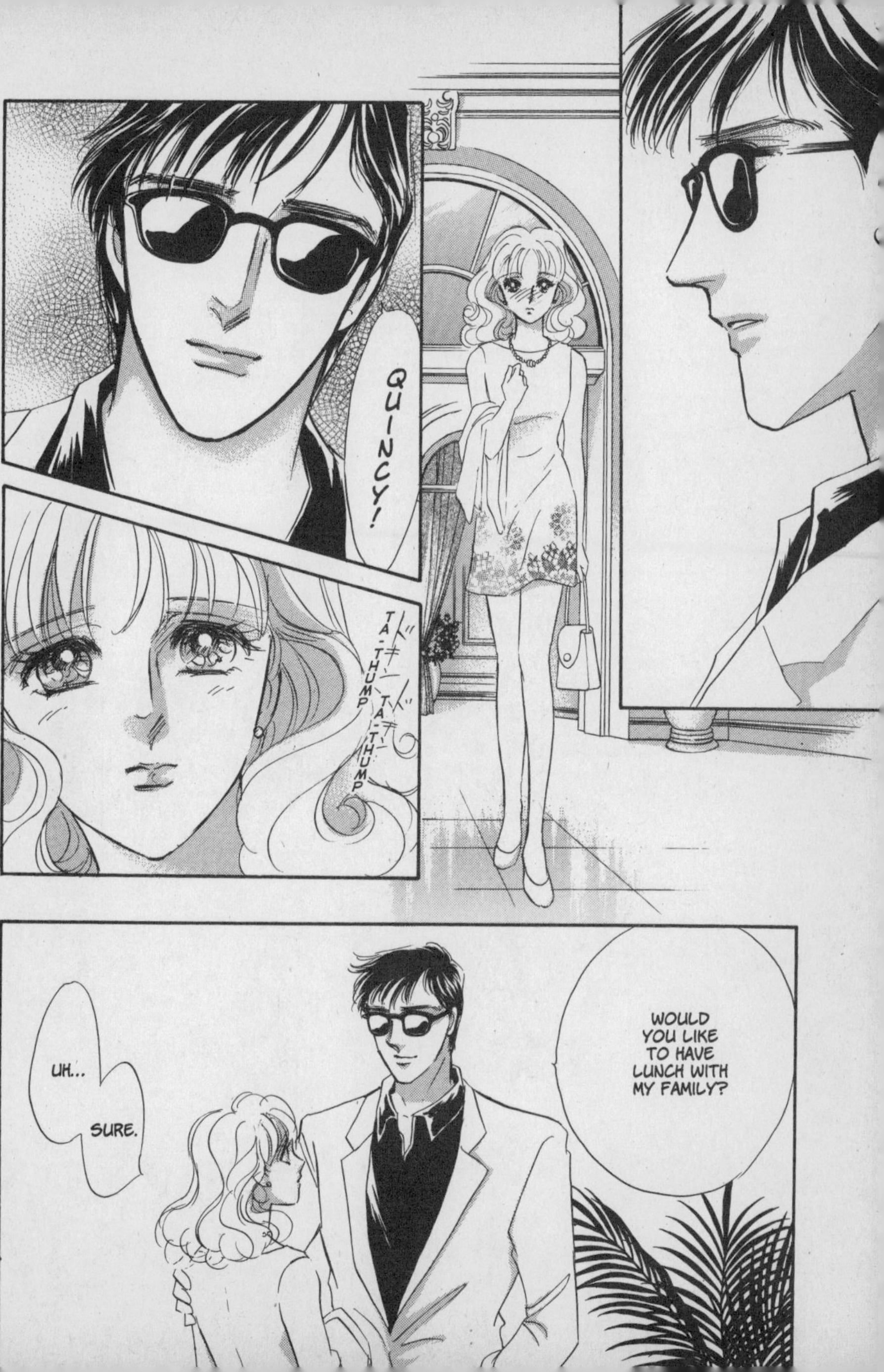
QUINCY!
TA-THUMP TA-THUMP
WOULD YOU LIKE TO HAVE LUNCH WITH MY FAMILY?
UH... SURE.

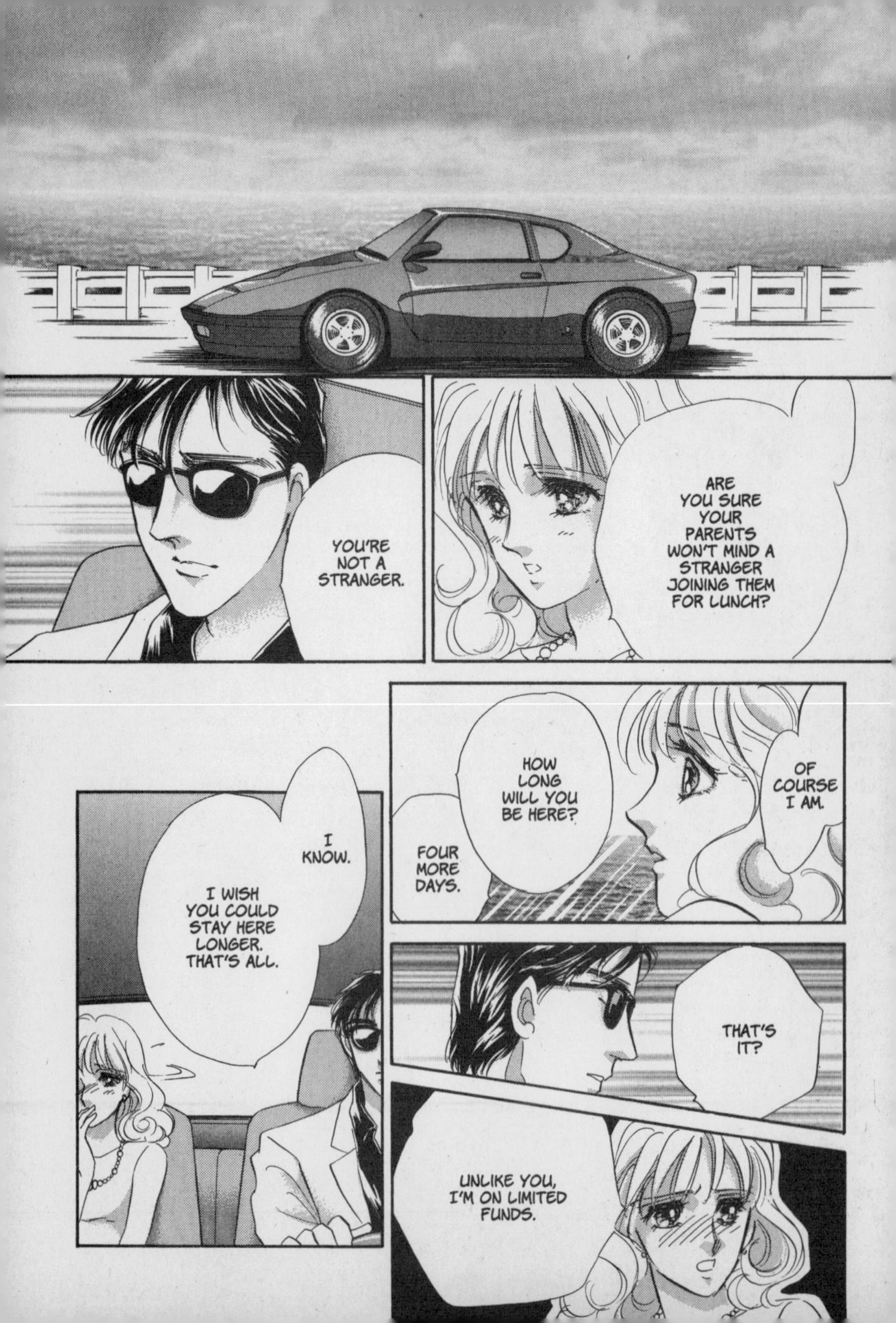
ARE YOU SURE YOUR PARENTS WON'T MIND A STRANGER JOINING THEM FOR LUNCH?
YOU'RE NOT A STRANGER.
OF COURSE I AM.
HOW LONG WILL YOU BE HERE?
FOUR MORE DAYS.
THAT'S IT?
UNLIKE YOU, I'M ON LIMITED FUNDS.
I KNOW.
I WISH YOU COULD STAY HERE LONGER. THAT'S ALL.

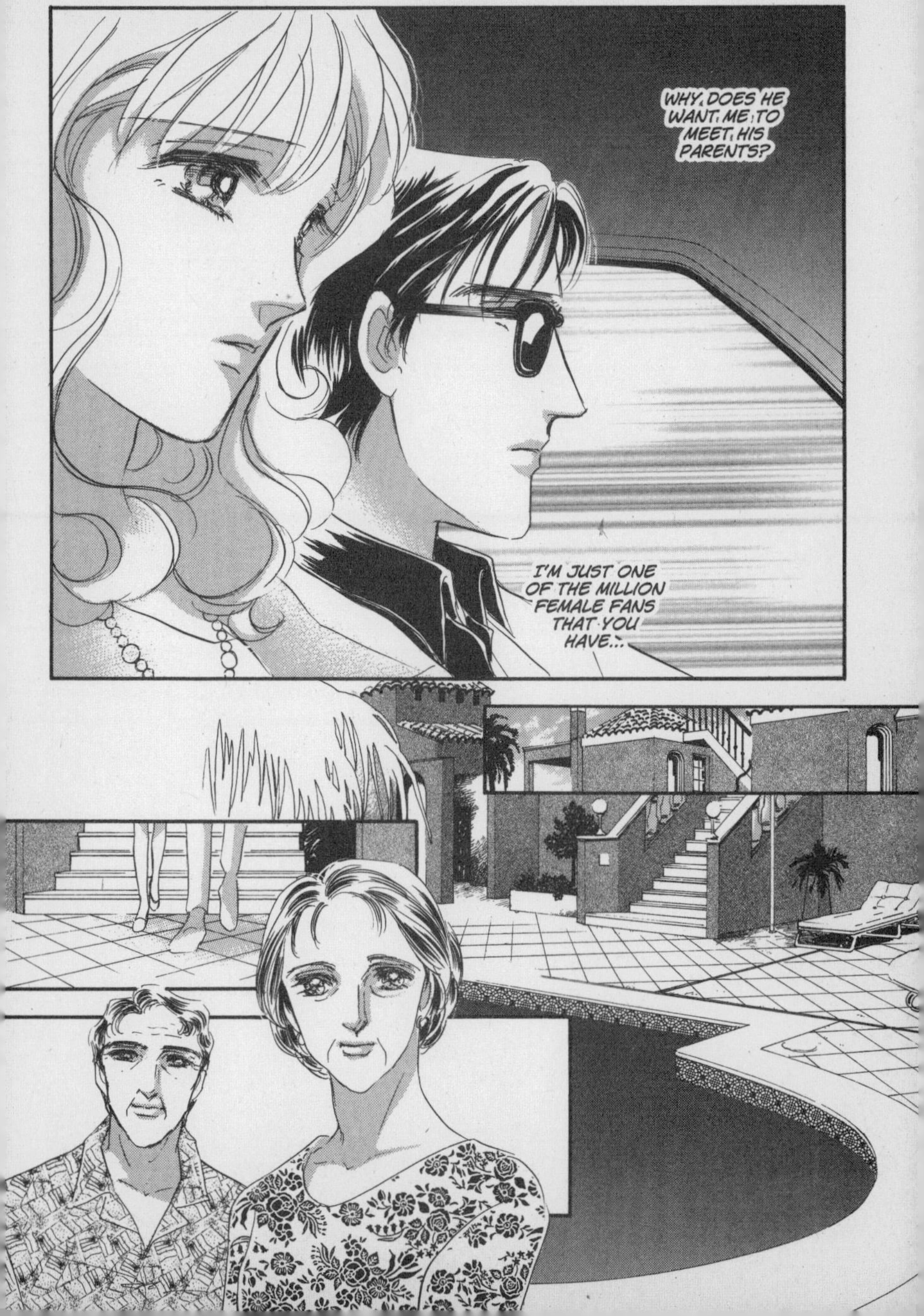
WHY DOES HE WANT ME TO MEET HIS PARENTS?
I'M JUST ONE OF THE MILLION FEMALE FANS THAT YOU HAVE...

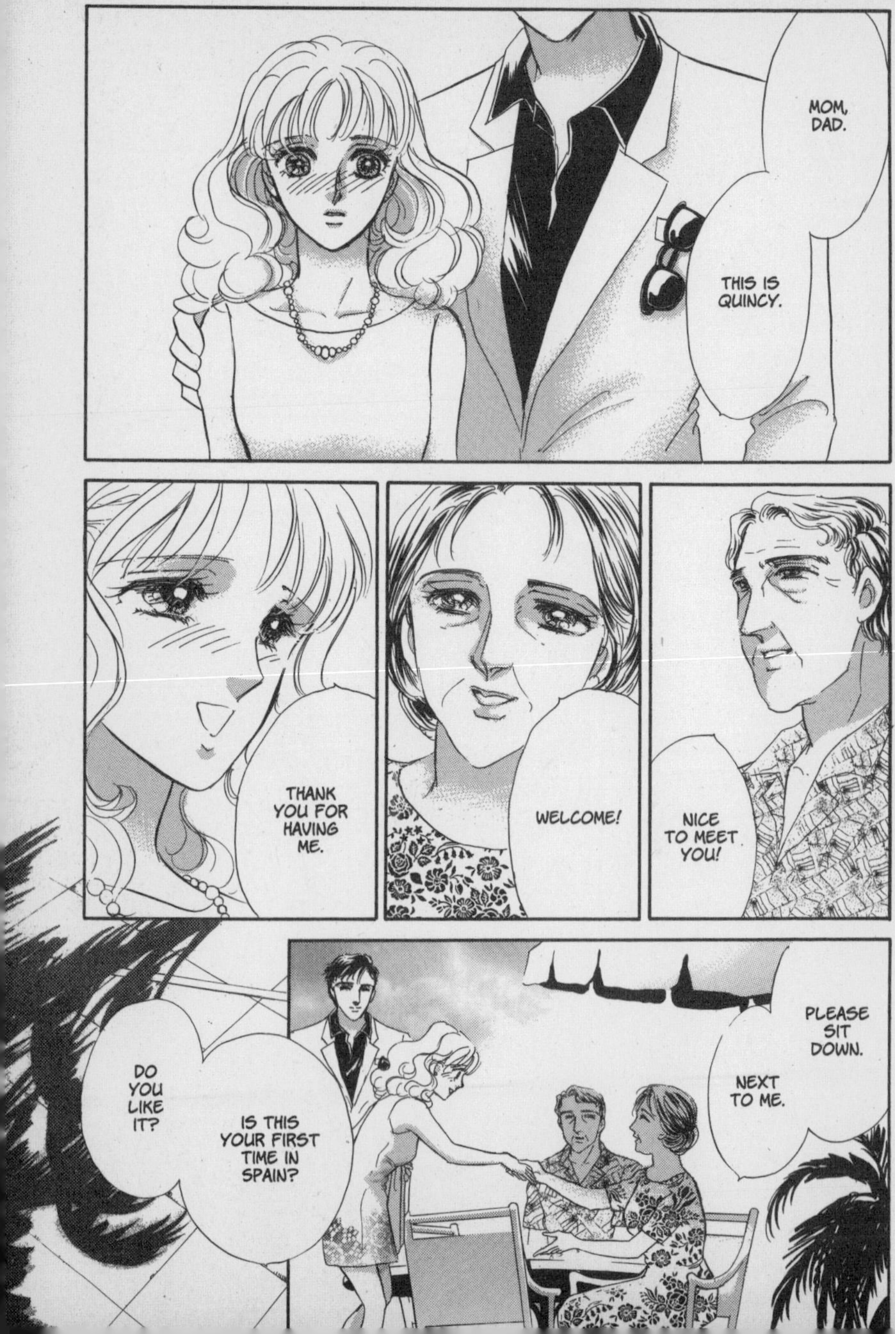
MOM, DAD.
THIS IS QUINCY.
NICE TO MEET YOU!
WELCOME!
THANK YOU FOR HAVING ME.
PLEASE SIT DOWN.
NEXT TO ME.
IS THIS YOUR FIRST TIME IN SPAIN?
DO YOU LIKE IT?

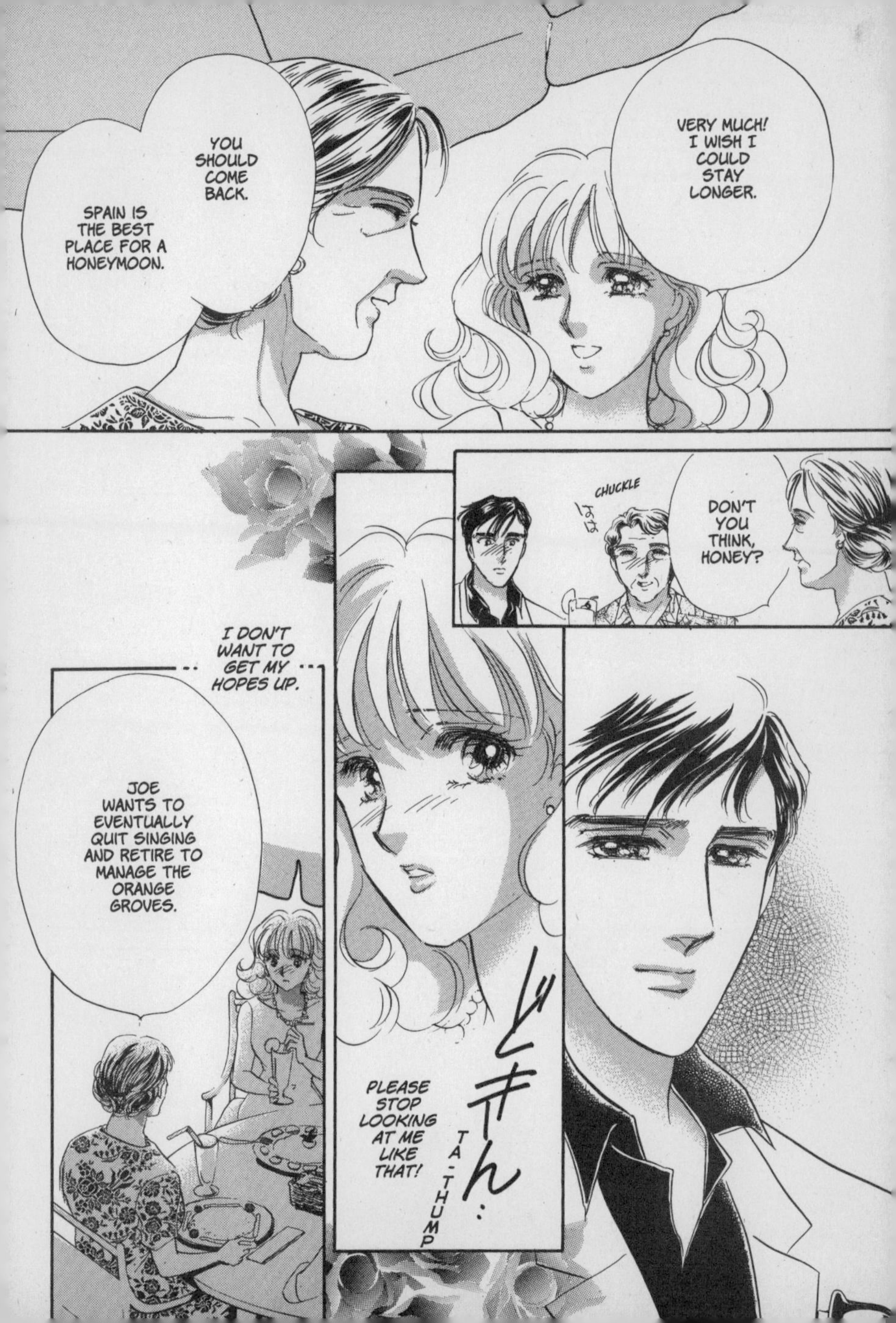
VERY MUCH! I WISH I COULD STAY LONGER.
YOU SHOULD COME BACK.
SPAIN IS THE BEST PLACE FOR A HONEYMOON.
DON'T YOU THINK, HONEY?
CHUCKLE
はは
ドキン
TA-THUMP
PLEASE STOP LOOKING AT ME LIKE THAT!
I DON'T WANT TO GET MY HOPES UP.
JOE WANTS TO EVENTUALLY QUIT SINGING AND RETIRE TO MANAGE THE ORANGE GROVES.

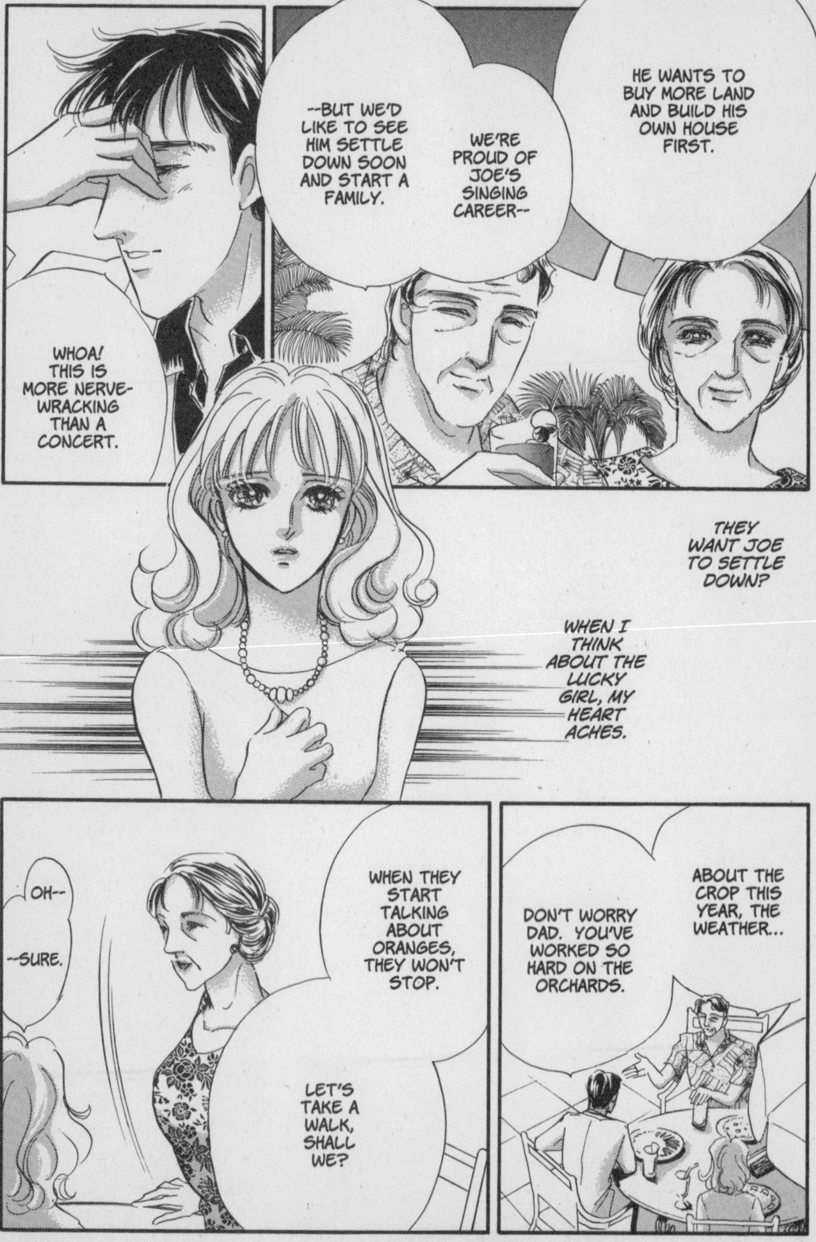
HE WANTS TO BUY MORE LAND AND BUILD HIS OWN HOUSE FIRST.
WE'RE PROUD OF JOE'S SINGING CAREER--
--BUT WE'D LIKE TO SEE HIM SETTLE DOWN SOON AND START A FAMILY.
WHOA! THIS IS MORE NERVE-WRACKING THAN A CONCERT.
THEY WANT JOE TO SETTLE DOWN?
WHEN I THINK ABOUT THE LUCKY GIRL, MY HEART ACHES.
ABOUT THE CROP THIS YEAR, THE WEATHER...
DON'T WORRY DAD. YOU'VE WORKED SO HARD ON THE ORCHARDS.
WHEN THEY START TALKING ABOUT ORANGES, THEY WON'T STOP.
LET'S TAKE A WALK, SHALL WE?
OH--
--SURE.

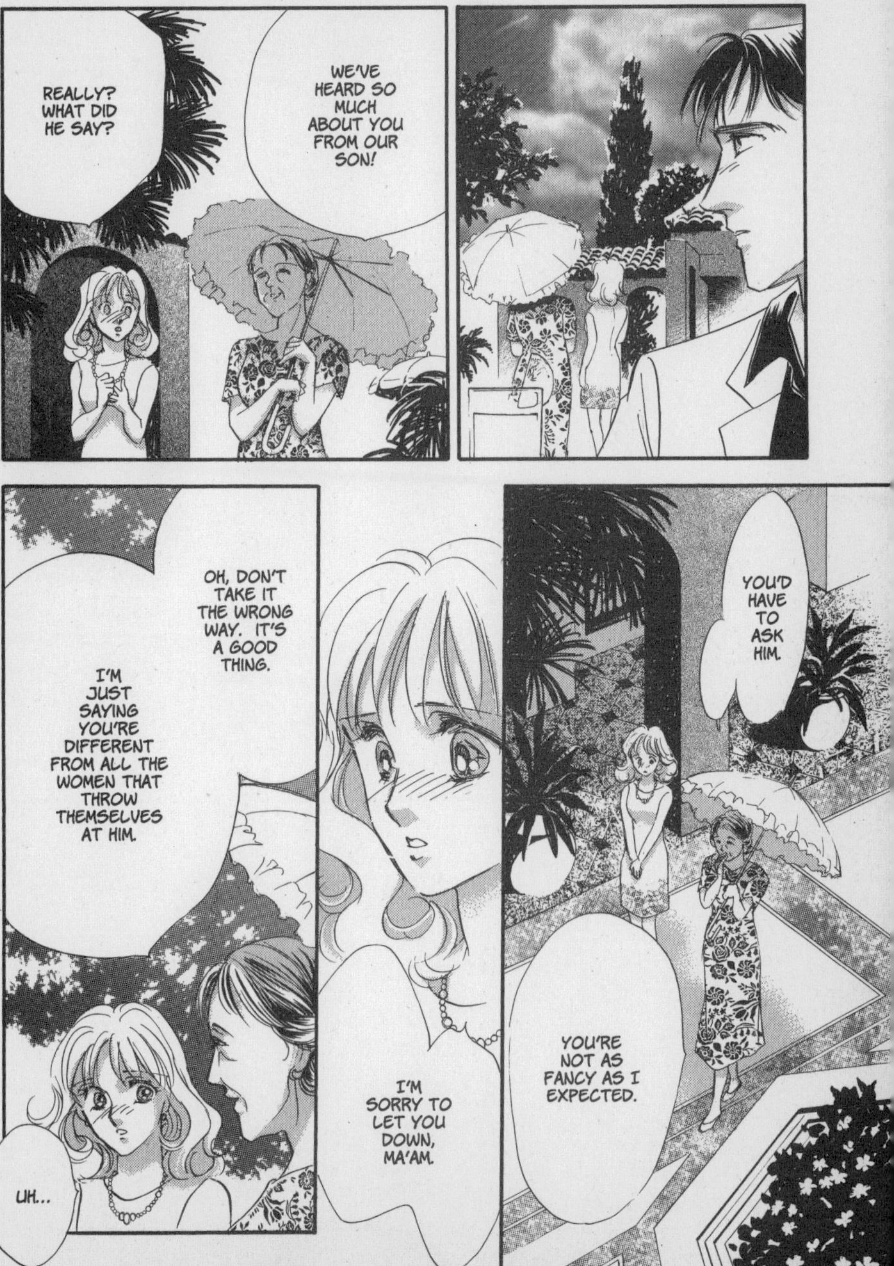
WE'VE HEARD SO MUCH ABOUT YOU FROM OUR SON!
REALLY? WHAT DID HE SAY?
YOU'D HAVE TO ASK HIM.
YOU'RE NOT AS FANCY AS I EXPECTED.
I'M SORRY TO LET YOU DOWN, MA'AM.
OH, DON'T TAKE IT THE WRONG WAY. IT'S A GOOD THING.
I'M JUST SAYING YOU'RE DIFFERENT FROM ALL THE WOMEN THAT THROW THEMSELVES AT HIM.
UH...

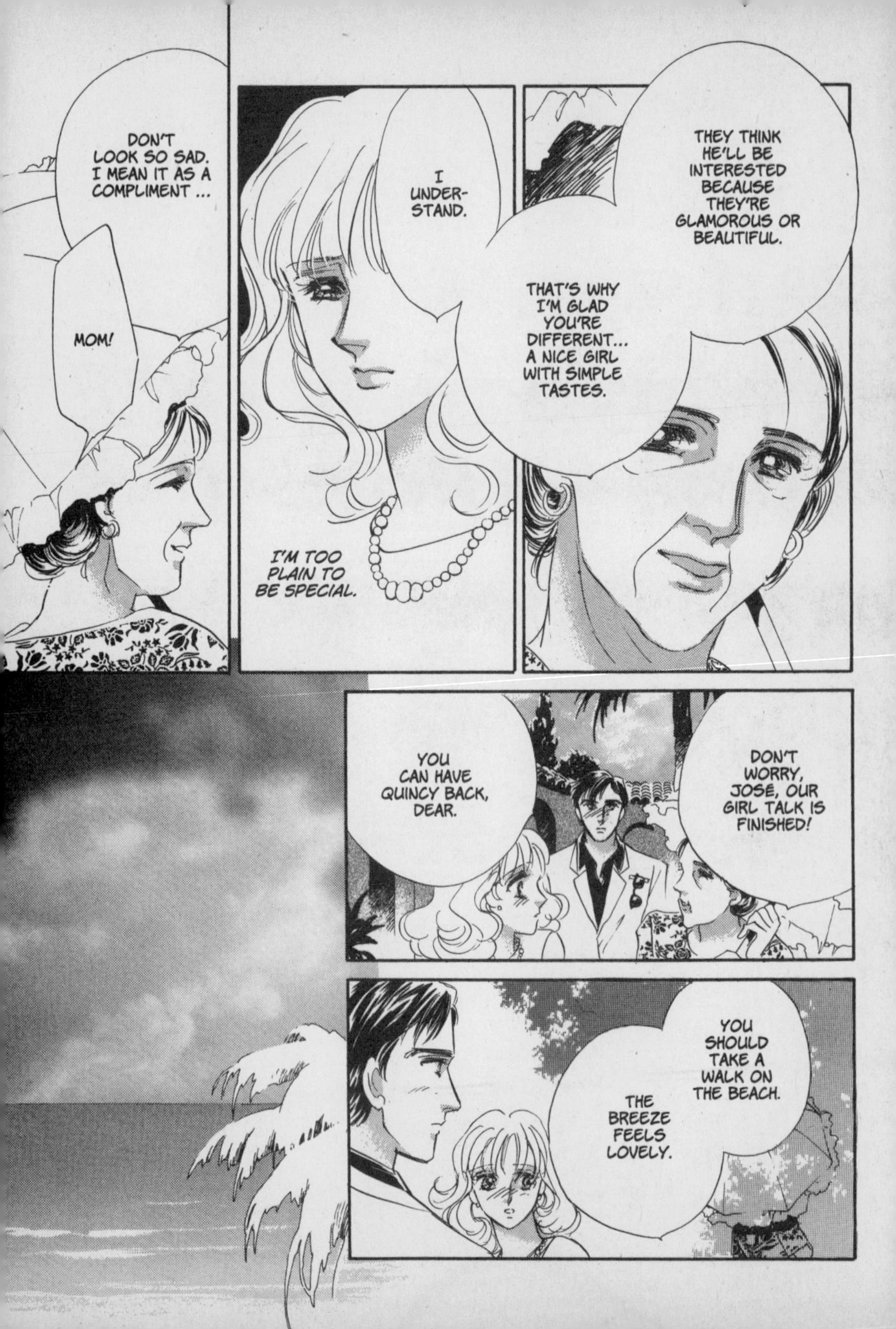
THEY THINK HE'LL BE INTERESTED BECAUSE THEY'RE GLAMOROUS OR BEAUTIFUL.
THAT'S WHY I'M GLAD YOU'RE DIFFERENT... A NICE GIRL WITH SIMPLE TASTES.
I UNDER-STAND.
I'M TOO PLAIN TO BE SPECIAL.
DON'T LOOK SO SAD. I MEAN IT AS A COMPLIMENT ...
MOM!
DON'T WORRY, JOSE, OUR GIRL TALK IS FINISHED!
YOU CAN HAVE QUINCY BACK, DEAR.
YOU SHOULD TAKE A WALK ON THE BEACH.
THE BREEZE FEELS LOVELY.

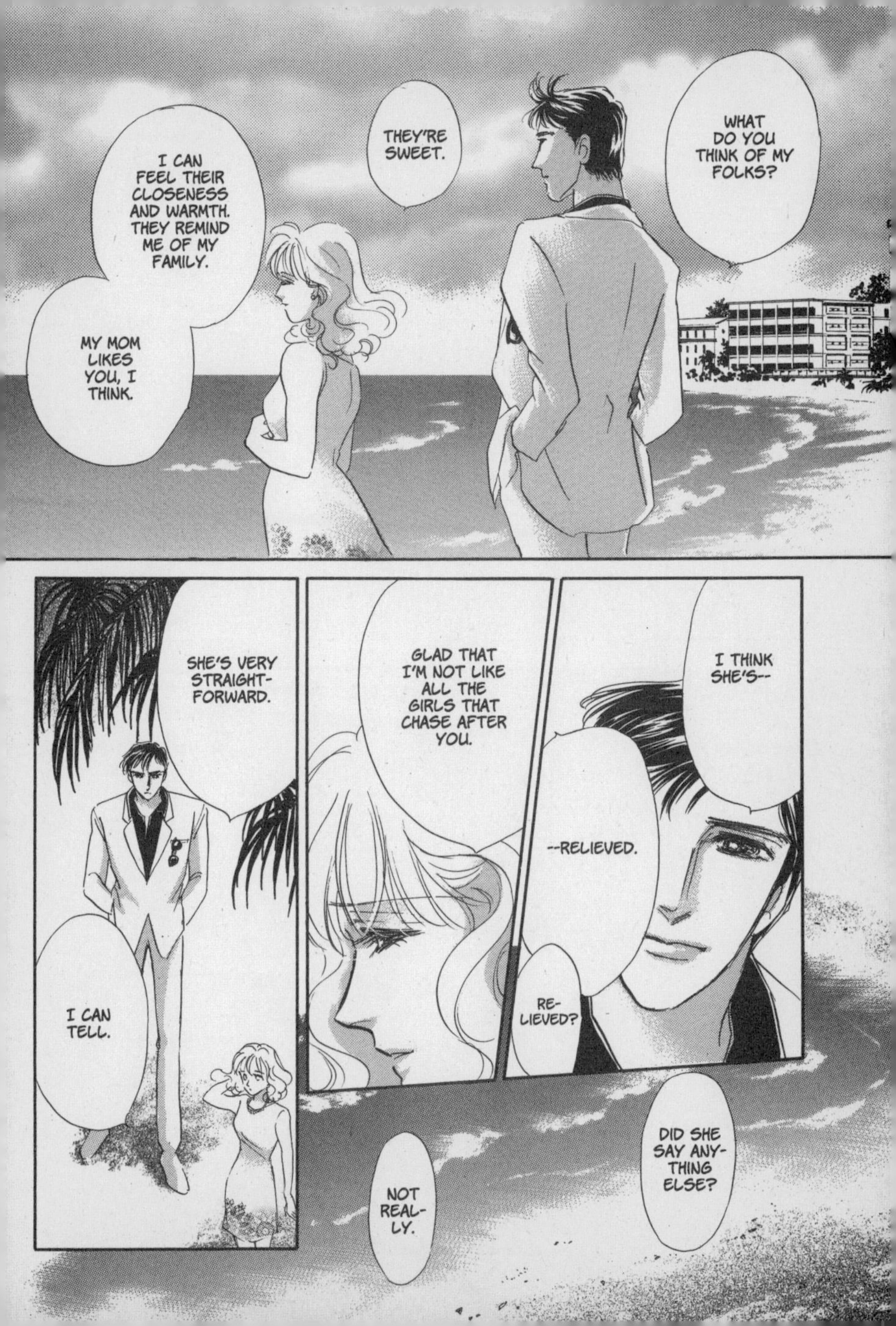
WHAT DO YOU THINK OF MY FOLKS?
THEY'RE SWEET.
I CAN FEEL THEIR CLOSENESS AND WARMTH. THEY REMIND ME OF MY FAMILY.
MY MOM LIKES YOU, I THINK.
I THINK SHE'S--
--RELIEVED.
RE-LIEVED?
GLAD THAT I'M NOT LIKE ALL THE GIRLS THAT CHASE AFTER YOU.
SHE'S VERY STRAIGHT-FORWARD.
I CAN TELL.
DID SHE SAY ANY-THING ELSE?
NOT REAL-LY.

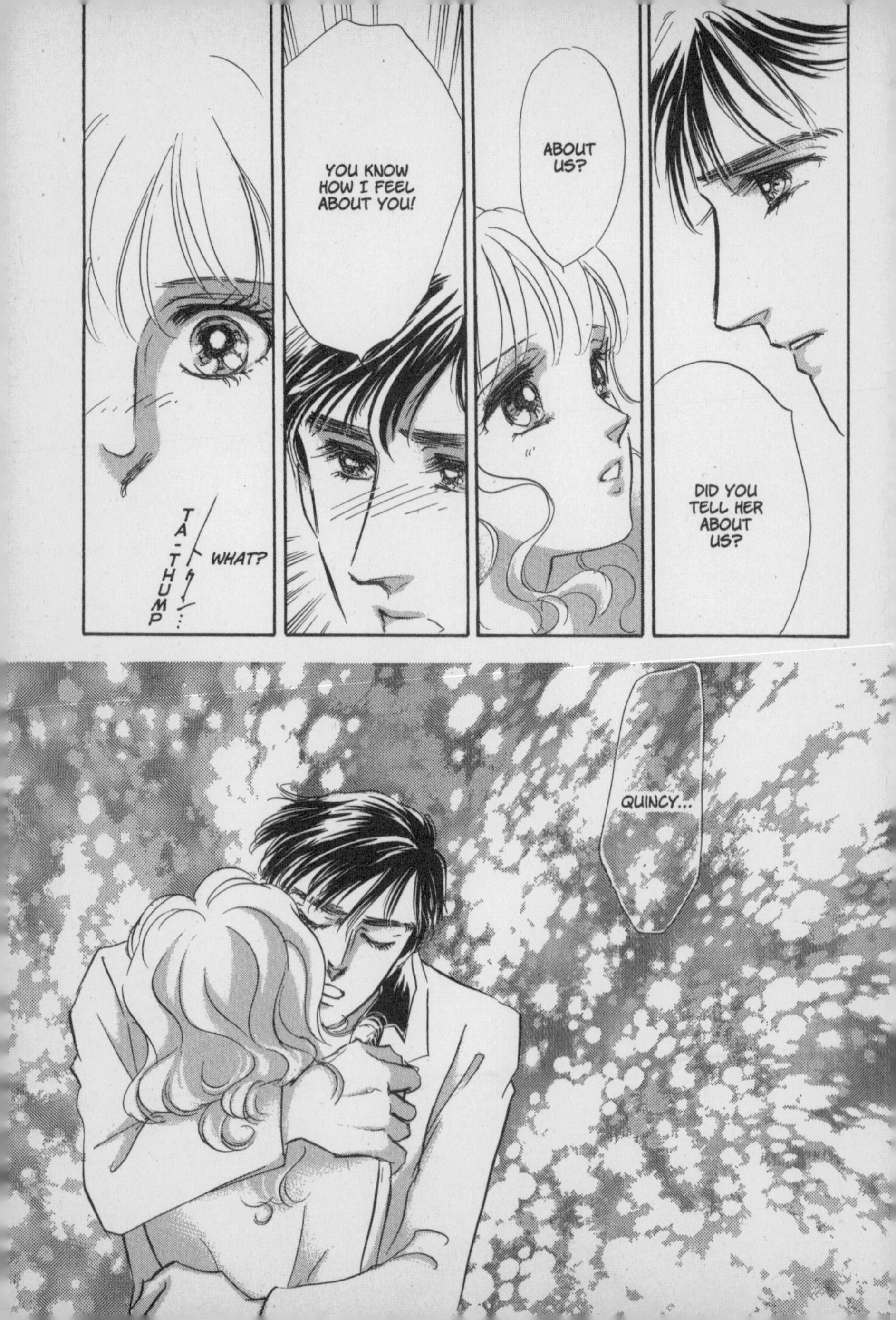
DID YOU TELL HER ABOUT US?
ABOUT US?
YOU KNOW HOW I FEEL ABOUT YOU!
WHAT?
TA-THUMP
QUINCY...

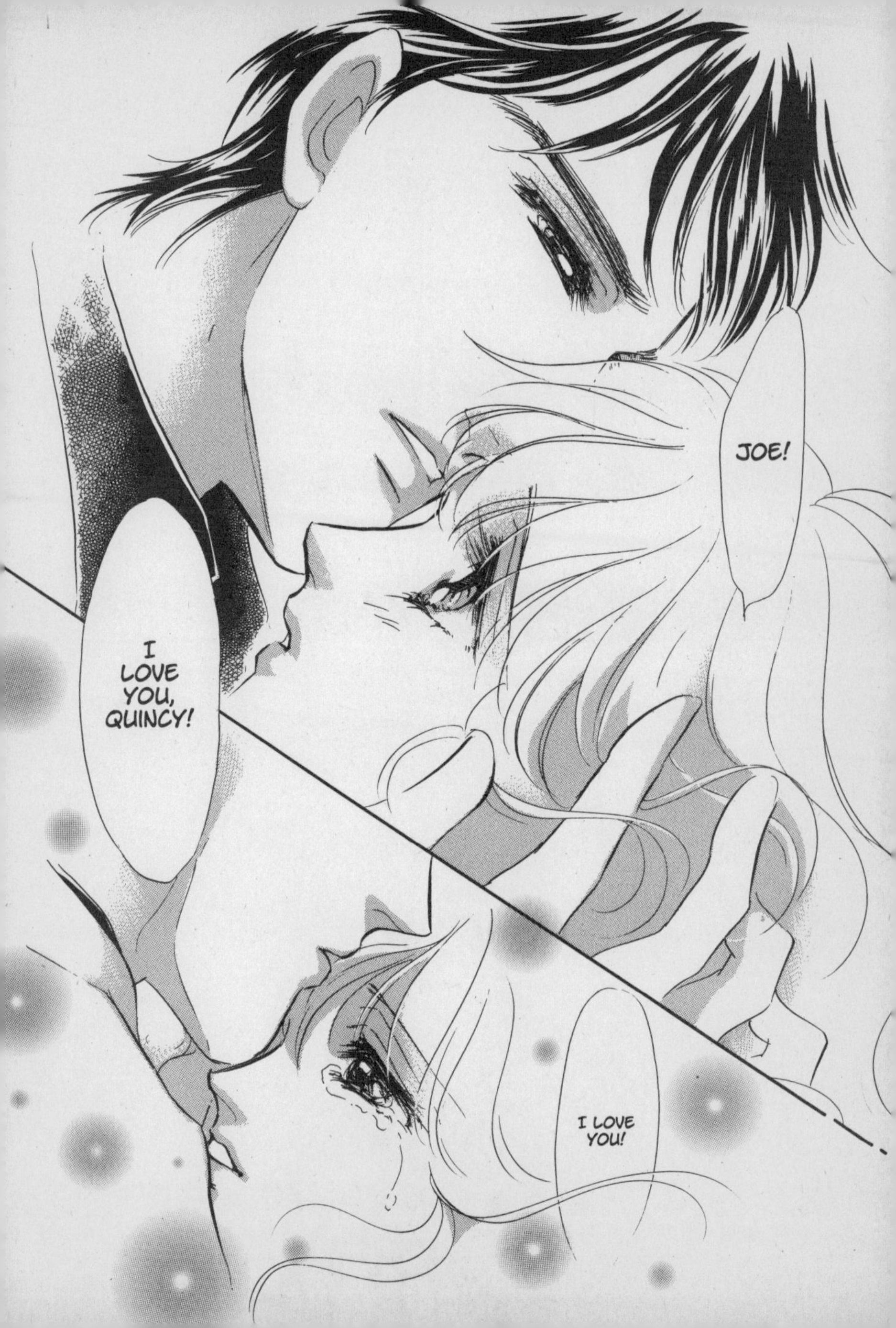
JOE!
I LOVE YOU, QUINCY!
I LOVE YOU!

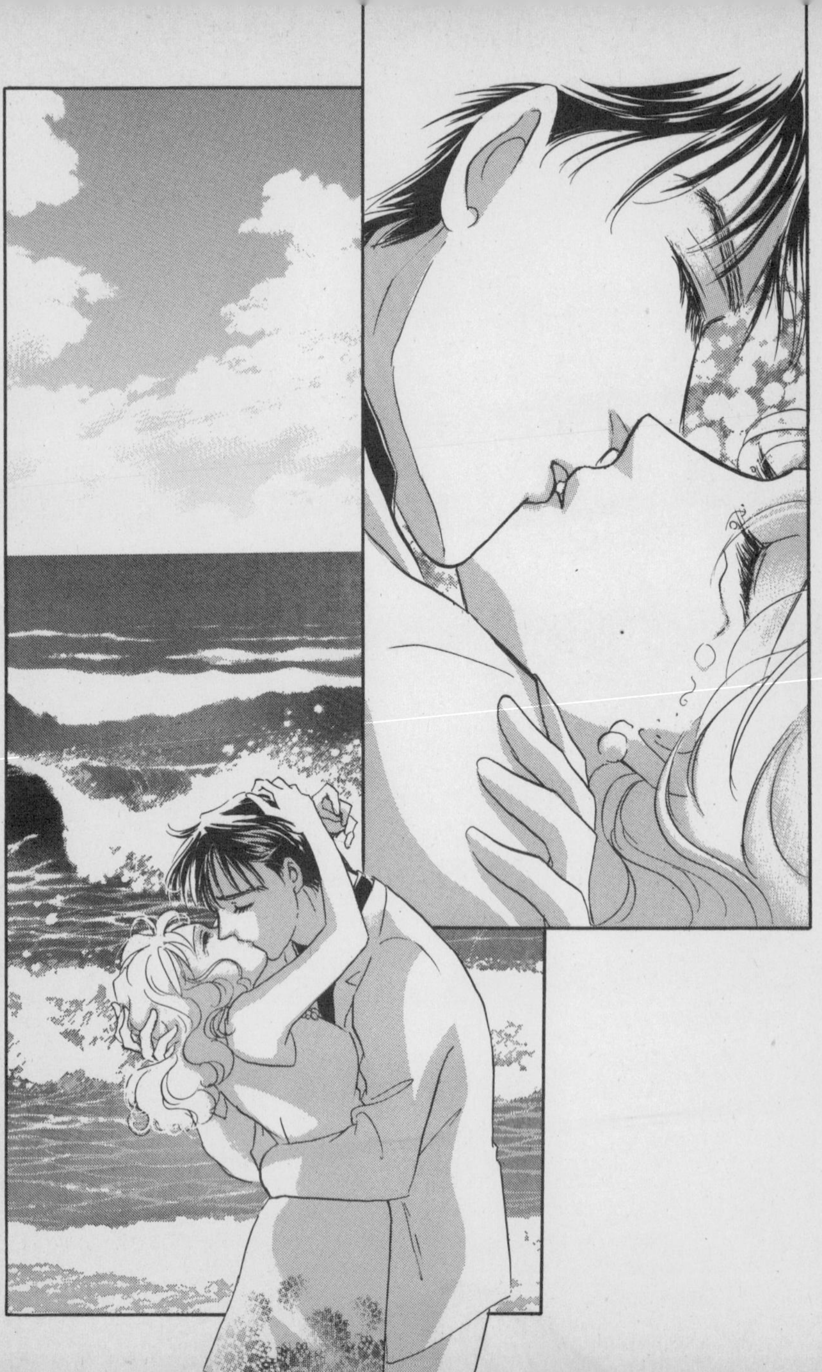

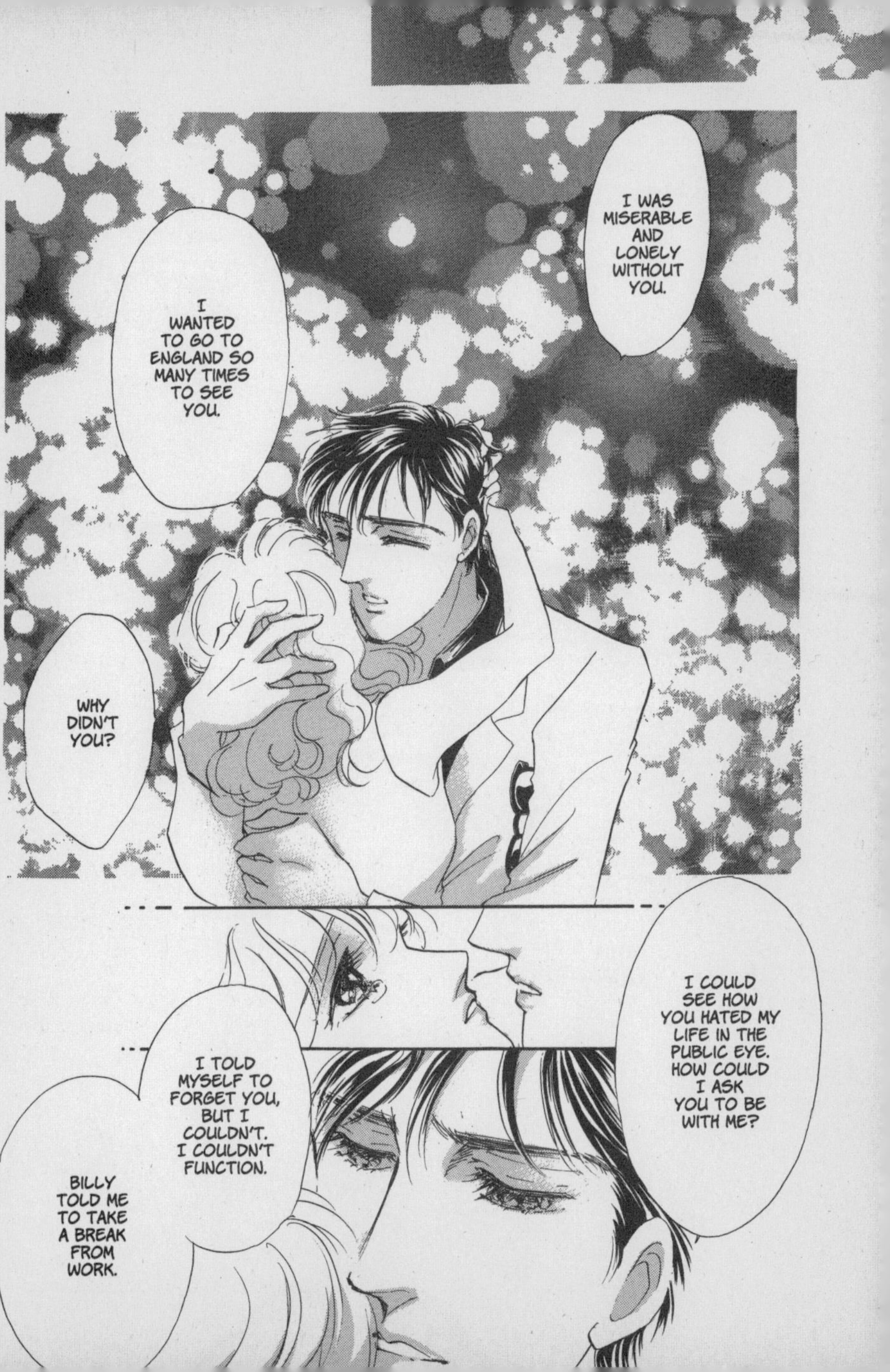
I WAS MISERABLE AND LONELY WITHOUT YOU.
I WANTED TO GO TO ENGLAND SO MANY TIMES TO SEE YOU.
WHY DIDN'T YOU?
I COULD SEE HOW YOU HATED MY LIFE IN THE PUBLIC EYE. HOW COULD I ASK YOU TO BE WITH ME?
I TOLD MYSELF TO FORGET YOU, BUT I COULDN'T. I COULDN'T FUNCTION.
BILLY TOLD ME TO TAKE A BREAK FROM WORK.

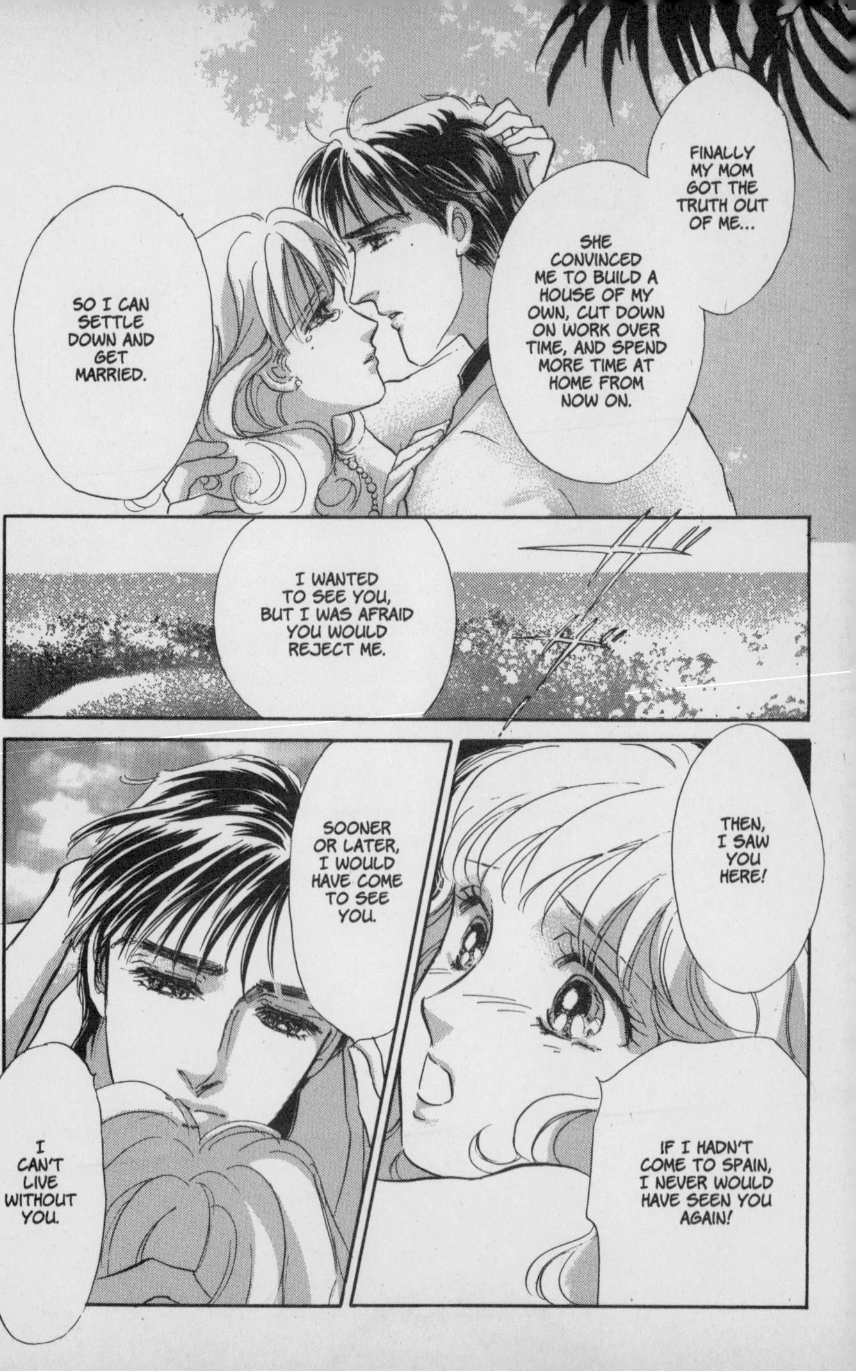
FINALLY MY MOM GOT THE TRUTH OUT OF ME...
SHE CONVINCED ME TO BUILD A HOUSE OF MY OWN, CUT DOWN ON WORK OVER TIME, AND SPEND MORE TIME AT HOME FROM NOW ON.
SO I CAN SETTLE DOWN AND GET MARRIED.
I WANTED TO SEE YOU, BUT I WAS AFRAID YOU WOULD REJECT ME.
THEN, I SAW YOU HERE!
IF I HADN'T COME TO SPAIN, I NEVER WOULD HAVE SEEN YOU AGAIN!
SOONER OR LATER, I WOULD HAVE COME TO SEE YOU.
I CAN'T LIVE WITHOUT YOU.

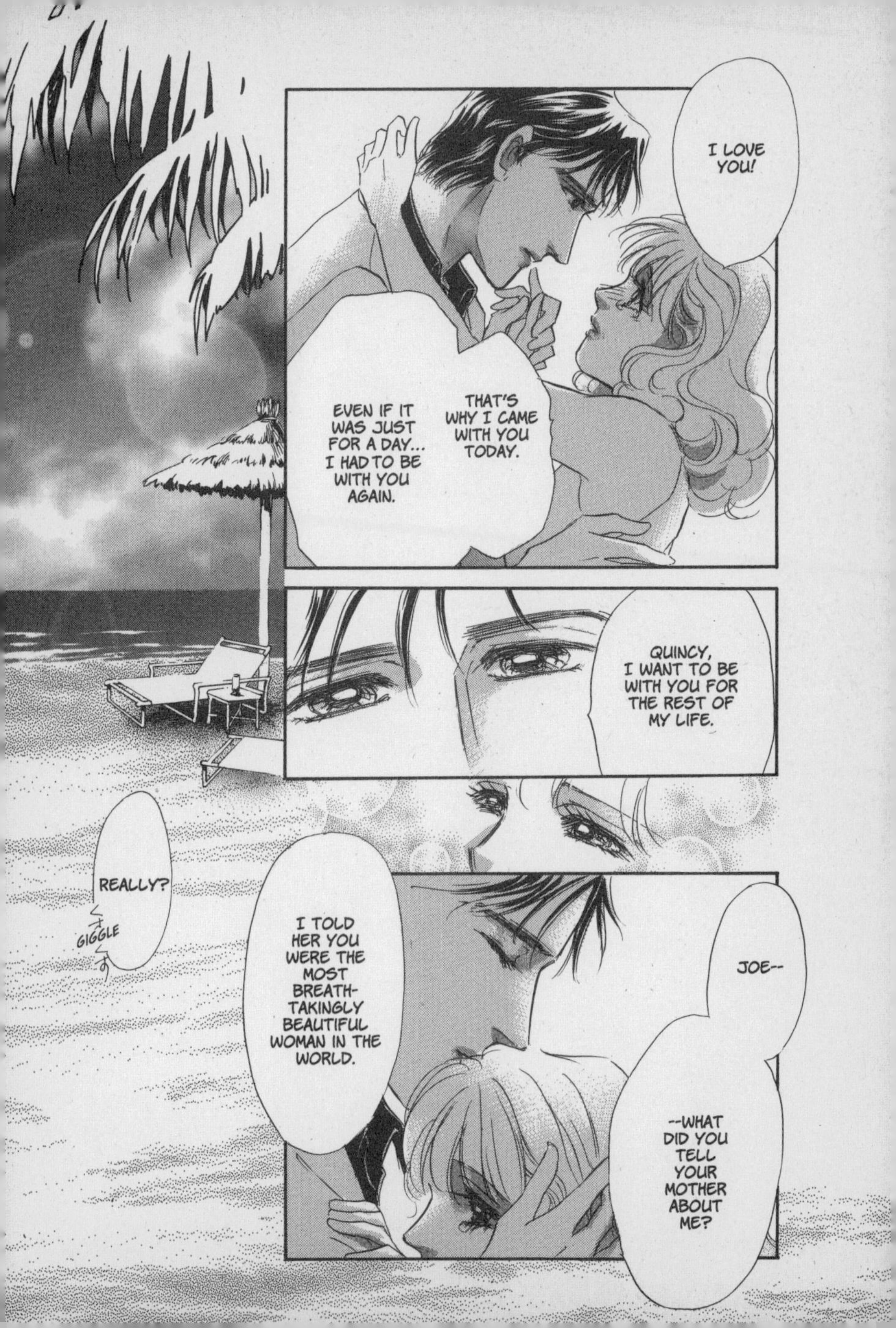
I LOVE YOU!
THAT'S WHY I CAME WITH YOU TODAY.
EVEN IF IT WAS JUST FOR A DAY... I HAD TO BE WITH YOU AGAIN.
QUINCY, I WANT TO BE WITH YOU FOR THE REST OF MY LIFE.
JOE--
--WHAT DID YOU TELL YOUR MOTHER ABOUT ME?
I TOLD HER YOU WERE THE MOST BREATH-TAKINGLY BEAUTIFUL WOMAN IN THE WORLD.
REALLY?
GIGGLE

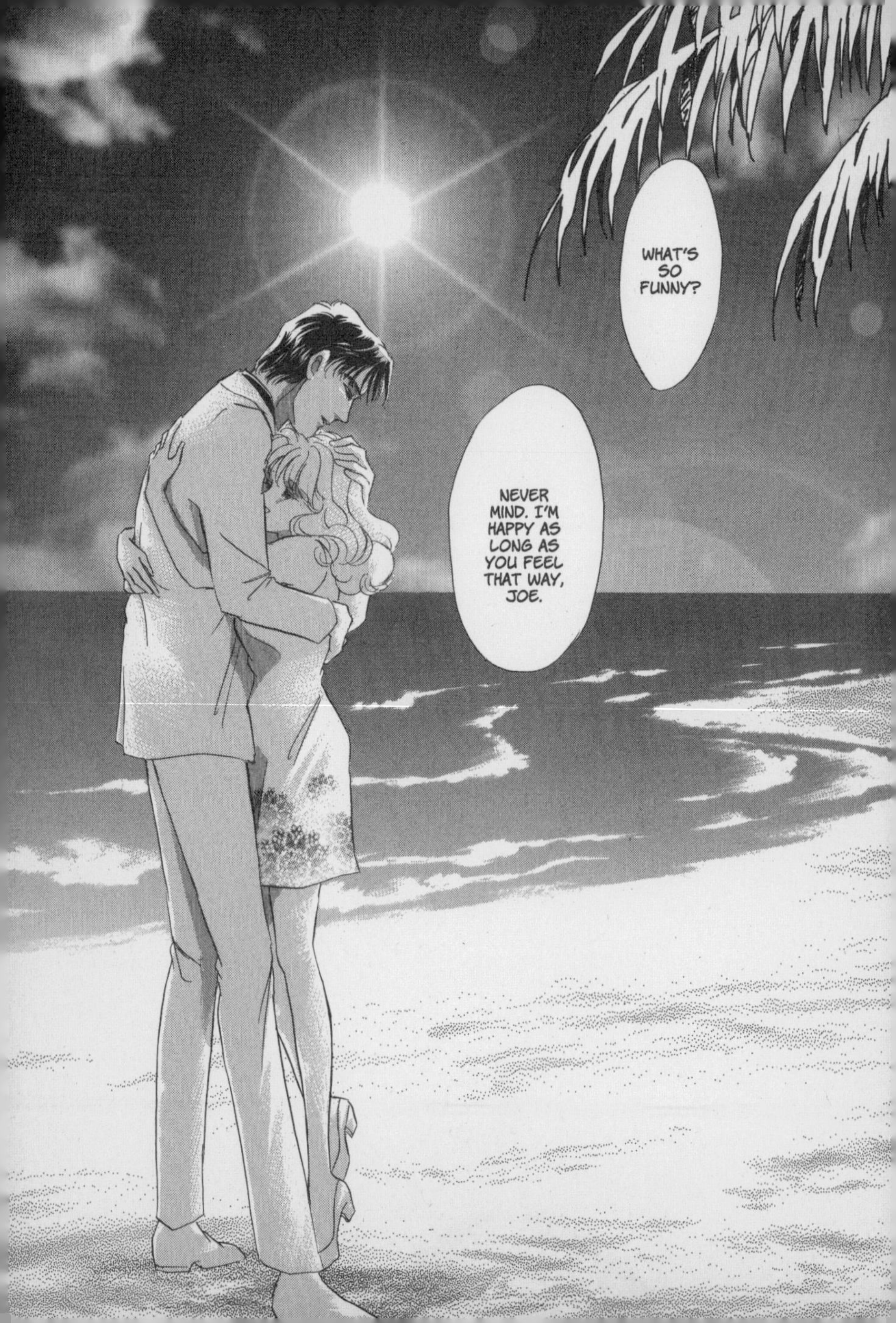
WHAT'S SO FUNNY?
NEVER MIND. I'M HAPPY AS LONG AS YOU FEEL THAT WAY, JOE.

HARLEQUIN®

Ginger Blossom

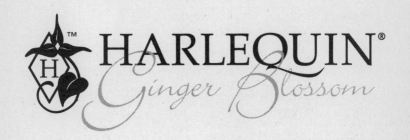

# Club 9

by Makoto Kobayashi
creator of **What's Michael?**

**VOLUME 1**
ISBN: 1-56971-915-2
$15.95

**VOLUME 2**
ISBN: 1-56971-968-3
$15.95

**VOLUME 3**
ISBN: 1-59307-322-4
$15.95

*Translation by*
**Ikoi Hiroe**

*Lettering by*
**Michael David Thomas**

*Edited by*
**Shawna Gore**

*Design by*
**Heidi Fainza & Lia Ribacchi**

*Publisher*
**Mike Richardson**

published by Dark Horse Manga
a division of Dark Horse Comics, Inc.
10956 S.E. Main St.
Milwaukie OR 97222

www.darkhorse.com

Harlequin Enterprises Limited
225 Duncan Mill Rd.
Don Mills
Ontario Canada M3B 3K9

www.eHarlequin.com

First edition: March 2006
ISBN 1-59307-460-3

1 3 5 7 9 10 8 6 4 2

PRINTED IN U.S.A.

# DARK HORSE .COM

# !STOP—

## *are you looking for the front of the book?*
## *This is the back.*

This Harlequin Ginger Blossom title is translated into English, but oriented in right-to-left reading format, following the original Japanese edition. If you're new to reading manga this way, please look at the diagram below for a quick lesson. It may take some practice, but you'll catch on quickly!

IT'S FOR YOU.
1
TOSS
THANK YOU FOR YOUR KINDNESS.
2
Thank
DON'T BE A FOOL!
3
HE ONLY LEFT A NOTE TO BE POLITE.
4
DING DONG!
5
BRENDAN!
6

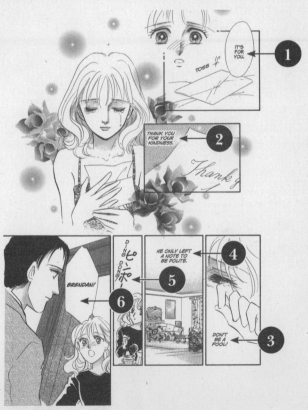